SWEE'PEA

SWEE'PEA

*The Story of Lloyd Daniels and Other
Playground Basketball Legends*

John Valenti

with Ron Naclerio

ATRIA PAPERBACK
New York London Toronto Sydney New Delhi

ATRIA PAPERBACK
An Imprint of Simon & Schuster, Inc.
1230 Avenue of the Americas
New York, NY 10020

First Atria Paperback edition July 2016

ATRIA PAPERBACK and colophon are trademarks of Simon & Schuster, Inc.

For information about special discounts for bulk purchases, please contact Simon & Schuster Special Sales at 1-866-506-1949 or business@simonandschuster.com.

The Simon & Schuster Speakers Bureau can bring authors to your live event. For more information or to book an event, contact the Simon & Schuster Speakers Bureau at 1-866-248-3049 or visit our website at www.simonspeakers.com.

Interior design by Paul J. Dippolito

Manufactured in the United States of America

10 9 8 7 6 5 4 3 2 1

Library of Congress Cataloging-in-Publication Data

Valenti, John, 1960–
    Swee'pea : the story of Lloyd Daniels and other New York playground basketball legends / John Valenti with Ron Naclerio
        pages   cm
2015050461

ISBN 978-1-5011-1667-4
ISBN 978-1-5011-1668-1 (ebook)

For Elizabeth, the love of my life, and for my son, Jarek,
who's honest and caring and tough as nails

And in memory of Nicholas "Nicky" Mann, a big-hearted kid and
passionate basketball fan, whom illness took far too young

(John Valenti)

"It's one thing to tell a man he must lift himself by his bootstraps. It's another thing to tell a bootless man he must lift himself by his bootstraps."

—Martin Luther King, Jr.

"A man got to survive. When you ain't got no money and you need clothes and food to eat, you don't think about it. You got to survive. Got to survive, got to eat, got to have sneakers."

—Lloyd Daniels, Jr.

Contents

Author's Note

It's hard to believe more than a quarter century has elapsed since *Swee'pea and Other Playground Legends* was first released, in November 1990.

Issued by a small, independent New York City publisher, we thought it a good story and felt like the luckiest guys in the world when it went into print.

This was the era before cell phones and home computers were common; before the invention of the World Wide Web, let alone Facebook and Twitter, blogging, email, and YouTube. Before e-books. Hard-core basketball fans, sports fans, had heard of Lloyd "Swee'pea" Daniels, a prodigy from the playgrounds of New York. But, more often than not, they'd heard just the basics: the rumor, the legend. Nothing more.

If you hadn't seen him play in person—and only a select few had—or caught some mention in one of the basketball or sports magazines, maybe an item in the local newspaper, much of his story remained unknown. As were the stories of players he'd played against. As were the stories of the environment they'd survived.

The telling proved incredible. Interest spread like wildfire. More than a hundred newspapers, magazines, and journals wrote about the book. It received praise from the *New York Times* Sunday Book Review. *People* and *Sports Illustrated* wrote about Lloyd. There were radio and television appearances coast-to-coast, including one on *Good Morning America* with Charles Gibson, Joan Lunden, and Spencer Christian. Lloyd's grandmother appeared on *The Oprah Winfrey Show*.

Other authors cited *Swee'pea*, the book, in their books.

A young father with daughters who were rising tennis players in

Compton, in inner-city Los Angeles, mentioned the influence of the book in a national article.

The feature by Sonja Steptoe about Venus Williams, ten, and her sister, Serena, nine, appeared in *Sports Illustrated* on June 10, 1991. Near the end was a paragraph about Richard Williams teaching his daughters not only about tennis but about life.

"He opens a desk drawer in his living room and pulls out *Swee'pea and Other Playground Legends*, a book detailing the troubled basketball career of Lloyd Daniels, a former New York City playground star," Steptoe wrote. "'They said he was Magic [Johnson] with a jump shot, but he didn't go to class and then drugs took him,' says Richard. 'That will never happen with my kids. Venus has already read this book.'"

Word from other readers who'd been moved by *Swee'pea* came to us more directly: navy man ABF-2 James D. Martinez wrote to share how the book kept him tied to home aboard the aircraft carrier USS *John F. Kennedy* in the Persian Gulf during Operation Desert Storm. A fan from Florence, Italy, sent a handwritten note to say he was reading *Swee'pea* for the second time—in a month. New York State prison inmate Joe Hammond, a legend known as the Destroyer on the fabled blacktop of Rucker Park, mailed me a letter, inspired to offer a bunch of stories I might not have known.

Might not have believed, had it not come from the *force's* mouth.

Then there was Kevin Ross, the former Creighton University star, who'd ignited a national controversy when he'd returned to elementary school once his college eligibility to play for the Bluejays had been exhausted in 1982—admitting he was a functional illiterate. I'd only seen a newspaper photograph of Ross squeezed into a child's school desk before all six-foot-nine, near three hundred pounds of him, a dog-eared copy of *Swee'pea* in hand, came walking into the studio at WGN Chicago, where I was to appear on a radio show.

First adult book he'd ever read, he told me. Loved it, too.

All that said, we—Ron Naclerio and I—were moved when Todd Hunter, an editor at Simon & Schuster imprint Atria Books, told us the publishing house wanted to reissue *Swee'pea*. The story of Lloyd

Daniels, of the players he'd played against, of the streets they'd come from, of the world that had shaped them, remained a good one, Todd said; a compelling one. One that still held value for the readers of a new generation.

This generation, to which the stories remained largely unknown.

What we have done, then, is to update *Swee'pea* while working hard to leave the manuscript as untouched and original as possible. That is, we've included new text in an effort to add to the telling without altering the flow and feel of the book. We wanted to keep the original as original as possible, to let it remain a period piece, a slice of historical reference, a testament to a time that no longer exists. From back when basketball could be as pure as the streets and playgrounds were impure; when word on the street was spread via word of mouth, not by text or tweeting or hashtag this. That is, from back in the day.

To do so—and we hope we've succeeded—we've held some developments since the book was first published until the Epilogue, specially added for this new edition. It helps answer questions unanswered where the original manuscript left off.

The story of Swee'pea has age behind it now; however, that doesn't mean its message is old. A quarter century later it remains a cautionary tale, its lessons invaluable. The need for education; for dedication and perseverance. The need to know when to walk away. For your own good; for the good of yourself. The need to choose your friends well.

We kindly thank our literary agent, Monika A. Taga, for believing and for bringing this project back to life; Todd Hunter for believing, too. I also want to thank the love of my life, Elizabeth, Beth, for her support—not to mention for putting up with me—and my parents, John and Dot, for teaching me and my brothers, Jim and Rob, well. My son, Jarek, was born the day I got the first contract for this book, back in 1989. He's done me and his late mother proud. Of course, there's my best friend, Tony Mills, Antone, who's been there through thick and thin, and *Newsday* cohort Neil Best, who first proofread *Swee'pea* as a favor more than twenty-five years ago. He said it was "good." High praise, if you know Neil. Thanks to Benjamin May, who's crafted a documentary about the life of Lloyd Daniels titled *The Legend of Swee'pea*, and to Matt Caputo, a regular Queens guy and gifted writer, editor, and filmmaker, who's worked for the *Daily News* and *SLAM*, and who once hunted me down on a street in Elmhurst just to tell me *Swee'pea* was his favorite book of all time—begging me, then pushing me, to get it back into print.

I'm thankful to know that our original editor, Kent Oswald, proved right when he told me all those years ago, "Twenty years from now, you'll pick this up and read it again—and it'll still be a good book." I didn't believe him; I'm touched to find others agreed with his assessment. I only wish our first publisher, good friend Michael Kesend of Michael Kesend Publishing, Ltd., were alive to see the day. He believed in *Swee'pea* and first made it possible. A character of the first order, he would have loved this.

Then he would have said, simply: Talk on you soon.

—*John Valenti*

Three-Shot Barrage

Blood was everywhere.

It had drained, crimson, into the corners of the torn and tattered shirt, as if it were trying to forever change the complexion of the fabric it had soaked through. Matted on the cloth and on the skin, it caked and congealed, gummy to the touch, and gave an eerie, surrealistic aura to the patient stretched out on the hospital gurney in the whitewashed emergency room.

It was two thirty in the morning and by now Dr. Daniel L. Picard had been up to his elbows in one mess or another for hours. Director of surgery at Mary Immaculate Hospital in Jamaica, Queens, he had been the primary surgeon on call for the better part of the night. And, in an area of New York City where treating the results of early-morning, drug-related street violence had long been as normal as the bandaging of minor cuts and wounds, nights were seldom quiet at Mary Immaculate.

Called to emergency fresh from working on another patient, Picard took little time disrobing, getting scrubbed, and exchanging his sweat-drenched, bloodstained outfit for a clean gown. Here was yet one more serious problem on his hands.

On a stretcher lay the six-foot, seven-inch victim, his size-thirteen feet dangling over one end of the emergency room hospital cart as if hovering at the edge of a precipice; eyes wide open, panic-stricken, like a mortally wounded fawn in search of some miraculous last-second reprieve from near-certain death.

Blood stained his coffee-chocolate skin. There was a bullet hole in the left side of his neck, just shy of the jugular. There were two bullet wounds in his chest: one just wide of his heart, the force of the other so sure, so brutal, that it had ripped its way across the distance of the cavity, exiting through a nasty opening in his back.

In its wake, the spent lead had left untold damage.

Picard caught his breath, drawing in hard as he considered the situation.

A major thoracic wound, he thought to himself as the fresh droplets of blood began to spatter his pristine gown. Tenuous red streams flowed across his surgical gloves. He had no idea who the patient was. Nor did he care. He knew just one thing.

"It's extensive." When you get shot, it always is.

On the table, twenty-one-year-old Lloyd Daniels, Jr.—the person countless basketball scouts had once called the best professional prospect from New York City since Kareem Abdul-Jabbar was known simply as Lew Alcindor—clung to life by a thread ever so much thinner than the strand of a well-worn playground net.

Already he had lost six pints of blood. He was almost dead.

The night had begun in rather unceremonious fashion. It had rained, poured actually, and Lloyd, bored and with nothing to do, had called one of his longtime friends and advisors, Ron Naclerio. A recovering addict, Lloyd was struggling to stay out of trouble, stay clean. Already he had been through inpatient and outpatient rehabilitation three times in an effort to beat an alcohol and drug addiction that had cost him a possible basketball scholarship to the University of Nevada–Las Vegas, as well as jobs as a pro with the Topeka Sizzlers in the minor-league Continental Basketball Association and a team called Waitemata in Auckland, New Zealand.

He had attended four high schools in three states before quitting his junior year at Andrew Jackson High School in Cambria Heights, Queens, without a diploma. His troubled academic past had caused teams to bypass him in the 1988 National Basketball Association Draft—despite not-so-subtle hints from a handful of general managers that he might be a first-round selection.

Although word suggested Lloyd had been blackballed by the

league, folks who had seen him play understood if only he might prove he could be responsible for his actions, if only he could stay clean long enough to at least earn an invitation to free agent–rookie camp . . . a job was all but his. Rules were often bent for stars.

"Yo, Ron," Lloyd asked Naclerio, "want to play some ball?"

A junior high school teacher, as well as the basketball coach at Cardozo High School in Bayside, Queens, Ron had known Lloyd for more than five years. He was a de facto guardian, someone who spent time with Lloyd, went to games with him. They'd play ball, talk the talk. Ron, a basketball junkie barely in his thirties, was tuned in to the streets and to their kids. He had been an athlete, an all-America baseball player at St. John's University, where his team made the 1978 College World Series. He roomed with future major-league star relief pitcher John Franco.

"Two-thirds of the world is covered by water," the former center fielder would tell anyone who'd give him a listen. "The other third is covered by Ron Naclerio."

He could be raw, coarse. But he understood an athlete's mentality; knew how to deal with them and with their problems. In college, he'd once led the nation in stolen bases and was a minor-league outfielder with the Chicago White Sox organization before a string of ankle injuries sidelined his career. Lloyd's relatives had grown so accustomed to him and respected him so much, in fact, they'd even given him a nickname. Lloyd's white brother, they called him.

"Nah, I'm watchin' the game," Ron told Lloyd. "I don't want to go."

"C'mon, Ron," Lloyd said, prodding. "Let's go work out."

Another time, another place, Ron would have gone. But he suspected Lloyd was again using drugs and they had fought just two days before, during a confrontation over those suspicions. Ron screamed at Lloyd and had come close to laying him out. He wanted to make it clear he would not tolerate such failure. Like so many others before him, he'd finally reached his breaking point. If Lloyd really wanted to succeed, if he really wanted to prove to the world he could turn his life around, he'd have to take the long-overdue first step. He'd have to prove he really could stand on his own.

"I'm tired," Ron said. "I'm stayin' home."

A short while later, Lloyd left home for a gym on Long Island.

It was Wednesday, May 10, 1989. The NBA Draft was almost two months away; rookie summer camps, little more than three.

———

Lloyd wasn't thinking about the NBA by the time he returned home to the green, single-family row house his grandmother owned on 203rd Street in Hollis, Queens.

His workout against a handful of locals had been relaxed—they hadn't offered much competition—and, bored, Lloyd was still looking for something to do.

On the surface, it was a quiet, residential neighborhood. A neighborhood that, over the course of generations, had given life to the dreams of a host of notables—from *60 Minutes* correspondent Andy Rooney, political humorist Art Buchwald, and political activist Rev. Al Sharpton to future FUBU founder Daymond John, Def Jam founder Russell Simmons, hip-hop megastar LL Cool J, and Reverend Run and his fellow members of Run-D.M.C. The fifty-fourth governor of New York, Mario Cuomo, and his son, Andrew, who would become its fifty-sixth governor, at one time lived in Hollis. So did the former U.S. ambassador to the United Nations Andrew Young. Brooklyn native Mark Jackson, who went on to become an all-America point guard at St. John's and the 1987–88 NBA Rookie of the Year with the New York Knicks, had ties to the neighborhood.

Still, when Lloyd was growing up there in the 1980s, Hollis and nearby St. Albans was an area with a more sinister, much less visible side.

For years Hollis had been a neighborhood in transition, one that day by day, block by block, was falling prey to drugs and to drug-related violence that skewed the community and disembodied lives. It was a crack neighborhood, crack cocaine being the latest inner-city scourge of the times. A neighborhood where dealers sometimes dealt from street corners down near Jamaica Avenue, Hollis Avenue, or

Francis Lewis Boulevard; where dealers sometimes dealt from the very house next door.

A neighborhood where the quiet of any given night might be shattered at the unlikeliest of moments, gunfire erupting in the middle of an otherwise quiet street.

Lloyd Daniels was about to become its next victim.

———

Outside, it continued to rain.

Lloyd and his aunt Sherry, herself only in her twenties, settled down in the kitchen with a deck of cards, a bottle of champagne, and some quart cans of O.E.—Olde English malt liquor. It was hardly a good start to a long night for a man with an alcohol problem.

For about an hour, the game went on. Hands were dealt, jokes were told. Laughter filled the room, alcohol was consumed. Soon Lloyd, feeling good, feeling that old feel, walked out to the living room. The clock was nearing midnight.

"Grandma," he said, "let me have one of them posters you got."

His grandmother, in her late fifties, hardworking, looked him in the eye.

The posters, made when Lloyd was in Topeka, were an ad for Gaines Cycle Dog Food. They pictured Lloyd in a Sizzlers uniform and, at the bottom, he lay stretched out amid a gathering of sad-eyed puppies and their dog food bowls.

Around the neighborhood, where Lloyd was a folk hero due to his ability, where he was known simply by his nickname, "Swee'pea," they were like gold.

"I'm not giving you any posters," his grandmother, Lulia Hendley, said. "You're gonna sell them to buy crack, you are."

Lloyd protested. "No, Grandma. Grandma, I'm not."

"Don't con me," she said. "I know what you're doin'."

"I ain't, Grandma. I just want one."

"Junior," she said, sharply, warning the grandchild she'd always called Junior after his father, her eldest son, "if you don't stop it, stop doin' those drugs, you're gonna get busted in the ass. You know that? You'll get busted in the ass, the cops will pick you up, put you in Rikers Island, and you know you can't deal with no Rikers Island.

"And you know you're gonna be dead if you get shot."

"Grandma," Lloyd said. "Grandma, I ain't doin' that stuff no more."

"You'd better not be," she said. But Lloyd, hardly interested in her learned, sage advice, had already turned his back on her—headed out to the kitchen.

He still had that hunger. And, facing the temptation and feeling weak as any recovering addict could possibly feel surrounded by a neighborhood filled with the bad stuff, Lloyd picked up the phone around midnight and paged his friend Moe.

The next day, the newspapers and police were rampant in their speculation about Moe, whose name and pager number were found on a slip of paper in Lloyd's bedroom after the shooting. In the days before cell phones became commonplace, pagers—used to alert someone to call you as soon as they could find a pay phone or landline—were carried primarily by folks who needed to be reached in emergency situations.

Doctors carried pagers. So did cops.

But in areas like Hollis, drug dealers and criminals carried pagers. They were their lifelines to their business clientele.

———

It turned out the number belonged to Kevin Barry, a man as far removed from the bad stuff as could be. Barry was almost forty. Still, it often seemed like he was from another time, back when life was far simpler. He believed in people. He believed they owed something to each other. And he believed in lending a helping hand.

Like countless others before him, he also believed in Lloyd.

He had met Lloyd not a month before. Ron introduced them. Immediately Barry offered support. He ran a small, independent school bus company. Lloyd called his bus, his ride, the Yellow Stretch. A man who had been friends with legendary boxing trainer Cus D'Amato, having met Mike Tyson when the future heavyweight champion was just thirteen and having seen what D'Amato had done for him, Barry had been inspired to found a nonprofit organization called the Give a Kid a Chance Foundation. He ran neighborhood basketball games, took underprivileged kids to the movies. He taught them there was a way other than what they saw on the streets of New York.

He taught them that they had a future.

Barry took Lloyd to his house in Brooklyn. He moved out of his bedroom, gave it to Lloyd, hung a sign on the door that said, "Lloyd's Room." Slept on the couch. He bought clothes for Lloyd, found him a trainer to get him into playing shape. He and his sons shared meals with their new housemate. They shared their lives. Their hearts.

Barry was trying to teach Lloyd to read, was teaching him responsibility. Lloyd called him Moe, mainly because Barry liked to watch *The Three Stooges*.

Then, one night, Lloyd showed up at a club game at St. John's. High.

"He was with a drug dealer," Barry said, later. "He was zonked out of his mind. Ron read him the riot act. I told him, 'You're fucked up. You're an asshole.'... We had a big fight. I went home, put a poster of Len Bias on the wall"—Bias being a star at the University of Maryland who had died of "cocaine intoxication" just two days after the Boston Celtics had taken him second overall in the 1986 NBA Draft.

As Barry said, "When Lloyd got home, I pointed at that picture. I said, 'Am I gonna be coming to visit you in a casket? Is that how this ends?'"

"He said, 'No, Kev. I'm goin' to make it.'"

Barry didn't believe him, threw him out. That was Monday, May 8.

———

Kevin Barry was out of the house when Lloyd called the pager number that Wednesday. But he was in a forgiving mood and, deep down, he knew Lloyd needed him. So, when he got the message, he called Lloyd back as soon as he could.

"C'mon an' get me," Lloyd said. "I got to get out of here."

"But I'm in Albany," Barry said, trying hard to sound serious.

"How far's that?" Lloyd asked.

"About four hours," Barry said.

"Okay," Lloyd said. "Can you come by and pick me up in twenty minutes?"

This time, Barry laughed. Even if Barry had been in Albany, Lloyd never did have a realistic conception of time. And even though it was somewhere around 1 a.m., Barry knew Lloyd needed him. Really needed him. So, without hesitation, without complaint, he hopped in the yellow stretch and drove from Manhattan to Queens.

For a while, Lloyd waited. But he had the urge. And so, when Kevin Barry arrived in Hollis little more than an hour later, Lloyd was nowhere to be found.

He searched the neighborhood in vain. Lloyd was gone.

As best as anyone could tell, Lloyd had remained in the house and continued to fight his temptation until near 2 a.m., when finally he decided to give in and wandered down to the corner of Hollis Avenue. There, according to relatives, he visited a local "businessman" who worked the corner. From him, relatives later told police, Lloyd picked up a little rock, the street name for crack—the smokable derivative of cocaine.

For years friends had told Lloyd drugs might someday be his downfall. But as one acquaintance said, "With him it always seemed to be a case of where the spirit is willing, but the flesh is weak."

So, when Lloyd returned to the house owned by his grandmother, he had the rock as well as the kind of company no man wants for friends, let alone enemies. Because no sooner had he closed the door than a white sedan arrived out front.

Two men got out of the car and stood at the front gate. Seeing them, Lloyd, who'd run inside to hide his crack vials, hide the rock, stepped outside to talk.

"Yo," one man yelled as Lloyd stepped onto the lawn. "Gimme my stuff."

"Ain't got your stuff," Lloyd yelled back. "Get out of here."

"Yo," the man said, again. "Gimme my stuff or the money. Don't play."

"I told you, man," Lloyd said. "Ain't got your stuff."

Unsure of what caused the confrontation, relatives described to police a scenario that would later prove somewhat incorrect. They said Lloyd, streetwise and king of the street con, had slipped the man, described only as a black male in his late teens or early twenties, two one-dollar bills—instead of the two fives required to buy the rock, sold on the streets by the vial. Now the dealer, finding he'd been ripped off, wanted his cash. Getting no satisfaction, he signaled for his friend, who'd gone back to the car.

With accuracy, though, witnesses told police how that second man had pulled a gun, pointed it at Lloyd. With no money and too far from the door to make a safe run for it, Lloyd made yet another bad decision in a life filled with bad decisions.

He reached for the gun.

Bam! And his body recoiled with the shot.

Bam! And, again, his body recoiled with the shot.

Four or five times, no one seemed sure, the gun went off.

Three times, for certain, its bullets struck Lloyd.

Have you ever seen a man get shot? It is almost mystical. Fire spews out the gun barrel. Skin tears, lead explodes. Shrapnel splinters and punctures organs as surely as spilled acid eats its way through metal. Powder residue hangs in the air: warm, moist, yet chilling. Its stench is powerful, spectacular even—like that of rotten eggs. Everything moves in slow motion. The body tumbles as if in instant replay. Blood shoots forth as if to replicate the motion of an oversize rock dropped into a pool of water; first, droplets splatter outward to reach escape velocity, then follows a steady stream. Screams, if there be, echo inside the brain until, finally, in agony, they hit home. Register.

And then the man falls, his innermost possessions most likely no longer locked away in secrecy. Body and earth, fused by violence, momentarily one.

"I looked out the window and I said, 'This joker's gonna shoot Junior,'" Lulia Hendley recalled, later on. "I gets to the door, I heard the shooting. And Junior grabs him, grabs the guy. One shot hit Junior; then two more."

"I was getting in the shower and my mother said, 'Lloyd, there are two people out there for you,'" Gary Hendley, an uncle who also lived in the house, said.

By the time Gary Hendley reached the lawn after the shots, Lloyd was sprawled out, writhing in agonizing pain, his lean, lanky body folded and contorted.

The two men and the car, going. Gone.

"I heard four shots," he said. "I ran outside and saw Swee'pea lying on the ground. I didn't even see the bullet holes at first. I said, 'Swee'pea, they ruined you.'"

Built like a bull and with shoulders like an NFL linebacker, Gary Hendley, with all the strength he could muster, pulled his nephew, already a bloody mess, down the driveway and in through a side door. He laid his broken body down in the hallway.

"My mom and my sister called the police and an ambulance," he said.

"I was like, 'Oh God, he's shot,'" Lulia Hendley recalled of the moment, days later. Then, she said, she yelled, "He's gonna die. Junior's gonna die!"

As they loaded him onto the stretcher, still conscious, the hundred-dollar sweatsuit Kevin Barry bought him having been torn apart, its turquoise fabric soaked almost pure scarlet red, Lloyd looked at anxious relatives and then at another uncle, J. C. Daniels.

"I don't want to die, J.C.," he pleaded. "Don't let me die."

New York City is known for the strange twists and turns it puts on life and the awkward, sometimes bizarre angles it brings to the fates, and this day certainly was no different. By the following nightfall, across the river in Manhattan, the crowd would be letting loose with a deafening roar as Mark Jackson and the New York Knicks met Michael Jordan and the Chicago Bulls in a playoff game at Madison Square Garden. But now, back in the operating room at Mary Immaculate, where the trauma team had assembled, Dr. Picard and his crew worked in virtual silence, save for the clattering of instruments and tools, as they fought to save the life of Lloyd Daniels.

There was a chance.

But honestly, Picard figured, it was a miracle his patient was still alive at all.

The average body has ten pints of blood and already Lloyd had lost 60 percent of that. His pulse was weakening, his breathing erratic. A bullet had punctured and collapsed his right lung. Another had barely missed his heart and embedded itself in his posterior chest wall. All around, blood spurted and seeped into the chest cavity.

This would be touch-and-go.

Around 6 a.m., as people in the neighborhood awoke, Lulia Hendley went outside to tear down the yellow police crime-scene tape drawn across her lawn from fence to house. She was angry. She couldn't stand it any longer. When she finally regained her composure, she went back inside and called Ron Naclerio. Bad news, she said.

Momentarily, Ron wrestled with his emotions, fought back his tears. Then he called Kevin Barry and Tom Rome, the Manhattan attorney who represented Lloyd.

Just the night before, Ron and Tom had talked about Lloyd's future.

They'd joked about the professional career waiting out there for him, waiting to be grabbed like a brass ring on some childhood merry-go-round. They'd joked about the movie that could be made about Lloyd's life. A soap opera, they'd called it.

"All we need is one of two things to happen," Ron told Tom Rome that night, amid laughter. "All he has to do is get killed or make the NBA."

When Rome answered the phone that morning, Ron tried his best to salve his guilt by putting the best face he could on what had happened to his troubled friend.

"Well, Tom," he said, "it looks like we can finally make the movie."

The Legend of Swee'pea

Lloyd seemed to be unconscious and, as far as anyone could tell, had been for the better part of the past half hour. Around him uniformed bodies raced with an almost nonsensical sense of urgency, their actions spasmodic and haphazard and brought forth with random precision; the result of their motions, in reality, was little more than energy wasted. He had viewed the scenario as if at half speed, watched it and visualized it as slow as sap runs from the cut bark. This was the biggest game of his life, he thought. He couldn't have someone else screw it up. Not after he had fought so hard.

Maybe it was heart; maybe just survival instinct. But inside something told him he couldn't go down without more of a fight. So he yelled, yelled like only a man who has an understanding of such grave nature can yell; calling hard and loud to be heard above the din, but trying his best not to sound like a man of desperation.

"Yo, c'mon!" he screamed. For emphasis, he clapped his hands twice in quick succession. "Ain't I said, 'C'mon'? Get me the motherfuckin' ball!"

The game was close, on the line. That Andrew Jackson still led was, in itself, nothing short of a miracle. A late run by Wyandanch had trimmed a 57–44 lead—a lead that once seemed near insurmountable—to one fragile point, 59–58. In that span, Lloyd actually had missed two straight shots from the field and a jam off an offensive rebound. Now, with little more than five minutes left, the crowd that had gathered on January 12, 1986, to watch the final of four consecutive games in the

Martin Luther King Classic at Nassau Coliseum in Uniondale, Long Island, had grown anxious, frenetic.

Most stood, awaiting the next move.

More than likely those in the crowd of about 8,500 had read accounts of his ability in the four New York daily newspapers and had heard what sounded to be tall tales of the skill possessed by this teenage all-America candidate from the streets of New York City. Stories, they thought, that must surely be pure exaggeration.

Yet, here before their very eyes was Lloyd Daniels, the player known simply as Swee'pea, his vast ability mocking the best efforts of the players around him.

A hush settled over the crowd as the pass came to Lloyd.

He had never played in front of so many before. And there were more than a few college scouts in the stands. Still, Lloyd took the ball near the top of the key, faked a pass, juked his man, spun off him—and posted up. From eight feet he let it ride with the smoothness of a seasoned con man putting the touch on an easy mark. In a move that was pure playground he laughed at his man as he did, trash-talking him.

"Real fine!" someone in the stands yelled from a few rows back as he let go the shot, banking it in easy off the backboard. Jackson led, 61–58.

Over the course of the next few minutes, when the game would be won and lost, when his inexperienced teammates appeared on the verge of panic before the raucous crowd who'd gathered for the most prestigious of all local regular-season metro-area high school basketball tournaments, Lloyd took control. He seemed oblivious to everything going on around him, except what was important. The game.

He zeroed in, focused on his mission. He never once lost his poise, never once let his concentration wander. He laid passes on all the right fingertips.

Down the stretch, he made all his shots.

Double-teamed—no, triple-teamed—he buried a pull-up twelve-footer in traffic to make it 66–60, then hit a clutch ten-foot banker to keep Jackson ahead, 68–65, after the lead had again been cut to just one. He sent home a short-range jumper—for him, child's play, really—with fifty-one seconds left to give Jackson a 70–67 advantage.

He followed it with passes that put two teammates in position to be fouled in the waning seconds, all of which gave Andrew Jackson a hard-fought 72–71 win, the score made close only on an insignificant basket at the buzzer by the team from Long Island.

"We knew we wouldn't be able to stop him," longtime Wyandanch coach Carl Gainey said, shaking his head, when it was over. "He had too much size, too much ability. We just tried to slow him down a little. . . . We couldn't even do that."

Unconscious?

By the time all was said and done, Lloyd had gone 17-for-26 from the field, as he scored a tournament-high thirty-six points, grabbed a tournament-high seventeen rebounds and blocked two shots—leaving those in the crowd, as well as most of his opponents, also shaking their heads in amazement. It was estimated he had also totaled at least ten assists, though it turned out no one had thought to keep track.

Named the tournament's outstanding player, he had played the unlikeliest of floor combinations: center on defense and point guard on offense.

"One hell of a player," Wyandanch point guard Sean Ramos said.

"That's why," Andrew Jackson coach Chuck Granby said of his junior all-America candidate after the game, "he's Lloyd Daniels."

The ironic part was that those who'd watched Lloyd in the parks and on the playgrounds, on the basketball courts in a host of band-box gymnasiums throughout New York City, understood one thing: the game had hardly been his best.

———

There was this litany of 1980s TV commercials. Spike Lee talking about legends, the bill of his baseball cap flipped up to reveal the word "Brooklyn."

"Yo," Lee said in one. "Mars Blackmon in the house talkin' 'bout my main man Money. Here's action photos of Money slammin' in Detroit."

All you'd see was a rim and sneaker-clad feet.

"In L.A." More feet.

"Boston." More feet. "Hmm. Must be Bird's-eye view," Lee, in his full-blown Mars character said, the reference to Boston Celtics all-time great Larry Bird.

"Denver." Feet and mountains.

"Some serious hang time. Must be the mountain air."

"The other L.A." (Meaning, the Clippers.)

"Paris. Oui, oui!"

Walla Walla. Budapest. The Sea of Tranquility. Yeah, the Moon.

Or, there was Spike Lee as some parkie, on the stoop of a brown-stone, talking to a bunch of kids about Lamar Mundane, the old-time park legend known as Rain Man or Money. "Money!" What he yelled at opponents as he rained thirty-footers down on them like layups. Burying them from each and every conceivable angle, nothing but net.

Like some god. Some playground basketball god.

You know the success stories, the guys who made it. Most every fan does.

They're the guys you hear about on radio sports-talk shows, on TV; that you read about in the papers. That you read about, nowadays, in the blogs and on the Web.

Back in the day, they were Larry Bird and Magic Johnson. Julius Erving, Bernard King. Then Patrick Ewing, Isiah Thomas, and Dominique Wilkins. Or Michael Jordan, Scottie Pippen, Dennis Rodman, Karl Malone, Moses Malone, and Hakeem Olajuwon. Later, Kobe Bryant and Tim Duncan and, not so long ago, Shaquille O'Neal.

In the here and now? That'd be Steph Curry, King James.

LeBron James. Of course.

And, of course, there are the exploits of those who came before, the ones most fans have only heard about in tellings down through the generations, in stories of the greatest who ever played. These are tales of Bill Russell and Pistol Pete Maravich, of Bob Cousy and the Big O—Oscar Robertson. Of Walt Frazier and Elgin Baylor, Jerry West and Earl "the Pearl" Monroe, known on the streets of Philadelphia as Thomas Edison—a nickname, legend has it, bestowed by the awe-struck for his illimitable inventiveness.

Best known on the playgrounds of New York as Black Jesus.

Just because.

These are stories about Wilt "the Stilt" Chamberlain, who millions of old-timers swear they "remember" seeing score a hundred points in a game, though almost no one saw that game that night in Hershey, Pennsylvania, back on March 2, 1962. Didn't see it because it wasn't televised; because it wasn't even filmed.

All of which often is the case of those other guys, the purest of playground guys; the ones with no records, no statistics, no film or movies or video to prove who they were, what they were. The ones who, without chronicles—without, ironically, concrete evidence—almost always have only word of mouth as testament to their careers. Their lives. Lives forever mythical, mystical, renditions of both the real and imagined.

Nowadays, if you're really lucky, you might be able to reference them online on ESPN or *Sports Illustrated*, on Wikipedia or on a handful of major metropolitan newspaper websites. In a book. Sometimes you might even find a few minutes of rare footage on YouTube. All of which is, in all honesty, about as close as most of you—as anyone who didn't see them in the flesh, with their own eyes—are ever going to get to knowing just what they were; just how great they were or might have been.

Every region has them. Hot Sauce Champion in Atlanta; Piggy Johnson and Electric Eye Robinson in Chicago. Bubbles Hawkins and Chain Williams in Detroit; Hook Mitchell, Worm Killum, and old-timer Wondrous Willie Wise in Cali; Chink Scott, Munchy Mason, City Lights Warrick, Sad Eye Watson, and Lionel "Train" Simmons in Philly. Pick a city, a neighborhood, a block. A playground. You'll get some localized version. Sleepy, Poodle, Drawers. Trouble, the Answer. Homicide, Bone Collector, One and Only, Killer Cross, Jeremiah "Carnival" King, Skip to My Lou, Ice Cream.

Yeah, Ice Cream. *Fucking Ice Cream.*

These guys represent the basic premise of what a playground legend like Lloyd "Swee'pea" Daniels was back then and still is today. The idea that people are remembered, are honored and talked about, on the streets and in the playgrounds, the way folks talk about Old West gunfighters like Billy the Kid and Jesse James; about old Prohibition-era gangsters like Al Capone, Baby Face Nelson, Pretty Boy Floyd, John Dillinger, and Bonnie and Clyde. The way they talk about old Negro League, Caribbean Winter League, and Cuban League baseball players, whose lives and careers often went undocumented. The way they talk about those old professional sports stars, whose careers—whose best moments in the game—often were hidden in plain sight.

Unfilmed. *Unseen.*

Those playground legends did—and, more often than not, still do—represent more, because you know a character like Money could have been any real street legend if only he'd gotten his shot at the big time. At the NBA. Because Lamar Mundane is the stark reality of the streets. Talked about only by those few who still remember.

Still, something about those legends was never explained; there was something about the real playground basketball legends that even a guy like Mars Blackmon never told us. Then. Or now. It was the part about why those guys never were able to escape the playgrounds, despite vast abilities. Why they never made it to the big time, too.

It was the part about how they are, how they were, real men in the real world. Real men with real problems, real concerns. Real flaws. Real men, not heroes.

Humans, not gods.

————

In legend, they are Swee'pea, the Goat, Red, and the Animal. They are folks like 88 James, so called because he had just eight fingers—four on each hand. They are Bullethead, Band-Aid, Boo, Booger, Bug, Future. The Terminator. The Truth. They are old-time folks like Fly, Helicopter, Pee Wee, and the Destroyer—Joe Hammond, aka an inmate identification number in some long-forgotten NYPD file somewhere.

Often, no one is quite sure how they came to be legends, whether it was a move or just a moment. In the end, it didn't matter. Doesn't matter. That they are remembered, that their nicknames alone still seem to evoke respect and regard, is enough.

Especially in the boroughs of a make-it-or-break-it place like New York City, a place where reputation alone can lift a man above the din. Especially here, in the Mecca of basketball, the place where the city game became *The City Game*. Refuse, and all.

In reality, they were folks like Lloyd Daniels and Earl Manigault, Tony Bruin and Richie Adams; men whose frailties meant they could never quite live up to their street status. Men who, despite some brief, shining moment, might not have been as good as the folks who made the NBA. Men who, in some cases, despite their downside, might have been better than the best who ever played the game. Ever.

Anytime, anywhere.

They were, and remain, men who became legends because, despite their talents, they weren't much different from the folks who came to watch them: the locals and the parkies, the addicts and the small-time entrepreneurs. They were just like them.

In some cases, they were them.

Joe Hammond once dropped twenty-five in a half against the good doctor, Dr. J, Julius Erving, and once scored seventy-three in a cable television game in the Rucker Pros, the famed summer tournament in Harlem. But he turned down a contract offer from the Los Angeles Lakers because it lacked a no-cut clause and, when a scout came to see him on the streets, Hammond told him to wait.

He was busy shooting dice.

And so Hammond blew his chance, turned to drugs, and wound up in Rikers Island, the New York City jail in the East River not far from LaGuardia Airport.

Later, he went upstate—to the state prison at Dannemora.

Pee Wee Kirkland had better things to do, too, than worry about the NBA. But in New York, his head-to-head battles with Tiny Archibald remain the stuff of legend.

"Pee Wee was a guard, Norfolk State. Got drafted by the Chicago Bulls," Archibald, who came out of a Bronx housing project to star in fourteen seasons in the NBA with the Boston Celtics, Cincinnati Royals, Kansas City–Omaha Kings, New Jersey Nets, and Milwaukee Bucks, recalled. "I used to go against him on the streets and in the playgrounds. . . . One of the best there ever was. His problem was he wasn't just an educated guy, but a street person, too. When Chicago offered him a contract, he laughed in their face and said, 'Hey, I could make more money in a couple of days out on the street.'" He was right, though as Archibald said, "He ended up in the federal pen."

James "Fly" Williams, the man from the 'Ville, Brownsville, Brooklyn, once set the NCAA major-college scoring record for freshmen, averaging 29.4 points per game at Austin Peay State University—a mark that stood from 1973 until the 1988–89 season, when it finally was broken by Chris Jackson of Louisiana State University.

His game was so spectacular, so full of flash, that it sparked the creation of what may be the most memorable of all college cheers: *"Fly is Open, Let's Go Peay!"*

Later, when he wasn't in Rikers, Fly, the man who once dropped sixty-three on future NBA great Moses Malone at the Dapper Dan Tournament, a high school all-star game, could often be found hanging around the Noble Drew Ali Plaza in Brownsville with half his lungs and a massive scar on the left side of his back—the result of an ill-fated robbery attempt that ended with a shotgun blast that nearly killed him.

Despite their shortcomings, they were also men who, on the playgrounds, brought pride to their neighborhoods. Men who played for honor and self-respect. Men who played because they had nothing better to do. Because they loved the game, nothing more. That they eventually fell hard, fell through the cracks in the concrete dream—failing in life, failing in their quest for success, failing to live up to the expectations, the hype; failing themselves—was, in fact, immaterial to what they accomplished.

After all, they couldn't do well in everything.

They were only human.

Legends, despite the lore that precedes them, are in fact just human.

Men who start life, live life, and sometimes—actually, more than just sometimes—end up like Lloyd Daniels. Losing their way, and sometimes even losing it all.

———

Sheets of tin and aluminum covered the building where its windows had once been, their glass having long ago been knocked clean away in the name of burglary, vandalism, and simple, honest old age. It was as if bandages had been placed on the running sores of a wound, and for all the protection they afforded against the elements, both natural and man-made, they had allowed it to become gangrenous.

Just a shell, the structure that remained served as a soulful, if tired, reminder of what had once been, standing among a line of ancient, beaten, and battered sentinels on this long-ago discarded block in East New York known as New Jersey Avenue.

Looking around, it was difficult to imagine this place had ever been beautiful, had ever been new or even clean. Everything about it, about this section of Brooklyn, in fact, painted a harsh picture of abject poverty. Just a block north, in an abandoned, weeded lot at the corner of Belmont and Jersey, old tires formed a mountain almost one-story high and bags of uncollected garbage sat decaying on the sidewalk, along a street lined with long-silenced doorways. On the streets walked the living dead, corpses who didn't know they were corpses, skeletons searching for salvation in the form of needles and nods and schemer's dreams. Reality here often came in the form of rat-infested hallways, roach-infested kitchens, and lice- and bedbug-infested bedrooms.

Here families often sat huddled in winter coats in heat-starved buildings in the frigid dead of winter, and were forced to broil in undershirts in congested, sweat-filled brick row apartments in the stifling, humid heat of summer—unable even to slip onto their fire escapes for relief, so powerful was the fear they, too, might become innocent victims of stray bullets from random shootings on the streets below.

Even the honorable folks—folks who, for lack of a better way but not for lack of pride, worked dead-end jobs, cleaning their cars, sweeping their sidewalks—remained stuck, as if by fate, in the middle of what had become a god-forsaken hell on earth.

It was here, on the first floor of a dilapidated walk-up among the boarded-up buildings that lined this stretch of New Jersey Avenue between Dumont and Blake, that Lloyd first came to be introduced to the world and to its nuances. It was a difficult way to start life. From here, it seemed, things almost never got better.

Usually, they only got worse.

———

Judy Stephens was a woman of considerable good looks, light-skinned and fine-featured.

She had been born in Brooklyn in a different time, before Brownsville and East New York had first gone to crack; back when people like her could live in those neighborhoods and work and go about their honest business in relative safety.

She had met Lloyd Daniels, Sr., while in high school. He was lean, a little bit over six foot tall, with a rich, even-toned coffee complexion, a handsome man with a knack for a good line. Even the gap between his front teeth lent to his appearance. She found herself attracted. The two soon fell in love and became an item in the neighborhood.

Lloyd had come to Brooklyn years earlier with his mother, Lulia, who had been born in Cordele, Georgia, a back-roads town about sixty miles south of Macon. He had been sheltered by family, his mother one of sixteen children—eleven of them girls—on a farm where they shucked corn, milked cows, and raised hogs and chickens.

Where they picked cotton.

In her teens, Lulia met a man named Walter Daniels. And in 1948, when she was just eighteen, the two of them had Lloyd, the first of six children. But Lulia was a strong-headed woman who, as she described it, "had ambition." Soon she grew tired of that farm in Cordele. "I wanted to better myself, make a better life for myself," she said.

So, in 1959, Lulia took her children and headed north. When Walter declined to go with her, she said, "I walked." As she defined it, "I'm a survivor."

Nothing would stand in her way, not even a man.

Lulia arrived in New York on a Sunday afternoon. By nightfall she had a job as a housemaid for a bed-ridden woman. Years later, she formally divorced Walter Daniels, married a man named James Hendley, and had five more children, the first three of them boys. Her second husband, she said, had a penchant for chasing women.

"So," she said, "I threw *him* out of the house."

Though on her own, Lulia worked hard to instill good values in her kids. She worked six days a week. Seven days a week she showered them with love and affection. She tried to understand their problems. All she ever asked in return was respect.

When she heard that Judy Stephens, then just sixteen years old, had become pregnant by her son, she went and paid her a visit.

"One day, I went to her work," Lulia said. "I said, 'You're pregnant, aren't you?' She said, 'How do you know? How do you know I'm pregnant?' I said, 'I know these things. I'm a mother. I can tell.' She said, 'Please don't tell my mother.' She was eight and a half months pregnant when she and Lloyd got married."

Lulia allowed the teenage couple to hold the wedding reception at her home in Brooklyn. She loved them. What else could she do? Theirs was not the best life, Lloyd's and Judy's. Like many in the neighborhood, they lacked money. But they were young and in love and had their son, also named Lloyd and otherwise known as Junior, who had been born on September 4, 1967. Lulia liked to tell folks how, when she went to the hospital, the nurse didn't even have to tell her which child was her grandson.

"The big, big baby," she said. "The one who got some good looks from his mother and that sweet face from his father."

But Junior was born while a tragedy was waiting to happen. Not long after his birth, Judy was diagnosed with uterine cancer. He was almost three when she died. It nearly destroyed his father, who, his mother said, in an effort to kill the pain, turned his attentions to alcohol. See, Lulia said, her son wanted to be strong, too. But like the rest of her children—who, despite Lulia's best efforts, all seemed to be finding problems of their own on the streets of New York—he just didn't know how.

"My son tried to commit suicide," she said. "He started drinkin', he started pickin' fights and stuff. It was rough. He wanted to die with the mother. My son, Junior's father, stayed drunk for two and a half years. I'm talkin' about he started drinkin' big. Then one day he fell out, right there on the avenue. I guess his blood pressure, whatever, it got so bad, that they had to put him in a straitjacket, because of the drinkin', the seizures he was havin'. Junior used to say when he see his father that he was embarrassed. That's why I figured Junior would never do drugs or drink. He was embarrassed to see his father. He'd say to me, 'Ooh, if I ever do that stuff like that, Gran'ma, I'll kill myself. I'll commit suicide. I won't never do no drugs or drink.'"

It was the first of many promises Junior wouldn't keep.

———

It is said a hungry tiger hides all indications of an impending strike. That it stalks its prey with an illusive, elusive touch; insinuates itself on a situation with purposeful stealth in order to gain the best advantage. Then, and only then, does it make its move.

Bold and impudent.

Watch footage of Lloyd Daniels on a basketball court and you will see such presence, such purpose. There is self-assurance in his game, a certain court awareness, perception; instinct that seems to let him know when the time is right. Almost never does he attempt to force a situation. Almost never does he tip his hand too soon.

His passes all seem to have that touch. Watch as he looks off the man, sends the ball in the opposite direction, as if he knew, felt, where his man would be. You can see how they are timed; so that his man is in a position of advantage, ready to strike.

All his shots, whether they come from two feet or twenty-five, seem to be released with a precision that cannot be taught, the kind that is felt deep within a man's bones.

In his soul.

Even rebounds are grabbed with just the right amount of authority; no wasted motion or effort, just what is needed to get the job done. To get his message across.

This is a man who understands the game of basketball the way Beethoven or Mozart understood music, the way Michelangelo understood painting. With a feel, a magic, that cannot accurately be described because, in reality, it is the stuff of legend.

Saul Lerner claimed he saw it the first time he ever watched Lloyd, back in the fall of 1983, when Lloyd was an eighth grader at Intermediate School 218 in Brooklyn. Lerner was a high school basketball coach who had spent three years as a pro player in Israel. He also headed the school's special education program. Lloyd was a special ed student who played ball and, as Lerner told it, sometimes attended class.

"He had one thing in his life," Lerner said. "Basketball."

As Lerner recalled: "I remember the first time that I watched him. . . . You could see that he had a certain brilliance on the court, one that he shouldn't have had because it was contradictory to everything he did in the classroom. Here was a kid who was on the pre-primer level in class—we're talking stuff like C-A-T—who was on the major-college or professional level on the court. You don't see kids graduating from college with the kind of on-court knowledge he had then. At that age, you're happy when a kid can put it in the basket. But he had vision. He knew how to balance out the floor. He knew how to find a kid cutting through the middle. He was something else."

Then again, Lloyd always seemed to be something else on the streets and playgrounds of New York, a place where the best often are known only by their calling card—a nickname, a moment, a move. Lloyd became known simply as Swee'pea. It was a nickname he acquired coming up in the Brownsville–East New York section of Brooklyn, where the locals—in particular, this guy named Yodel—noticed that his peculiar-shaped oval head, skipping-stone flat cheeks, high, receding hairline, and skintight hair gave him a curious resemblance to the baby-faced character from *Popeye*.

He was something else out on New Jersey Avenue, where, after his mother died, he lived with his maternal grandmother, Annie Sargeant Stephens, in that apartment a block from Thomas Jefferson High School and not far from where former heavyweight boxing champion Mike Tyson was born. And he was something else at Thomas Jefferson—Jeff—where, as a ninth grader, he broke his ankle playing ball and missed most of the regular season, then returned for the last seven games to lead a seven-man team into the playoffs and, after scoring twenty-nine points in a first-round upset of Tilden High School, netted thirty to almost single-handedly beat Abraham Lincoln.

Swee'pea owned Lafayette Gardens, a park that often showcased some of the best talent in Brooklyn. There he once scored fifty-four points to win a head-to-head battle with the brother of former Utah Jazz and Knicks forward Carey Scurry; Moses Scurry later went on to become a star for the 1990 NCAA national champion University of Nevada–Las Vegas Runnin' Rebels. And Swee'pea owned Five-Star Camp, where, in 1985, he buried J. R. Reid, then the most highly touted player on the planet, one who would become an all-American at the University of North Carolina and fifth overall pick in the 1989 NBA Draft, taken by the original Charlotte Hornets.

Swee'pea was slick, refined. He was confident, but not cocky. In an era when, and in a neighborhood where, taking it to the hoop and jamming it home with thunder was considered to be the real deal—it was once written a New York City guard "will give up his gold and his girl before he'll give up his dribble"—he was secure enough, knowledgeable enough, to lay off a pass or lay it in when the moment called for it. In one game he might control things with his passing, making no-look feeds or simple bounce passes, something rarely seen in an age of glitter and flash. In another he might dominate with scoring, firing jumper after jumper with consistency from twenty-five feet.

"He was born to play basketball," East Coast recruiting expert Tom Konchalski said then. Konchalski, who for decades evaluated high school talent for many of the nation's college coaches, first saw Lloyd play ball back in junior high school.

"He just had a special gift, almost a mystical grasp of the game. I don't think it was anything he was even taught. He had a great instinctive feel for the game, such sophistication, such pedigree. Maybe the best way to describe it is to compare it to the Socratic ideal of knowledge as remembrance, almost as if he had inherited it as knowledge learned in a previous life. His biggest problem on the court was that he was such a sophisticate, had such an understanding of the game, that he had little tolerance for others who were not as sophisticated and so he easily became querulous with others who could not do what he could. But, aside from that, not many have ever possessed his ability to read the game, had his understanding of how to let the game come to him and of how to let the game dictate what he should do. He understood you could not predetermine what to do with the ball. No one saw the floor like Lloyd."

The closest comparison?

"Maybe, Magic Johnson," Konchalski said. "Maybe." And, as Konchalski pointed out, not meaning to sound facetious, that was being kind to Magic.

As Larry Davis, who in 1984 briefly coached Lloyd on the prep school basketball team at Oak Hill Academy in rural Mouth of Wilson, Virginia, said: "God just said one day, 'I'm going to laugh at the rest of the basketball world,' and he made this kid."

———

Of course, Swee'pea wasn't without flaw. He didn't care much for playing defense, didn't like to lift weights, didn't like working to stay in shape. He didn't like practice and could be lackadaisical, sometimes so bored with the competition he didn't give an honest effort. But those deficiencies were minor in comparison to his skills.

"Talent is our narcotic," Al Menendez, who'd watched Lloyd often back when he scouted for the then–New Jersey Nets, said. "We are addicted to basketball. I've watched Lloyd play since he was a sophomore in high school. He's as good as there is."

"He is a tremendous talent," longtime NBA team executive Donnie

Walsh said back in the 1980s. "No doubt, he has the talent to play in our league."

That ability made Lloyd a *Parade Magazine* all-American his junior year at Andrew Jackson, where he averaged 31.2 points, 12.3 rebounds, ten assists, and five blocks. It made him a much-sought-after player by college coaches, who were willing to overlook his well-documented academic deficiencies—including undiagnosed dyslexia, a third-grade reading level, and frequent truancy—for the chance to get him into their school's uniform. It made him a hot commodity in Topeka, Kansas, where he averaged 16 points, 3.5 rebounds, and 4.7 assists as a twenty-year old rookie in the CBA.

It also made him a playground legend on the streets of New York, one often mentioned in the same breath as a pantheon of basketball gods.

"Sometimes, people talk . . . but, I seen him play," Chris Brooks, an all-America candidate at West Virginia University who played with Lloyd on the New York Gauchos, an Amateur Athletic Union club team in the Bronx, said. "He can shoot, he can dribble, he can play defense when he wants to, and he's [six foot seven]. They say he is the next Magic Johnson and I tell you what, I think he is. Is he the best I've ever seen? I don't know. I like Michael Jordan. But, next to him, it's Lloyd. Hands down."

Basketball Hall of Fame inductee Nate "Tiny" Archibald said when he was young, playground stars like Joe Hammond and Earl Manigault were the best. But, he said, it turned out they had "no direction"— except when they were on the playgrounds.

Lloyd, he said, had those same shortcomings, a player who could be the next George Gervin, Gervin being an all-time NBA great known to millions as "the Iceman," but who was just as likely to end up on the streets. A player who might've been.

The difference between the outcomes, between success and failure? *Reliability.* That's what Archibald said.

"He has the ability to play on the pro level," Archibald said of Lloyd. "He has the talent to be great. But management—coaches and general

managers—want someone who's reliable, who will show up for practice and work, who will show up at a game and do his best. There are
a bunch of guys in the NBA who are not as good as Lloyd. But they're
reliable."

———

In his day Howie Garfinkel, the basketball superscout who also served
as the director of Five-Star Basketball Camps, had seen too many su-
perstar high school players come and go. He liked some, disliked others. Precious few did he hold in as high regard as he held Lloyd Daniels.
Garfinkel first saw Lloyd back in the summer of 1985, when he broke
onto the national scene as only the second high school junior-to-be in
fifteen years to be named outstanding player at the weeklong camp in
Pittsburgh.

Lloyd was a magician; Garfinkel was hypnotized.

So enamored was he that Garfinkel proclaimed to broadcaster and
former star coach Al McGuire, "Lloyd Daniels is the best junior alive,
dead or yet unborn."

"The first time I saw him, I nearly fell out of my seat," Garfinkel
said. "He was just incredible back then. He was great. I remember one
time where he was on a three-on-two break and, as he came down I
thought, 'Is he going to shoot, going to pass?' He went to shoot, drew
the defender. No one was free. At least, *I* didn't see anyone. Then, all
of a sudden, *bingo*! While he was in midair he hit someone for an easy
layup. I was like, 'How did he find that man?' *I* hadn't seen him. After a
while, every time he touched the ball you would lean forward in your
seat in anticipation of a great play."

Seldom did Swee'pea fail to deliver.

"Calvin Murphy, inch for inch, pound for pound, shot for shot, was
the greatest high school player I ever saw," Garfinkel said, citing the
Hall of Famer. "I saw him get thirty-four at the Dapper Dan on a Friday
night, then score sixty-two in twenty-nine minutes the next at the Allen-
town [Pennsylvania] Classic. After that, you can choose between Connie Hawkins, Lew Alcindor, and Lloyd Daniels. It's a pick 'em for second.

"I call Lloyd 'Magic Johnson with a jump shot.'"

To which Stan Dinner, who coached now-closed Benjamin Franklin High School in Harlem, a team that one season fielded five NCAA Division I college stars in Kenny Hutchinson, Richie Adams, Gary Springer, Walter Berry, and Watkins "Boo" Singletary, said: "He is Magic Johnson with a jump shot, all right. Larry Bird's jump shot. Lloyd Daniels can do everything with a basketball except one. . . . Autograph it."

And that was a problem.

School Daze

P.S. 218 sat on the corner of Fountain and Blake about twenty blocks from Lloyd's home in the heart of East New York. It was a hazardous walk for a kid, even one as street-smart as Swee'pea. It was even more hazardous for those who weren't as streetwise, for the kids who had to walk past the Cypress Houses, the Pink Houses, and Linden Plaza—housing projects once built in an effort to provide shelter for the poor and underprivileged, now all-but-forgotten worlds, seen but unseen. Left to the drug dealers and to their clientele. Left to the wind and the rain. To the fates.

The neighborhood had the highest murder rate in New York City, one of the highest in the nation. Over a span of little more than two years, the area, which measured just over six square miles, had seen more than a hundred murders, most of them drug related. As a takeoff on the local all-news radio station, 1010 WINS, whose motto was "You give us twenty-two minutes, we'll give you the world," New York Police Department officers from the embattled 75th Precinct often told visitors: "You give us twenty-two minutes, we'll give you a homicide." Real-world humor, they called it.

But there was nothing funny about East New York. Not if you were an adult, a lifetime of experience under your belt. Certainly, not if you were just a kid.

As the then–chief executive officer of the Local Development Corporation of East New York, Vivian Bright, told the *New York Times* in a January 5, 1989, article about the neighborhood fighting for its very life, "We have four main problems here—abandoned housing, sanitation, crack, and unemployment." As the *Times* reporter Felicia R. Lee wrote in that article: "Statistics fail to convey the hopelessness of East New York." She added: "No one can say definitively why East New York is such a murderous place, but crack gets much of the blame from police and residents."

School provided a sort of safe haven in that turbulent world, one of the few places kids could learn skills that might help them escape the environment. Unlike some public schools in the city, where students had to walk through metal detectors and be searched for weapons by the school security guards just to enter the building for class each morning, I.S. 218 wasn't as bad as imagined. It didn't have a principal like Matthew Barnwell, who, while head of a public school in the Bronx, would be arrested for possession of crack. It didn't have a substantial amount of hard-core, violent students—though, honestly, that was mostly because those kids almost never came to class.

"The school, I would say—considering its neighborhood, where it was—was not as bad a school as you might think," Saul Lerner, head of the special education department at I.S. 218, said. "It was clean. It was relatively new. In many senses it was not a bad place. It was a shelter from the problems that surrounded the school."

Trouble was, those problems seemed to undermine and overwhelm much of everything teachers and faculty were trying to accomplish inside the building.

"They're not coming out of middle-class homes," Lerner said of students in neighborhoods like East New York, noting some come from families where there isn't even a book in the house. "And, as teachers, we can't handle the social issue, only the academic and so, right off the bat, we start off failing these kids. It only gets worse from there. The kids who do get out, who simply make it through school and get out, are the ones who beat the system. They got out of school more than it could offer them. It's a shame it has to be like that."

———

The streets are no place for a kid. But, by the age of seven, Lloyd knew them, inside and out. He knew East New York. He knew neighboring Brownsville, knew Bedford-Stuyvesant. He knew how to panhandle money and how to take the train to the amusement park at

Coney Island, where he would spend an afternoon alone by himself on the rides. Knew how to take the subways and buses to the Hollis–St. Albans section of Queens, where his grandmother Lulia had moved when he was still an infant.

He knew how to sneak out at night from the first-floor apartment on New Jersey Avenue, where he lived with his other grandmother, Annie Sargeant.

Back then, Lloyd would leave at midnight, basketball in hand, and head down the block to the local park. And after he slipped through a cut in the chain-link fence—"Soul in the Hole," he called it; the Hole being the name of the playground—he'd stand in the darkness, stand amid the broken bottles and shavings of glass, amid the rocks and debris that would coat a man's hands black with dirt just from dribbling the ball. He would shoot baskets for hours. Just a kid, alone in the world, an island unto himself, trying to make sense of his situation. Some afternoons he took time to watch the older kids on the playgrounds, where they'd go five-on-five, three-on-three, or just one-on-one—sometimes playing H-O-R-S-E, sometimes just getting in runs. But the rule in New York is that every player—no matter how good—has his age, his time. And unless you own the only ball on the block, you don't get to play with the big boys until you've grown, paid your dues.

And so, being just a kid, Lloyd almost always practiced by himself out in the park at night, stopping only to run for cover when he heard gunfire on the block.

He taught himself how to dribble on those darkened, glass-strewn courts. Taught himself how to pass, bouncing the ball off the chain-link fences. Taught himself to shoot jumpers in the park, which had no lights, banking them home in the dark. He said it developed not only his eye for the basket, but his feel for it. He'd take a hundred shots. After a while, despite the darkness, he could make ninety-eight, ninety-nine.

"Nobody helped me," Lloyd said. "I practiced myself. Shootin', dribblin', passin' off the gate or the fence. Sometimes, twelve, one o'clock in the mornin', I'd be out playin' ball down the block. If I was lucky, I'd get to the lighted park on Thirty-Sixth Street in Manhattan right next to the mouth of the Queens–Midtown Tunnel.

"Usually, I stayed right in the neighborhood."

"Lloyd would disappear for hours on end and just play basketball," said Annie Sargeant, who'd simply let him go do what he did. "At first, I'd worry about him. But then I always figured I could find him down the block, shooting. About the only time I saw him was the weekends when we'd go shopping on Pitkin Avenue."

Lloyd was, in effect, on his own. Annie Sargeant worked. When she left the house in the morning no one was around to watch Lloyd, who then went off and did what he wanted to do. Because of the trauma he had experienced, Annie was reluctant to punish Lloyd when he did do something wrong—like cut school or hang out with a crew that was headed for trouble. "What he found out," one childhood friend said, "was that, when he got older, he had to take care of *hisself*. He didn't have no choice. It was like people pushed him out into the world and said, 'Okay, take care of *biz*. Take care of yourself.' It was like he didn't have no chance. . . . He was on his own."

When Lloyd needed sneakers, he had to get them for himself. When he needed clothes, he had to find a way to come up with the cash. When he wanted to eat, he had to figure how to get food. It was a simple fact of life. Annie didn't have much money. She had her own life to manage. She had her own kids to support, first and foremost. She did what she could for Lloyd, but she couldn't do much. Lulia, knowing her own son had abandoned Lloyd, left him with Annie. She didn't want to interfere. And Lloyd didn't want to be a burden. So he did what he had to do. No questions asked.

"I had to support my own self," he said. "That's just the way it was. I had to buy my own clothes comin' up, so some days I had to go to the grocery store and pack bags to make money. I'd go to Waldbaum's and Key Food. I had to survive, man. My grandmother had it rough. My father wasn't around, my mother died. I had to go there to pack bags. I had to buy me sneakers and some fancy clothes. The boy didn't want to go to school with the same shit on every day. Some days, I had to work.

"Some days, I had to survive. 'Cause I was an only child," Lloyd said, "my grandmother, she tried to spoil me. I didn't have no mother, so she let me get over. I'd get a little hittin', a little spankin'. But she'd punish me and I still would go out; sneak out the back door, walk out the front door. As soon as she'd go to sleep, I'm gone. Swee'pea down the block somewhere shootin' ball. She'd let it slide."

Annie let it slide and Lloyd soon learned that he could do as he pleased. When he didn't know the rules of the game, when no one bothered to tell him what the rules were, he improvised. Made his own. If something was beneficial to him—be it legal or illegal, moral or immoral—he did it. No second thoughts, no questions asked. Like a scene straight off the storyboard for some inner-city remake of *Lord of the Flies*.

As one observer said, "People tell kids, 'You should know better.' But how? Children are born blank. How are they supposed to know if they are not told?"

Like his grandmother before him, Lloyd was a survivor, doing what it took to survive. Except, unlike her, he didn't always do things by the book.

"I never stole shit," he said. "I never stole shit. I never robbed, never stole."

But one relative said that wasn't quite true.

She said Lloyd was taught by other family members to shoplift. They would take him to the local stores and, while one family member occupied the cashier, Lloyd, in an oversize jacket, would tuck away the merchandise. It all made for quick cash.

Asked about that, Lloyd admitted, "I did what I could. I got into trouble, a lot of trouble." But he also said he often seemed to have luck on his side. He seldom got caught, and, even if he did, unlike his friends, he was able to talk his way out of a situation. He had style. He had a rap. He was a smooth operator; *sweetness*. He made people laugh. He made people *like* him. Even folks he did wrong by.

After all, he was just a troubled kid trying to make it. So they'd give him the benefit of the doubt. They felt he deserved it.

Now, give a kid, any kid, an inch and he'll take a mile. It's the nature of the beast, the nature of growing up. Except, when you have responsible role models, they'll put you in line when you step out. But
Lloyd had no one. As he grew, Lloyd mastered an old trick: how to get
over on folks. He became lord of the street con: begging money, talking
folks into "lending" him things. He learned to play on sympathies and,
due to his situation, he found those were many. What he also learned
was that packing bags didn't earn him much. If he was going to get by,
he needed to find another way.

And, in the neighborhood, mostly what he saw was drugs.

It is a lesson learned early on in the harsh environs of just about any
inner city. Take all you feel you're entitled to, and expect nothing in
return. Do what you can to survive. Figure you'll have to look out for
yourself, because everyone has their problems; no one has time to
waste worrying about yours. Everyone knows only the strong survive.

It's the law of the urban jungle, where tomorrow morning you may
wake up to find you're in a body bag. Which likely was why the ultimate put-down on the streets and in the playgrounds of eighties New
York was the phrase "You're weak."

As in no muscle, no power. No survival instincts. No "juice."

Juice was what then separated new-jacker dopeboys—hip-hop culture's description of trendy, but lethal, new-wave, new-money drug
dealers of the era—from the burger boys working the greasy golden-
arch grills down at Mickey D's. McDonald's. It's what separated cools
who'd *got* a nice ride—as in BMWs, Benzes, Samurais, Maximas, and
Jeeps—from bummyboys who took the bus or the subways. Who
walked.

If it meant going illegal, so be it. The creed of the street was as pure
and as simple as it was absolute: a man *gotta* do what a man *gotta* do.

It may sound hackneyed, stereotypical even. But more often than
not it's power that equals success on urban streets, and in turn, it equals
survival, because it's the strong who get to dictate the rules, who get to

feel invincible, *be* invincible, even if it's not for long. It's the guiding force behind gangs, behind posses. Behind thug life.

Just as certainly, power is what separates class from mass on the playgrounds, where a 360-degree tomahawk dunk often means more than a lay-in; where a rejection is viewed as the ultimate insult to masculinity. It is why dissin' someone—a term come to life in the mid-eighties to characterize treating a man with disrespect—often calls for retaliation. It is about macho, *machismo*. Reputation and regard.

In a societal setting where wearing finger-thick gold—being able to hang it all out front; dare someone to snatch it from you—was the ultimate sign of success and prowess. It was the reason you always had to show how much juice you had.

It is the same reason why, when you were on the playground back then and made a move that wasn't strong—a move not geared toward declaration of your manhood, not geared toward survival—the chant would rain down on you.

"Runnin' low on *Tropicana!*" the crowd might yell. Or, worse. "*Word up!*" they'd scream. The *truth*! "You're *weak*!"

Except, when you're not strong on the streets, when you don't look out for number one, you don't hear put-downs. Often, you just end up dead.

───────

There were 184 days in an average school year in New York City. And, though no records were available for his first year at I.S. 218, which Lloyd entered as a thirteen-year-old seventh-grade student in September 1980, records for his subsequent years there paint the picture of a chronic truant.

For the 1981–82 school year, New York City Board of Education records indicated Lloyd was present just 62 days; absent, 122.

"And I don't think he was there that often," Lerner said, "because, what happens is you have your attendance taken in the morning and, after that, you could not attend any of your classes and still be considered in attendance. If I remember, we were lucky to see Lloyd two times a week, if at all. And that was good weeks."

Records also showed Lloyd was marked present just 32 times during the 1982–83 school year, when he was absent a staggering 152 days.

Nevertheless, the next October, when Lloyd was a just-turned-sixteen-year-old student in eighth grade, he was "promoted" to Thomas Jefferson High School.

"*Promoted* is a bad word," Lerner said. "Because he never really graduated, per se, but instead was kind of pushed on despite the fact that he probably was present fewer than a hundred days, in my opinion, over the course of three full school years. He was 'pushed on' because there was nothing else we could do with him. Here he was, sixteen years old, six foot seven, and almost too big for the desks. He could not read and he was in classes with twelve-year-old kids. What else were we supposed to do?"

It was a situation that seemed to summarize the problems plaguing an ancient, underbudgeted, overburdened school system in the 1980s.

It seems to summarize problems still plaguing the system today.

"This isn't just Lloyd," Lerner said, noting the problem was systemic. "There must be thousands of no-show truants in the city. Thousands and thousands. And there are something like four attendance teachers in each district to keep track of hundreds and hundreds of kids and, even if they can keep track of them, in reality they are powerless to do anything to make sure they get to school. You can't babysit them. You can't call up ten times a day. When Lloyd stopped showing up, when he did not come to school for a couple of days, we'd make a call. . . . But, really, that was all you could do."

The reasons vary why kids don't go to school. Some, because of problems with their home lives, turn to the streets. To drugs, to prostitution; to crimes that cause them to be sent away. Some, because they lack educational skills, leave school to pursue legitimate, though low-paying, dead-end jobs. Others, whether out of fear or frustration, maybe even out of self-consciousness, simply don't want to go. For Lloyd, the reason admittedly was, in part, laziness; in part, embarrassment.

Due to what would be diagnosed years later as dyslexia, Lloyd had fallen so far behind in school, which labeled him instead of helping him—he was classified, Lerner said, as "Neurologically Impaired, Emotionally Handicapped"—he never really had a chance. Was never really given a chance. No one bothered to figure out what was really going on with him. No one ever bothered to figure out a method to help him learn.

Lloyd was thrown into remedial classes. Frustrated, because he couldn't read due to his undiagnosed dyslexia, he avoided the work. Later, that frustration with his inability to do the work grew into embarrassment and then boredom with school.

By the time Lloyd reached the eighth grade he still could not read, could not handle even the most basic school work. School had failed him. Educators had failed him. The system had failed him. All he had been taught, really, was how to fail.

"I didn't have no mother at home to help me with my schoolin' when I got home," Lloyd said. "I had no one to ask, 'Is this right?' How was I supposed to have felt? What was I supposed to have did?"

"He was in with special ed kids, kids who were two, three years behind in reading level and *those* kids were calling *him* dumb," Lerner said. "How was he supposed to react? He was, and please forgive the scientific explanation, labeled 'dumb.'

"He got so frustrated he would not go to class."

Most mornings, Lloyd pulled stunts on Annie Sargeant. He'd sleep late and not go to school or he'd cut the backstreets and not go to school. He'd pretend he was getting washed and dressed, run the water in the bathroom, and, once his grandmother left the house, for work, he'd go back to bed—and not go to school.

"Some days," Lloyd said, "I would sleep 'til nine o'clock and I wouldn't go. There was days she'd wake me and I would act like I'm sick and I wouldn't go. She would baby me. She'd say, 'You don't have to go to school today.' And so, I wouldn't go. Then there was days when she say, 'Hey, you can't pull none of that sick shit on me.' Then I would go, but maybe when I got there I would cut class.

"The big thing was you had to get me out the house. You didn't do that often. I would be sleepy from shootin' ball late at night. See, there was days I wanted to go to school, days I didn't. Some days I felt good goin' to school, like I should try to do well. Then there were some days I just didn't want to go to school 'cause, you know, there was a lot of frustration. Whenever I sat there and put my head to it, when I wanted to learn, I felt I could learn. When I wanted to catch on, I felt like I could catch on. Like that." He snapped his fingers. "But there was times when I didn't try."

Instead, Lloyd acted like a kid. Like most kids, he looked for the easy way out. He'd try to get into trouble—maybe disrupt a class, take someone's jacket; maybe just get caught roaming the halls—because he knew it would get him out of school.

He would get sent to the guidance office, where he'd sit around most of the afternoon talking or just hanging out. If he was lucky, Saul Lerner and the other administrators would get called away and he'd have a chance to escape.

For yet another day.

"I ran with the wrong crew," Lloyd said. "Got caught up in the wrong crew. Like the old gangs, we went around school takin' kids' jackets, runnin' around school. I used to go to school and look for trouble, so I could go home. It was like, 'Send me home.' 'Cause when they put me in that office, I could cut out. 'Cause, you know, Lerner'd have another kid fightin' in another class and the second he walked out to go there, I would walk right out the side door. And I'm gone. Once I hit the streets, I'm gone. You don't see me for weeks."

"He was a kid without supervision, who grew up on his own," Lerner said. "When that happens, you fall into things. I would call one grandmother and she would say, 'He's with his other grandmother.' I'd call the other grandmother and she'd say, 'He's with the other grandmother.' What that meant was he was on the streets by himself. This was not your Harvard-bound scholar. Just a kid who grew up without guidance."

"It's a shame, right?" Lloyd said. "For a little kid like Lloyd, it's a shame 'cause everybody in the world I had around me then, there was a lot that wanted to see me make it for me. They didn't want nothin' from me back then. They just wanted to see me do well. I had teachers that used to beg me to come to school. I mean teachers that, when I was in junior high school, wanted to pick me up from my house to make sure I got there. But I denied them. I would not let them pick me up.

"I'd tell them, 'I'll be all right. I'll be there,'" he said. "I had teachers drop me home after school and talk to me, give me lectures. They would tell me, 'Lloyd, they is nothin' in the streets. Come to class. Be a good athlete. Try to do your work. All you got to do is come to class and learn a little bit 'bout education.' But I wouldn't."

Wouldn't, Lloyd said, because he was embarrassed. Embarrassed by the fact he couldn't read; embarrassed by his home life. Embarrassed by the fact he mostly was on his own.

He was embarrassed by the fact he didn't know how to solve his problems.

"A kid who is dyslexic, who can't read, is not going to try to do the work," Lerner said. "He is going to become bored and go on to something else. The general impression was that he was turned off by school. That he didn't belong there. [But] his hatred of school was completely justified, because the system did not serve this kid. The system was just not capable of helping this kid. There was not a whole lot of learning going on. How many times can you ask the same kid to do his ABCs? From the first to the eighth grade, this kid had learned nothing. Somewhere along the line, he had to say, 'I'm not going to do it.'

"What can you do? Hold him over in kindergarten? Then what, first grade? *Second*? Instead, you put him in special ed. But that's not the answer, either. What we have then are addicts, muggers, rapists, murderers, and kids just hanging out on the corner with nowhere to go, nothing to do. What you end up with is kids with no direction."

Mostly, Lerner said, born of frustration.

———

The Jamaicans down the block had cornered the market on marijuana. Business was sweet, the list of clientele ever-expanding. They could always use extra hands to distribute their product. Young boys preferred, the man told Lloyd. No complications, he said; no problems for juveniles. Now, Lloyd had made a promise never to use drugs. He did not want to sell them, either. But he was now ten years old. And promises did not begin to fill the holes that burned in his unfilled stomach. Promises did not begin to clothe a kid who had no clothes to wear, or begin to ease the burden of a child who felt embarrassed over his impoverishment. Besides, Lloyd said, almost all his relatives used drugs. He had watched them smoke marijuana, snort cocaine.

It didn't seem so terrible, didn't seem to hurt anyone. So Lloyd put aside his promise to his grandma—and became a businessman. An entrepreneur.

"I would sell a little marijuana, sold a little cocaine," he said.

"When you doin' it and you ain't got no money and you need clothes and food to eat, you don't think about it. You got to survive. A man got to survive. Got to survive, got to eat, got to have sneakers. I didn't believe in takin' from my grandmother. She had it rough, too. She had to support her kids. She did her best with me. But a lot of times, I needed my own money in my own pocket. That's how I got caught in that shit, smokin', sellin' drugs. That's when I first started smokin' weed. I was smokin' weed when I was ten years old. Bein' around that shit, man, you say, 'I'll try a joint.'

"Next thing I know," Lloyd said, "I caught myself every day smokin' weed. Weed, weed, weed. You know how it feel. You just feelin' nice. . . . I'm goin' to tell you the honest truth. . . . I wake up in the mornin', I smoked. I thought it was okay. I said, 'I'm young. I could smoke weed. It ain't goin' to hurt me.' I didn't have nobody to tell me not to do it."

Like everything else in his life, Lloyd said he just figured it was all right. "It was almost like," he said later, "it was in my genes. Like I let it be in my genes."

———

The kid had it in *his* genes, too. He knew it, understood it. The college scouts could tell—even if he was just twelve, playing in a Catholic Youth Organization game at a local gymnasium. It was apparent in the way he handled himself under pressure.

He had innate talent. He had the potential for greatness. "He was," scout Tom Konchalski recalled of the moment he first saw him, "amazing. Just amazing."

The kid would later concede he was in the process of "gettin' a little name." But where would that recognition, where would basketball, lead Kenny Anderson?

A handful of years earlier, when Anderson was still just a baby, basketball had captured the imagination of his uncle, James McLaughlin, who had thrown himself into the game, had earned a little name, too, in some of the local parks. But that name, the reputation, had also attracted the hangers-on, folks looking to see what they could get from a man headed for success. Some were folks of not so fine moral stature.

But James McLaughlin was really just a kid then, too—and, in them, he saw the easy life. He was a star and they had befriended him. Before he knew it, James McLaughlin was cutting school to hang out. Before he knew it, he was a man going nowhere fast, another kid who had fallen for the old routine and gotten sidetracked.

It also happened to his nephew, Ricky Anderson, Kenny's older brother.

Though no one will talk about just what happened—"He got turned around the wrong way, that's what happened," Kenny's mother, Joan Anderson, said back then—those associations left Jimmy Mac a lost, broken man, dead at the age of twenty-seven; left Ricky Anderson the next-best thing to it, having dropped out of school to pursue "other interests." And now here was Kenny Anderson, a little left-handed guard with a game bordering on brilliant, seemingly headed down the same path.

He was in sixth grade, struggling in intermediate school in South Jamaica, where he lived not far from the notorious Forties Projects.

He was throwing himself into basketball but skating on his academics, which he said he didn't like. As he said, "There were temptations out there in the world. I saw them and I can't say that I hadn't thought about them, because I did."

All of which worried his mother, as well as others who saw his potential and did not want to see it go to waste.

"My brother had some troubles," Joan Anderson said then. "He played for Jamaica High, but he never pursued it. He had a *bad* heart. He didn't do what he should have done. My other son, Ricky, he didn't do the right thing, either."

Luckily, Joan Anderson did. With the assistance of some acquaintances who were also concerned about her son's future, she moved from South Jamaica, which had already claimed two members of her family. The idea, she said, was to give her young son a chance for a future.

So she moved with Kenny to Lefrak City, a huge apartment complex along the service road of the Long Island Expressway in Corona, Queens.

The tenants at Lefrak were sometimes a bit short on income. But the apartments were in a middle-class neighborhood thriving in ethnic diversity. That proved to be a good influence on her son, as did a man he met there: Vincent Smith.

Smith, like those college basketball scouts, first saw Kenny Anderson in a youth game at Lost Battalion Hall on Queens Boulevard in Rego Park. Smith knew a bit about basketball. His brother, also Kenny, better known around New York as "the Jet," was an all-America guard at Archbishop Molloy High School in Briarwood, Queens, and was leaning toward attending the University of North Carolina to play for the legendary Dean Smith. (Kenny Smith would become a two-time NBA champion and a star basketball analyst on *Inside the NBA* on TNT.) Vincent Smith understood Kenny Anderson needed guidance if he was going to find success, too. So he lent a helping hand.

First, he talked to Joan Anderson.

"She told me about Jimmy Mac and Ricky," Vincent Smith said.

"How they played and how they didn't do as well as they should have. I told her Kenny would be different. Kenny had a lazy attitude. You could tell that he knew he was good. I always told Kenny, 'You have to be a student first, ballplayer second.'

"I stressed that if he didn't keep working, he'd slip and then all he'd have left were people talking about what he could have been."

Kenny Anderson, just a kid, could have done what Lloyd seemed to be doing, could have done what Jimmy Mac and his brother, Ricky, had done before him. He could have nodded in agreement and gone about his business. After all, he was good. He knew that. He saw the way people fawned over him when he worked on his game on the court at Lefrak or the one at Lost Battalion. He saw the admiration; that he was something special. He also remembered what happened to Jimmy Mac and Ricky.

"My brother was real good," Kenny, nine years younger than Ricky Anderson, recalled. "He had a lot of talent. He was like, you know, a legend in the parks. He had a reputation. I heard stories about my uncle Jimmy, too. A lot of people said he was real good, that I reminded them a lot of him, you know, of the way he was in the playgrounds. My moms told me stories about him all the time. She said that he and my brother, they got sidetracked. She said that they didn't want it bad enough."

They couldn't see the future. But the people beginning to hang around Kenny Anderson back then could. They said it wouldn't be easy. They said it would take a lot of work. But, Kenny Anderson wanted it. Badly. So, unlike his predecessors, he decided to listen.

———

Some people tried to point Lloyd in a new direction, too. They tried to lead him down a new path. Tried to start him on the road to success. And if it wasn't teachers trying to convince him if he only did a marginal amount of work he could be a success, it was coaches. The teachers did it because they wanted to see him get an education. The coaches did it because they wanted to see him play ball. In some way, though, both groups were doing it for him, as well as for themselves. There was ego involved.

Each wanted to be the one who saved Lloyd.

One person who tried was Arnie Hershkowitz. A special ed teacher at Westinghouse High School, a vocational school in Brooklyn, Hersh was a basketball junkie who ran a summer league team called Albie's Trimmings. Hersh recruited players for Westinghouse, mainly because he liked to associate with up-and-coming stars, feel he had some control over what happened to them. He also did it because, though married, he had no kids of his own; players were his surrogate children. He did it because he liked his school to win, so much so that he often went to games—usually, he sat in the first row of stands on the side opposite the team bench—and shouted instructions to "his" players; instructions often in direct opposition to orders from the then–high school team coach, Irv Turk.

It was difficult to tell if there was more to it than that, especially since many street-level recruiters also befriend kids in order to steer them to certain colleges, which then pay the recruiters what are known in the trade as "finder's fees"—illegal kickbacks, which can range from a few hundred dollars to several thousand, depending on how good a player the school receives. Hersh didn't seem to be about that, though it was difficult to tell exactly what he was about. He was in his forties, a small-time horse player; strictly dollar, two-dollar stuff. Balding, he wore a scraggy beard; he was one of the most manic, frenetic people around. His middle-aged teeth were cloaked in braces.

Some fashioned him an outlaw; he liked the image.

Often, he gave players money for food, taxis, or the subway. Sometimes he gave them as much as fifty dollars, mainly, he said, just because he knew them. It was his entertainment, like a night out on the town, like taking in a movie. Unlike most known street recruiters, he seemed to have no ties to specific colleges. He seemed, instead, to be more like a groupie, a man who did it to be respected. To be liked.

Hersh knew Ron Naclerio. And, in fact, it was Hersh who'd made the first introductions between Ron and Lloyd. Hersh had met Ron at a high school game. Between them, they knew almost every legitimate big-time player in New York City. Players knew them, too.

Players listened to them; to their advice, guidance.

"I would attend a game, see a youngster play, and try to corral him one way or another," Hersh said. "It's a simple procedure; you're dealing with kids on the junior high school level. You give them a little attention, they feel obligated to you, feel closer to you. Most of the time, they had never been recruited before. . . . The first impression is lasting."

Still, there was something about it that sounded, well . . . perverse.

"The kids didn't know anything," he said. "You could do anything you wanted with them. If I took a kid to McDonald's or said, 'Here's twenty dollars,' or bought him a pair of sneakers, that was it. What else could they have wanted? If you pay a kid attention or take him to a game, that's all you have to do. It doesn't take that much. It's not like recruiting a kid for college. Say I give him fifty dollars. He learns to have money in his pocket. When he gets to college, he's going to be around kids with money in their pockets. At least I'm giving him a sense of how to spend money, what it's like to have money. One thing you learn, you never ask for anything in return. If you're looking for monetary value in return, you shouldn't be in it in the first place."

Among the players Hersh befriended were a host of future star collegiate and NBA players, including Mark Jackson, John Salley, and the late Conrad McRae.

He met Jackson back at Bishop Loughlin High School in Brooklyn; met Salley at Canarsie High School in Brooklyn. Met McRae back at Brooklyn Tech.

McRae went on to star for Jim Boeheim at Syracuse University before dying at age twenty-nine of an apparent irregular heartbeat while working out as Orlando Magic summer league player in Irvine, California, in July 2000. Salley, the former Georgia Tech star, became a four-time NBA champion—one of only two players in history, along with Tim Duncan, to win league titles in three different decades: two with the Detroit Pistons (1989, 1990), one each with the Chicago Bulls

(1996) and the Los Angeles Lakers (2000)—before becoming an actor and longtime host of *The Best Damn Sports Show Period,* back when it was on Fox Sports Net. Jackson, of course, starred for St. John's University before launching an NBA career that spanned from 1987 to 2004, later becoming a notable television analyst and coach of the Golden State Warriors.

Hersh claimed he once "lent" Salley more than five hundred dollars—"Just to help him out," he said—while Salley was at Georgia Tech. It could have been seen as a significant NCAA violation; which could have cost Salley his scholarship, maybe his future.

Which could have gotten Tech sanctioned, penalized.

And still, for all the players he knew, Hersh had met Lloyd by accident. He was eating at a restaurant in Brooklyn one afternoon. Lloyd walked by wearing a jacket from Bishop Loughlin, a jacket given to him by someone he said *had* tried to recruit him.

"Hey!" Hersh yelled to Lloyd. "I know you don't go to Loughlin."

That stopped Lloyd cold.

"We talked for a while," Hersh said.

Hersh learned Lloyd was Swee'pea. He knew the nickname.

"I took down his phone number," he said.

A week later, Hersh took Lloyd to see the Philadelphia 76ers. *In Philadelphia.* Then, he recruited him for his team, Albie's Trimmings.

Hersh also tried to convince Lloyd to attend Westinghouse.

"I just went out and recruited five kids to come to the school," he said, "and, if they had all been in the school at the same time, we probably would've had the number-one team in the country." One of those players was Lloyd. Another was Jamal Faulkner, who went on to become a *Parade Magazine* all-American at Christ the King in Queens.

Eventually, Hersh decided Lloyd might be more trouble than he was worth at Westinghouse. So, while he remained an advisor to Lloyd, as did Ron, he quit trying to recruit him. Instead Lloyd enrolled in his zoned school, Thomas Jefferson.

That Lloyd was even able to be "pushed on," as Saul Lerner put it back then, was because he finally decided to come to school beginning in September 1983.

Not that he really had a choice.

Lerner knew how badly Lloyd wanted to play high school basketball. So he lied to him, told Lloyd the school would hold him there forever. That school administrators would refuse to promote him unless he attended school on a regular basis.

Where talks about education and the future failed, using basketball as the carrot to entice Lloyd worked. For the better part of a month, Lloyd came to school.

Every day.

And in October, he was sent on to Thomas Jefferson.

"The only reason we ever saw Lloyd was because he wanted to play basketball and he had been told that, if he didn't get out, he was not going to ever play," Lerner said. "Otherwise, it would have been impossible to reach a kid like this."

As Lloyd said, "They knew how good my talent was, they knew I was a good ballplayer. Teachers told me, coaches told me, 'All you got to do is come to school and we'll make sure you get a passin' grade, even if it ain't nothin' but a seventy.'

"They told me that in junior high school," he said. "Teachers said to me, 'I'll pass you if you just come to class.' That's the system."

But, placed in Jefferson, Lloyd again rarely went to school—even though it was just a hundred yards from his house, across the vacant lot from New Jersey Avenue to Pennsylvania. Worse, Lloyd broke an ankle that fall and missed the first half of the season. Still, because of the way the marking periods fell and because he had a medical excuse, after Lloyd recovered he became eligible for the final seven games of the regular season. His high school debut was against Wingate—ironically, coached by Lloyd's counselor at I.S. 218, Saul Lerner.

Wingate had a senior forward named Dexter Campbell, who would go on to play at Xavier University in Cincinnati. Lloyd weighed just 150 pounds but he used all of his battle-tested basketball knowledge to exploit the weaknesses in Campbell's game; used his finesse, his smarts, to negate Campbell's strength.

"He did not start," Lerner recalled of Lloyd, later on. "But once he got in, he ate Campbell for lunch. It was a complete domination of the game. And this was against a kid who played for what was a Top Twenty program. It was impressive."

So were his performances against Tilden and Lincoln in the Public Schools Athletic League Playoffs. Problem was, his problems were again catching up.

"I would just wake up in the mornin' smokin' weed," Lloyd said. "Goin' to practice, smokin' weed every day. It wasn't a day I didn't miss smokin' weed. It was like that was the only way I'd get through practice; like by feelin' good, goin' through the motions. At one point, I thought nobody could stop me if I smoke a joint before I play. I thought nobody could hold me. I'm sure I ain't the only guy who thought like that. Like, soon I just got tired of all that school stuff, though. After basketball season, I was history anyhow. I didn't like that place. I called it 'Baby Rikers Island.'

"A kid came up to me once in the halls," Lloyd said. "Showed me a gun and said, 'This is my school. This ain't your school. So what you play ball? You could still get killed here.' I was like, 'Get me out of here.' I wanted to get out."

And so he just stopped going to school.

Miles to Go

E ven as the crow flies, Mouth of Wilson, Virginia, seemed more than a hundred miles from even the faintest hint or trace of civilization. A one-horse town in the damn-near most literal sense, it lent new definition to the term "isolation."

There were no traffic lights in Mouth of Wilson. A run-down mill, a general store, a car dealership, and a U.S. post office formed the entire downtown business district.

There were three pages in the local telephone book.

"There are," a writer once wrote, "only a hundred stories in this naked city." And perhaps even *that* was exaggeration.

Along a deserted stretch of road known as Highway 58 in the foothills of the Iron Mountains—somewhere between the Appalachian and Blue Ridge Mountains along the state's southern border, a stone's throw from North Carolina and Tennessee—Oak Hill Academy stood in a place some referred to as "the End of the Earth." But Mouth of Wilson, known as such because the locals used to tell each other, "Meet me at the mouth of Wilson Creek," and its school served as a refuge of sorts, a place where a struggling student could salvage his faltering academic career. Could salvage his future before it fast became his past.

"Most of these kids are at the end of their rope," then–school basketball coach Larry Davis once said of his players at Oak Hill. "It's their last stop. If they don't make it here, they're going to junior college or not at all." As his then–assistant coach, Steve Smith, said: "This is the last road out." The court of last resort. It was here that Lloyd, entering his sophomore year of high school and having quit school at Thomas Jefferson, found himself in September 1984.

The task at hand would be difficult, especially for someone with his track record. Lloyd had shown that, due to his lack of family structure and his lack of self-discipline, left to his own devices he just was not capable of doing what was necessary to ensure his own success. Enrollment at Oak Hill might eliminate some of the variables and increase the odds of him making the grade. It had to. Without improvement, and with the National Collegiate Athletic Association (NCAA) tightening entrance requirements for student-athletes, Lloyd might never become eligible to play college basketball.

Once, enrolling in a preparatory school to improve weak academic skills had been a practice reserved for the financially well-to-do. It gave those students another year of refinement, gave them a chance to gain maturity and discipline in the classroom.

It gave them the chance to bolster academic standing, improve their college entrance exam scores; enhanced their chances of gaining admittance to Ivy League universities, service academies, and other prestigious academic institutions.

A few schools specialized in dealing with more-troubled students from less suitable economic backgrounds, kids desperately in need of improving their academic skills. Fewer still, most notably Laurinburg Institute—a traditional black prep school in Laurinburg, North Carolina, whose alumni include Dizzy Gillespie, basketball all-stars Jimmy Walker and Charlie Scott, and Hall of Fame inductee Sam Jones, named to the NBA's 50 Greatest Team in 1996; not to mention Earl Manigault—even gained a reputation for helping troubled athletes navigate an otherwise perilous road to college.

But, in reality, the opportunities for success were few and far between.

At the time, it had been only a handful of years since major-college basketball had exploded into the national consciousness, creating a national obsession.

With one game—that being the famed 1979 NCAA Championship Game between Michigan State and Indiana State, the first of many hard-fought battles between Magic Johnson and Larry Bird; then the single-most-viewed college basketball game in television history—the sport became big business in the United States. And with it, the attraction with prep schools blossomed in inner-city environs.

Suddenly cable television stations were scrambling to broadcast college games. There was a call to expand the postseason NCAA tournament field from 40 teams to 48, then to 64. Now it's 68. The increase in tournament revenue, which by 1990 was about $1.4 million for teams making the Final Four, was bound for the stratosphere.

In 2012, it was $9.5 million for each Final Four team, according to *Forbes*.

To ensure on-court success and remain in the hunt for all that gold, schools suddenly needed to find athletes who could meet more stringent entrance requirements; athletes who could remain eligible. Coaches of high school, college, and club teams understood that new NCAA legislation such as Proposition 48—a rule that enforced tougher entrance and eligibility standards for high school recruits, and had become an NCAA bylaw in 1986—meant they needed to guarantee the best players in the nation the best possible chance for academic success.

After all, the NCAA, conscious of the beating its image was taking because of the questionable enrollments and eligibilities of underqualified athletes—athletes like Kevin Ross, who starred for the basketball team at Creighton University, then went back to grammar school to learn how to read—was scrambling to raise the academic bar. A recruit had to achieve a 2.0 scholastic grade-point average on a 4.0 scale and a minimum score of 700 out of the then-maximum 1,600 on the Scholastic Aptitude Test to become what was being called "a predictor." That is, to be eligible for competition in Division I, the highest level of major-college athletics, as a freshman.

That didn't bode well for many inner-city athletes, who often had educational backgrounds not much different than Kevin Ross's. Or from Lloyd's. Cheating to make sure players became eligible was the last resort for desperate schools. Some had stand-ins take the test for their troubled recruits; others just cheated, as the NCAA declared University of Kentucky recruit Eric Manuel did in June 1987.

Still, for most athletic programs, the first choice was simply to identify the right kids and get them immediate help. Overnight, any high
school recruit with an academic problem who could shoot, dribble, rebound, or score was becoming a preppie.

Headed to the University of Pittsburgh, recruit Brian Shorter
passed on his senior season at Simon Gratz High School in Philadelphia, where he was just 384 points shy of the all-time city scoring record set by Wilt Chamberlain. He enrolled at Oak Hill.

Dennis Scott, who would take Georgia Tech to the 1990 NCAA
Final Four, left his home in Reston, Virginia, to attend Flint Hill in
Oakton, Virginia.

Which only touched on the number of big-time high school basketball players suddenly making their way to a bunch of previously
unheard-of places, like Fork Union (Va.) Military Academy, Solebury
(Pa.) Prep, and Maine Central Institute.

———

Of course, Lloyd didn't choose to attend Oak Hill. That was the idea of
an advisor, Lou d'Almeida, who ran a Bronx-based Amateur Athletic
Union club team called the New York Gauchos.

A wealthy real estate developer who claimed to have been born
in Paris, raised in Buenos Aires, and educated at Yale University,
d'Almeida said he once worked as an actor in off-Broadway produc-
tions as well as in 1950s television on *Playhouse 90* and *The Dinah
Shore Show*. He said he first became involved in youth basketball quite
by accident, when a friend with whom he was playing squash asked
him to purchase a few T-shirts for a team run by another friend.

That was 1967.

One thing led to another and soon d'Almeida had laid the cornerstone for a program that would become the Gauchos, operated
through a nonprofit organization called Teamwork Foundation Inc.,
whose trusted advisors included Leonard Bernstein, Lauren Bacall,
Lou Carnesecca, Jeffrey Lyons, and Willis Reed.

D'Almeida was a slightly built man with short hair almost as white as his Jaguar, which was adorned with vanity license plates that read GAUCHO. An immaculate dresser, he was always well groomed. Congenial to a fault, he seemed to have a genuine interest in his players, his kids; later there would be revelations that he had a criminal history. Other, unsubstantiated accusations included child abuse.

It was, however, revealed that d'Almeida once was indicted on manslaughter charges in connection with the shooting death of a twenty-year-old college student, Gerald Gerardo, in a parking garage on East Eighty-Second Street in Manhattan on October 2, 1969. Accounts in the *Daily News* reported that d'Almeida allegedly told police he had tried to commit suicide and that Gerardo tried to stop him. That during the ensuing struggle his pistol, a .32-caliber Spanish Llama, had gone off—accidentally killing Gerardo.

In 1995, d'Almeida told *Sports Illustrated* it was Gerardo who was trying to kill himself. Whatever the case, d'Almeida eventually pleaded guilty to a lesser charge—criminally negligent homicide—and received five years' probation.

Still, back in the eighties, all anyone in basketball circles knew was that his Bronx gym, an ultramodern $2.5 million facility built in the shadow of the original Yankee Stadium, sported a massive orange-and-brown logo of a snorting bull with "Gauchos" alongside—the sign was visible from the Major Deegan Expressway. That it had a deluxe, all-wood, regulation-size court; a wall, covered in imported African mahogany.

A bachelor, d'Almeida had lived in the same two-bedroom penthouse apartment at Fifty-Seventh Street and Seventh Avenue in Manhattan almost all his adult life.

He liked to tell folks how he had given away "more sneakers than Imelda Marcos had shoes" and that the purpose of his club was, through basketball, to offer hope to those who because of their environment and because of their lot in life have been raised without it. He said his goal was to give kids—his players, his kids—a chance.

"A gaucho," he once said, "could build his house, catch or hunt his food, cook his meals, tame horses. The connotation is of an outlaw, but the reality is not. A gaucho is a peaceful person, a conqueror of nature. These kids should look up to gauchos.

"They are," he said, "the ultimate survivors."

Which was why, he said, he chose to work with these kids to begin with.

Some critics alleged the purpose of his program was ego gratification, claiming the club insulated players, demanded their prime concern be basketball and winning games, not education. Some alleged the driving force behind the program was not a concern for those players but for kickbacks from colleges who signed those players. After all, like college basketball, club teams throughout the nation had become big business, often receiving funding from sneaker companies as well as alleged behind-the-scenes financial support from the very colleges who coveted their best players.

No longer associated with the Gauchos, d'Almeida declined during his time running the program to discuss his financial background or real estate holdings and investments. Instead, he said only that he spent about $100,000 in tuition each year for players and denied his program received kickbacks or other outside funding.

He denied that he paid players—other than to give them team jackets, sneakers, or meal money—in an attempt to lure them to the Gauchos.

D'Almeida also denied allegations—to the best knowledge, none ever proven—that his players had been caught using drugs, shoplifting, and trashing hotel rooms at various club basketball tournament sites. He called such allegations "bullshit."

Still, in New York, where almost every elite player in the five boroughs belonged to one of the big basketball clubs—Madison Square Boys Club, Elmcor, Dyckman, the Gauchos, and Riverside Church, which, built in the 1920s by John D. Rockefeller, Jr., ran its program out of community service, as well as to enhance its image among minorities in bordering Harlem—his program often attracted the most talented of all.

Former club members included NBA players Dwayne "Pearl"

Washington, Sidney Green, Ed Pinckney, Rod Strickland, Jerry "Ice" Reynolds, Mark Jackson, John "Spider" Salley, and Chris Mullin, elected to the basketball Hall of Fame in 2011. Former Andrew Jackson star Greg "Boo" Harvey, who went on to St. John's, was a Gaucho. So was Tony Bruin. Richie Adams was a Gaucho, then became the two-time Player of the Year in the old Pacific Coast Athletic Association at the University of Nevada–Las Vegas. More recent stars include Felipe Lopez, Jamal Mashburn, Doron Lamb, Taj Gibson, and Kemba Walker. Back in the eighties, Salley credited d'Almeida for his success.

"We talked about business, we talked about life and the future. When we went to dinner on trips, he'd even sit the players down and teach them how to eat properly; you know, what eating utensils to use, how to hold your knife, how to hold your fork.

"He cared."

"I care about the lowliest and the worst kid," d'Almeida said, adding, "I get them launched into the real world and teach them how to take hold of the advantages."

The lesson wasn't lost on Lloyd, always cognizant of taking whatever advantage he could. Lloyd had joined the club in 1983, after going to one of the other local clubs, promising to play there. "Everybody wanted me," Lloyd said. "I knew that everybody wanted me. So, I went to [one team] and said, 'The only way I'll play for you is if you pay me.' They gave me a couple of crispy hundreds. But I never showed again."

Instead, Lloyd went to the Gauchos. Arnie Hershkowitz claimed that "Lloyd was always getting money from the Gauchos. Lou would give him money all the time."

Rumors had it at $250 a game, if not more. Possibly more than $2,500 for an out-of-state tournament, a figure not as absurd as it sounds. After all, AAU tournaments—tournaments like the Las Vegas Invitational and the Basketball Congress International in Phoenix, Arizona—guaranteed appearance money for teams.

And if your team won or made a good showing in those tournaments, they got invited back. So good players, it would appear, might have gotten paid.

D'Almeida said none of his players, even Lloyd, ever got paid to perform. He said he didn't even know who Lloyd was when he first arrived at the club, then run at P.S. 197 in Harlem. "He came into the gym while I was there," d'Almeida recalled, years later. "I didn't know who he was. I had no idea. I asked my assistants, 'Who's that?'

"He said, 'His name's Lloyd Daniels.' But even then he looked like he was better than a lot of the kids," d'Almeida said. "He must have been for *me* to notice. I'm not a basketball genius, but even *I* could tell he was better than the other kids."

D'Almeida said he soon realized Lloyd also had more problems than the other kids, especially when it came to education. "You could see he was much less prepared than most of the kids," d'Almeida said. "That was probably the biggest problem he had.

"I felt this kid, with the right education, had a chance to go anywhere that he wanted. That's why I wanted him out of the city, wanted to get him into an environment where he could learn. So, I sent him to Oak Hill."

Lloyd said there was also another, more sinister, reason d'Almeida was willing to spend more than $5,000 on his education at Oak Hill. Lloyd said d'Almeida knew he had little loyalty and, therefore, might lose him to another local club team.

"Want to know the real reason I went down there? Lou was tryin' to keep me away from Riverside Church. They said they was goin' to send me to school on a bus and Lou said, 'I ain't goin' to send you on a bus. I'm goin' to send you on a plane.'"

So, Lloyd said, "I took that deal. You know, 'bigger and better.' Comin' from where I come from, you have to get what you can."

That was how Lloyd first came to be a student at Oak Hill, though maybe *student* is the wrong word. As school coach Steve Smith said, "We've never had a student like that before. We've never had anybody here who was like Lloyd."

For almost one hundred years, Oak Hill Academy deviated little from its original mandate. Founded in 1878 by the New River Baptist Asso-

ciation, it was built as a school for locals, one that, through the teach-
ings of the church, tried to steer its troubled teenagers away from
outside distractions and toward a more humble, more respectable,
more academic life. That it went coed in the 1950s was more out of real
necessity than true desire—its enrollment on the wane, its till growing
less and less full.

By the early 1970s, its demise seemed imminent. Enrollment was
down to eighty-five students. The operating budget used to support its
dwindling faculty, its thirteen worn and wearied buildings, and its lone
two varsity sports—a baseball team that almost never played actual interscholastic games and a basketball team that played against the likes
of the Virginia Baptist Children's Home—was a mere $200,000.

Oak Hill was in dire straits.

Until, that is, then–athletic director Chuck Isner got an idea. What
if, taking a page from the major-college and big-time private high
school programs, Isner asked his father, Robert, then the school's president, Oak Hill invested in its miserable basketball team and used the
squad to promote the school? Four scholarships would be all Chuck
Isner needed. His father's first reaction was that the school could not
afford to do it. Before long, he came to the stark realization his school
couldn't afford not to.

In New York City, Chuck Isner found three players. A team was
born.

That was 1976. By the 1980s, the enrollment at Oak Hill had grown
to nearly two hundred, the operating budget to almost $2 million. As
one sportswriter put it, Oak Hill had used interscholastic basketball to
"spread the word of the Mouth."

Hearing what the school could do for troubled kids, Lou d'Almeida
paid to send academically troubled Rod Strickland to Oak Hill Academy in the fall of 1984.

Like Lloyd, Strickland hardly appreciated the move. Strickland had
just established himself as a consensus all-American, having led Harry
S. Truman High School in the Bronx to city and state titles as a junior. But, with an offer from DePaul University hanging in the balance,

Strickland could ill afford to gamble with his 1.94 grade-point average
when he needed a 2.0 to become eligible for a scholarship.

"It was do or die," Strickland said. He didn't like it, but he went.

Oak Hill offered the perfect environment for athletes like Rod
Strickland and Lloyd. "The same like Rod, I went there because I
needed my grades," Lloyd said. "But I was, like, shocked when I got
there. I was in a town with nobody and nothin'."

Nothing that would hinder a man's chances of attaining success.
Nothing that would hinder him from getting his life back on track.

Nothing, Strickland once noted, except "blackboards and backboards." Nothing except the chance for education and maturation
with a dose of big-time high school basketball thrown in on the side.
Oak Hill offered a chance to learn what it meant to be responsible, to
become successful despite past failure. It taught that lesson through
structure. Breakfast was at 7 a.m. Class was from 8 a.m. to 3:25 p.m.,
with tutorial from 3:30 to 4:15. After dinner at 5, there was study hall
at 6, practice from 7:30 to 9:15—lights and televisions out at 10. No
exceptions.

For some of these kids, it would be the first time in their lives that
they'd have positive role models. They would see kids who went to
school, kids who wanted to learn. More important, for the first time
in their lives they would have no excuse not to attend class. If you slept
late, Davis and Smith came and woke you in the morning.

In Mouth of Wilson you were force-fed knowledge. Like it or not.

"The kids there go to class because they have to," Tom Konchalski,
the basketball recruiting expert, said. "The dorm is across the street
from the buildings where you go to class and, if you don't go, they
come and drag you out of bed. They don't give you a chance to goof off.
It's not like the city. They make you work."

Newcomers often were of the misconception, Davis said, that
if you went to Oak Hill you automatically were going to get your
grades. "But," he said, "nobody's going to give you a grade. It forces
you to do things. If you don't do your homework, you don't get a zero
like public school. You have to keep coming after school until you do

it. The kid decides he'd rather do it the first time than keep coming after school."

Lloyd could not read more than a few words when he arrived at Oak Hill. He understood neither phonetics nor the basics of grammar. Teammates recalled how he would take a book and pretend to read it and how they laughed because he was holding it upside down. Or how he once tried to read a magazine—written in Spanish. Unlike most students, who needed minor refinements due to deficiencies in their educational backgrounds, Lloyd needed to restart the entire process from scratch.

"I hate to label him," Smith said, sounding all too familiar. "But I wouldn't even want to speculate on how low his reading and writing skills might be."

In an effort to improve those skills, Lloyd was assigned a private tutor, Lisa Smith, the coach's wife. She said that while Lloyd wanted to learn, there was "no real desire" to do actual work. Partly it was because of his dyslexia, which, possibly due to a lack of specially trained counselors, remained undiagnosed. Partly it was because he just didn't like school. School, after all, meant work. And Lloyd didn't like work.

"It just wasn't in him," she said. "I tried to tell him that every spare moment he had to read and write. Of course, he wouldn't. For him he was doing a lot."

But not nearly enough.

"I didn't expect it to be that deep," Lloyd said. "Like, you just went to class, then back to your room. I thought at least you go down there, go to a little party. Like a college thing. But it wasn't that type of thing. It was like, check your books, then go back to the dormitory. That wasn't Lloyd Daniels' style. I was like, 'I got to get up at seven, got to eat breakfast, and then I got to stay up from like seven to three thirty?' I was like, 'Excuse me, sir.' You know, that wasn't me every day like that, man. I wasn't into my books that hard. I felt like I was thrown into, what you call it, formation—no, *reform*—school. It seemed like that's what they threw me in. Oak Hill was a good school. But you couldn't take a kid like me, from the ghetto, out to that type of country.

"I couldn't deal with no mountains. I couldn't deal with Oak Hill."

Few could. Like countless others, Strickland fought the idea—threatening to quit after he'd gone home for Christmas. "I'm not coming back," he called to tell the coaches. "I'm just going to forget it and go to a junior college." To which they responded: "You've got a full scholarship to *DePaul*. You're going to throw it all away?"

Convinced that wasn't in his best interests, Strickland came back. But he was promptly placed on academic probation for two weeks—meaning he couldn't play ball. "I was walking around with a chip on my shoulder," he said. "I didn't want to be there. But it helped me realize that I had to get down and do my homework."

Academics were screwing up his basketball career.

But homework wasn't what concerned Lloyd. He had other concerns. After all, at Oak Hill male students weren't even allowed to be in a room with a girl if the door was closed. That meant no kissing. *No sex.* Violation of the rules had caused one city player to be expelled after he had taken the girl out of town, to a motel, for a weekend.

"You can't be expectin' a guy like me, who is just start learnin' about girls, sayin' I can't kiss a girl," Lloyd said. "I mean, I got to get restricted? I couldn't take it, man. I couldn't take it.

"You couldn't get caught tryin' to get your rocks off. How was I supposed to deal with that? What was I supposed to have did?"

Unable to understand the need to exercise restraint or be mature enough to obey the rules, even if he disagreed with them, what Lloyd did instead was turn to drugs. If he couldn't get action, satisfaction, at least he could get high. Smith said he always suspected Lloyd had a drug problem at Oak Hill. "I knew he had some drug-related problems when he was here," he said. "There weren't that many drugs down here and that was his problem. The only thing you can find down here might be some marijuana. A new kid would come onto campus and he would be the first one to say hello to him. It was always, 'Hey, you got anything? Can you get me some?'"

If you were a basketball player, you could make connections. At Oak Hill, Lloyd had juice. "White guys that go home on the weekend, we used to pay them to get us a twenty-five-dollar bag of marijuana," Lloyd said. "And they'd bring it in."

After all, the kids who weren't athletes, who weren't there because of club coaches and athletic affiliations but because of parents who wanted to teach them responsibility, liked the idea that they could associate with the players. It gave them prestige, just like those hangers-on on the city streets. That is, it gave them a chance to mingle with the stars, to live out their fantasies, all while making some cash money on the side.

For the players, however, what it came down to was differences in maturity, in their priorities. While Rod Strickland went back to his dorm to do homework after class, Lloyd was going back to his room to get high with his newfound "friends."

Until, that is, one afternoon in October, when he was caught by a school dean in a room where students were found smoking marijuana.

"I swear to God, I wasn't doin' no drugs," Lloyd said, trying to minimize the incident.

"You ask me, 'Were you puffin'?' and I would say, 'No, I didn't do no puffin'. But I was in there, so who's goin' to believe me? I mean, I ain't sayin' I wasn't gettin' ready to take a toke. But I wasn't smokin' yet. Still, I was here. What could I do?'"

"He was not caught red-handed," Smith recalled. "But there were drugs in the room and school officials felt this wasn't something they could condone."

As punishment, school officials decided that, since he was a player and since he had not actually been caught smoking marijuana but had only been in the room when it was being smoked, Lloyd would not be expelled. This time. Instead, as penance, he was ordered to run laps at six o'clock every morning for a two-week period.

It was a minor punishment, one requiring minimum effort to fulfill. But, with the shot at a successful future in hand, Lloyd made his choice. Instead of redeeming himself through an option offered only because he was a basketball player, he refused.

After all, he was Swee'pea. Why should *he* have to run?

"It ain't about listenin'," Lloyd said. "It was just a lot of times Lloyd wanted to do what he wanted to do." As he said: "I told them, 'I ain't runnin', I ain't goin' to run. This ain't like the *slavey* days. And I ain't no *slavey* boy.'"

It was, at once, both an absurd and intriguing comparison—though, school officials argued, what it really boiled down to was the need for rules and discipline.

"We had suspected him for a long time," Smith said in the high-profile aftermath. "But he said so many times that he didn't have a problem that I think he seriously believed that he didn't have a problem. He'd say, 'No, I'm clean. I'm clean.'"

Having left school officials with what they saw as no other acceptable options, finally Lloyd was asked to leave Oak Hill. He did so without hesitation.

Lloyd had lasted all of six weeks at Oak Hill. Now, he figured, after that stretch, which to him resembled a prison sentence, he would be headed back to New York—where he could sleep late, cut class, play ball, do drugs, and, as he said, "get fucked by all the pretty ladies." It would, no doubt, be adolescent paradise.

Except, Lou d'Almeida had other plans. He'd heard of another prep school with a big-time basketball team, a school that specialized in problem kids, in getting them eligible. The season before, the school was home to one of the most heavily recruited players in America, Chris Washburn, who had gone on to North Carolina State. So what if in recent years the school, Laurinburg Institute, had seen its academic reputation wither as its basketball program blossomed into a national power, becoming known among basketball cognoscenti as a haven for short-cutters, a diploma mill?

Lloyd needed a school, needed a team. Laurinburg was always looking for star basketball players. It seemed like the perfect match. Lloyd liked Laurinburg.

For good reason, it turned out.

"I was smokin' pot every day there. I could smoke in my room. No one checked. I was the man on campus, that was my school. I was the new Chris Washburn."

It was a morbid comparison, especially since on the night of December 19, 1984, about the time Lloyd was finishing his second month at the school, Washburn, an admitted frequent drug user, was arrested for breaking into a dorm room at North Carolina State and stealing a stereo. In the wake of charges of second-degree burglary—he later pleaded guilty to misdemeanor charges—it was revealed Washburn had scored just 470 on the SAT. Test takers got a minimum of 400 for signing their name correctly, which led to a joke among coaches, who told players: "Just sign the test twice."

Washburn, it was said, had managed at Laurinburg because he was such a highly recruited player; one allegedly pushed through, given grades, despite being a functional illiterate. As one basketball scout who knew the school alleged, "The place is a total zoo. A trained parrot might have been able to pass class there."

Lloyd agreed. In addition to smoking marijuana at Laurinburg, he said he did anything he wanted. Pretty much anytime he wanted.

Lloyd even warned coach Frank McDuffie, whose mother, Sammie, was the Laurinburg principal and whose ancestor, Tinny McDuffie, co-founded the school in 1904, that if things didn't work out in his favor, he'd just leave.

"It was a wild zoo," Lloyd said. "It was so fucked up. But they listened to me because I was a hell of a good ballplayer, I was the man. They knew if they didn't listen to me, I would go. Everybody knew my record. I was goin' to leave if things didn't go well for me. I always kept a school under my belt. That may sound funny, but that's the truth. I knew if I left this school, somebody was goin' to take me. Those days, I knew everybody wanted me then. A lot of times I threatened them that I was goin' to leave and they said that they'd work things out. Then they'd sit me down to talk to them, take me out to dinner, somethin'. Next thing you know, I'd sit down and chill."

Lloyd averaged 25 points and 15 rebounds a game at Laurinburg, where he earned immeasurable respect as a big-time player. He also earned a C academic average and five credits, the most he'd ever earn in a single year of high school.

"You know," Lloyd said, "I stayed there for a whole year. For once in my life, I went to a place and stuck it out. I lasted a year, got my grades."

As Frank McDuffie later said: "If a person tries, should he get an F?"

———

The best high school basketball player in America in the summer of 1985 was J. R. Reid. A shot-blocking, rebounding machine, Reid was built like the Incredible Hulk and every bit as intimidating. Every college coach in the nation wanted him.

He would later attend the University of North Carolina and become the first-round selection of the original Charlotte Hornets in the 1989 NBA Draft.

But that summer at Five-Star Camp, according to camp director Howie Garfinkel, Reid got "served"—street slang for getting his ass busted—by Swee'pea.

"Here was Lloyd, this skinny [six-foot-seven] guy, and you figured he would get crunched," Garfinkel recalled. "But he guarded him, defended him nicely. He outshot Reid, outhandled him, and played him even on the boards. Here was Reid, considered the best senior in the nation, a man who was playing for his reputation, and Lloyd outplayed him both weeks of the camp. Clearly, they were the two best players in camp and it was never worse than even and, in most cases, Lloyd was superior."

Lloyd toyed with J. R. Reid, often scoring at will. He would come down, freeze Reid with a head fake, then blow by him for an uncontested layup. He would take him down on the low post, spin off him, sink his shot. He couldn't outmuscle Reid. That was improbable. But Lloyd could use his infinite basketball knowledge to best him.

And he did.

"He was a real good player," Reid, who even got rejected once by Lloyd, said later. "They called him the next Magic Johnson. And he was pretty good. I played against him a couple of times. He checked me for a while. He was a really smooth player.

"He had the skill, I sure remember that."

Ron Brown, then an assistant coach at West Virginia, said there was no doubt Reid remembered even more about Lloyd from that camp that he wanted to forget.

"Everyone going in was talking about the great J. R. Reid," Brown, a Bronx native who had watched Lloyd throughout high school, said. "But, coming out all they talked about was Lloyd Daniels. Lloyd took him to the free throw line a couple of times, head-faked him, then took him to the hoop, smooth as can be. He did a little passing, he ran the break. He scored a few on fingertips to the basket.

"He made the great J. R. Reid, the man who was supposed to be the best on the court, lose his reputation. Lloyd was phenomenal. A few coaches were walking around going, 'They could put him in the pros right now.' When people say that Lloyd can play five positions, it was because of that camp. He showed he could play. He was just a little slicker, just a little sweeter, just a little better than anyone else there. He was playing basketball at his own level. When camp was over if you asked, 'Who's the best player in the country?' people would have told you: 'Lloyd Daniels, without question.'"

Garfinkel remembered something else, too, about that camp. Something that also had to do with the battles Lloyd had with J. R. Reid. It was about Larry Brown, the future Hall of Famer, then the basketball coach at the University of Kansas.

"His mouth was open for two days," Garfinkel said. "He wanted to take the kid home with him. . . . Wanted to adopt him. He kept telling me: 'I'll find a place for him. I'll find a family for him to live with.' He said he could get something worked out.

"Believe me, this kid was the real thing."

———

Larry Brown, who had ensured the recruitment of then–high school all-American Danny Manning when he hired Manning's father, Ed, a truck driver, to be his assistant at Kansas, never tried to adopt Lloyd that summer. And, with Ronnie and Hersh arguing against Lloyd going back to Laurinburg because they felt he needed a "more structured environment," Lou d'Almeida again made contact with officials at Oak Hill.

Rod Strickland had stuck it out, graduated, and gone on to De-Paul. Chris Brooks, a senior from Samuel Gompers High School in the Bronx, was being sent to Oak Hill by d'Almeida. D'Almeida asked Smith, who had become the head coach after the departure of Larry Davis, if the school would consider taking another chance on Lloyd.

It was a risky decision.

But Smith, as well as the school administration, decided to be practical. The school needed whatever students it could attract. Even ones like Lloyd.

And, of course, it always needed players. *Especially* ones like Lloyd.

"He was a paying student," Smith said, "and we felt, 'Hey, let's give him another chance.' He was a good basketball player. The school would get some publicity. Now, that wasn't the only reason. We were genuinely concerned. Besides, he really didn't have a whole lot of places he could go." So Lloyd headed back to Mouth of Wilson.

Once again, it wasn't long before he ran into problems.

Lloyd was a god on the court, where it seemed every coach in America had become enamored with his abilities. (That included University of Nevada–Las Vegas [UNLV] assistant Mark Warkentien, who flew from Las Vegas to Chicago to Pittsburgh to Tri-Cities Airport in Bristol, Tennessee, then drove two hours in a rental car—just to watch Lloyd *practice* at Oak Hill.) Still, Swee'pea remained a hellion off the court.

"I've never seen a high school player who has the talent he has," Smith said. "It's like he's not human. . . . He could have been my point guard, my shooting guard, my small forward, my power forward, or my center and we don't have such a bad team. Just to watch him play, you'd never know he has any problems. . . . Until, he steps off the court."

The problems, at first, were minor. Lloyd began to doubt he could ever do his schoolwork, so he refused to make the attempt. He slept late. He created disturbances in class—talking during lessons, telling jokes, cutting up. He disrupted team unity, went against orders. He became rebellious. He refused to play with certain players, who he felt weren't good enough to be on the court with him. And, though he might have been correct in his assessment, teammates were hardly appreciative of his candor.

"Oak Hill was no joy ride," Chris Brooks said. (Brooks, who played with Lloyd on the Gauchos, won the president's award for academic progress and good citizenship at Oak Hill—though he later failed to achieve the minimum SAT score, making him ineligible as a freshman at the University of West Virginia.) "But you had to think of the future. I tried to appreciate what they were doing for me there. But Lloyd acted as if school was something he was allergic to. If you said, 'Lloyd, do this,' he would do it. But if you said, 'Lloyd, don't do this,' then it was almost like he had to try to do it. He just got out of hand. It was like he had made a decision, like, 'I don't really belong here. Why try? I'll only do bad.' So it seemed like he tried to be out of control, almost as if he figured, 'They'll send me home.' It was like that was what he expected.

"I figured it was what he wanted. To be sent home."

It was a familiar refrain. As Smith said, "The things he would do, you would say to him, 'Why'd you do that?' It just compounded itself daily. You kept on saying, 'You're blowing your only chance to make it.' He didn't seem to understand."

The problems soon multiplied. Teammates were missing possessions from their rooms. They began to blame Lloyd. There was dissension on the team. People began to blame Lloyd. "A lot of things started to go wrong on the perimeter," Smith said.

As Brooks said, "People started to say, 'Lloyd's a bad apple.'"

Lloyd denied the allegations, but he did nothing to ingratiate himself to his coaches or his teammates. "People on the team started saying, 'Lloyd is a shady character,'" Smith said. "I thought it was tearing our team apart. It wasn't just one player. It was ten against one. And if they suspect you, and they had good reason to, it will eventually show up on the floor, in the classroom, and in everything they do. It just got to the point where I didn't want to have to fool with his everyday headaches."

So one day, Smith just asked Lloyd to leave. This time Lloyd had lasted eleven weeks. Lloyd *never* played a basketball game for Oak Hill.

"It just shows you that Lloyd Daniels is his own worst enemy," one high school scout said.

"It is difficult to understand," d'Almeida said, when asked about the turn of events. "But it's like people on a life raft out in the ocean. Why do some die and why do some survive? Maybe what it all comes down to in the end is willpower."

As Smith said: "At the rate he is going, he is a prime target to be one of the biggest athletes, one of the biggest names, never to make it. . . . When people hear the name 'Lloyd,' they think of trouble. The funny thing is that I still like him. I care about him. When he pulled out of here, I watched him go down the road and . . . I wondered if this was his last chance. If Oak Hill was his last chance. I wondered if I could have saved him."

He wondered if anyone could.

Andrew Jackson

A lvis Brown was in class when he heard the news. New kid in school, basketball player. Good one, too, word was. Already there was talk that with this kid Andrew Jackson High School was a cinch to defend its New York City title in the Public Schools Athletic League (PSAL). Some said the kid might even be the best ever to wear a Jackson uniform.

Brown wondered just a bit.

His cousin Boo Harvey had graduated after the previous season. A two-time all-city player at Jackson, Harvey was listed in the school hall of fame right next to Bob Cousy, the Boston Celtics guard and member of the Basketball Hall of Fame.

"Who's the new kid?" Brown asked a classmate. "Don't know," the kid told him. "His name's Swee'pea. That's all I know, he's called Swee'pea."

Brown thought a moment. When he was younger, maybe six, seven years old, he and a cousin used to play ball with this kid over at St. Pascal's in Hollis. Brown couldn't remember the kid's name, just that folks used to call him "Sweets." He'd been real good. "I was sayin' to myself, 'Couldn't be the same kid, could it?' It couldn't be Sweets."

Right after class, Brown bolted for the gym, anxious. It was time for practice; the kid would be there. Brown walked in. There he was, on the floor, alone. Shooting.

"Sweets," Brown said to himself.

"This," Jackson coach Chuck Granby told his guys, "is Lloyd Daniels. He's going to be on our team." Players in the stands watched, whispered. "We're goin' to win the title," Brown recalled a teammate said. "We got us another city championship."

"Here was Lloyd, out on the court by *hisself*, dribbling, shooting the ball where the three-point line would be if we had a three-point line—which, at that time, we didn't, 'cause the rule wasn't put in until two seasons later," Brown said. "He hit all the way around from the left side to the right, shooting right-handed all the way, and then, when he got done, he went back around the other way, hitting every shot left-handed.

"Again, he didn't miss."

Left hand over his heart, Brown pressed his thumb to the forefinger and middle finger of his right hand, kissed them. Held them aloft; gestured to the heavens.

"I swear to God," he said, "he didn't miss not *one*."

The new kid was good, all right.

And if that little shooting exhibition in the gym hinted to the kids at Jackson the skill this new kid possessed, the first game of the season against Moses Scurry and his team, Brooklyn's Eli Whitney High School, offered irrefutable evidence of what Lloyd could really do with a basketball. Actually, it defined the very essence of his game.

Another man, his first big contest with his new team on the line, might have panicked and rid himself of the ball too soon, the result being one of disaster—or, at least, not one of benefit to himself or his club. But Lloyd, now a junior, was no such man. And so, as time wound down and with Jackson down by two, he glanced at the clock and calculated in his head, it seemed to all in attendance that night in Cambria Heights, Queens, just how far he could go before the ball would need to be released.

He'd been buried deep in his own backcourt, having taken the inbound pass. He'd dribbled to within a few steps of the midcourt line when he first looked at the clock. There were three seconds left in regulation. Jackson trailed Whitney, 62–60.

Lloyd had been in this situation hundreds of times before, in his imagination, during those lonely nights in the park back in East New York. He'd done fine then. He would do fine now. He was Lloyd Daniels, damn it. *Swee'pea*. This was *his* game.

Undaunted, he dribbled once. Then again. And then, once again.

Having used all the time he'd allotted for movement toward his goal, Lloyd pulled up and, to the amazement of all, squared his body to the basket.

He was at half-court. The buzzer was about to sound. He fired.

No sooner had he released the ball then the buzzer sounded its alarm, the shot in midair, mouths hushed among the patrons. The shot could easily have missed the mark and, despite the toughness of the crowd, all would surely have been forgiven. Even the legendary Cousy had sometimes failed in his quest for heroics as a schoolboy in this gymnasium. Here even Harvey, who as a senior at St. John's would hit four buzzer-beating shots to tie or win games, had sometimes come up short.

Besides, Lloyd already had thirty-seven points, a more than fair performance, even for a player of his stature, in this, the season opener for both teams.

What more could the crowd expect?

But those who knew him knew that, deep down, Lloyd always seemed to have something in reserve, a bit of extra magic with which to command the situation.

"We was going to lose our reputation," Brown, then a sophomore, recalled of the moment. "It was all on Lloyd's shoulders with that one shot.

"We all felt we would lose the game," Brown said. "All of us had our heads down. But Lloyd was telling everybody, 'Y'all move out the way. I got the game under control. I got the game under control. Just leave it to me.' Then he took it—and let fly."

It was the stuff of miracles, the stuff of legends. Because as the crowd and his teammates looked on, stunned, the ball hit dead center in the backboard box—and, an instant later, fell clean through the hoop. The gym echoed with delirious applause.

Swee'pea had tied the game.

Still, Lloyd was not finished. With Jackson down, 63–62, in overtime, he hit two free throws, the last two points of the game, to win the contest, 64–63.

He had gone 16-for-20 from the field and 9-for-9 from the foul line, scoring 41 points with 12 rebounds. *Go down, Moses!* Lloyd had outshone Scurry, who, despite scoring 28, could only shake his head at what he'd just seen.

"You know," scout Tom Konchalski said later on, "the most impressive part was that, when he hit that half-court shot against Whitney, he released the ball at the precise moment of best advantage. He wasn't going to release it a dribble too soon. He timed it in his head, got as close as he could, then shot. It was pure Lloyd Daniels.

"It told you right then just what kind of player he was."

––––––

Coaches throughout the five boroughs already knew what kind of player Lloyd was and accepted that he was a star with talent unparalleled. At the same time, they also knew what kind of student he was—and questioned whether he should, in fact, be allowed to remain eligible to play based on his perilous academic record.

Several suggested the PSAL investigate.

Two, Paul Dallara of Far Rockaway High School and Howie Warhaftig of Beach Channel High School, even filed protests after division games against Jackson.

"The kid is jumping around from school to school to play basketball, not get an education," Dallara said. "Someone has to be held accountable for the procedure which allowed him to get into school and then be eligible to play basketball. When I think of it, I feel cheated. I feel bad for my kids. I feel bad for my whole division. I feel bad for the whole system. I don't mind losing. But I like to lose fairly. This is a travesty for everybody. I have to question a system that allows this to happen."

The controversy began long before that first game against Whitney, long before Jackson split its season series with Far Rock, a team featuring future Seton Hall University guard Oliver Taylor, Jr., who would lead the city in scoring during the 1986–87 season at 35.2 points per game. It went back to the first week of that November, when Lloyd first returned to New York after his dismissal from Oak Hill.

Back then, Lloyd called Ron Naclerio's house. Left a message. "Tell Ron I'm comin' to Cardozo," he told Ron's mother, Gloria. "Tell him I'll be there tomorrow."

After a brief conversation with Lloyd, Lou d'Almeida had decided Cardozo would be the best fit for him. It had a notable academic reputation. It had a tutorial program that could assist Lloyd in his studies. And Ron, who by then had known Lloyd more than three years and who knew how to handle him perhaps better than anyone who'd ever dealt with him, was its coach. But, there was one problem: Cardozo was in Bayside, Queens. And Lloyd did not live within—or, even near—the school zone.

According to the New York City Board of Education, several methods allowed students to attend a school out of zone—areas defined by a complex geographic grid system that delineated enrollment districts. A student could request to major in a specific subject offered only in a school out of zone, such as a vocational school or one with a specialized academic program; education options programs, or ed-op programs, as they were known. A student also could request a safety transfer, usually to protect him or her from some sort of harassment. They could request something known as a guidance transfer. But Lloyd's case didn't fall into any of those defined areas.

Still, Ron wasn't about to argue when d'Almeida arrived the following morning with Lloyd. They all expected to find some route, conventional or otherwise, by which Lloyd, now high school basketball's prodigal son, could enroll at Cardozo.

Like those before him, Ron believed he could help Lloyd get his life in order. Like those others, Ron also had selfish reasons. As he said later: "I knew if I had him I would either have an ulcer or a city championship. Or, probably, I would've had both."

Lloyd was given the guided tour at Cardozo. Baseball coach Ed Tatarian, who served as coordinator of student affairs, even talked with him about coming out for his team, something that interested Swee'pea—since he had shown hints of major-league potential in the local youth league before quitting to concentrate on basketball.

Ron introduced Lloyd to his starting guards, Greg "Skate" Scott and Kevin Story, whose game was all flash and glitter and straight out of a playground circus. The two were known, affectionately and not-so, as "the Psycho Twins." Then Ron and Lloyd ran into Duane Caus-well, his seven-foot senior, bound for Temple University, who'd later be a first-round selection of the Sacramento Kings in the 1990 NBA Draft.

"Duane was in an office, studying, when I walked in with Lloyd," Ron recalled. "I go to Duane, 'Duane, this is Lloyd Daniels. There's a good chance he might come to our school.' Duane looks at me and goes, 'Yeah.' I go, 'Duane, he's a pretty good player.' Duane goes, 'Yeah.' It was obvious he didn't know who Lloyd was, so I go, 'Duane, he has a nickname.' Duane goes, 'Yeah. What is it?' I go, 'Swee'pea. This is Swee'pea.' Immediately, his eyes lit up. He goes, '*This* is Swee'pea?'

"You could see he understood what it meant."

Others at Cardozo knew what it meant, too. It meant trouble, Cardozo assistant principal George Rosenberg said. In fact, Rosenberg said later, it meant so much trouble that he decided to let the officials at the New York City Board of Education High School Placement office make the final decision on where Lloyd would attend school.

"If he gets clearance from High School Placement to come here, that's fine," Rosenberg said, explaining his decision. "It's not unprecedented for kids out of district to come here because we are one of the best schools in the city and have a very good tutoring program. But he is not going to come here just to play basketball."

As Ron later said, "Maybe I should have told Lloyd to tell them he wanted to come to Cardozo because he wanted to study Russian."

––––

Of course, Ron never did that. And High School Placement followed the book when it ruled that Lloyd, who was no better at reading English than he was at Russian, should attend Jackson—not Cardozo. Placement also ruled Lloyd immediately eligible at Jackson. That, because the PSAL, the organization that oversees interscholastic sports among public schools in New York City, mandated that to be eligible a student-athlete only had to attain a passing average the previous semester. Lloyd had.

Some argued those marks were questionable. But, fact was, Lloyd had passed his classes at Laurinburg. And though another rule stated a transfer must be enrolled in school no later than fifteen days after the start of a new term to be eligible to play sports—and, truth was, Lloyd had not been so enrolled—in the end he remained unaffected, because he was considered by the system to be an out-of-state transfer.

The situation, some argued, was indicative of just how bad, how widespread, the problem of illegal recruitment and illegal transfer had become in New York City. Here was Lloyd, a gun for hire who had little more than one-quarter of the credits needed for graduation, shopping around—at the request of his summer-league club coach, Lou d'Almeida, no less—for what would be his fourth high school in three states in two years. Shopping for a school that could offer him basketball and an education—though, if his past was indicative of the future, certainly not with an equal emphasis.

"My initial reaction is one of anger," Ken Gershon, coach of Hillcrest High School in Jamaica, Queens, said, though some called it sour grapes—noting Hillcrest was one of the schools Lloyd had considered during the whole transfer saga. "Since when did we go into the recruiting game? There has to be something wrong with a kid being in four schools in two years. How can he be a student? Here is a kid who, every time he fouls up in a school, leaves that school and still he has been allowed to play ball.

"He has not been penalized because of his academic problems," he said. "He just went where he could play basketball. In this case, it brought to the forefront problems with the system because of the type of player he is. The fact that he was allowed to play said something about our whole athletic system. We, the basketball society, continue to use these kids as much as we can. We stress that they belong in an academic background, when they don't, because we only want them to play basketball."

It was an all-too-common problem. Within the two-year period when Lloyd attended those four schools—and, truth be told, also had considered transfers to Westinghouse, where Hersh worked in Brooklyn, as well as to Brooklyn's Wingate and John F. Kennedy in the Bronx—a handful of other players had also jumped ship several times. Kenny Eato, a guard from Queens, went from Forest Hills High School to Oak Hill, where he was dismissed, then to Long Island City High School. Forward Adrian Carter went from Christ the King, a Catholic school in Queens, to St. Agnes, the Catholic school in Rockville Centre, Long Island, where former University of Florida and current Oklahoma City Thunder coach Billy Donovan first made his name as a player, then to Jackson and finally Long Island City.

Guard Darin Worsley left Hillcrest for Richmond Hill. Forward Royal Miller left Richmond Hill for Jackson. Even Duane Causwell had transferred, leaving Jackson—for Cardozo.

Some of the moves were made for personal reasons.

One, the transfer of Miller, was made after claims he'd been the victim of "racial harassment," though Richmond Hill basketball coach Eric Greenberg and Theresa Oropallo, the assistant principal in charge of guidance, both said neither the school nor the NYPD had records of racial threats against Miller—a six-foot-five, 220-pound forward, who left perhaps the worst basketball program in the city to join a Jackson team that would go on to win the New York City title in 1985.

And those were only a handful of the documentable transfers during that period, according to Joe Varone, chairman of the Eligibility Committee for the PSAL. No doubt, Varone said, there were many others that were never brought up for review. "This happens all the time," he said. "The Board of Ed rules and regulations allow this to happen, because of the way those laws are written. People take advantage of it and, even though we know what goes on, there is really not anything we can do about it."

The reason it happens is simple: coaches want to win games.

Winning games can lead them out of the high school ranks and into college coaching. Having a great player can sometimes mean a college will offer that player's coach a chance to come along for the ride—hiring him as an assistant, part of a package deal. Because winning can get a high school team into national tournaments.

It could even get a high school coach sneaker and clothing deals.

As a result, the best players often were given inducements in the form of sneakers, sweats, cash, and an easy path through school or, at a minimum, they were coddled by coaches who understood that without them, their teams couldn't win.

It led to a battle between the local club teams, which bid for the services of players to ensure their participation in national tournaments. It led to a battle between local high schools, which competed for out-of-zone players—even if sometimes those players used false addresses to enroll in a school out of their assigned zone.

Rod Strickland did it when he attended Truman, which was not his zoned high school. "I used another guy's address," he said. "I don't remember who."

A playground legend in Brownsville, Pearl Washington did it—first attending Norman Thomas High School in Manhattan because a friend of his knew the coach at the open-enrollment school. But, after scoring thirty-seven points in his high school debut, Washington was convinced to leave Thomas, which had a weak team, to attend perennial power Boys & Girls in Brooklyn. As Bernie Gober, an assistant principal at J.H.S. 8, the school where Ron worked as a teacher and one known well for producing talented players, said, "Throughout the city of New York, if a kid is known to be a ballplayer, he is going to be approached and asked, 'Why don't you come to my school?'"

Their values corrupted by club teams, which gave them money, and by a school system that often demanded little more than their attendance, if that—considering the atmosphere in their very neighborhoods and, sometimes, their very households—many times kids did. They left whatever school they were in, went to another.

(Consider, that just a few years after Gober's assessment, the starting backcourt at J.H.S. 8, the intermediate school, would be the pairing of two future NBA stars: Rafer Alston and Stephon Marbury, both of whom were little-known players when the original version of *Swee'pea*, the book, was dedicated to them back in 1990. And consider that, en route to college and the NBA, Alston, a magical ball handler known on the playgrounds as "Skip to My Lou," would play his high school ball at Cardozo in Queens, while Marbury went to Abraham Lincoln in Brooklyn—his story chronicled in *The Last Shot* by Darcy Frey.)

"What you do," Gershon said back before any of that unfolded, "is give a kid a false sense of values. A kid like Lloyd Daniels says, 'Hey, if I'm not happy at Jackson, I'll go to a school in Wisconsin or Ohio or somewhere,' because he has no allegiance to anyone. See, these are high school kids. They're impressionable. From the time a kid like Lloyd— any of these kids—was a grade schooler, he was exploited because of his basketball ability. People saw something in him. Coaches took care of him, gave him money, bought him things, found him a place to go to school. When do these kids realize that is not the way life is? When do they learn to deal with life on their own level?"

Stan Dinner was seated at a table in the Sports Page, the café he owned and operated on the Lower East Side of Manhattan, a place frequented by Ron and Hersh, as well as college coaches and even members of the Knicks—among them back then, Mark Jackson and Charles Oakley. Once, Dinner had been a high school basketball coach, one regarded, often with disdain, as New York City's most able recruiter. No one was better at finding kids and getting them eligible than Stan Dinner. Certainly, no one was more flagrant in his "creative manipulation" of the high school recruiting rules.

Dinner's claim to fame was that he once assembled what was considered by many the most troubled scholastic team *ever* in America, an ungovernable band of truants and rowdies that transformed Harlem's Benjamin Franklin High School into the nation's top-ranked high school squad back in 1979. "I recruited all the maniacs, the knuckleheads," Dinner said with a laugh. "But those guys, they could sure play."

There was Gary Springer, a two-time high school all-American who made two trips to the NCAA tournament at Iona College before his career gave way to bad knees. There was Richie Adams, who later became the two-time player of the year in the Pacific Coast Athletic Association at UNLV before he found himself in the big time; prison, that is. And there was Kenny Hutchinson, a pure shooting guard who made it to the University of Arkansas before substance abuse problems robbed him of his game. Truth was that Walter Berry, who won the Wooden Award as the NCAA Division I National Player of the Year at St. John's in 1986, and who played three years in the NBA with the Portland Trail Blazers, San Antonio Spurs, New Jersey Nets, and Houston Rockets, was no more than a practice player on that Franklin team. A sophomore who had transferred in from DeWitt Clinton High School in the Bronx, Berry rode the bench. Ineligible. Hardly missed. An assortment of others made the roster, though: respected high school and playground players such as Wayne Alexander, Lonnie Green, Darrell Davis, and Watkins "Boo" Singletary, later a starter at the University of Utah.

Dinner recruited them all through a shadowy network of assistants, summer league coaches, and friends, his kids often using "acquired" addresses as their heads filled with visions of the NBA. Dinner admitted those kids often developed a false sense of values, believing they were above the law. Then again, Dinner said, even though some saw him as a minor-league Larry Brown or Jerry Tarkanian, what they didn't truly understand was that he wasn't alone. *Everyone* recruited high school players in New York City.

"I was just the only coach who was willing to admit it," he said. "In New York, so many fucking guys get a piece of the kids that it isn't funny.

"But everyone else was sneaking around."

An affable, good-natured New York guy—Dinner was rumpled, liked his beer and Buffalo wings; was happiest sitting in his café talking sports, which he did no end—he spoke his mind and never skirted the issue. Rules, sure. *Never* the issue.

"I remember Dinner coming up to our star player at a game once, saying, 'Why are you wasting your time at Stuyvesant? You could be on my team,'" one player later recalled of Dinner's approach. "At least with Dinner, he was open about it."

Sure, Dinner said, maybe he sent the wrong message to some kids, allowing them to play when they weren't eligible. His 1980–81 team, after all, had to forfeit all its victories for using an ineligible player, iron-ically, not Berry or Hutchinson, but one using his real address—which was across the street from the school zone boundary.

Still, Dinner said, at least he made an effort to teach his kids to be responsible. He didn't give them money for nothing. If they needed it, they had to earn it. He made them sweep floors and wash dishes at his café or at a deli he owned. His players were welcome to borrow his car, though not without asking his permission first.

He couldn't be their parents, couldn't be their guardians. He couldn't make them become good citizens—though some did, finding success. Dinner said he was just a coach. All he could do was use bas-ketball to give those kids the chance to get off the street, be on his team; give them an enticement to get them into school.

The idea, altruistic or otherwise, was to get them more exposure than they could garner somewhere else to give them a fighting chance at college, success.

Sometimes it worked.

After Iona, Springer became a counselor for the Job Corps, while Green worked for the Transit Authority. Still, it seemed that more often than not, kids who came to Dinner found trouble more often than they found the classroom. Adams, Berry, and Singletary never graduated; each was forced to pursue an equivalency diploma.

The problem, Dinner said, was that most of his players, like most of the students at Franklin, were beyond help by the time he got them.

"We were a turn-back school," he said, adding: "Other schools would send us kids they didn't want."

His kids were lawless. Because of their environment, he said, they had grown up without discipline in their lives. They were addicted to the streets. His 1979–80 team, for instance, should have easily won city and state titles and was regarded as the leading candidate to finish the season as the national high school champion—a mythical title then based on polls in a host of basketball publications.

Gary Reedy, coach of Lake Braddock High School in Burke, Virginia, remembered playing that Franklin team—and being in awe. "They were amazing in the warm-ups," Reedy said. "After watching the first few dunks, we were like, 'Let's get on the bus and go home right now.'"

But, considered best in the nation, Franklin lost in overtime in the city semifinals to Adlai Stevenson. Then again, Dinner said he'd expected to lose.

"When they came in you could tell they were high," Dinner said. "I said, 'What are you guys doing? This game is for [a berth in] the city championship.' They said, 'Don't worry. We beat them once.' It turned out the night before was Richie's birthday. . . . The players got to the game straight from the party, about an hour before tip-off. At halftime, I'm pouring coffee down their throats and giving them cold showers to keep them awake." Franklin lost after a turnover by Hutchinson in overtime allowed Stevenson to score the game-winner.

Twelve times, Adams was called for goaltending.

Adams was typical of the players recruited by Dinner. An incredible talent, he was nicknamed "the Animal" for his shot blocking and take-no-prisoners approach around the basket. Then–Orlando Magic forward Sidney Green, himself a notable New York playground player who played against Adams in high school and with him at UNLV, said, "It was a thrill to watch him. He could snatch shots out of the air."

But Adams was a terrible student. Not a dumb one, because when he went to class, he did well. He just never went. In fact, Adams transferred to Franklin from Alfred E. Smith High School in the Bronx, where he had been assigned for two years—but had *never* attended class. "It took me two years not only to get him to come to Franklin, but just to convince him to go to school," Dinner said. When Adams entered Franklin, he did so as a second-semester sophomore, one who still had *no* high school credits.

But Dinner needed Adams to win. So he got him eligible.

"I'm probably guilty, as a coach, because I'd bend the rules for the good players to make sure there were no problems," he said. "Maybe that gave them the wrong idea, the wrong perception. Maybe, every time a kid failed a class, I failed a little, too.

"But," Dinner said, "at the time, it seemed like something that was helping them; helping them stay eligible, helping them get to college."

The alternatives were either to slide an unprepared kid into college and hope he could learn something—even if just from being exposed to that atmosphere—or let him stay on the street, where his future was already bleak. As Tom Konchalski, the high school basketball scout, said, "I think people like Stanley try to help these kids. I don't think he did anything malicious or with bad intent. He might not have done everything right, by the books. But I don't think he tried to harm anyone. He meant well."

Then again, the road to hell is paved with good intentions, right?

Consider that the example Dinner set only reinforced the notion that his kids were criminals, thugs, kids out of control. The image most of those kids had of themselves. Kids saw their coach bending the rules—and weren't about to argue it.

Look at Adams. He didn't like school, but he liked cars. And there was one time during the season that Adams, Springer, and Hutchinson "borrowed" Dinner's.

It was hours before a game when Dinner, sitting in his office with a recruiter from the University of California, Los Angeles, then coached by Larry Brown, got the call from cops at the local NYPD precinct. Could he come around when he had a moment and identify half his team?

"I got the call," Dinner said, "and the sergeant asked, 'Do you know a Richie Adams?' I said, 'Yeah.' He said, 'Do you know a Gary Springer?' I said, 'Yeah.' He said, 'Do you know a Kenny Hutchinson?' I said, 'Yeah.' He said, 'Do you know a Darrell Davis?' I said, 'Yeah.' He said, 'Do you know a Wayne Alexander?' I said, 'Yeah, *yeah already*. Why do *you* want to know? What the hell did *they* do now?' He said, 'Please come down here and identify them. . . . They stole your *car*.'"

"We were on our way to pick up someone else and all of a sudden a policeman is sticking a gun in my face," Springer recalled of the incident. "When the police saw we were Ben Franklin basketball players, though, they didn't really handcuff us. But they put us in a holding cell for a while. We were all like, 'Richie, didn't you tell Dinner you were taking the car?' He said he *forgot*. The police called Dinner to come and get us from the station, and he's got a coach from UCLA in his office who'd been there to recruit *me*. We figured it would make a great episode for *The White Shadow*."

The difference, of course, was that the coach in *The White Shadow*—a period TV show about a white coach at a fictional high school in South Central L.A.—would have suspended his players for pulling such "pranks." Dinner was living in the real world. He said he felt nothing he could do would make a difference in the end.

After all, there was the time his team was ahead by nine with about a minute left in a game and, in the era before the shot clock, he elected to go into a stall.

"I'm sitting on the bench and the team manager goes to me, 'Coach, what are you doing?'" Dinner recalled. "I go, 'It's a stall, why? What's the matter? We're up nine.' He goes, 'But the spread is ten and a half. And I got *money* on this game.'

"I mean, what can you do?" Dinner said, echoing a familiar refrain. "Most of these kids are living in a different world, one that has its own rules. You have to play by them if you want to survive. I was coach of the top-ranked team in America. I had all-Americans. I got wined and dined by the recruiters. I admit it, I was impressed. Maybe you just lose sight of what's important. You lose sight of your job as a coach. Maybe you take a look at these kids and realize you're helpless to change them and so you just decide you have to be practical."

Even, he said, when you know it's wrong.

———

Jack Curran had no need to be practical. He had been around too long, had built too good a program at Archbishop Molloy, to have to bend a few rules. His workplace, after all, was exclusive: an all-boys' school, one of the most-respected academic institutions in New York City. It attracted only the best students, only the best athletes; a Harvard of high schools. In a time of growing moral corruption, in a time when most public schools in New York more resembled Benjamin Franklin than Benjamin Cardozo, Molloy, the private parochial school remained well ordered, refined. Its students still obeyed a dress code that demanded of them blue blazers, button-down shirts, and ties. The halls were immaculate. Should a stray piece of litter dare appear, it was not beneath a student—or Jack Curran, for that matter—to bend down and pick it up.

Curran was a respectable gentleman with an old Irish face and a brush of fading red hair. He didn't curse, was a regular churchgoer, and yet his voice, his mere presence, commanded respect, authority. He had been at Molloy forever, it seemed, having come to the school in 1958, the year it changed its name from St. Ann's. He had replaced the former basketball coach, a guy named Lou Carnesecca, who'd moved a few exits down the Grand Central Parkway to become an assistant coach at St. John's.

A former minor-league pitcher, Curran had once been a baseball and basketball player at St. John's, where he'd been recruited by the legendary Frank McGuire and played on a team with Mario Cuomo, the future governor of New York.

But at Molloy, Curran was part of a then-two-man athletic staff; his partner, Frank Rienzo, later became athletic director at Georgetown University.

It wasn't long before Curran built himself a reputation, though. His baseball team was always among the best in the nation, once winning sixty-eight straight games during the 1960s. His basketball teams, too, were renowned. By the fall of 1985, Curran had coached six all-Americans, including Kevin Joyce, Brian Winters, and Kenny Smith.

Even Lew Alcindor had once sought enrollment at Molloy.

Alcindor, later known as Kareem Abdul-Jabbar, lived in Manhattan then and told Curran he thought it might be too far for him to travel to Molloy on a daily basis. Curran said that was a shame and wished him well. "I told him, 'Lewie, I think you're right,'" Curran recalled. Alcindor enrolled in Power Memorial. The rest is history.

"It cost us three championships," Curran said. "If we had to do it all over again, we might not tell him it was too far."

Really, though, it wasn't Curran's style.

Jack Curran was not going to bend the rules for anyone, even if, like most private schools, his received most of its players from the local club teams, which often paid their tuition to attend. He told Kenny Anderson as much when the freshman guard arrived at Molloy in September 1985. Freshmen, Curran said, even freshmen as good as Anderson, didn't start games at Molloy. Often they didn't even get a chance to play. If the kid didn't like that . . . well, like big Lew Alcindor, he was free not to come.

Period. End of discussion.

Though just five foot ten and 150 pounds, a wisp of a kid, Anderson decided he had come too far and worked too hard not to give it a shot. With Vincent Smith and an ever-expanding group of advisors prodding him on, Anderson not only tried out; he made varsity. By the winter of 1985, while Lloyd was tearing up the PSAL, the reputation of Kenny Anderson also was beginning to grow. In the parks, they called him "Chibbs." He was getting himself a household name.

———

There were four major daily newspapers in New York City in the 1980s—the *New York Times, Daily News, New York Post,* and *New York Newsday*—and three of them, the tabloids, fought each other for space on the newsstands.

After all, New York is a competitive town. There are two Major League Baseball teams, two National Football League teams, three National Hockey League teams, and two National Basketball Association teams—all within a twenty-mile radius.

And, with the papers fighting each other over coverage, the trickle-down effect often even dictates how they cover high schools.

High school sports were not—and are not—as important in New York as they are in most smaller cities and towns across America. But high school basketball has, to some extent, always been taken seriously. After all, basketball is and always has been the City Game. So, when a player of Lloyd's ability and stature, one with his history, goes through the kind of situation Lloyd was going through at Jackson, well . . . understand that the New York tabloids know a good story when they see one.

Be assured, Lloyd was a good story.

"A High School Star Out of His League" was the headline of one column in the *Daily News*. "Daniels 'used' Jackson, PSAL," cried a headline in the *Post*.

"The Strange Case of Lloyd Daniels," read the headline over a story in *Newsday*, which chronicled Lloyd's movement from school-to-school, from state-to-state.

Even the normally aloof *New York Times* got involved in the growing coverage of the story. "Schoolboy Star: Fit to Play, But Where?" it politely asked.

It was a sure bet Lloyd couldn't read any of those headlines, or the stories. But his friends could. And they did. That caused embarrassment; Lloyd's travels and travails were on public display. Friends, classmates, even the public at large, now knew not just that Lloyd had jumped from school to school but also that he couldn't read. Lloyd tried to remain polite to people who were polite to him, but he refused to speak with reporters on the record. And, in some cases, off the record as well.

One reporter who especially got to Lloyd was a guy from the *Post* named Steve Barenfeld. He had ripped Lloyd in a column, had written about how he couldn't read, about how he had used the PSAL only for basketball. Now, all of that was true. But Lloyd felt Barenfeld had taken a bunch of cheap shots at him en route and, one afternoon, in the locker room at Jackson, Lloyd decided to confront him. There was no violence, nothing physical. In fact, Lloyd just wanted to poke fun at him. Put him down.

The problem was, in the process, he dissed himself.

"Is this the guy who wrote I can't read?" Lloyd asked teammate Anthony Johnson as he pointed to Barenfeld. Johnson shrugged. "I guess so," he said.

"Yeah," Lloyd said. "You're that guy from the *Post*. Steve Barenfeld. You're the guy who wrote I can't read. Well, if I can't read, how'd I *know* you wrote I couldn't read if I couldn't read it?" Barenfeld looked at Lloyd in pure disbelief.

"Someone read it to you?" he said.

Lloyd's teammates started to laugh. They knew it was true. You could almost see Swee'pea wince in what was a most terrible moment—especially since, no matter what anyone thought of him, Lloyd was, in reality, still just a lost kid.

"The kid's been going through a tough time," Chuck Granby said when asked why Lloyd refused to speak with reporters. "People keep calling asking for interviews and he's not ready for that now. So far we've had no problem with him, on the court or in the classroom. I've told him he has to do certain things, because if things don't go right here, everybody is really going to come down on him. He seems to understand."

Certainly, Lloyd continued his incredible play, something later confirmed by his postseason selection as a *Parade Magazine* all-American—an honor that, strangely enough, was partially due to all the coverage he received in the press, which extolled his virtues as a player if not as a student. There was a 27-point, 12-rebound, 15-assist performance in an easy 83–67 win over August Martin—a team that, led by a tandem of terrific guards, Sean Green and Brent McCollin, would reach the 1986 PSAL Semifinal Game.

"He intimidated us," Green said. (Consider that Green would later play at Oak Hill, then the second-ranked high school team in the nation, before playing at North Carolina State and Iona College, then in the NBA with the Indiana Pacers, Philadelphia 76ers, and Utah Jazz.) "Just the name Lloyd Daniels is intimidating," he said.

There was the half-court shot Lloyd made—it hit nothing but net— at the third-quarter buzzer later that season against Beach Channel. And there was a tournament in Trenton, New Jersey, when Lloyd went out and made a mockery of the opposition.

"We had won the first game," Alvis Brown, who shared a hotel room with Lloyd on the trip, recalled. "But the crowd was getting on him because he didn't show them nothin'. That night, in the room, Lloyd and I was talking. He had like five hundred dollars on him and I had forty-five. He said he'd bet me his whole five hundred against my forty-five that he wouldn't miss a shot the whole first quarter of the championship game, against Trenton Central." Brown had no idea where Lloyd got all that money: a club team, a drug deal, a recruiter. Still, he told him: "It's a bet."

"Well, he didn't miss a shot the whole first quarter, the whole second quarter. He didn't miss 'til the third quarter. In fact, he was going to the guy guarding him, 'Where you want me to shoot it from? Right about here? Here?' He was pointing to marks on the floor, going, 'Here? Here?' then shooting and hitting all net."

Lloyd finished with fifty-six. "I lost all my money," Brown said.

Understandable, performances considered: 41 points, 12 rebounds, in a 93–83 win over Far Rockaway; 43 points in an 82–61 win at Franklin K. Lane; 21 points, 18 assists, in a 104–37 rout of Richmond Hill; 21 points, 11 assists, 10 rebounds, in a 73–57 win over John Adams; 38 points in a 61–56 win over August Martin; 33 in a 75–53 win at Long Beach on Long Island; and 34 in a 64–63 loss against Far Rockaway.

Perhaps the most important game all season, though, was in the Martin Luther King Classic at the Nassau Coliseum. And it wasn't because Lloyd dominated that game against Wyandanch. Rather, it was because it was at that game, Arnie Hershkowitz alleged, that he informed UNLV assistant coach Mark Warkentien of plans for Lloyd to visit the school on a trip that would lead to his enrollment there.

Despite Granby's statement about Lloyd meeting his scholastic obligations at Jackson, certainly that was not happening. According to Lloyd, he rarely attended class at Jackson, though he still remained eligible to compete. Some mornings, Lloyd said, he would make some token effort to attend school. Others, he would simply pretend he was getting ready to go and, once his grandmother went off to work, he would go back upstairs and go to sleep—just like he had back at I.S. 218.

"At Jackson, I couldn't understand why he was sleeping when he was supposed to be in school," Lloyd's grandmother, Lulia Hendley, said, also telling a reporter how Lloyd constantly smoked marijuana—sometimes even before games.

"Granby would call and say, 'If he's not at practice, I won't let him play,'" Lulia Hendley said. "But he would let him play anyway. See, that's the thing with Junior. If he had respect for you and didn't lose it, he would respect you to the highest.

"I think Granby knew Junior was smoking, but he let him play anyway because he wanted to win games," Lloyd's grandmother said. "And Junior would say, 'He's goin' to let me play anyway, 'cause he needs me. I don't need Granby.' He would get up, like one o'clock, take a shower, smoke his stuff, and he would still play."

"When I first got into Jackson, I was goin' to classes," Lloyd said, "Even he couldn't believe it, 'cause Chuckie knew my background. The first half, I was goin'." But, Lloyd said, when he saw Granby was going easy on him, because of his talent, he took advantage of the situation; cursed Granby out, cut school. "See, the days I did go to class, I went to class. But there was days I went to school and I just hung out in the lunch room all day. And Chuckie knows it. If you ask me, I should have been ineligible. I should've flunked out of Jackson."

While Granby refused comment on Lloyd—"All I can say is that he was never mine," Granby said, when pressed; "I'm not going to say anything else"—Brown said that, though Lloyd rarely went to class, Granby tried in vain to help him. "The reason Lloyd doesn't like Chuck is because Chuck was always staying on him, calling his house in the morning, trying to help him," Brown said. "He would call his grandma.

He was going out into the neighborhood looking for him. He was looking out for him. But soon he just realized there was no helping the boy. See, it just got to the point that, no matter what you did, Lloyd just wouldn't show up. Most of his classes were remedial classes and he was embarrassed that people might find out his reading level. He'd see his picture in the newspapers and, because he knew what his name looked like, he knew it was about him. He'd say, 'Yo, read the article.'

"If you call someone a dummy over and over and over, they're going to tend to withdraw. People said that about him and he went into his little shell."

As one Jackson teammate said, "He turned to drugs. It was the only thing he had left in his life." Drugs. And basketball.

———

Lulia Hendley said her grandson was "high when he left the house" the afternoon of February 20, 1986, the day Andrew Jackson met Cardozo in the first round of PSAL Playoffs at Hillcrest High School. Lloyd protested that wasn't the case, claimed he was sick, instead. "That was like one of the times, one of like the only times, I wasn't high," he said. "I just didn't feel good. I had a little cold."

Lloyd had missed two previous games, one of them, he said, for a good reason. "I was gettin' laid by a cheerleader," he said.

But now he was back. And, despite his "cold," he was virtually unstoppable. He'd drive down the floor, dribbling past defenders like Cardozo guards Greg Scott and Kevin Story, both all-borough selections, to swoop in alone on center Duane Causwell.

Now, Causwell wasn't much of an offensive player. In fact, he scored just two points in the game. But he was seven foot tall and was a bigtime shot blocker and defender. And yet Lloyd rattled him that afternoon, put every park move he could on the big man, getting him into early foul trouble. Getting him out of the game.

One time, he'd score on a fingertip roll. The next, he'd pull up against Story or Scott, bank one home from twenty. He'd back in against Causwell, spin off him.

Force him to foul.

But it wasn't enough. Though Lloyd went 9-for-11 from the field and 11-for-14 from the line, one of his missed field goal attempts coming on a fierce rejection by Causwell, it was Cardozo that upset Jackson, 69–63. Despite a game-high 29 points with 9 rebounds, 2 blocks, 2 steals, and 2 assists, on a team where three of his teammates were marginal, at best, Lloyd could only do so much.

After the game, Granby refused to shake hands with Ron, the two continuing a feud that stemmed from the situation with Lloyd—and the transfer of Causwell.

But Lloyd walked over and congratulated Ron and his players, including Story and Scott, who had combined for thirty-six points against the Hickories.

Later, Lloyd said, Chuck Granby yelled at him.

"He thought I threw the game," Lloyd said. "Can you believe that? He figured since I wasn't all broke up after the game, that I must've gotten paid by Ronnie to throw the game. The team beat us, straight up. I did everythin' I could have did against them. So I went over and shook their hands. Chuckie didn't like that. But what was I supposed to do, get on my knees and cry? Chuckie's daughter came over to me after the game and said, 'How much did the coach pay you?' I had a cold. So, I just coughed on her."

Afterward, for the first time all season, Lloyd elected to talk to reporters. "Definitely," he said, "I'm comin' back next year." No more jumping around.

The next day, true to form, he dropped out of school.

Kenny Anderson cut through traffic on the congested floor of Rose Hill Gymnasium on the Bronx campus of Fordham University. It was the Catholic High School Athletic Association City Championship. Molloy trailed Tolentine High School, 66–65, with little more than a minute to go in overtime. Already the lithe, left-handed freshman had dominated, scoring five straight points near the end of regulation to take the Stanners from a 60–59 deficit to a 64–62 lead with seventeen seconds left. It had taken future St. John's and NBA star Malik Sealy to tie the game and force overtime.

Now, as Anderson weaved through a host of defenders, a raucous crowd of almost four thousand, packed into the old-time bandbox gym, stood and screamed.

Anderson dribbled into the lane, backed up his man, spun off him, lifted from the floor. When his leap reached its apex, Anderson, his arm already cocked, shot the ball in his most peculiar fashion—fired almost as if by a shot-putter. Still, it went in, smooth, the basket proving to be the deciding points in what would become a 69–66 championship win for Molloy. "It wasn't an incredible shot or anything," Anderson said with a flash of his characteristic sly smile when it was over. And, he was right.

But he had shown poise enough to take it, and make it. To take control of such a huge game at such a crucial moment, that said a lot about him, about his game; about how far he had come since his days as a raw talent back at Lost Battalion Hall.

Tolentine coach John Sarandrea, a firefighter who later went on to become an assistant coach at the University of Pittsburgh, said, "He did some incredible things. I know, without him, we would have won the championship. Hands down."

When it was over, Anderson's teammates gathered under the basket and lifted him to cut the first strand from the net. Just fifteen years old, Anderson had become the first freshman ever selected the MVP of the CHSAA Tournament, a feat never accomplished by Lew Alcindor, Dean "the Dream" Meminger, or Chris Mullin.

"He's the greatest," Jack Curran said later, outside the championship locker room. Then, in reference to the 1984 Robert Redford film, based on the old Bernard Malamud novel, Curran said of his lithe freshman guard, "He's *The Natural.*" Anderson smiled when he heard. "Not bad, right?"

Not bad at all. Because not only had he been named MVP, but he also hit the game-winning shot in his next game, converting a three-point play with four seconds left in overtime, as Molloy beat St. Anthony's High School, 89–88, to win the CHSAA State Championship—Anderson grabbing a rebound, firing it, and drawing a foul against Tom Greis, a seven-foot-one senior center headed to Villanova.

When the season ended, Anderson had averaged 16.7 points, 4 rebounds, and 7.8 assists. True to his word, Curran never started the freshman, whom he referred to always as Kenneth; never once allowed him to appear in the first quarter of any game. Lloyd averaged 31.2 points, 12.3 rebounds, 10 assists, and 5 blocks to be named a *Parade Magazine* all-American. But Steve Barenfeld, who hated Lloyd, took a moral stand and wrote that, since Lloyd dropped out of school, he wouldn't be named to *his* All-City Team. Anderson, meanwhile, would be selected All-City by *New York Newsday* and the *Post*. It was the first of four straight years Anderson would be named to the All-City Team. At the time, he was the only player in history ever to have done so.

Not far from Andrew Jackson, Lloyd sat in a booth at McDonald's, eating a cheeseburger and french fries. It was an April afternoon and he had just been asked if he'd been to school in the previous six weeks, since the end of basketball season.

"Of course, I stopped goin' to school," Lloyd said, dumbfounded, acting as though the question was a ridiculous one. "I'm here now, ain't I?"

He set the burger down, pushed back in the seat, stiffened himself. It seemed to be a defensive position. He licked his lips, then motioned with his hands, spreading greasy fingers to expose his palms as if to say "stop"—the gesture surely designed to cut the legs off any question that might follow.

"I ain't allergic to no school," he said. "I just don't want to go."

Within a month, despite the fact his high school class was not to graduate until June 1987, despite his inability to read, Lloyd would make an unexpected and unprecedented move: he'd elect to pass up his remaining year of high school, declaring *himself* eligible for college, and sign a letter of intent to attend UNLV.

The entire notion was absurd. According to Rick Evrard, then-director of Legislative Services for the NCAA, there was almost no chance Lloyd could ever become eligible to play for the Runnin' Rebels. Evrard believed that even if Lloyd could somehow gain his General Equivalency Diploma (GED), the earliest he could become eligible was the 1988–89 season. Still, Lloyd said that afternoon back at Mickey D's, he was going to give it a shot. After all, Lloyd said he had been "shocked" when he found out he could even get into college; quite understandable, considering he had earned little more than one-quarter of the credits needed for high school graduation.

Considering he was, at best, borderline illiterate.

"But, you got to handle it," he said, between interruptions from a host of well-wishers, among them freshman Jackson guard Dave Edwards, who would later play one season for John Thompson at Georgetown before transferring to Texas A&M. "If you can get in, you get in," he said. "You got to take an opportunity like that. Nobody can turn it down. They givin' it to you, you take it. I'd be a fool not to, right? You'd take it, wouldn't you? That's why I'm goin'. That's why it ain't worth goin' to no high school now.

"I *can't* worry about it. I got goin' to college to worry about."

The statement begged the obvious, Tom Konchalski said.

"Does Lloyd have the wrong perception of how the world works? No. His perception of the system has been correct. It is the system that is not correct. But he is a product of the American athletic system. It spoils kids. It leads athletes to think that they can break the rules that they feel don't affect them. A kid like Lloyd has come to realize that, if he screws up, someone will cover for him and find an escape hatch.

"Some say he is a con man, that he will say, 'Yes,' and then go out and do whatever it is he wants to do," Konchalski said. "But I think it is more of a case where the spirit is willing, but the flesh is weak. . . . So far his athletic talent has kept him from being just another kid hanging out on a street corner going nowhere with his life. But that talent will only keep him from that so long. With the gifts that God gives out, he gives responsibilities. Lloyd Daniels has such great talent that, to not use it would be a sin. It would be a tragedy for him, but it would also be an oblique tragedy for the others he deprived of having the joy of watching him play."

"We've told him nothing about life," Ken Gershon, the Hillcrest coach, said. "All we've told him is that he is a great ballplayer. And the minute that Lloyd Daniels cannot bounce that basketball, that is the moment these guys give back their piece of the rock. . . . We never forced him to mature. Instead, we let him do what he wanted and, sooner or later, he'll probably wind up in the parks, talking about his glory days, trying to pick up a few bucks here and there.

"See, you have to try to steer these kids. . . . With Lloyd, a lot of people often just tried to take what they could get. He has abused [the system] because he has been allowed to abuse it. But he has also abused it because people used him to abuse it. He has been taught to use people the way people used him. It's a terrible thing, a sad case."

It figured to get sadder still.

Swee'pea and the Strip

The University of Nevada–Las Vegas was one of a hundred schools pursuing Lloyd. That it landed him was only because its staff conjured up a most creative—and, unprecedented—solution to the problem of how to get a high school dropout eligible for college. Enabling, in the end, Jerry Tarkanian and his Runnin' Rebels to survive the hard-fought recruiting war, a war of attrition that counted among its vanquished the likes of Kansas and Kentucky, St. John's, Syracuse, Seton Hall, and a host of others, including Providence College and its then-coach, Rick Pitino.

The process had begun as it usually does for potential major-college recruits. As far back, that is, as eighth or ninth grade, when Lloyd first surfaced among those in the know as a player with legitimate big-time skills. Once identified, he became the subject of incredible letter-writing campaigns—letters, his first came from Syracuse—as well as the subject of recruitment visits, which began in the tenth grade at Oak Hill and Laurinburg and continued during his one season at Jackson.

While no one actually sent him $1,000 stuffed into an Emery air-mail package, as it was alleged Kentucky later had in an effort to entice recruit Chris Mills of Los Angeles, that didn't mean Lloyd's recruitment was not often out of hand. Basketball coaches and street-level sources alike called him dozens of times a night just to say hello and to mention their schools remained, as always, interested in him.

Often, coaches and assistant coaches even flew in from around the country just to see him practice, as UNLV assistant Mark Warkentien had back when Lloyd was a junior at Oak Hill. Always, coaches wrote. Sometimes, to absurdity.

There were letters about how their school was "one of the finest" in the country, as then–University of Missouri coach Norm Stewart wrote. Or what an asset Lloyd would be to their university, then–Louisville coach Denny Crum thanking him for his "interest" in exploring the possibility of coming to the school that rivaled Kentucky.

Michigan assistant Mike Boyd wrote: "I sincerely enjoyed the opportunity to watch you work out this past week. Without a doubt, you have great talent and we have a very strong interest in you."

Then–Alabama coach Wimp Sanderson wrote: "The University of Alabama is always searching for the type of young men that will represent our University well on the court and in the classroom. We have been told that you are the type of person and player that we need to continue to be successful."

It was hard to believe anyone who'd ever talked to Lloyd honestly thought he'd be swayed by the promise of a good education or that a kid who'd been to four high schools in three states, dropping out the day after his junior season ended, promised to be a good representative of *any* academic institution. No surprise then that the most shrewd, guys like Pitino, a Long Islander who'd just arrived at Providence fresh off a stint as an assistant coach with the NBA New York Knicks, simply cut to the chase. Noting that "hundreds of people have asked me how I could possibly leave the New York Knicks and the glamour of the NBA," Pitino wrote that the answer was "simple and from the heart."

He told Lloyd that player-coach relationships in pro basketball often were "impersonal" and "purely business-oriented," that he'd come back to college to "satisfy a personal hunger" of developing players—and developing friendships.

Then, of course, Pitino made his real selling point clear—and it wasn't Providence College or its academics.

"My NBA experience will prove invaluable," he wrote Lloyd, "as I can now help develop future pro draft choices."

"All the schools tried to get in on him, but, because of his background, most never thought they had a shot so they backed off," Ron recalled. "A lot of coaches came around and just watched and waited, looking for some way to get him, but not wanting to tell him he had a weakness, tell him, 'Hey, you're not that bright. But we got a not-too-bright program, you know, a remedial program, we can get you in.'

"They figured that would offend him and then they'd have no chance. So they just waited to see what happened."

One coach who tried in vain to land Lloyd was Larry Brown, then at Kansas, who'd wanted Lloyd since he first saw him back at Five-Star Camp. He wrote, saying: "I thought you might enjoy this article about our recent midnight scrimmage. It was a huge success + is getting a lot of nat'l. [national] attention. I hope practices are going well for you. I hope you have a great year. Good luck! Sincerely, Larry Brown."

And one night, when Kansas was in New York City for the National Invitation Tournament, Hersh said he took Lloyd to the Essex House—a posh Manhattan hotel that overlooks Central Park—to meet Brown in person. It was late when Hersh said he called Brown from the lobby of the hotel. "Hey," he said, "I got Lloyd Daniels down here. Do you want to talk with him or what? If you do, you got to get down here."

Minutes later, Hersh said, Brown, the man who brought thousand-dollar designer suits to the world of collegiate coaching, arrived in the lobby in his *pajamas*—a robe hastily thrown over the top. "He knew who Lloyd was," Hersh said of Brown, "and he wasn't about to keep him waiting while he changed into his clothes."

In the end, Lloyd barely considered Kansas. He said he didn't want to live in the middle of nowhere. And he also barely considered Syracuse, despite what some said were the best efforts of alleged street-level recruiter Rob Johnson, who, it also was alleged, had been responsible for delivering a handful of New York recruits to the Orangemen—among them Eugene Waldron, Tony Bruin, and Pearl Washington.

Syracuse officials denied Johnson had ties to the school. Johnson, too, denied ties to the Orangemen. But Hersh alleged that Johnson offered Lloyd "sneakers and sweats" just to attend Syracuse practices. "I think I did give Lloyd some sneakers," Johnson later confessed, adding: "But it was Rob Johnson doing it. Not Syracuse."

Semantics, some argued. Par for the course, the cost of doing business, others said, noting one could find similar stories in all corners of
the country.

As Ron put it, "Lloyd always had money and a fresh pair of kicks.
. . . After a while it was difficult to tell where any of it came from."

For a while, St. John's seemed to have the best chance at Lloyd. Ron,
after all, was a graduate and friendly with legendary St. John's coach
Lou Carnesecca. Lloyd liked St. John's, too; liked the idea of staying
close to home. And Ron and Lou d'Almeida had seen how St. John's
had taken interest in players who'd first found themselves ineligible,
been forced to get GEDs, among them Walter Berry.

Berry earned his equivalency diploma in a program affiliated with
St. John's and then transferred to the school after a stint at San Jacinto
College in Pasadena, Texas, where he had been selected player of the
year after leading the team to the 1984 National Junior College Athletic Association Championship.

"It was at their Hall of Fame dinner," Ron said, recalling how he first
informed Carnesecca of Lloyd's interest in playing for St. John's.

"Lou was having a cocktail with some big-timers when I came
up and told him I had a player for him. He asked, 'Who?' When I
said, 'Lloyd Daniels,' he excused himself immediately—and I mean,
immediately—and took me into his office."

The two agreed that Lloyd would stop by the basketball office to
meet the staff at St. John's. Soon Lloyd began receiving tickets to St.
John's games at Alumni Hall in Jamaica, Queens, where he often sat in
the third row—behind the team bench.

Carnesecca and his staff allegedly began making arrangements that
would enable Lloyd to earn his equivalency diploma, enroll in junior
college, and gain admittance to St. John's. But then, d'Almeida said, St.
John's assistant coach Ron Rutledge bummed the works. He told Lloyd
to talk to Ernie Lorch, who ran the AAU team at Riverside Church,
which had assisted Berry.

The Gauchos and Riverside were bitter rivals.

And Lloyd didn't like Lorch.

"He took Lloyd aside and told him to disregard all of us and work through Ernie," d'Almeida said of Rutledge. "That didn't cut it. It was wrong."

"I would never tell anyone not to listen to someone he's comfortable with," Rutledge said later on, trying to defend the move. "I just told Lloyd about how Walter Berry got his GED through us and that Ernie would be the one to talk to about it. I don't think there was ever any big deal about Lloyd and St. John's, anyway."

What else could he say? Due to his lack of political sense, Rutledge had blown a sure thing. As d'Almeida said, "Lloyd came to me and said, 'Lou, you got to know this.' When I called Lou [Carnesecca], he made Rutledge get on the phone and apologize." But by then it was too late. After all, recruiting is a sensitive business. In the interim, Lloyd had reached his decision. He was headed to Las Vegas.

UNLV coach Jerry Tarkanian had made a career of recruiting and coaching misfits and vagabonds. He and his assistants often scoured the nation—its inner cities, its cracks and crevices—in search of the unwanted and the unwilling, the scorned and the scornful, the maligned and the malignant. The outcasts.

They looked for players other coaches wouldn't take. They looked for players other coaches, because of guidelines established by their schools, *couldn't* take.

Year after year, it seemed, they coveted those castoffs, took them in, and, acting much like a shelter for wayward men, cared for them, nurtured them. In the process they molded the unmoldable into something cohesive. Unified them. Took renegades and from them made what most perceived to be a renegade basketball team.

Turned them into *"Your Runnin' Rebels!"*

Tarkanian did this, he said, because once he'd been just like them. Been them. Had been a hell-raiser, the kid who was an underachiever, the kid voted least likely to become a brain surgeon. One whose entire life revolved around basketball. As he once admitted: "My wife got me to some plays and ballets, trying to get me into culture. I went to the ballet and everybody's standing up clapping. I wondered who *scored*."

He'd spent most of his teenage life at parties, rarely thinking about school, which in his case turned out to be Pasadena City College in Pasadena, California.

"It took me six semesters to get through junior college," Tarkanian said. Then, after three years at the two-year school, Tarkanian went on to a four-year school, Fresno State. "It took five more [semesters] to get through Fresno State. I went to every party I could find. I didn't care about school." Until, that is, he met his wife, Lois. She was a good student. She prodded him to go to class. He did. He got all A's and one B and even went on to get his master's degree at the University of Redlands.

"That convinced me that with a lot of these kids, it's not that they can't do the work, it's that their priorities aren't in the right order," Tarkanian said of the lesson he'd learned. "Sometimes, you just have to be more patient with certain people. I wasn't perfect in college, and I know that they're not, either, and I don't expect them to be. I do what I think is right. I'm not a hypocrite. I'm not on an ego trip. How many players have been the same way, have had their priorities changed and become good students, too? But if someone doesn't give them a break, where would they be right now?"

He pointed to Ricky Sobers, recruited to his first team at UNLV, back in 1973. Sobers had gone to DeWitt Clinton in the Bronx but quit, saying he was "too good" to waste his time. So he'd ended up at the College of Southern Idaho. But Tark believed in Ricky Sobers, made him his first "project" player at UNLV, and Sobers made good on the deal—achieving huge success with the Runnin' Rebels, going on to a long NBA career with the Phoenix Suns, Indiana Pacers, Chicago Bulls, Washington Bullets, and Seattle SuperSonics, scoring more than 10,000 points.

"Ricky Sobers was a non–high school graduate from DeWitt Clinton High School," Tarkanian said. "He went to junior college in Twin Falls, Idaho, and he got his degree. He came to UNLV and played for two years. He made all-American. He played twelve years in the NBA. . . . He did the broadcasts of our games. He's the most articulate, well-mannered, well-adjusted human being you'll ever meet. He's a credit to our institution, he's a credit to himself and his family. He is just great. And, here's a kid if somebody didn't take a chance on him, what would he have done?

"The way I look at it," Tarkanian once said, "if you bring a kid in that can't read or write—somebody nobody else would touch—and you keep him here four, five years, teach him to follow the rules, make him responsible for what he does, and, at the end, if he can read and write a little, you've done him a favor. Even if he doesn't have the piece of paper [the diploma], you gave him a chance to straighten out.

"I don't see anything wrong with that."

The National Collegiate Athletic Association did. And, at the urging of Warren S. Brown, then–assistant executive director of the NCAA, Tarkanian was first investigated at Long Beach State back in 1972. He had taken over a losing program there and, in five years, amassed a 122-20 record—never losing a home game. The NCAA suggested that Tarkanian had worked his so-called miracle at Long Beach State because he'd bent a few rules, namely, players had been provided fake test scores, among other things.

The feud between Tarkanian and the NCAA, which would last the rest of his life, really began when Tark wrote a column for the *Long Beach Press-Telegram* back in 1972 chiding NCAA officials for their investigation of Western Kentucky University while failing to take action against schools like Kentucky. "The University of Kentucky basketball program breaks more rules in a day than Western Kentucky does in a year," Tarkanian wrote. "The NCAA just doesn't want to take on the big boys."

Four days after Tarkanian left to become the coach at UNLV, the NCAA announced it had begun an "official inquiry" into the situation at Long Beach. Nine months later, the program was charged with seventy-four NCAA violations.

And it was placed on probation.

In 1977, the NCAA had done the same thing at UNLV, placing the school on probation and urging that Tarkanian be suspended for two years. Tarkanian fought the suspension, received an injunction, and, seven years later, embarrassed the NCAA—a U.S. district court judge ruled the NCAA had violated his constitutional rights by denying him due process. It would take the NCAA four more years before that ruling was overturned and it earned the right to enforce its original action.

That happened in December 1988, when, in a 5–4 vote, the U.S. Supreme Court ruled the NCAA was not a public entity, but rather a "private actor"—and therefore not bound by the U.S. Constitution to provide due process for college coaches. Back in 1986, however, the outcome still hung in the balance. "You hear Vegas and you think of gambling and the Mafia and cement shoes," New York native Al McGuire, the ex–NBA player, coach of Marquette, and star broadcast analyst, said. "Mother Teresa couldn't coach there without looking tainted."

"Every time I say something like, 'You can help a kid without graduating him,' it gets me in trouble," Tarkanian once told *Sports Illustrated*. "That's the biggest problem you got with education today, the hypocrisy. You say what you think, you get murdered. You talk like that guy [then–football coach and athletic director] Vince Dooley at Georgia, they [the NCAA] leave you alone, at least until some newspaper or magazine investigates the program and makes them come in. You ever heard Vince Dooley speak? About building character, preparing kids for life, teaching them honesty and values? He says, 'My kids are the kind of kids you'd want to go out with your daughters.'

"I *never* had a kid yet I'd want going out with *my* daughters."

It was understandable. Among his players at UNLV, Tarkanian had once taken on Richie Adams. Tarkanian and his assistants had seen Adams at Massachusetts Bay Community College, where, after failing to graduate from Ben Franklin, he averaged 25 points, 18 rebounds, and 15 blocked shots a game as a freshman.

Such ridiculous numbers brought Tarkanian and an assistant to the South Bronx in the summer of 1981. "That was frightening," Tarkanian recalled. "I remember the elevator didn't work and we had to run up eighteen flights of stairs. I wasn't in very good shape, but I ran as fast as I could to keep up—just so I wouldn't be alone. We were yelling, 'We're

Richie's coaches. We're Richie's coaches.' We didn't want the kids in the halls to think we were detectives. That's the first thing they thought when they saw two white guys with ties on, smiling at everybody."

Perhaps that was why, when Adams first encountered problems at UNLV—drug problems that would later rob him of his career, and his freedom—and Tarkanian's son, Danny, volunteered to room with his teammate, Tark told him, "Hell no, you're not living with Richie." Then he assigned the job to a grad assistant.

———

Considering the recruiting class of 1986, graduate assistants were again worrying their fates and, no doubt, Jodie Tarkanian thankfully wasn't going to have to worry about dating any of the players. Tark and his staff not only recruited Lloyd in 1986, they also recruited Clifford Allen, who, after failing to gain admittance to UNLV, would attend three junior colleges and be convicted of second-degree murder in the stabbing death of a sixty-four-year-old guidance counselor in Milton, Florida. Allen, who committed the crime while in Florida for a tryout with the CBA Pensacola Tornados, told police he killed the man during a fight after the two had sexual relations.

In May 1990, Allen was sentenced to forty-five years in prison.

In 1986, Tarkanian had called Allen "my first valedictorian"— something based, no doubt, on his ability as a student in El Paso de Robles, a detention center in Paso Robles, California. Allen was six foot ten, 235 pounds and was not even eligible for parole from the center at the time he was recruited. Like Swee'pea, there were indications Allen had a substantial substance abuse problem. Only, in the case of Allen, that problem had led to petty crimes and stints in halfway houses. He once stole a car that belonged to his foster father, robbed a man, and was convicted of armed robbery. Allen signed his letter of intent from *behind bars* at El Paso de Robles.

Still, to some extent, the recruitment of Lloyd was no less difficult.

Since he was still technically a high school junior, under NCAA rules Lloyd was not allowed to take an official visit—one paid for by the school, that is—to UNLV. If Lloyd was to get to Las Vegas, he needed to find a "rabbi." And quick.

Arnie Hershkowitz had just the man. As he, Ron, and Mark Warkentien sat in Nassau Coliseum watching Andrew Jackson take on Wyandanch in the Martin Luther King Classic that afternoon in January 1986, Hersh outlined the plan.

His friend was Sam Perry, whom Hersh described as a "commodities broker" he knew from the local racetracks. Perry, Hersh told Warkentien, was a basketball fanatic who helped him run a summer league team that counted Ron among its players. Perry lived in Staten Island during the summer but he spent his winters in Vegas.

He knew Lloyd. And he had money, lots of it.

Hersh said Perry would not only be willing to fly Lloyd out to Vegas; he would also be willing to make lodging and transportation arrangements.

There was just one problem. There was a strong chance the plan was a violation of NCAA rules, which forbid a booster or a representative of the school—or someone merely *perceived* to be acting in such a capacity—to assist in the recruitment of a player. That meant that once Hersh and Perry made it known they were willing to provide these arrangements, they could be construed as being representatives of the school's athletic interests—and could have nothing further to do with Lloyd.

Still, this was the recruitment of Lloyd Daniels. *Swee'pea*.

Despite knowing nothing about Perry, something Tarkanian and his assistants, as well as Ron, all would soon come to regret, the plan was implemented.

Which was why if viewers watching the national telecast of a game between Memphis State and UNLV that winter had known just who to look for, they would have seen Lloyd and Sam Perry sitting behind the team bench.

It was why Lloyd signed a letter of intent with Las Vegas.

"He contacted the school," Hersh said of Perry. "He was working hand in hand with Warkentien at that time. The next thing we knew, they [UNLV] said [to Lloyd], 'If you want to come out here for good, then you can come back [for summer school].' . . . Sam contacted Warkentien. I told him to. He was the middleman. He [Perry] figured that would be a good way to get in with Tarkanian. Why? He likes basketball. . . . He liked UNLV, I guess."

As Ron said, Las Vegas thought they'd caught a lucky break, landing Lloyd. But, in Vegas, fortunes can change in the blink of an eye.

———

Sam Perry was straightforward, no-nonsense, a serious man. Serious, meaning he got what he wanted, when he wanted it. The kind of man who never saw the need to raise his voice.

The kind of man, it turned out, who never had to.

Back at Erasmus Hall High School in Brooklyn, Sam Perry had been known by his given name, Richard. That was 1963. He'd also gone on to gain a reputation as a gambler with a criminal record and a nickname among those in the know: "Richie the Fixer."

He'd twice been convicted on federal charges of sports bribery.

In 1974, Perry was convicted in connection with a major New York betting scandal involving fixing harness races at both Roosevelt Raceway and Yonkers Raceway.

In 1984, he pleaded guilty to conspiring to commit sports bribery as part of the notorious Boston College point-shaving scandal—a scheme masterminded, in part, by Henry Hill, the infamous mob guy played by Ray Liotta in the 1990 Martin Scorsese classic, *GoodFellas*. The mob turncoat called Perry a gambling "genius" in *Wiseguy*, the 1986 book by Nicholas Pileggi that served as the basis for the film. Hill once told *Sports Illustrated*, "Richie does everything for a reason. He wouldn't even talk to a player unless he had something going."

Long before anyone even considered it, Perry made contacts around the nation—folks who watched the college sports scene for him, Hill said. He knew the condition of the field, the condition of the players; he even knew "whether the quarterback had been drunk" the night before a big game. He knew things that gave a handicapper an edge, things he found out from sources as basic as college newspapers, Hill said.

Hill called Perry "the brain" who'd figured out how to increase the odds at the horse-trotting tracks. A wiseguy's wiseguy, Perry worked out the scheme with the understanding that by having as few as two or three drivers get their horses boxed in, a betting man could eliminate almost half the betting combinations—and make a killing on a race.

Edward McDonald, former head of the U.S. attorney's office's Eastern District Organized Crime Strike Force, said Perry became involved in the Boston College point-shaving scheme when Hill, putting together the scheme in 1978, went to clear it through the late mob boss Paul Vario. McDonald said Vario, the onetime head of the Lucchese crime family, claimed Perry had an expertise in "fixing things."

When the whole thing fell apart, Perry was convicted for his role in the racing scheme and sentenced to a $10,000 fine and two and a half years at the Allenwood federal prison camp in Montgomery, Pennsylvania. For his part in the Boston College game-fixing scandal, Perry pleaded guilty to sports bribery charges that September in U.S. district court in Uniondale, New York. He was sentenced to time served and was given probation. He became a free man.

A year later he met Lloyd.

Hersh introduced the two one night at his favorite hangout, the Entourage Cafe in Manhattan. Within hours, Hersh said, Perry had handed Lloyd "a few bucks."

As Hersh explained it, "You want to show you have an affection for great players. Why do you love your parents? Because they take care of you. If they didn't, you would find someone else. That is what the world is about. So, he gave him some money. He likes basketball. What do you think he's doing, getting involved with these kids for betting [on] games? That was years ago. It is nothing of that sort now.

"He doesn't even bet on sports anymore."

Even if that were true, it was hard to argue there wasn't something sinister about a convicted gambler being associated with a high-profile soon-to-be college athlete—especially considering the history of basketball and gambling in New York City.

In fact, it's an NCAA violation. And for good reason.

The potential for disaster first became evident in 1945, when a game between Brooklyn College and Akron had to be canceled after word leaked out that five members of the Brooklyn team had each accepted a $1,000 bribe to guarantee a loss.

Six years later, Junius Kellogg, the first African-American player at Manhattan College, told school officials he'd been approached by an ex-player and offered $1,000 to guarantee at least a ten-point loss to DePaul. Kellogg found it an offer he *could* refuse. And, to his credit, he did. But he told officials he'd learned the player and a teammate had thrown three games the previous season, each earning $5,000. The allegations began an investigation by then–New York district attorney Frank Hogan.

The results would shock a nation.

Eighty-six games in twenty-three cities, Hogan said, had been fixed by thirty-two players from seven colleges between 1947 and 1950. Among the schools involved were Long Island University, New York University, and Manhattan College—at the time, all national powers—as well as the University of Toledo, the University of Kentucky, and Bradley University. The biggest shock was the involvement of players from City College of New York. Just the season before, City College, known as CCNY, had defeated Bradley twice—once to win the 1950 National Invitation Tournament and once to win the 1950 NCAA Tournament, the only team in history to win both titles the same season.

The fixes, Hogan said, had been arranged when players were offered cash during summer league games in the Catskill Mountains, where many of them worked in the resorts to earn money for school. By the time the full extent of the scandal was uncovered, seven City College players, including NCAA tournament MVP selection Irvin Dambrot and fellow stars Ed Roman, Ed Warner, and Floyd Layne, had been accused of shaving points or fixing games; so had four starters at Bradley, all-America Gene Melchiorre, among them, and Alex Groza and Ralph Beard of Kentucky. College basketball was in ruins. In New York City, it never really recovered.

That was 1951.

Ten years later, while home on Christmas vacation from the University of Iowa, a teenager named Connie Hawkins took a $200 loan from a guy named Jack Molinas, who turned out to be a gambler. "Maybe he was trying to set me up," Hawkins said later. "But I was out of money and he was the only one who came to my aid."

Hawkins was the best-known playground player of his era. But he was banned from the NBA for eight years, until he won a $1 million lawsuit allowing him to play.

A $200 handshake almost cost him his career.

Still, Perry did have a genuine interest in basketball. According to McDonald, he had coached a prison team in Allenwood. He coached Albie's Trimmings, the summer league team run by Hersh, as well as a team sponsored by the Entourage. In fairness, Perry, who refused to comment on the situation with Lloyd, did work to teach his club team players a lesson about the ills of prison. Every summer, Perry, Hersh, and Ron took a few guys to Comstock Correctional Facility for a game against the prisoners—though, as Ron said: "Lloyd always managed to finagle his way out of it."

One time the three brought their best team to Comstock, including Mark Jackson and Marcus Broadnax of St. John's; Cardozo center Duane Causwell, bound for Temple; and, August Martin guard Brent McCollin, bound for Long Island University.

"We didn't tell them where we were going 'til we were in the van," Ron said. "We were like, 'Okay, Mark, you got the axe murderer.' Duane, you got 'Son of Sam.' And Marcus, 'You got the rapist.' They were like, 'Who're we playing?' We showed up and they saw it was a prison and they were like, 'You got to be kiddin'."

"But it was good for them," Ron said. "It was like out of that movie *Scared Straight*. The inmates talked to them, told them to do the right thing. Of course, we walked in and Sam Cutchins and Mark Jackson, who both come from the same park, are walking and some guy, one of the inmates, yells, 'Yo, Sam! Mark! *What's up?*' They knew two guys there—a murderer and someone who got nailed for dealing drugs—so they walked over and started bullshittin' with them."

Another time, they brought a team with Wilfred Kirkaldy, a hulk of a center who would play at Oak Hill, and Lawrence "Future" Pollard, a guard from Boys & Girls who later attended West Virginia University with Kirkaldy—before their college playing careers were sidetracked by a terrible car accident that cost Kirkaldy his leg.

"In one of the games, Future got hit so hard he got nineteen stitches," Ron said. "With no foul called."

When the team was leaving, someone took Kirkaldy's visitor's pass. Hid it. So, the guard detained him, saying he'd have to "stay overnight" until the authorities could determine whether or not he was a prisoner.

"He was going, 'Ron, Sam, Hersh, tell them who I am,'" Ron said. "We were like, 'We never seen you before.' The kid was crying. It taught him a lesson."

Still, it was hard not to be skeptical of Perry's interest. McDonald said the situation should at least have raised eyebrows. Here was a convicted gambler, a *fixer*, palling around with some of the most highly recruited basketball players in America.

"Sure, the guy could have a conversion," McDonald said later. "He could say, 'Hey, look, I want to be a decent guy now.' The guy really loves basketball. He could be a straight arrow. But you have to have doubts about that, given the guy's background. How many people in this country have been convicted of fixing *two* different sporting events? I mean, the number of prosecutions brought under the federal sports bribery statutes, you could probably count them on one hand."

When Lloyd arrived in Las Vegas that spring he had a friend with him from back on 203rd Street, Steve Cropper—a friend who, among others, would later allege in a prize-winning investigative series by *Newsday* that the basketball staff at UNLV had committed NCAA violations during the recruitment of Lloyd.

Cropper was twenty-two years old and had briefly attended Hofstra University in Hempstead, New York, where he'd served as manager of the school basketball team. He was working for the U.S. Postal Service when Lloyd asked him to go to Vegas. Cropper saw it as his big chance, a chance to get in good with Lloyd and maybe get taken care of somewhere down the line. He saw it as a "management position." So he went.

"Well, to me, college basketball as a whole was going to use Lloyd," Cropper said. "They needed Lloyd just like Lloyd needed them. They didn't want to face up to that, but I let them know that. I let Tarkanian know that he needed Lloyd there and don't think that, you know, he did him a favor by letting him come there even though he didn't have the grades, because he needed him there. He was going to bring money to Las Vegas."

In exchange for that service, Cropper said, he told Tarkanian that he and Lloyd needed assistance. Helping them find a place to live would be nice. Helping them find jobs would be better. Cropper alleged that, on the basis of those requests, he received a job interview—allegations both Tarkanian and Warkentien later denied—and was lent a hand finding an apartment, though he and Lloyd paid the rent.

"The first time I saw Tark, it made me laugh," Cropper said. "He looked like Yoda from *Star Wars*. I was just trying not to laugh and he said, 'What's so funny?' I said, 'Nothing I can talk about right now.' But he said to me, 'Now everything has changed because you've come out here with [Lloyd].' He was like, 'So, what has to be done?'

"I was like, 'Could you just tell people that I'm out here with a recruit of yours and that, um, I'm a good worker and that I could prove myself.'"

Cropper said he soon found himself at an interview with Mike Sloan, the general counsel for Circus Circus, a well-known hotel and casino on the Strip. Sloan, Cropper said, took him to see Tony Alamo, the hotel's vice president and general manager.

As Cropper found out, it paid to know people. Soon he had a job as a money runner at the casino and, later, after he quit, he and Lloyd allegedly were set up with interviews at an ad agency. They got the job. Warkentien had also helped them find a place to live at the St. Tropez

Villa Apartments. Another assistant coach, Tim Grgurich, allegedly provided the two with a used color television set and kitchen utensils.

Those situations seemed like small potatoes, all things considered. But, though the alleged enticements appeared inappreciable, all of them could be construed as NCAA infractions—and, if the NCAA had anything to say about it, blatant ones.

And it didn't end there.

Cropper also claimed both he and Lloyd received small "loans" from Warkentien—allegations that were later denied by the assistant coach but were supported by a former player, Ricky Collier, who was then a reserve guard for the Rebels. "He never told me how much," Collier said, then. "He was always like, 'Bald-head blood likes me, Ricky. Bald-head blood loves me.' I'd laugh when he'd say that." So would Lloyd and Steve Cropper. All the way to the bank.

———

As he stood in the terminal at McCarran International Airport, it hit Ron that he had committed a cardinal sin, one he never thought he would make. He'd trusted Lloyd.

Earlier in the week, when he'd last talked with Lloyd, this had seemed like a good idea. It was late August. Ron needed a vacation and he also wanted to see how Lloyd was doing in his new environment. He figured he'd catch a weekend flight to Vegas. Lloyd said he'd meet Ron at the airport. Simple, right? Except for one thing.

Ron had now been standing in the terminal more than an hour and Lloyd still hadn't arrived. That alone wouldn't have been so bad, but Ron also realized he had no way to contact Lloyd. The phone had been disconnected because Lloyd hadn't paid the bill. Worse, Ron realized he'd forgotten to ask Lloyd for his address.

Annoyed, Ron called the athletic department at UNLV. He figured if he could at least explain his predicament, someone there could give him an address. Then he could catch a cab. Problem was, it was Sunday. No one was at school.

Ron considered a hotel. He could find Lloyd on Monday. Exasper-

ated, he decided to check one last option: dialed information. Maybe
he could find Jerry Tarkanian.

"So I get the telephone operator and I go, 'Could I have the number
for Jerry Tarkanian?'" Ron said. "I figured, at least if I could get Tark,
then I could find out where Lloyd lived. But instead of giving me the
number, the operator goes, 'Why do you want it?' I'm thinking, you
know this operator isn't asking 'cause he figures I'm a friend of Frank
Sinatra. I mean, you could tell I was calling from a phone booth at the
fucking airport. So, I figure, maybe he thinks I want to make a crank
call or something and won't give it to me. I explain the situation. I go,
'Look, I just flew in from New York. I used to coach this guy named
Lloyd Daniels. I'm trying to reach him.'

"I figure, no way the operator buys my story. Instead, he goes,
'Oh, I know Lloyd. He lives in the apartment downstairs from me.'
I'm in shock. Next thing I know, the guy tells me he'll call his apartment and get his friend to run downstairs and tell Lloyd to come and
get me."

A half hour later, outside the terminal, Ron heard this horrible
noise and turned to see an old rust bucket of a car speeding along the
access road, Lloyd's head poked out the side window.

"*Ronnie Boy!*" Lloyd screamed. "Hey, *Ronnie Boy!*"

"You had to see this," Ron said. "This car was a wreck. Junk. I mean,
even if the school gave this car to him for nothing, it wasn't a violation,
that's how bad it was. But here he is, winging it down the wrong side
of the street doing about fifty miles an hour. He's got his head out the
window, looking like *E.T.*, not looking where he's going, but looking
at me and yelling, 'Yo, *Ronnie Boy!* Hey, *Ronnie Boy!*' After he goes by
me, he makes a U-turn, forgets to give this truck the right of way, and
nearly has an accident. He pulls up and goes, '*Ronnie Boy! Yo, Ronnie
Boy!* I finally got my license.'

"I yelled back, 'Lloyd, give me your address.' He goes, 'Why you
want my address, Ron?' I said, 'Because I'm taking a cab.'"

It seemed everyone in Las Vegas knew Lloyd. Not just the telephone operator and the attendants at the local gym or the workers at the school. But everyone. It was one of the first things Ron noticed. Lloyd had contacts, had power. Lloyd had a name.

"When I was in the airport," Ron said, "I saw Jesse Jackson get off a plane and two, maybe three people knew who he was. When Lloyd met me, everyone knew him. People were going, 'Hey, it's Lloyd Daniels.' It was like that everywhere we went. Everyone knew who Lloyd was and, if they didn't, once his name was mentioned they knew what it meant. In the casinos, in the restaurants. He was a celebrity."

When Lloyd first arrived in Vegas, Ricky Collier had taken him on a guided tour of the town. He had shown him the places to hang out, places to avoid. Had shown him the places where a ballplayer—more specifically, a member of the Runnin' Rebels—could put the touch on folks because of his situation. The community loved the Runnin' Rebels, a team that seemed to reflect the very soul of Las Vegas. They loved their run-and-gun style, loved their outlaw image. They loved that they won.

Better still, they loved the players, because in Vegas, like in Hollywood, everybody loves a star. The team even had a section known as "Gucci Row," where season tickets sold for around $1,500 a piece, a hefty price back in the mid- to late 1980s.

"The thing is," Tarkanian once said of the relationship, "Las Vegas doesn't have anything else of its own. You know, they got things coming in all the time, the greatest entertainers in the world. But everything else leaves after the show. UNLV is part of the town. None of the boosters' kids go here. They go to Southern Cal or Stanford. The boosters never went here. The *alums* didn't even go here. But they love us."

In true Las Vegas fashion, Collier taught Lloyd how to capitalize on that newfound stardom. He took him out on the Strip. He took him to at least ten hotels for meals, always, he said, making sure to introduce him to the right people.

"I'd say, 'This is Lloyd Daniels' and they'd flip, because Tark talked about him so much," Collier said. "They were like, 'Come anytime. If you need anything, call me.'"

Like most players, Lloyd was not about to let his status go to waste. Free meals, free drinks, free time at the Las Vegas Sports Club, where members paid an initiation fee plus monthly dues, but where players could use the facilities—including a regulation-size basketball court— at no charge, according to a club executive.

This was heaven for Lloyd, who had the soul of con man and who was always trying to get something for nothing. It was the way he had been taught in school, where, if he performed on the court, he was allowed to slide in the classroom. It was the way he'd seen some in his old neighborhood spend their entire existence.

Las Vegas offered him a perfect forum to perform his routine to the fullest. Minimum effort, maximum gain. Lloyd knew the score, could name that tune.

They didn't call it fame and fortune for nothing.

"He had a tremendous amount of juice," Ron said. "It was incredible. We went to one or two casinos where we got a steak and all he had to do was sign for it. He went to jewelers, looking to get the best deal he could on gold. In fact, Lloyd was always trying to make a deal with the local jewelers, going for his con. He wanted to find out jewelers where he could get a ridiculous deal. With everything, he was always looking for a guy who *knew* a guy. You know, anyone in that position is going to take advantage of the situation, try to work his con. But with Lloyd, he does it to the nth degree."

There was a reason Lloyd had so much juice in Vegas. It was because Tark had been quoted in the papers saying what people had said about Lloyd for years, that he was the second coming of James Naismith. You know, every time he touched the ball, he *reinvented* the game. "When they write the final chapter on guards," Tark once said, "they'll start with Jerry West, Oscar Robertson, Magic Johnson, and Lloyd Daniels. He's the best I've ever been around." Folks took those words to heart on the Strip.

Ron recalled how when Lloyd walked into the Sports Club, where he practiced daily on the immaculate indoor court, people would give him the once-over.

"By the time he had laced up his sneakers," Ron said, "a crowd would be filing around." And Jarvis Basnight, then a junior forward for the Runnin' Rebels, would tease Lloyd. "You better get eligible," Basnight said. "You better do the right thing, because you're putting me in the NBA with those alley-oop passes."

Then there was a bystander who told Ron, "What's he doing in college?"

"I figured," Ron said, "the guy's going to tell me, 'He's not smart enough. He's not a student.' Instead, he goes: 'This guy should be in the NBA.'"

Consider the time Lloyd and Sam Perry, then well into his forties, teamed to face future U.S. Olympic team members Stacey Augmon and Barry Young, then both recruits who'd later sign with UNLV. Lloyd and Perry won. Consider the game when Lloyd busted Sidney Green, the former Rebels star out of New York City who was then with the New York Knicks. As Green struggled, Lloyd toyed with him— banking home jumpers, talking trash about how good he was, how it wasn't *nothin'* for him to hit a few J's.

"This kid always shoot like this?" Green asked in disbelief.

Consider the game when Lloyd, Ron, future Arizona recruit Matt Othick, and two guys who had been working out in the gym went against Armen Gilliam, Freddie Banks, Gerald Paddio, Mark Wade, and Eldridge Hudson—the backbone of a UNLV team that would go on to be ranked number one in the nation.

"We won," Ron said. "That's when I knew Lloyd could be ungodly, that everyone else next to him was a joke."

Maybe that was also the reason, when the two ran into then–Georgetown coach John Thompson in the Barbary Coast Hotel, Thompson told Lloyd: "Stay out of trouble and I think you've got a good chance to be the two-guard on the Olympic Team." To this day, Ron still swears Lloyd cost the U.S. team the 1988 Olympic Gold Medal.

———

Lloyd signed his national letter of intent on April 11, 1986.

Despite dropping out of high school, by the time Ron left Vegas,

Lloyd had earned fourteen college credits. Though he left UNLV that fall and didn't return until spring, before Lloyd left Las Vegas for good in 1987, he even had a tutor.

"He had trouble reading and we felt that, if we could get him with a reading specialist, we could monitor his work academically," Tarkanian said. "We thought we had a chance. . . . We knew it was a small chance. But I felt we had a chance." Mark Warkentien said Lloyd was "in absolute wonderment over the dictionary." He was even "amazed at punctuation marks, at what they could do."

Some suggested the inference that Lloyd was learning was, at best, misleading. Ron recalled how Lloyd would have one book open to his left, another open to his right—each on different subjects. He would attempt to answer one question out of the first book, then attempt to answer a second question out of the other book.

And it wasn't long before Lloyd "fired" one tutor.

The reason? The tutor, who'd once told Lloyd he had a "primitive style," also had the nerve to tell the star recruit that he had a learning disability.

"He, of course, has done nothing as far as his education is concerned," the tutor told Ron. "He refused to work with me anymore because I said he had a learning disability. He was appalled at the fact that I would say anything like that about him. He fired me as his tutor. We laughed our brains out about that one. It is the joke around here: Lloyd Daniels fired his tutor. It never ceases to amaze me what he'll do next."

Still, at least Lloyd was going to school on a regular basis during the summer of 1986. "What was he taking?" Ron said. "He was taking premed, what do you think? At least he looked good going to class. I mean, he sat in the apartment and tried to do his homework. He carried his books. It was like he was trying to be normal.

"Imagine that."

Guardian Angel

Larry Brown had suggested to Howie Garfinkel back at Five-Star Camp that he had a family Lloyd could live with in Kansas.

But UNLV assistant basketball coach and "recruiting coordinator" Mark Warkentien took the idea one step further. On August 26, 1986, Warkentien filed a petition in the Eighth Judicial District Court of Clark County, Nevada, stating his desire to become the court-appointed legal guardian of Lloyd Daniels.

It was a strange request, considering his position and considering Lloyd already had two guardians—grandmothers Lulia Hendley and Annie Sargeant—and that, though he'd signed a letter of intent with UNLV, the NCAA still viewed him as a "potential recruit" until his actual enrollment on a full-time basis.

Some said the proposed arrangement would violate NCAA rules; if not in fact, then at least in theory. That it would provide UNLV with an unfair advantage in the recruitment process. Common sense said it must, since in his petition Warkentien asked the court for the power to borrow money and obtain loans for Lloyd, as well as assist him in his financial affairs—all potential NCAA violations. Others simply found the request to be unethical, at best. In bad taste—or, at very least, dumb.

Pacific Coast Athletic Association commissioner Lew Cryer had "concerns" over the situation and initiated an exchange of correspondence between the university and the NCAA. The NCAA notified athletic department officials at UNLV that the matter would be investigated by its Legislation and Interpretations Committee.

Still, Warkentien—or, as Lloyd called him, Stein—elected to move forward with the legal process. "The proposed ward has the potential to be a successful human being, student and athlete," Warkentien stated in his petition to the court. "He has shown great promise in athletics, and, given the right direction and encouragement, has the potential to be a successful professional athlete. However, the proposed ward, despite being eighteen years old, barely reads at a third-grade level. Without the guidance, support, encouragement, and counseling of a special guardian, the potential for exploitation of the proposed ward is great." *Um* . . .

Okay. So the petition painted a sad, tragic picture of a kid born into poverty, a kid raised in a situation where he seemed to amount to little more than an afterthought. A kid passed through an educational system that showed little concern for whether or not he actually was educated, no more than a pawn in a societal system where concern for his well-being seemed to begin and end with his ability to play basketball.

What the petition did not mention—not *anywhere*—was that Mark Warkentien was an assistant basketball coach at the University of Nevada, Las Vegas.

Warkentien said he couldn't understand how outsiders could view the situation as unethical or exploitative. But Warkentien and his wife, Maureen, hadn't become the guardians of other poor, disassociated students at UNLV. In fairness, Warkentien seemed to have a genuine affinity for Lloyd. "I loved him," Warkentien said later. "He has the key to my house. He babysat my daughter. Around my house, I consider him family. In the human existence, you do what you can for people."

Still, Tarkanian admitted, Warkentien made the move so UNLV could exercise "greater control" over Lloyd, monitor him more closely, and, therefore, have a better chance to get him to do the things he needed to do to become eligible to play basketball. Lloyd went along with the proceedings because, while he genuinely wanted to "be part of a real family," as Warkentien put it, he also realized the situation could provide him with access to money, to a car; access to material things he did not have, including a shot at the pros via a career at UNLV.

Though Lloyd, as usual with what he viewed as "that negative stuff," said he would not discuss the situation, team members at UNLV, among them reserve guard Ricky Collier, alleged one of the things Lloyd seemed to like most was that Warkentien gave him money, usually in the form of an allowance. He said Lloyd sometimes stopped by the athletic offices for closed-door meetings with Warkentien. When Lloyd needed cash, Collier said, he'd say, "I'll get some money from Stein." After those meetings, Collier said Lloyd told him, "Yeah, I got some money now."

The "guardian angel" was the "goose who laid the golden egg."

There was no need for Kenny Anderson to have another legal guardian. He had his mother, Joan, who worked hard to keep him in line.

Still, it was certain that Kenny needed more support, needed someone to keep him in check, keep him from letting success go to his head. That job fell to an organization that scout Tom Konchalski called Team Anderson—a network of advisors headed by Vincent Smith and his friend, a lawyer named Pierre Turner.

What members of the team did was keep track of Kenny at all times. If he was in the park, they knew it. If he was talking to the wrong people, they knew it.

"Vincent became his security blanket," Jack Curran said of Smith, who had also become an assistant coach at Molloy—all in order to keep an eye on Kenny Anderson. "He had everything covered." The network was so extensive it even included Kenny's barber. "We even know when he gets his hair cut," Curran said.

If the guardianship situation with Lloyd and Las Vegas smacked of exploitation, the network established by Smith and Turner seemed a welcome alternative. Despite rumors on the street of ulterior motives in the deal, such as ensuring themselves of a cut if and when Kenny ever turned pro, the two were the main reason he had been able to find as much success as he had. And he *had* found success.

Kenny Anderson was the best player in New York City by the fall of 1986, an intriguing notion, considering he was still just sixteen, a first-semester sophomore—one who'd yet to *start* a high school game.

Already calls had come in from coaches around the country and, in his office closet, Curran had a box filled with recruiting letters from places like Kansas and Kentucky, Stanford and Syracuse. The goal now was to ensure all that "pub" didn't get to Anderson, didn't give him what teammate Ralph James, a Harvard-bound senior swingman, called "an ego overflow."

The cure was simple. First, Curran met with Anderson on a regular basis, the two talking about the recruitment process as well as about the development of the star guard. Second, Curran called on Team Anderson to make sure things didn't get blown out of proportion with recruiters and the local club teams—though Kenny did eventually play for three: Madison Square Boys Club, Riverside, and the Gauchos.

"It could become a problem," Curran said of the chances of Anderson being spoiled by success, getting sidetracked. "But I don't think it will happen. We talked about it and I told him the situation could be good for him, as long as it doesn't affect the way he behaves. He's not a wiseguy and doesn't act like this is a big deal, though he could have. But, what I told him is you have to be suspicious of people. A lot of people want to be connected with Kenneth, because they realize that he is going to be something. It's up to Kenneth not to associate with those people—you know the old story, 'Show me your friends and I'll show you who you are.' The problem is, at his age, he thinks he can just say hello to them and not be affected. But you can't."

"What I've done is take everybody's advice, use the information I thought I could use and sort it out," said Anderson, who, despite remaining traces of street in his voice and in his actions, was a likable kid with a quick wit and sharp sense of humor. "It's always good to listen to people and hear what they have to say. The people around me help keep me levelheaded. I don't think I'm great because I'm a good basketball player, because there are people who can do things I can't do. Some people here can't play basketball like me, but they have academic skills I don't."

Of course, primarily due to the efforts of Team Anderson, Kenny had been able to achieve a B-minus average as a freshman. And because of that support, throughout his time in high school Anderson would never stray far from the straight and narrow. "People here had a fear he might slack off, but I think he really grew up and realized the world doesn't revolve around basketball," Ralph James said. "Besides, if he would ever start to stray, people would pull him aside and make sure he did things right."

"His salvation," Tom Konchalski said, "is that he has enough people around him who will keep his hat size the same." As Curran said, "I think he really understands the dangers of being this good, this young."

"Maybe some people think I'll get a swollen head," Anderson said. "But I'm not like that. I just want to be myself. People can say you're great all they want. But you have to remember that every time you step on the court you can prove them wrong." But not all kids get such good advice or learn those lessons as well as Kenny Anderson.

———

In order for Mark Warkentien to obtain legal guardianship of Lloyd—at one point, in an oxymoron to end all oxymora, identified by the court as "an adult minor"—it had to be proven that Swee'pea was not able to make "all of the decisions necessary to his own care." In other words, that he could not survive on his own, that more or less, without the aid of yet another in a seemingly endless string of benefactors, one who would vow to act "out of concern" for him and in his "best interests," Lloyd would become just another lost soul on the streets.

To support those contentions, Lloyd underwent examination by a family and marriage counselor, Dr. Joan Elaine Owen, the director of the Center for Diagnosis and Development in Las Vegas. In a five-page affidavit, dated August 7, 1986, and attached to the petition filed by Warkentien, Dr. Owen outlined the findings of her exam.

She testified Lloyd had been presented with "a full battery of diagnostic tests" and that he was "quite easily discouraged during the test taking."

Several tests were administered, among them the Bloom Sentence Completion Survey, Wechsler Adult Intelligence Scale–Revised, Leiter

International Performance Scale, Bender-Gestalt Test, Wide Range Achievement Test, and Peabody Individual Achievement Test. All were designed to test intelligence levels, as well as verbal and nonverbal communication skills. The results indicated Lloyd was a dyslexic who needed to be tutored as would "a blind or deaf student."

"He has made numerous school moves which have interfered with continuity in his life," Dr. Owen stated in the affidavit. "He admitted that he had substantial absenteeism and had felt humiliation and embarrassment with the limited academic growth. Thus, he avoided school rather than face the continued failure."

As Dr. Owen wrote: "He admits that he is angered by the media for embarrassing him due to his poor academic success. He stated that what bothered him more than anything else was not being able to read. He stated further that if he only had a mother and a father, 'These school things would have been different.'" According to the sworn statement, Lloyd also told Dr. Owen, "I feel that this is my last opportunity to get an education before I am too old. I know that I will not be able to play basketball for all of my life and I must prepare for another career as well."

How someone like Lloyd would be able to attain a college education prior to being provided years of tutorial assistance was beyond all comprehension, especially since Dr. Owen said that, while Lloyd possessed an understanding of "addition, subtraction, multiplication, division and simple fractions," his math skills were that of a sixth-grade student. His reading comprehension tested out at a grade level of 2.8.

The entire situation seemed to make a mockery of the college athletic system. But, based on the testimony presented by Dr. Owen, Warkentien, and Lloyd, district court judge Thomas A. Foley appointed Warkentien legal guardianship on October 24, 1986. By that time, though, Lloyd was already living in Walnut, California.

He had become a "student" at Mount San Antonio College.

Mount Sac

E ven though it was three days after his nineteenth birthday, Lloyd still could not read when he arrived at Mount San Antonio College in September 1986.

Basketball coach Eugene Victor said Lloyd was dyslexic and described him, candidly, as "educationally disabled." Still, neither Victor nor the school administration felt compelled to let any of that interfere with his quest for a formal college education.

Lloyd was going to be a "normal" student, school officials said. He was going to attend classes on a regular basis. He was going to pass courses.

And, if all went according to the elaborate plan laid out by Jerry Tarkanian, Mark Warkentien, and Gene Victor, Lloyd would graduate with a junior college degree from Mount Sac, as it was known, and become eligible to play at UNLV.

It was masterful. And, by design, it all would neatly circumvent NCAA eligibility guidelines. Those rules, then-director of Legislative Services for the NCAA Rick Evrard said, required that a student be a high school graduate or hold a GED in order to receive a major-college athletic scholarship.

Lloyd had neither.

Back when Lloyd was at Andrew Jackson, Evrard said the earliest Swee'pea could receive that GED would be one year after the graduation of his high school class—or, at best, in time to become eligible for the 1988–89 season at UNLV. If then. *If ever.* But the plan conceived by Tarkanian, Warkentien, and Victor took into account one obscure and all-but-overlooked fact: California law mandated admission to state-run institutions for *any* adult "who can profit from the instruction offered."

A student need not be a high school graduate, need not prove competence in scholastic areas. A student need not even be a state resident. The *only* requirement was that a student be *breathing*—and be at least eighteen years of age.

Lloyd, it turned out, qualified on both counts.

Although admission policies suggested a prospective student take a minimum three years of college prep courses in mathematics and four years in English, and even though Lloyd had *never* spent even one full year in any high school or come close to learning how to read on the high school level—had made little or no progress toward receiving a high school degree—he was eligible to become a full-time junior college student in California. With a junior college degree, he wouldn't need a GED.

And he'd be eligible to transfer to Las Vegas—on full scholarship.

The entire notion was ludicrous. But, with additional credits from intersession classes, Lloyd even had the chance to graduate *ahead* of schedule—making him eligible to appear for the Runnin' Rebels in 1987–88. It was brilliant. Better, it'd work.

As an additional slap in the face, it turned out that even his tuition to Mount Sac, $90 per credit for out-of-state students, would be paid for through federal grants.

"Is this a loophole?" Warkentien said, sounding appalled at the mere suggestion when questioned about the developing situation. "No. The bottom line is that Lloyd is doing what he is supposed to be doing. It is his expressed desire to become a student. At this point, he is more excited about reading than about basketball. And, if it's for the kid and it's the right thing to do, then I really don't worry what people think."

The explanation seemed, well . . . *implausible.*

Especially since it was apparent Lloyd had shown little desire to be a student—*even* if it meant he could play basketball. Yet, it *had* happened; *was* happening.

"I guess we were wrong, that he *will* be able to play next season if he is a junior college graduate," Evrard admitted with great reluctance after being informed of the scenario by *Newsday*, which had launched an investigation into the recruitment. "It is pretty clear what [Nevada–Las Vegas] has done and why it was done, but there is nothing within the legislation to prohibit it. It certainly seems they have found a way to bend the rules."

Still, there was little concern about threats made by the NCAA back at Mount Sac in the fall of 1986. There were more pressing concerns.

The first was to get Lloyd a class schedule, one he could handle.

It proved a challenge, but after a great deal of effort, Lloyd was assigned a full course load—eighteen credits. Among his classes was an ethnic studies course called the Black American. There were physical education courses: Strength and Conditioning, Recreation and Fundamentals of Sports, and Fundamentals of Team Sports. Lloyd had four other classes, as well. Two of them also were in physical education, one in biology; the other, remedial English. The remedial class, Reading 67, was, according to the Mount San Antonio course catalog, required for students who'd failed a placement test for freshman composition, basic first-year English—or the placement exam for the basic remedial course, English 68. It soon became evident Lloyd couldn't handle either biology or the reading course. He was forced to withdraw from both.

"I had placed him in Reading 67," Victor said. "It was not even remedial reading. It was just *trying* to read. But Lloyd couldn't do the work."

There were no such problems in the other classes. As Victor said, "I dropped him from all the classes he wouldn't attend. All he had left was PE classes. Lloyd did all right. There was no heavy reading. Just say they were all 'activities courses.'"

One of those "activities courses" was Fundamentals of Team Sports, a class open *only* to members of the Mount Sac basketball team; a course taught by Victor and his assistant coach, Ralph Osterkamp. The Mount San Antonio course catalog stated the class offered "instruction in the skill and technique of playing basketball, including offensive and defensive strategy." The catalog stressed that students who took the course would "receive more advanced instruction leading to skill improvement."

Bizarre as it seemed, Lloyd Daniels, the *Parade Magazine* all-American and one of the most sought-after basketball recruits in the nation, was scheduled to receive two *college* credits—for being a member of his junior college basketball team. *This* was his "education." Of course, Lloyd wasn't the only city kid in junior college back in the fall of 1986. Boo Harvey and Moses Scurry were "doin' time," too.

———

Graduation day was May 10. Boo Harvey had marked it on his calendar. He'd been waiting for the day almost two years, since he'd first come to San Jacinto College in search of a second chance. He'd have traded the junior college national championship he'd won his freshman season, when the team was unbeaten in thirty-seven games, just to have back the scholarship to Syracuse—the one he'd forfeited when he left Andrew Jackson in the spring of 1985 with a New York City title, but no grades.

In fact, he would have traded it all just to be anywhere except San Jacinto, a school nestled between oil refineries in the Houston suburb of Pasadena, Texas.

"When I first got down here," Harvey said, "I looked around and said, 'What am *I* doing *here*?' It hurt. I remember when I first came home. Everybody said, 'Where you goin' to school? I kept on thinking, 'I shouldn't be here. I shouldn't.'

"But," he said, "being here made me realize that basketball might not be there all the time, that I needed something to fall back on. This place helped me mature.

"I took a fall. But now I'm coming back."

Coming back was what junior college was all about. For years junior colleges, like prep schools, had served as a home for wayward student athletes. A place where the academic indigent could—if they just learned to use their heads and show even faint dedication in the class-room, in their studies—stake a claim to a higher education, as well as to their rightful place in the world of major-college basketball.

A place where they could earn a second chance.

It was far from a simple process, since many of the athletes who found themselves in junior college—called the *thirteenth* and *fourteenth* grades by the hopelessly cynical—were much like Lloyd. Few cases were as dramatic, mainly because few players involved in such situations tied all the major elements—the incredible talent, as high a profile and as poor a scholastic background; in this case, all compounded by the involvement of UNLV and Jerry Tarkanian, whom the NCAA had been after for more than a decade—into one neat package the way Lloyd did. That didn't mean there weren't, wouldn't continue to be, hundreds of others in all-too-similar situations.

"We get kids for three reasons," San Jacinto coach Ronnie Arrow, who later served as head coach at University of South Alabama and at Texas A&M–Corpus Christi, said. "First, because they aren't doing it academically; they have the big-time tools, but they didn't predict. Second, because they've had problems off the court. Third, because they're just not ready for Division One.

"Mostly, for the first reason."

San Jacinto was perhaps the most renowned junior college in the nation, even better known than Hutchinson Community College in Hutchinson, Kansas—site of the annual junior college tournament. Just about every inner-city player in America had heard of San Jac. Though they all admitted it probably wasn't such a bad place, they still didn't want to go there. Just down the block from the bar Gilley's, home of the original *Urban Cowboy,* San Jac specialized in big-time, small-time college basketball and the education of the theretofore uneducable; the new urban cowboys.

Since it opened back in 1960, San Jac had won three national junior college championships—including the previous season, when Harvey, then a freshman, helped the Ravens go 37-0. In fact, since 1966, when Ollie Taylor came from the Bronx en route to a Sweet 16 NCAA Tournament appearance with the University of Houston and the New York Nets in the old American Basketball Association, San Jac had given a second chance to eleven future professional players, among them Tom Henderson, who came out of the Bronx to attend San Jacinto before heading to the University of Hawaii, the NBA Houston Rockets, and the Washington Bullets.

Even Walter Berry, who had gone on to St. John's and the NBA, found himself at San Jac after failing to graduate from Franklin. Denied enrollment at St. John's, he earned his equivalency diploma, led the Ravens to the national junior college title as a freshman, and headed back to St. John's, helping it to the 1985 NCAA Final Four.

"I was told by more than one Big East guy," Arrow recalled of his 1983–84 team, "that we could have finished fifth, maybe fourth in the Big East."

Of course, most of those kids—kids like Harvey, kids like Scurry—should have gone to major colleges in the first place. It's just their academic pasts wouldn't let them. "Some of these kids you call up keep telling you they got their grades and you know they don't," Arrow said. "But they'll go down to the last minute saying that until someone slaps them silly and says, 'Hey, you big dummy. Who you kidding? You ain't going to graduate, so what you going to do now?' The problem is, a lot of these kids live in a dream world."

Which means, more often than not, that they don't realize the academic trouble they're in—until, Arrow said, it smacks then upside the head. Until they end up in junior college.

"Everyone thinks that these are dumb kids," assistant coach Scott Gernander, who would later become head coach, said. "But for the most part, they're not. It's just that a lot of them didn't go to class. I bet most of them have never studied in their lives. It was just easier to hang out."

That transformation was difficult for both Harvey and Scurry, a freshman during the 1986–87 season, when Harvey was finishing his second year at San Jacinto. The first inclination of both was to resort to their old ways, to cut class. Go hang out. But, unlike the old days, they couldn't get away with it.

"If they miss a class—and, if they miss one, we find out—Scott gets them up at six a.m. and runs them," Arrow said. "If they don't turn in a paper on time, Scott runs them. The third time we have to run them, we add an eleven o'clock curfew. Now, Scott's a runner. He gets up at five thirty every morning and he's going to run whether he has company or not. But we've had guys who run with him twice a week, and one year we had guys who could've gone out for the track team. But we tell them, 'We damn sure didn't bring you here to get you up at six every morning to run.'"

Some, like Harvey and Scurry, got the message.

Maybe they didn't change completely—as Harvey admitted, "I had to run once or twice"—but at least they changed some. As Scurry said: "I'm here trying to make it. I never thought it would come to this, but now I realize my mistake. It's a real big change. But I found out that when you work hard, you can do it."

"A lot of these kids have never been punished," Arrow said, "and so they are one-dimensional. With them it is, 'I'm going to do what I want to do when I want to do it.' We teach them to accept structure in their lives. If they don't accept it, they may end up on the street spending their whole lives blaming their problems on someone else. But if they can accept that their reason for being here is their fault, then they can succeed. We give them a horizon to shoot for. The rest is up to them."

Despite his success back then, Harvey, whose teams combined to go 73-1 in his two seasons at San Jacinto, would later be ruled ineligible at St. John's, missing the 1988–89 season before leading the team into the 1990 NCAA tournament. Scurry, too, would later be ruled ineligible for part of his senior season at UNLV.

Still, at least those two got *something* out of junior college. They earned a chance to regain a foothold on futures that seemed theirs for the taking. Some, though, never learned enough to even make that jump. They got as far as junior college.

But they couldn't clear the streets.

The Terminator stood perched, momentarily, at the foul line, analyzing the situation. Three defenders, nowhere to go. The perfect scenario for a man of dangerous means, a man with an outlaw heart who did what he wanted, when he wanted.

The kind all too willing to take his chances, to roll the dice.

He dribbled once, then again. He wanted to score. He was *going* to score. He knew that. But why go easy on them, he thought? Why not have a little fun?

Terminator dribbled again, then flashed that half grin of his, the one a gambler flashes when he's been called, knowing he's got an ace up his sleeve, ready to drop it on the unsuspecting field, all of whom figured he was about to fold. He looked at one defender, glared at another. Glowered at the third. He didn't say a word. Didn't have to. He just gave them that look. *Go on, stop me if you can. I know you can't.*

He stutter-stepped one man, *juked* him, slid past the next before there was time to react. Finally, in the boldest of moves, he took the ball right at the third—over the third, in fact—spun 360 degrees, and dunked. The crowd erupted. People fell out of the stands, rolling about, laughing at the opposition. Jeering them, taunting them. Then Terminator turned and slowly trotted up the court. Mission accomplished.

Behind him, the trio of defenders—Eric Brown, a six-foot-six forward from the University of Miami; Eric Johnson, future member of the Utah Jazz and younger brother of Detroit Pistons guard Vinnie Johnson; and, Darryl Middleton, a six-foot-nine center who teamed with Eric Johnson at Baylor—shook their heads in disgust.

And wonderment.

"Hey," Terminator said after that summer league game in the gymnasium at the City College of New York, "sometimes you got to make a point out there. You got to show you're hard-nosed, that you're not going to take nothing from no one."

Ron Matthias, aka Terminator, had always made it clear he wasn't weak, that he wouldn't be pushed around on a basketball court. He'd learned the importance of being strong back when he was comin' up, having to fight to get his due in a household of eight kids, five of them brothers. "They'd push me around," he said. "I was told what to do *all* the time. If I wanted something, I learned I *had* to assert myself."

Much to his detriment, Matthias made it clear he would not be pushed around off the court, either, an act that didn't often play well with those who didn't understand the realities of his daily fight just to survive on the streets of the inner city. The reluctance to trust anyone but himself, the reluctance to back down even an inch, was a big reason why, after a lifetime of earning a name on the playgrounds, he still couldn't escape them. And so what if, once, he'd scored more than a hundred points in a game?

In the end, Matthias had done what no opponent ever seemed able to do: he stopped himself. Became a has-been before he'd had the chance to be an ever-was.

Back then, opponents couldn't touch his game. And then, all of a sudden, no one in basketball would. Too many problems, too many headaches.

"I did have a rep," he admitted. "And I still have one. Problem was I would get defiant. But now I'm learning how much I messed up."

The future seemed bright back at Evander Childs High School in the Bronx. Sure, Matthias rarely attended class. But he averaged twenty-four points a game, leading Evander to the city title in the division for small public schools. Even though he failed to graduate, he managed to get his GED and a spot on the team at Palm Beach Junior College. But, wherever he went, his unbridled rage forced people to shy away from him.

He was leading the National Junior College Athletic Association in scoring during the 1985–86 season, averaging 41.4 points, shooting an absurd 69.6 percent from the field, when he was dismissed from Palm Beach. It seemed the school administration frowned upon his taking textbooks he'd received for free and trying to sell them to the bookstore. Frowned upon him making sexual advances toward a female professor. Frowned upon him showing up at halftime for one game. Matthias admitted his part in the incidents. He claimed he was merely being an entrepreneur, that he needed the money from the books to pay his tuition, and that the professor had it in for him because of the book situation and because he was an athlete.

As for missing part of a game—well, he had a good reason.

"I was a victim of circumstance," he said, in all seriousness. "I had to visit my probation officer in New York." What's a guy supposed to do?

A six-foot-three, 195-pound guard who rippled with muscles, biceps bulging, thighs taut, calves ready to spring him skyward in an instant, Matthias launched awkward, running one-handed shots from every conceivable angle, yet somehow made them fall. Out of control, he had the knack for making the right play at the right time, even if, when one was watching him, it seemed like he'd gone about it all wrong. Almost bored on the court, he'd explode on a moment's notice; explode with the fury of someone trying to prove a point—to himself, to the world.

Problem was, it wasn't just on the court.

As a freshman at Palm Beach, he once scored 63 points in a game against Miami-Dade North, which had a front line that averaged six foot eight. He once scored 81 in a Rucker League game against a team that had Walter Berry. And once, back in 1985, he scored 107 points in a game in the Upward Fund Tournament in Manhattan. "Hey," he said, "sometimes you get hot."

"The kid can't shoot a lick," said former Palm Beach coach Howard Reynolds, a graduate assistant to the legendary University of Kentucky coach Adolph Rupp. "He just takes it to the hole. But, I tell you, I seen a whole lot of good basketball players when I was at Kentucky. This kid was good enough to start for *any* Top Twenty team. Miami-Dade had a six-foot-nine kid and a six-foot-eight kid and that night he dared those two kids to step out in front of him.

"He has no fear of anyone."

Maybe that explained why Matthias received five years probation on assault charges after he "punched out a drug dealer" in front of his Bronx apartment in 1985. He refused to say whether he did so because he despised drugs or because he despised drug dealers who'd given him a bad count. Whatever the case, at Palm Beach, Reynolds said, that attitude fast made Terminator a student out of control.

"You would sit and talk with him and really feel like you were getting through to the kid," Reynolds said. "But once he got away from the office, on campus, and things went against the grain with him, he just lashed out." No one was spared. Not professors, not coaches. "Not even the president of the college," Reynolds said. "It was like he just went out of his way to paint himself into a corner and, after a while, you just couldn't get him out. Finally, he just had to be dismissed from school."

"They said it was in the best interests of both of us," Matthias recalled.

Until his dismissal, Terminator had been recruited by a host of major-college teams. But seeing all the problems he got himself into at Palm Beach—his reputation was so bad that he wasn't even named to the NJCAA all-America team—those schools stopped calling. Saying he had learned a lesson and pledging to make a new start, he turned up in the fall of 1986 at South Junior College in Savannah, Georgia.

He soon made his presence felt—on and off the court. He averaged thirty-four points a game, again, best in the nation. But the unruliness continued.

"He passed class," Brien Crowder, then coach of the team, said. "That is, as long as he went to class. And, on the court, you couldn't stop him." One-on-one, one-on-two, one-on-three, Crowder said, Matthias could score on anybody, anytime, anywhere. "His problem is that you have to follow rules. And Ron doesn't always like to do that."

The problems started small. Matthias had his girlfriend in his dorm room, which was forbidden under school rules. "You would tell him not to have a girl in the room and then he goes and does it," Crowder said. "You tell him not to do it again and so he does it again. And again. And again. Finally, he was kicked out of the dorms."

Then, Crowder alleged Matthias became a suspect in several dorm break-ins, though he was never charged. Finally, Crowder said, he was asked to leave.

Matthias was supposed to attend St. Mary's College, a school in Orchard Lake, Michigan, that competed in the National Association of Intercollegiate Athletics (NAIA). He never showed up. Later, he made a commitment to play at St. Thomas Aquinas, an NAIA school in Sparkill, New York. Again, he never arrived.

For the longest time after that, you could find Ron Matthias hanging out in the parks around New York City, still hoping to make it. "I'm trying my best to keep things under control," he said, adding he was working hard to turn it all around. "I still have a temper, but now I try to catch myself. You've got to grab a hold, concentrate. A lot of people might not want to take a chance on me because of my past. But that's up to them. Either they're right, you're right, or no one's right. That's just the way it is."

Based on the results of his first collegiate game, and considering the course requirements, it seemed Lloyd fully deserved those two credits for being on the team at Mount Sac. The game was at Santa Monica College on November 19, 1986, and though Mount Sac lost, 84–77, in overtime, the loss had little to do with Swee'pea.

He dominated, scoring thirty; had a game-high sixteen rebounds.

"He played every spot on the floor," Santa Monica assistant coach Bill Smith said after the contest. "Center. Forward. Even point guard. He brought the ball down, shot twenty-five-footers like *layups*. He had about ten turnovers—and I'd say *nine* of them were because his guys weren't ready for his passes."

After that, Lloyd appeared in just one more game for Mount Sac, against Orange Coast College in Costa Mesa. Victor said that, due to "a conflict" with his tutoring sessions, Lloyd had missed too much practice time. So, when he scored just five points with eight rebounds against Orange Coast, Victor, who'd embraced Lloyd because of a long-time friendship with Tarkanian, decided he was no longer welcome.

"I decided that was enough," Victor said, implying that Lloyd also had created disturbances, much like he had back at Oak Hill. "He had to make a commitment and his commitment was to get into UNLV, which I don't blame him for. When I saw the handwriting on the wall, I just backed off. When I found out he couldn't sincerely go to practice like the other players—I've got a lot of nice kids here—I could not deal with it. So, I made that decision. And Lloyd agreed. He badly wanted to play at UNLV."

Though Lloyd refused comment on his situation at Mount Sac—"I ain't talkin' 'bout none of that"—it was obvious Tarkanian and Warkentien also wanted Lloyd at UNLV, and ASAP. "Our plan was to put him in junior college, watch him in junior college, and get him eligible," Tark said then. And Victor even told *Newsday* back then: "Hey, if Jerry sent him here, I'll make sure he gets him back."

Allegations leveled by two Mount Sac players and reported in the investigation by *Newsday* indicated Lloyd also clearly understood to what lengths Tark and his staff were willing to go—and that he planned to milk it for all it was worth.

Consider that Lloyd arrived at Mount San Antonio driving a car that, according to Nevada Department of Motor Vehicles (DMV) records, was leased to R&R Advertising—a firm owned by UNLV booster club member Sig Rogich. Sure, the car, a 1983 Dodge Aries K, was low on the list of desirable sets of wheels; maybe at the bottom. But it was Rogich who had hired Swee'pea and his friend, Steve Cropper, as runners—errand boys—at the firm the previous summer. And Rogich was a man of power.

"Ronald Reagan used to call him all the time," Cropper recalled. "Marvin Hagler, Bill Cosby. Everyone who was anyone knew Sig. . . . He had an awful lot of juice."

Published reports indicated Rogich had been "instrumental" in bringing Tarkanian to UNLV in 1973. Later he'd become a Regent at the school.

He'd also helped a lot of folks secure gaming licenses in Nevada—among them Ol' Blue Eyes, Frank Sinatra. Rogich also had been one of the three directors on the Tuesday Team, which conducted the $20 million advertising campaign that secured Reagan's landslide 1984 presidential election win over Walter Mondale and Geraldine Ferraro. Later, Rogich served as the so-called quiet partner in a team with Roger Ailes, supervising television commercials for the 1988 presidential campaign of George H. W. Bush. Most notable among their endeavors were negative commercials about pollution in Boston Harbor and the tale of ex-con Willie Horton, who'd committed a rape after being paroled by Bush's opponent—then–Massachusetts governor Michael S. Dukakis. As a result, Rogich came to be included in the inner circle of White House advisors to President Bush. He would even come to hold a position in the Bush administration. His title: Assistant to the President for Public Events and Initiatives.

Strange, then, how people are connected.

Because, back in the fall of 1986, Lloyd Daniels—an uneducated, illiterate basketball player from New Jersey Avenue in the crime-ridden, poverty-stricken section of East New York, Brooklyn; a player who'd been brought to Las Vegas via arrangements made by a gambler who'd done time in federal prison for fixing horse races and college basketball games for the Mafia—just happened to be driving a car leased by a major national advertising agency owned by a future presidential advisor and one of the most powerful, most influential men in America. As one school official said, "What power. I have never in my life seen anything like this kid. If he runs for mayor, he'll win."

And Swee'pea said Rogich sometimes even let him live at his house.

"He saw the good side of Lloyd Daniels, when Lloyd Daniels was straight," Lloyd said, adding: "He saw a lot of fucked-up days, days I would call in, say, 'I'm sick.' And how can you be sick in a hundred degrees? But he saw the good side. When have you ever known a man like him, who works with the president, let you stay in his condominium with all big, fancy stuff? He even let me drive his cars."

Records indicated one of those cars, the Aries K, was leased by R&R Advertising through Master Lease Plan, owned by another member of the UNLV booster club, Norm Jenkins. Rogich said he'd leased it in June 1986, when he'd hired Lloyd. He also told *Newsday* that he'd let Lloyd keep the car at night, but that he'd allowed his other runners the same privilege—thereby distancing the school from possible NCAA infractions. He also said that the only reason Lloyd still had the car when he was at Mount Sac, long after his employment at R&R had been terminated, was a "slipup" in paperwork. "We notified the lease company that we wanted out [of the lease]," Rogich said, "and they said they would. They said someone else was going to take it, and that's the way we left it." Then, on September 14, six days after classes began at Mount Sac, Swee'pea was involved in an accident and ticketed for failure to decrease speed at an intersection in Las Vegas, according to municipal court records.

His car had passed another car, sideswiped it, and left fifty-two feet of skid marks, the accident report said. That report described the car as a blue 1983 Dodge. The license number, according to records, confirmed it was still leased by R&R. Little more than two weeks after the accident, Lloyd brought the car to a Chevron service station in Pomona, California—about eight miles from Walnut, from Mount Sac. The mechanic, Jose Flores, said the engine needed to be rebuilt. He also said a rental car company later sent a truck to take the car. On the work order, Lloyd had listed the vehicle as an "84 DOD ERZ," his description of his Dodge Aries.

Ricky Collier said his UNLV teammates teased Lloyd about the Aries. They called it a "cereal box car" or a "detective car," because it looked like the kind used by undercover cops. Lloyd always said he was getting a new Nissan Maxima.

"He was bugging them about that Maxima, too," Collier said, explaining that Lloyd mostly bugged Warkentien. "I know he was, because I was there when he said, 'Stein, when am I getting my Maxima? Rick doesn't believe I'm getting it.' He kept saying it. And Stein would say, 'Lloyd, just wait. Just wait.' Lloyd said, 'Watch, Rick. I'm going to have a Maxima. You guys rap me in my blue car. Wait 'til I get my Maxima.'"

Warkentien denied he ever promised a Maxima. But records on file in Pomona Municipal Court showed Swee'pea was nevertheless driving a vehicle registered to Warkentien when he ran a stop sign in Wal-

nut on November 12, 1986. Records obtained from the Nevada DMV
showed Warkentien bought that vehicle for $1,792—on November 5.
The dream car wasn't a brand-new Maxima.

It was a motor scooter.

In the wake of claims Lloyd had been provided with a car, two Mount
Sac players—James Jones and Cletus Jarmon—said that, at the request
of Gene Victor, they'd allowed Lloyd to live rent-free in their three-
bedroom apartment in Pomona. Jones said Warkentien would visit
Lloyd at the school "maybe three to four times" a week.

"When Lloyd first came, he really didn't want to [attend Mount
San Antonio]," Jones said. "Mark was coming down constantly. Mark
and Lloyd would talk. Mark would ask, 'Are you going to class?' Lloyd
would say, 'Yeah.' But if Lloyd said, 'No,' then Mark would be on his
case about that. The things that Lloyd wanted Mark to do for him, if
Lloyd didn't go to class, Mark wouldn't do them."

Jones said Warkentien gave Lloyd clothes and small amounts of
cash as rewards for attending class. As incentive, Warkentien later said,
he also told Lloyd: "If, in a year, your reading is better, your mode of
transportation [may be] better."

Needless to say, the NCAA took keen interest in the situation,
which investigators construed as a possible violation of recruiting
rules, rules that, if broken, would give UNLV an obvious advantage in
the recruitment of Lloyd, whose letter of intent had become void when
he enrolled in junior college. After all, NCAA rules limited the number of times a coach could contact a prospective recruit to three visits at the prospect's school—and three away from it. Those rules also
barred a coach or booster from supplying financial aid or other benefits to a recruit, his family, or his friends.

For their part, athletic department officials at UNLV protested that
the school and its staff had done nothing to violate those rules.

"I'll guarantee we didn't do one thing," Tarkanian said. "We were
not involved in one thing. Believe me, we would not have stuck our

neck out on anything on him. I mean, you've got to be a damn fool to think that anything with him wasn't going to be checked out, wherever he played. I don't care what school he went to. And particularly being us, there was no way we would stick our neck out in any way."

Warkentien, meanwhile, continued to defend his actions because, as he said, he had only acted in his role as legal guardian. "It was all perfectly legal," he said.

And from a legal standpoint, he was right. It was just that: legal.

But the law of the land isn't necessarily law when it came to the NCAA, which has its own standards and rules. Which has its own definition of what is legal.

And what isn't.

On January 22, 1987, the NCAA informed UNLV athletic director Brad Rothermel that the guardianship arrangement was not allowable, based on a decision by its Legislation and Interpretations Committee. That committee ruled coaches could not become legal guardians of recruits, unless the guardianship was based on factors unrelated to recruiting and that it predated the recruiting process. In other words, Warkentien would had to have been Lloyd's guardian before he ever recruited him—"recruited his skinny ass," as Warkentien so kindly put it—back at Oak Hill.

"The [guardianship] question has come up a number of times in the past, and the interpretation from this department has always been that a coach could not be involved," Evrard said of what later became known as "the Lloyd Daniels Rule," adding, "It wasn't like this was the first time this was ever interpreted or reviewed."

Two months later, in March, the school administration announced it would conduct an internal investigation of the entire situation and association.

None of the developments seemed to concern Lloyd. Neither did the final exams at Mount Sac, which were scheduled for January 21–28. Lloyd knew how badly people wanted him to play basketball. So, even though he left campus right after finals and moved back to Nevada to enroll for the spring semester at Las Vegas, when grades were posted on the glass-enclosed bulletin board in the administration building at Mount Sac, Lloyd was listed with the other students who had passed their courses.

And he didn't only pass. But there, alongside the names of students who had aced courses in analytical trigonometry, bacteriology, microbiology, physics, foreign languages, and literature, was the name of the star dyslexic: Daniels, Lloyd.

Swee'pea had made the dean's list.

But the farce didn't end there. Having become a full-time student at UNLV, one who'd amazingly earned twenty-six college credits at Mount San Antonio despite being illiterate, Lloyd found himself assigned a class schedule: Elementary Composition, Appreciation of Theater, Internship in Sports Management, and Juvenile Delinquency in the Juvenile Justice System. With any luck, it wouldn't be long before he found himself eligible to play ball. At least, those around him thought so.

It turned out, soon Lloyd would *really* get a chance to gain insight into the justice system; its inner workings. Too bad this knowledge would all be firsthand.

Gone Bust

Lloyd," the television cameraman asked as Swee'pea was escorted from the house to a waiting van by an officer from the Las Vegas Metropolitan Police, "do you realize what you may have done to your career?"

Lloyd stared blankly for a moment as it all sank in.

A rising national star, here he was, hands cuffed behind his back like a common criminal, an undercover officer holding him. He had just been arrested for attempting to possess a controlled substance, rock cocaine. He appeared to be under the influence of drugs. His world was coming apart at the seams. Worse, he was on television, a crew from WVBC-TV Channel 3 Las Vegas filming his arrest.

Swee'pea lowered his head. This was real, this was bad. No doubt about it. From inside the van, where a handful of other suspects, also handcuffed, were seated, came the voice of another arrestee. "Fucked up," the man said as he watched it unfold.

"They're goin' to put me on the news," Lloyd said to the other detainees as he reached the side of the van. "They like that."

The officer guided him to the open side door and, as Lloyd ducked his head under the roofline, leaned in, and stepped toward the crowded rear seat, he twitched and twisted his hands. As he did, his left hand slipped free of the cuffs, which were formed from a simple notched plastic tie fastened to bind his wrists.

"He's out of his cuffs," someone said immediately as Lloyd continued to make his way toward one of the remaining seats as if nothing had happened.

"Lloyd," the officer said. "*Daniels*. Come on back out here."

As Lloyd backed out of the van, the officer grabbed his hands, calling to another undercover officer: "You got some regular cuffs? We need some regular cuffs."

For a few minutes, Lloyd was held outside the van. As others looked on, he presented a curious study of a man trapped between his immortality and mortality, his destiny and his demons. What of his career, he thought. His future. What would happen now? He licked his lips. His mouth was parched. The cool night desert air seemed to swallow and consume him as he stood there and waited for the next move.

Was this how it ended?

"Oh shit!" he said out loud, shaking his head in a moment of frustration and self-contempt as he cursed himself for being so stupid as to let this happen.

As the officers again cuffed him, this time his wrists bound too tight for them to move, Lloyd watched the cameraman again focus in on him.

"Hey. Yo, man," Lloyd said as the light illuminated his face against the dark winter night. "Want to move that camera? You goin' to end my career."

"That's the idea," another arrestee, a man inside the van, said—before adding a dose of his own wisdom. "It sells *newspapers*."

Lloyd stood, defeated almost.

"That's life, man," he said to the other arrestee finally. Then he shrugged his shoulders as if to indicate he didn't care. He was here now. What's done was done.

What could he do about it?

"Like I said, we'll get you," a female undercover officer told Lloyd as he was once again placed in the van—this time in the front seat. "Every time."

Of course, Lloyd was not the first basketball star ever to run into trouble because of problems related to drugs, drug use, or the streets. Countless pro players had—from Denver Nuggets all-star guard David Thompson, whose cocaine addiction led to problems with the Internal

Revenue Service, to Micheal Ray Richardson, the former all-star guard for the New York Knicks and New Jersey Nets whose addiction earned him the distinction of being the first player "banned for life" from the NBA.

And playground legends like Earl Manigault, Joe Hammond, Fly Williams, and Pee Wee Kirkland had often been arrested in connection with an assortment of crimes—from petty thefts to bank robberies—stemming from their drug involvement.

The streets have—have always had—power. Some can't resist. Not Thompson, not Richardson. Not Hammond, Williams, or Kirkland. Not Lloyd.

Not a two-time high school all-American from Astoria, Queens, named Red Bruin—a man whose life once was described by a friend as "a picture from a storybook." A man whose fall said a lot about how a man's weakness can ruin his life.

———

Handcuffs and chains shackled the woman's wrists and bound her hands fast to her waist as she stood before the judge on what was a hot and unpleasant midsummer morning in Onondaga County Court in Syracuse, New York. She had been charged in a homicide and, what with her attorney in the midst of making pretrial motions and without many places to go considering her state, she stood and watched, bored almost, as nearly indecipherable legalese was exchanged between barrister and bench.

The courtroom was crowded, nearly full, and considering the number of sinners present and the choice of boxlike seating formed to resemble pews, it could have passed as church during penance. A legion of the hard-core sat, five together, off to one side of the court, bound by a length of linked steel and their common disregard for the law. Their times had come and gone and the decisions rendered had been largely unfavorable. Now they awaited their return home—to life behind steel bars; to their cubicles, their hardened beds, to their stainless steel toilets with no real seats.

To their unclean sinks that smelled of urine.

Here, amid the world of the incorrigible, sat Tony Bruin. He looked out of place, more than just a bit, as he awaited his turn before the bench. Truth be told, he was.

"Are you Abraham Bruin?" Judge William J. Burke asked when Bruin was finally brought before him on that morning, August 4, 1987.

"Yes," Bruin answered in a quiet, almost hushed tone.

"Do you understand," the judge asked from his lauded seat on high, "that there are allegations that you were in violation of your probation?"

"Yes," Bruin said again.

The judge looked down from his bench. He had piles of papers, which outlined details of the case, but had little need to look at them, knowing quite a few of the particulars from personal experience. Still, he looked to see that Bruin, who had tested positive for drug use while on probation on drug charges, had just completed forty days of inpatient care and rehabilitation for a substance abuse problem. He read recommendations from a multitude of municipal agencies that suggested the man now before him had a chance, this time, to succeed in his full rehabilitation.

The judge again turned his attentions to the man before him.

"You're a troublesome person to deal with," Burke said, having announced he had restored Bruin to full probation, allowing him to avoid jail time. "You're a high-visibility person, looked up to by the members of the community. You have to make an effort to live up to that. I trust you will. . . . I don't expect to see you back here again."

"Believe me," Bruin said, once he had made his way outside the courtroom and into the corridor, "I don't want to see him again, either."

How Abraham Anthony Bruin III came to be in court that morning was testament to how some of each new generation never learn from the mistakes of ones previous. Because, like many fallen stars, the streets once offered an easier, smoother road.

He had been the all-American boy-next-door and that was not rumor left open to interpretation, but fact twice proven if you believed the reports in all the magazines, which—despite the fact that one of his teammates was Vern Fleming, who went on to the University of Georgia and the Indiana Pacers; that another was Dwayne Johnson, who would star at Marquette—had named him among the best in the nation two consecutive seasons at Mater Christi High School in Astoria, Queens.

He was the man with the untouchable game then, the man who seemed destined to soar to new heights. "The elastic man," his coach, Jim Gatto, called him.

He was six foot four with a forty-two-inch vertical leap. He could dunk at will, do pretty much whatever he wanted with a basketball.

"He could just go up and up and up and stay up," Gatto said.

Superscout Howie Garfinkel once called Bruin, a guard-forward—in basketball terms, a swingman—"the Benny Goodman of swingmen." It was a reference to the legendary 1920s and '30s clarinetist known as the King of Swing.

But, while all the attention he received for possessing such abilities was very nice, it put quite a strain on Tony Bruin. Subjected to the unrealistic expectations—as Jim Boeheim, who coached him at Syracuse, said, "There had been such incredibly high hopes"—Bruin, like most legends, turned out instead to be an ordinary kid who one day found himself up on a pedestal, only to find out he didn't know how to get down.

"I feel like I'm coming back from a war," Bruin said as he sat in the office of his attorney, Donald J. Martin, after his court date. He seemed tired, used.

"I don't know how to react, what people are thinking about me. I feel bad for the embarrassment I caused. I feel like I'm still on eggshells."

Court had reminded him how fast his life had spun out of control, he said; just how far he had fallen. He had once been Red Bruin, the man who had it all. He was the one who had been named to the Big East all-tournament team as a sophomore, the one who'd scored twenty-five points on national television against DePaul; the one who'd finished his collegiate career with 1,294 points, then fourteenth best in school history.

What that all counted for in the aftermath, no one knew.

He had turned his back on the goodwill wrought by those accomplishments long before pro scouts realized he was a forward trapped in the undersized body of a guard—Philadelphia made him a seventh-round pick, 162nd overall, in the 1983 NBA Draft; the move effectively ended his professional basketball career before it ever began—and long before he ever pleaded guilty in May 1986 to having sold $420 worth of cocaine to an undercover detective in Syracuse on separate occasions in April 1984.

Since he first began college and maybe, some said, since earlier even than that, Bruin had wagered high stakes on his ability to withstand the seductive force of cocaine and, in a game of Russian roulette, had committed career suicide.

He had forsaken most of his options in basketball and even forfeited a good job as a youth counselor at the Spofford Juvenile Center in New York City after he was named in an indictment on October 28, 1985. He had lost his self-esteem.

Under a plea bargain he was given a probated sentence. Five years. Less than seven months later he was stabbed in what police termed a drug-related incident. On March 21, 1987, he again tested positive for drug and alcohol usage—in violation of his probation—and underwent rehabilitation at the Benjamin Rush Center in Syracuse. What he had when he emerged was nothing. He was twenty-five years old and in debt, the unmarried, unemployed father of a three-year-old son.

"How this happens is hard to figure out," his father, Abraham Bruin, Jr., said.

The elder Bruin had worked as a laborer on Rikers Island, the main jail complex for New York City, which sits in the East River adjacent to LaGuardia Airport. Because of where he worked, the elder Bruin had been more aware than most parents about the dangers of the streets. While Lloyd and others had no parents to teach them right from wrong, Abraham Bruin, Jr., had advised his son to be careful. He saw those of bad influence, of bad faith; had warned his son about the dangers of association.

He assumed the message had gotten through. He assumed wrong.

"You know," he said, "every day on the streets of New York there are hundreds of kids selling drugs. Near our apartment, on Thirty-Sixth Avenue, there are five, six kids every morning. The same on Thirty-Fifth Avenue. The same on Thirty-Fourth. And this is Astoria. A good neighborhood. I used to see those kids and wonder how come nobody stopped them. Then I realized they have parents, too, and they couldn't stop them.

"After all, I didn't see it coming."

"It is a real scary thing," then–commissioner of probation for Onondaga County, Robert Czaplicki, said. Czaplicki had been one of those officials who'd recommended to the court that Red Bruin be restored to full probation. "Tony is the kind of guy who, if you ever met him, you'd say, 'This is not a bad guy.' Now, I'm not a believer that someone else is at the root of your problems. But I think it is real easy to see how this could happen to him or someone in his situation. We put athletes on a pedestal they may not deserve. They're subjected to a dream world. Everyone told Tony he would be the next Dr. J. Then, when it didn't pan out, what did he have left?"

The undercover detectives at first thought their eyes had deceived them. Just a few hours earlier on February 9, 1987, the narcotics officers from Metro Police had staged a raid on the pink-and-white single-story house on Clayton Street in the downtrodden section of north Las Vegas and had seized "several" cigarettes laced with PCP as well as a "small quantity" of cocaine, and had arrested four persons for selling drugs.

Having established a sting operation at the house, they watched as the latest of the clientele walked toward the door. "Looks like we got trouble," one officer said.

"What do you mean?" another officer asked, slow on the uptake.

The members of UNLV basketball team were well known in the community, almost as famous as the stars on the Strip, if not more so it seemed at times. It was no surprise, then, that the first officer had immediately recognized the man headed to the door of the crack house. At six foot seven, he was hardly inconspicuous. And he wore a sweatshirt that read "UNLV Runnin' Rebels" and a hat that read "N.C. State Wolfpack." This was the prospective big-time recruit everyone in town had heard about. The one Tark had spoken of time and again. The one he'd raved about.

"Lloyd Daniels," the surveillance officer mumbled under his breath as Swee'pea walked to the front of the house and knocked on the door.

No sooner had he said the name than an undercover officer answered and the attempted purchase commenced—recorded on a video camera in the room.

"Is Neil there?" Lloyd asked, already on tape.

"No," the officer said.

"Well, I *need* a rock," Lloyd said. "I *want* a rock."

According to Lieutenant Jerry Keller, head of the Las Vegas Metro Police Street Narcotics Unit, Lloyd then paid the undercover officer inside the house twenty dollars in an attempt to purchase the crack, known on the streets as rock. He was arrested on the spot, one of sixty suspects busted during the sting operation at the house that night.

"Lloyd Daniels appeared to be under the influence of a controlled substance," the police report read. "Based on [his] actions—[he was] for example, very talkative, fidgety, licking his lips and constantly sniffling—and physical signs such as dilated pupils, red and runny nose, it appeared that he was possibly under the influence of cocaine. Daniels told [the arresting officer] he was under the influence of cocaine."

Lloyd was remanded to the Clark County Detention Center. It was there, he later said, that he came to realize just how serious this business was.

The charge of attempting to possess a controlled substance was a felony and carried maximum penalties of three years in jail and a $5,000 fine, Clark County deputy district attorney Bill Koot said, noting the charge of being under the influence, also a felony, carried maximum penalties of six years in jail and a $5,000 fine.

Despite his well-chronicled history of problems, Lloyd had never been arrested. Now he was searched, fingerprinted, photographed, processed, and placed in a holding cell to await a bail hearing. It scared him. But, really, not because of the jail cell. Not because he felt isolated or because he felt like that scared little kid who had been left to fend for himself. Not because of the jail term that awaited him if convicted.

Rather, he said, it was because—based on his experiences back at Andrew Jackson—he knew what the newspapers would do.

"I ain't goin' to lie," Lloyd said. "Jail didn't scare me. You know what scared me, know what hit me the hardest? When I realized it would be in the papers, nationwide. I swear to God on my mother's grave, if they had just kept that quiet, I would have goed out the next day and got high. What shook me up was when I realized it was goin' to be in the papers and everybody would know; that my grandmothers, that Ronnie would know. I told the cops, I swear to God, I told the cops, 'Beat me up, man. But don't have it in the papers.' I would do six months if they would keep it out the papers.

"I wasn't worried 'bout jail. I knew how to get over in there."

Lloyd remained in jail for some time; it was hours before Mark Warkentien found someone to arrange his bail. Records showed it was Sam Perry's signature and $1,500 cash that got Swee'pea released in the early hours that Tuesday morning.

"He was petrified and very embarrassed," Warkentien said. "He knows how many people have been in his corner wanting him to do well. Then, this happens. I told him, 'You're going to carry this with you, whether you get off or not, for a very long time.'"

Though he was scheduled for arraignment in Clark County Court on March 3, when Lloyd left jail that morning he said he figured the worst part of the nightmare was over for him. "Once I got out," he said, "I thought I was home free."

———

Tony Bruin thought he was home free, too. He had cocaine, enough of it in his possession to make a deal. He'd been in the car with an acquaintance. The acquaintance had brought a friend. Bruin sold the friend $110 worth of coke.

Another time he sold him an amount worth $310.

But the friend of a friend, a man named Paul Pendergast, turned out to be an undercover officer with the Syracuse Police Department. Eighteen months after the two first struck a deal, Bruin was named on two warrants charging him with third-degree sale of a controlled substance and third-degree possession of a controlled substance—felonies that carried a maximum sentence of twenty-five years in prison.

Records showed Pendergast once asked Bruin why he'd sold drugs.

"You got to make money somehow," Bruin said.

But there was more to it than just money. Bruin had first used cocaine, he said, because it was available, because his friends did it. He used it because he felt good and wanted to feel invincible, because he felt invincible and wanted to feel immortal. Later, he said, he used it because he felt depressed and just wanted to feel normal again.

"There are plenty of bad characters who missed their boat, who are not going anywhere, who want to steal some of your shine," Bruin said. "They're like parasites and leeches. But they're taking you to parties and there is drinking and drugs and they're giving it to you for free, and you don't think about it. It smooths right in.

"Pretty soon, you're overcome.

"With cocaine, no matter how bad you feel, it makes you feel good. No matter how hungry you are, it makes that hunger go away. No matter how tired you are, it makes you feel like dancing all night. If you were a businessman you'd say, 'Let's package this and sell it. We'll get rich.' You just don't realize how bad it is for you."

Bruin admitted he "occasionally did coke" at Syracuse, but denied rumors that he ever used cocaine in the locker room at halftime, that he had played games with coke stuffed inside his socks; that he had served as the middleman in several drug deals for other players in the Big East—a vague implication made by former Villanova University guard Gary McLain in an eighteen-page, first-person account of his own drug problems in the cover story of the March 16, 1987, issue of *Sports Illustrated.*

There had long been indications Bruin might have had a problem, even though, as Boeheim, among others, said, "Tony was one of the nicest kids we've ever had in the program. I didn't know about him using drugs. It came as quite a shock to me."

But, like Lloyd, Red Bruin—the man of whom Gatto, the coach, said, "Everyone who knew Red knew he was a nice, down-to-earth kid. Even *refs* liked him"—turned out to be a drug addict. On probation after having pleaded guilty to reduced charges in his drug case, Bruin was ordered to donate five hundred hours of community service at the Southwest Community Center in Syracuse. He was asked to work with disadvantaged kids, to help them overcome the obstacles presented by the neighborhood.

Bruin liked working with those kids. They liked him.

"I taught them ball," he said. "But I also tried to give them a message. I'd tell them, 'Learn from other people's mistakes so you don't have to go through what I went through.' I figured if you could talk to ten, you might be able to reach one."

"I am strictly against drugs," acting director of the center Carmelita Boatwright said. "Drugs ruined my family and that was in the back of my mind when I heard about Tony and so I figured I wouldn't want to get to know him. But, as the months went on, I realized he was a thoughtful, caring person. Just a good person. He was the type of person who just took time. You take time with kids and they don't forget."

The community center was located on South Avenue in Syracuse, just down the block from Fredette's Lounge, the Tadros Market, and Chicago Market, which long before had had its windows boarded to keep out the trespassers. It was not far from Rezak's Silver Star Grocery and the Pillar of Truth Church of God in Christ, Rev. Benjamin Jamison, pastor—a parish more than needed to assist the sinners here, it seemed, seeing as how across the street was an adult movie theater sandwiched between the Tippin' In Lounge and an enterprise known as J+J Liquors.

Near the center, over on Marginal Street, folks lay in the littered grass in the park, drinking at the otherwise respectable hour of three thirty in the afternoon.

Faced with the constant assault on his senses, the constant temptation, Bruin gave in to his weaknesses. He forgot to listen to his own advice.

The trouble occurred in the wake of a car accident, when Bruin received two thousand dollars from his insurance company. That same day, he had a fight with the mother of his son—longtime girlfriend Tracey Johnson. Angered, Bruin cashed the check and headed out to a local club that, Czaplicki said, was a known drug location. There Bruin met a man named Phillip Stokes and the two went back to his house, allegedly to do some coke.

Not long after midnight, two men wearing ski masks burst into the house and demanded Bruin give them all his cash. According to Stokes, Bruin told the two would-be assailants, "Hey man, I got cocaine here. You don't have to do this."

Bruin then stood and said, "Hey, I'll give you some money."

But instead of turning over the cash, Stokes said, Bruin rushed the pair as he yelled, "Let's get them." Problem was, the pair turned out to be Elmer "Butch" Stokes and his brother, Leroy, who, in a move of comic proportions, had used their own brother in a desperate attempt to set up and rob Bruin. Leroy, holding a knife, slashed Bruin in the arm; Bruin lost a significant amount of blood as the assailants ran off. Later, under threat their younger brother would testify against them, Elmer and Leroy both pleaded guilty: Elmer to second-degree robbery, Leroy to attempted first-degree assault.

Because the situation was viewed as one-time incident, Bruin remained as a worker at the community center, but he was ordered to submit to regular drug testing.

"Think about what happened," Boatwright said. "He was arrested for a drug problem, then he comes into an area with all the poverty, drugs. I don't think it was wise to put him in that environment. It just don't seem right to have put him there."

"There was too much temptation."

It was a delicate situation, one Boatwright understood from first-hand experience. She had seven children. One daughter, she said, worked for a lawyer. One son, she said, was in prison on robbery charges stemming from his involvement with drugs. Her husband, she said, had been a drug addict when he died. She knew the pain.

"The thing is you have to remember that all these addicted folks got a problem, that they are really just like you and me," she said back then.

"They have the same weaknesses. Maybe the problem was they just didn't want what society said they should have. Maybe they just didn't know what it takes to become a success or how to handle the disappointment when they failed. When my husband died, I saw junkies and winos come to pay their last respects. Anytime a junkie takes time from a fix or a wino takes time from a drink to come see a man in a coffin, that person can't be all bad. Must have a bit of good in him to pass them things up.

"Like, I'll never forget this wino I always used to see in the neighborhood. Used to call me 'lady with the smile.' One day he said, 'Hey, lady with the smile, how come you ain't smilin' today?' I said, 'I ain't got no money to pay the grocer.' . . . When I went to pay the grocer the next time, he said, 'It's taken care of.' That wino had come and took care of my bill. I haven't seen him since that day. But that shows you how there can be good and bad in every man. . . . I always say, don't never look down on a man, unless you stoppin' to pick him up."

With that in mind, Boatwright sat and talked to Bruin on a regular basis. She'd give him advice, lend him support.

"I had no direction," Bruin said. "And the problem was, every time I got that empty feeling, I went to look for 'those guys.'"

The big relapse came in late March and early April 1987, just after the *Sports Illustrated* story by McLain. Bruin tested positive for drug and alcohol use on three separate occasions and was ordered into the inpatient drug treatment program.

"Red is a very honest and moral person, but he got a little frustrated with some of the things in his life," said Hank Carter, who ran a charity basketball game in New York called the Wheelchair Classic and who had known Bruin since his days at Mater Christi. "He saw that golden fleece over the rainbow and then, when he didn't get it, well, he gave in to temptation. I see that every day in my community. What you have to learn is to keep doing the right thing. If you're consistent with it, they can't get to you.

"But you have to continue asking yourself, 'Who am I hurting by doing this?' If you know the right answer, you'll stop."

It wasn't—and, still isn't—always quite that simple, though. For Tony Bruin the road proved long and hard. He understood how fragile his situation remained, would always remain, and tried to use that knowledge to make a commitment to himself.

To his future; to the future of his son.

"I used to be happy-go-lucky and that was my problem," he said. "I trusted people. You had to do wrong by me before I would write you off. Now, I'm more cautious, more of a realist. . . . I have no room for stumbling now. I have to say, 'No.' The things I did can't cause you nothing but trouble. I know that now. The thing is, when the spotlight is on you at a young age like that, you immediately think everyone is your friend. You don't see all the angles. You don't realize this guy might have a friend who's an agent, that this guy might hope you get into a college so he can go along, too, and get a coaching job; that this guy may want to deal you drugs. You lose perspective. All of a sudden, ten White Castle hamburgers don't satisfy you anymore. You want lobster.

"The hard thing is to learn to be strong. I think I've learned that."

"You know," Boatwright said, "when you have kids, you have these dreams that the boys will grow up to be doctors, lawyers, have good jobs and that the girls will grow up and get good jobs or find a good man and get married.

"Nowadays, in this world, it seems like you just got to hope that the boys grow up to be boys and the girls grow up to be girls."

As Abraham Bruin said, "If Tony hadn't gotten arrested, who

would have ever known this was happening? If Len Bias hadn't died, who would have ever known about his problem? He would have been in Boston, just another all-American. It makes you realize this can happen to anyone. It happens down on the stock market. Geraldine Ferraro was running for vice president of the United States and it happened to her son. As a parent, that's scary. You start to think maybe there is nothing you can do."

———

There was nothing Lloyd could do, either. The footage of his arrest was shown on the television news that night and was reported the following day in newspapers from coast to coast. But despite the evidence—as Sergeant Ed Pitchford of the Street Narcotics Unit said, "It's not the strongest case, but it's not the weakest case, either"—and the bad publicity, Lloyd maintained that the entire incident was a simple misunderstanding.

"This is somethin' serious," he said. "But I'll be all right, 'cause this was nothin' I done. I didn't try to buy no drugs. I was just in the wrong place at the wrong time. That's all it was. People can say, 'He fucked it up.' But I didn't do nothin' wrong. I didn't buy nothin'. I just got caught in the house. How was *I* supposed to know it was a crack house? If *you* had knocked on that door like I did, *you'd* be under arrest, too."

Truth was, Lloyd said, he had gone to the house in search of a former summer league coach who was to have supplied him with tickets to a basketball game. Truth was, he said, he knew the man only as "Tony." "I went there to get some tickets. I get to the door. I'm knockin'. I walk in and a guy said, 'What you want?' I said, 'I want Tony.' He said, 'Well, Tony ain't here and you're under arrest.' I said, 'What I'm under arrest for?' He said, 'Comin' to a crack house.' There was nothin' I could do. The motherfucker cop pulled a piece and said, 'Freeze.' I just said, 'Whoa.' I ain't goin' to get shot. I didn't know what was goin' on."

The truth also was, no one, least of all the members of the Clark County district attorney's office, believed the scenario. Especially since Tony Milner, identified as the "summer league coach" Lloyd described, also was arrested for allegedly attempting to purchase crack at the house—just twenty minutes after the arrest of Lloyd.

Especially since, just two weeks before, on January 29, a sting operation at the residence had resulted in arrests and the confiscation of thirty-four "Sherm sticks." That is, joints dipped in PCP—better known on the streets as "angel dust."

"Everythin' was goin' real good," Lloyd said. "But this one incident could end my career. I thought about that when I was in the slam. I said, 'Think Lloyd. *Think.*' Whatever I do now, it got to be correct. My feelin' is that the papers are goin' to write what they want and people are goin' to say what they want. But my life ain't goin' to change because of that. They got people out there doin' murders and shit. As long as I know deep down that I ain't guilty, I'm not goin' to feel like I killed four people.

"When my day comes, we'll see who's right."

UNLV coach Jerry Tarkanian did not share that optimism. He had always worried Lloyd might be using drugs and had confronted him several times with his suspicions. Time and again, Lloyd had denied the drug usage. "Give me a test, I'll take a test," Lloyd told Tarkanian. "C'mon, I'll piss in a bottle right now, Tark. Right now, I'll piss. *Right now.*"

"It was only later, after the arrest, that Lloyd admitted to me he was just doing that to cover himself," Tarkanian said. "He told me, 'That's the way us drug guys are, Tark. You got to be a good liar if you want to get away with it.'

"He must have been a good liar, because we believed him."

Part of the problem was that, like Jim Boeheim, Tarkanian was not an expert on drugs, on drug use, or on the warning signs. He was a basketball coach and, lacking expertise on drugs, was misled by a seasoned con man. Likely, he also didn't want to look too hard; if he had, he might have found a problem, whether he understood drugs or not. No doubt that would have affected his chance to win basketball games.

But, confronted with the arrest, Tark understood the situation was bad—and not only because it was apparent Lloyd had a problem. Tark had a problem, too.

A big one. One that called for damage control.

His team was 24-1, ranked number one in the nation. He was still locked in that court battle with the NCAA. As if all that hadn't focused enough attention on the Rebels, the arrest had sent a host of curious reporters rushing to Vegas to find out how a player with such suspect academic credentials had been admitted to UNLV.

Then, of course, there was the most immediate problem. Three years before, in an effort to clean up its image, UNLV had begun a drug-testing program that tested, at random, the members of all its athletic teams. It was a state-of-the-art program, implemented two full years ahead of the program designed by the NCAA. The university had not only used it to benefit the athletes, it had also used it as a public relations tool. Players went around to the local schools and warned students about the dangers of illegal drug usage. Tark spoke out about the perils of drugs.

Players wore T-shirts that backed the antidrug campaign being conducted by then–first lady Nancy Reagan. "Say No to Drugs," the shirts read.

On one wall in the basketball office there was even a section dedicated to newspaper clips about the drug-related deaths of athletes. The most prominent article was the one about Len Bias, "cocaine intoxication" in June 1986, little more than a day after he had become the first-round draft pick of the Boston Celtics.

Above that article, a sign read: "Are You Next?"

And so, Jerry Tarkanian was forced to make a decision. He could either wait for the outcome of the arraignment hearing and subsequent court case and then, based on whether he was convicted or acquitted on the charges, decide if Lloyd would remain eligible to be on his team. Or, in an effort to save face for both his program and UNLV, Tark could view the situation as a worst-case scenario and make an immediate announcement: Lloyd was banned regardless of the outcome.

On Monday night, when news of the arrest first became known, Tarkanian went with his gut instinct and immediately tried to distance Lloyd from the basketball program at UNLV. "Lloyd Daniels," he said then, "is not a member of the basketball team or on scholarship. He was a potential recruit." That was it, he said.

Then, on Tuesday morning, Tarkanian acknowledged that Lloyd was, for better or worse, associated with the team. However, he stressed that Lloyd would be dismissed from the team "if proved guilty." Later that afternoon, after lengthy discussion with school officials, Tarkanian considered the athletic department policy—which called for an immediate suspension of an athlete who has been arrested, pending trial—and decided he would, indeed, take those recommendations one step further.

"We have been extremely proud of our position on drugs and of the young men on our team who have similarly taken a strong stand against drugs," Tarkanian said at a news conference in his office at the school arena, the Thomas & Mack Center.

Which was why, Tarkanian said reluctantly, that because of the arrest Lloyd would never play basketball for the University of Nevada, Las Vegas.

———

With his weathered features, forever half-closed eyes outlined and accentuated by thick brows above and darkened bags below, Tarkanian almost always gave the appearance of being worn, haggard. His nickname, "Tark the Shark," acquired for the way his teams devoured opponents, was reinforced by the way those eyes never seemed to focus on one thing—but rather seemed to cut through a man's very soul, as if he weren't there. The way a shark does when he comes at his prey, in search of a meal.

Something about those eyes often made it impossible to tell what Tarkanian really felt or thought. But, after most of the reporters at the news conference had gone, Tark sat and talked with the stragglers. Those eyes said he was genuinely sad.

"Lloyd is very hurt by what happened," Tark said. "He made a big mistake. It's really sad because the guy is so talented. This was such a great opportunity for him to do something with his life. He had made great, great progress but he went the wrong way. It's unfortunate he made the wrong turn [because] we never had a player come close to his ability. He's the best basketball player I've ever been associated with, the most talented kid I've ever been around. If I had a Top Ten, he'd be my First Nine.

"But," he said, "we told him if he messed around with drugs he'd never play here. All of our kids know our position on drugs. I won't tolerate *that* in any way."

Tarkanian said he made the decision after a closed-door meeting during which Lloyd admitted he had gone to the house to purchase crack.

"How could you be so stupid?" Tarkanian said he'd asked.

"I don't know," he said Lloyd told him.

"He was in tears," Tarkanian said. "He said he had never used anything harder than grass before. He said it was his first time. But he was there, it's on television. It's not like it was a case of mistaken identity. We checked with Metro. They told us there was no doubt he was guilty."

———

The school was in the third year of its drug-testing program. And while Tarkanian said he believed in giving everyone a second chance, the bottom line is that it would have been hypocritical *not* to kick Lloyd off. The decision, Tark said, was final.

It took less than twenty-four hours for the coach to soften his stand and announce that his decision to ban Lloyd had been a "knee-jerk" reaction. "You should never use the word 'never,'" Tarkanian said. "It doesn't give a guy a chance to recover."

Tark also said he "could neither confirm nor deny" Lloyd told him he'd gone to the house to purchase crack. "You must have misunderstood me," he told a reporter.

School athletic director Brad Rothermel said Tarkanian regretted having used the word *never*. That Lloyd would "never" play for UNLV "I think very few things in life are final," Rothermel said. "I would hope in any case that, if the facts are overwhelmingly against the decision that was made, we'd at least take the time to reconsider our decision.

We may not render any different decision, but we must be willing to consider other possibilities. That would be the truth in any case."

The reason for the sudden about-face was twofold. And obvious.

Everyone at UNLV still wanted Lloyd to play for the Runnin' Rebels. And, hearing that Tarkanian's first reaction was to ban Lloyd from the team based solely upon his arrest and not his conviction or acquittal, Larry Brown came out and said Kansas would still be interested in trying to "assist" Lloyd en route to the NBA.

"It all depends on his grades and transcripts and things of that nature," Kansas assistant coach Mark Freidinger, who'd called Warkentien "just to inquire about Lloyd's whereabouts," said in an interview with radio station in Lawrence, Kansas. "[Brown] saw the immense talent he has. He knows his future is in the NBA."

Even though it was remote, a possible scenario that ended with Lloyd in a Kansas uniform bothered folks at UNLV. They had already made too much of an investment in Swee'pea, had taken too much heat in the form of bad public relations, to then have to watch him play somewhere else. Besides, David Chesnoff, the Las Vegas attorney representing Lloyd, said he might be able to get charges against him reduced—giving officials at UNLV good reason to soften their stand.

Chesnoff was then thirty-one and from Sea Cliff, an affluent section on the North Shore—or Gold Coast—of Long Island, the land of *The Great Gatsby* and not far from New York City. Chesnoff said he liked to play basketball. In fact, he told *Newsday* he'd first met Lloyd during a game at the Las Vegas Sports Club. Chesnoff said he'd given Lloyd his card; told him if he ever had a problem, give him a call.

It just so happened he specialized in criminal law. "Federal criminal law," he told *Newsday*, when pressed. Federal sting operations, to be exact.

Chesnoff said he had faith Lloyd would be acquitted or, at worst, because he had no previous convictions, would be granted a light sentence, likely a suspended sentence or probation. That took into consideration that, while Lloyd had admitted he had taken cocaine, he also had refused to submit to urinalysis at the time of his arrest.

Without proof of drug use, the district attorney's office probably would have to drop for lack of evidence the charge of being under the influence.

"I'm not a big fan of sting operations, because they have their own inherent problems," said Chesnoff. "The people involved often don't commit the crimes, though ofttimes the police running the operation report that they do. They want people to think that someone is doing something that they might not have done. They might as well have asked him to walk over hot coals and, if his feet were burned, then found him guilty.

"Everybody is eager to condemn a young kid. But I care about this kid. He is a great kid. I'm confident in Lloyd as a young man and hopeful that this rush to judgment—after all, his arrest was on television—will not prejudice his case, that people will give him a fair chance. I told Lloyd, 'Go back to school. Keep your head held high.' I don't think he has anything to worry about. I don't think we're worried. . . ."

As usual, someone figured out how to save Lloyd—bailing him out of a bad situation. For others, it was already too late.

The Life

Cigarettes in hand, the locals lined the walls of the building in search of an ever-fleeting patch of shade and a brief respite from the searing rays of the midday sun. They sat, leaned hard against cool bricks, talking, drinking, laughing amid the smell of this place. Its odor hung in midair, hovered over the littered asphalt; the smell old, unfaithful. It smelled of warm beer and of stale tobacco, of urine and of bodies and of their sweat. It smelled like life, in all its impurity. It smelled, it seemed, of death.

Only the morning before, Len Bias had been buried down in Maryland. Friends, as well as strangers, had cried at his funeral. He'd been too young to die, they'd said, over and over; just twenty-two, in fact, when his life came to its unexpected end.

Though no one would ever know for sure, he had, in a moment of arrogance or weakness, taken one false step in a life filled with an array of sure-footed moves.

If Lloyd's lapses in judgment and the lapses in judgment by Red Bruin brought both arrest and shame, then the result of the lapse in judgment by Len Bias brought the harshest of revelations on the morning of June 19, 1986.

Less than forty-eight hours after he'd experienced the high of being the first-round draft pick of the Boston Celtics, who'd taken him second overall in the NBA Draft, Bias, the all-America forward out of the University of Maryland, had felt the wrath of what authorities would later call "cocaine intoxication"—a lethal buzz, if you will—and died a sudden, premature death. An astonishing death; a historic death.

"Lenny was vulnerable," Rev. Jesse Jackson said as he eulogized Bias, using his passing to measure the tragic extent of human fallout from the use of illegal drugs. "But all of us are. It takes years to climb a mountain; one slip and we face oblivion. God sometimes uses our best people to get our attention. He called him to get the attention of this generation. On a day the children mourn, I hope they learn."

The message seemed to have fallen on innumerable deaf ears that afternoon in the neighborhood that surrounded the courtyard at I.S. 59 on Springfield Boulevard. Barely a block north of Merrick Avenue in Springfield Gardens, Queens, on its face this appeared an area far different from the then-destitute backstreet environs of Brownsville, Bushwick, East New York, Harlem, and the South Bronx.

The school stood amid a well-ordered middle-class neighborhood, home to a host of single-family and two-family homes as well as several relatively well-kept apartment complexes just a few miles from where Lloyd's grandmother, Lulia, lived in Hollis.

As it was in Hollis, the illusion created—one of a safe, serene environment—was shattered with a ride a few blocks west, where Guy R. Brewer Boulevard crossed the Belt Parkway and headed north from Kennedy Airport through South Jamaica.

There, an incalculable amount of drugs were dealt to motorists and the walk-up crowd alike in an almost open-air-market atmosphere; distributions made by teenage sellers outside ramshackle storefronts, their routines, replete with "def" hand signals, body language, and street jingoism that hinted at a sort of blue-collar stock exchange—business risks weighed between the sporadic patrols of passing police cars, instead of the trading bell. Even as kids ran an informal five-on-five game on the basketball court that bordered the school, an herbal essence wafted over from the local viewing audience and doctored the air with the thick, pungent aroma of marijuana.

Underfoot, the crunching of vials once used to store rocks—pellets of crack cocaine—provided physical evidence that one death, no matter how notable, how significant, would do little to change the nature of the beast overnight.

"It might get to certain people," Marlon Crawford, a sixteen-year-old from the neighborhood, said as he took a moment between games.

"But not a lot. They'll keep doin' it, because a lot of people live to get high. They'll do anything for the fifteen minutes of action. Some might say no. It may get to the athletes with a chance to make it. But for the others, well . . . I don't think there's nothin' you can do."

If the cocaine death of Len Bias down in Maryland, the arrests of Lloyd Daniels and Red Bruin, and the rise and fall of other playground basketball legends—not to mention the apparent apathy of those whose hopes they represented—seemed indicative of a larger problem, it's because they were. The statistics were grim. According to the Institute for Advanced Study of Black Family Life and Culture, in Oakland, California, best estimates were that 1 in 10 black males in America would die by murder, compared to 1 in 80 for comparable white males.

And the institute found that, for black men between the ages of fifteen and twenty-four, the leading cause of death was homicide.

One out of every three African-American men who died in the 1980s between the ages of twenty and twenty-four, the institute estimated, died a homicide victim. (The figures were even more dramatic in 2010, according to National Vital Statistics Reports released by the Centers for Disease Control in December 2013.)

Some were the innocent victims of street crime. Some not.

But most had a common thread, statistics showed: related in some way, shape, or form to drugs. To what was known on the streets as "the life."

"Not since slavery has so much calamity and ongoing catastrophe been visited on black males," then–health and human services secretary Louis W. Sullivan, founding dean of the Morehouse School of Medicine and one of the highest-ranking African-American officials in the Bush administration, said in the 1980s. "I do not think it is an exaggeration to suggest that the young black American male is a species in danger."

According to a 1980s study conducted by two doctors at Harlem Hospital and published in the *New England Journal of Medicine*, drugs were a significant reason why the life expectancy of a male born and living in Harlem was likely to be shorter than that of a male born in Bangladesh, one of the Third World's poorest nations.

And almost half the deaths, they found, were linked to violence and drugs, as well as to AIDS, which, in most inner-city environments, was often not related to sexual encounters but to drug use.

Not that danger hadn't always been inherent in such environments. But in the past, it had come in different, much less caustic forms. It came in the form of poverty, which continues to plague the residents of inner cities, and in the form of resultant poor medical care—factors that made life hard even in the best of times.

As it had with the heroin epidemic of the 1960s, the harsh realities of the streets seemed to have become harsher still in the 1980s with the advent of mass-appeal drugs like crack cocaine, which often caused increased stresses on a societal framework already stressed to the breaking point. Black families had seen a significant breakdown in their structure. According to the U.S. Census Bureau, almost 6 out of 10 African-American families with children under age eighteen were headed by a single parent, usually female, by the mid- to late 1980s. Factor in other components—the fiscal crisis of the 1970s, which led to the closing of hundreds of inner-city community centers; the lack of a father figure, impoverishment, poor education, and low-paying honest work when available—and the result was that a growing number of youths in the inner cities of America had become sidetracked by drugs, either as users or as dealers.

Or both.

Surviving by making "cash money," as it came to be known on the streets, brought with it a new social class: the new-jacker. The nouveau riche.

New-jacker dope-boys—and girls—were new-world entrepreneurs. They could make hundreds, thousands, of dollars a day manufacturing crack; selling it, stashing it. Better still, to do so they didn't need a formal education. All that was needed was the raw ingredients to make it or to find a way to acquire the merchandise to be dealt—and, for new businesses, this could be accomplished through a modest investment.

About $1,000 got you an ounce of cocaine, which would make enough crack pellets to fill a thousand $5 vials. Find the street workers to sell it and the enforcement arm to protect against the threat of street-level takeovers, and there you had it.

The risks were high; often the result of a bad business decision was death. There were rival crews, rival posses to contend with. But considering the possible gains and considering the alternatives, more than a few decided it was worth the gamble.

"We are dealing with an economy that has its own rules and order," one assistant district attorney in Queens said then, noting, "It makes sense to deal drugs."

"Take crack, for instance," said Bob McCullough, Sr., a man once drafted by the old NBA Cincinnati Royals and who for decades directed the celebrated Rucker Pro Tournament, which matched pros against street players on an outdoor court in Harlem, before it gave way in the 1980s to something called the Entertainers Classic. "These people are dealing with survival. Their attitude is, 'If people are willing to buy crack, I'm going to sell it to them.' They are not dealing with the morality of the situation. They are dealing with putting food on the table. Now, after a while, that changes. Then it becomes a quest for a new car, new clothes, something for their woman. But it usually doesn't start that way. It starts with trying to find a way to survive."

Drugs related to inner-city basketball because often the playgrounds reflected life on the streets. The lone difference was that sometimes, if a player was receptive enough to want to learn, basketball could teach him order, something that might have been otherwise missing from his life. It could earn him an education, teach him a work ethic and responsibility. It could teach him maturity, stabilize his life.

A life for many that was otherwise filled with instability.

For those who needed it—and not all did—basketball might just enable them to sidestep the street element and to find success. It opened doors that seemed otherwise forever closed to them. Still, faced with a shot at success, a number continued to fail.

"The thing is, out here, you've got to be strong-willed because you can't plan twenty years into the future," former playground star Sonny Johnson said. "There are too many ways to get sidetracked. So, what you have to do is set short-range goals.

"And," he said, "you have to be extremely careful."

Once Johnson was a member of Young Life, a team that featured Earl Manigault and was unbeaten for several summers on the playgrounds of Harlem.

Back in 1964, Johnson had played ball with Manigault at Laurinburg Institute—the school Lloyd later attended—and he was the first African-American player to attend Gardner-Webb College in a place called Boiling Springs, North Carolina. Years later, he became recreation director for the New York State Division for Youth, in Brooklyn. His job was to work with kids who had been through the judicial system.

"One out of every hundred kids at the center have skills to play college ball," he said. "But they have no goals, no expectations. On the playgrounds, the number of kids who can go on to college ball is probably more like one out of ten. They have the tools to get by that street element. Basketball in the city, in particular, keeps a majority of kids out of jail. See, kids at the Division for Youth talk about basketball. They don't play it. But most of the kids on the playgrounds have decided that when the guy comes and says, 'Hey, let's go stick up the candy store,' they can say, 'You take *let's* and *I'll* stay here.' They have an alternative. Their thrill for the moment is in the park, basketball. They have a work ethic, where the other kid ain't working for nothing.

"The problem is the bad guys find a way to pick off the good guys," Johnson said.

———

He walked with a comfortable gait. Not an attitude walk, the kind fashioned by new-jack punks and assorted common street hoods, but rather a step like that of a man who'd once been a king but had never quite found it to be his role in life. It was humble, dignified, a walk that cut the fine line between self-assurance and self-doubt.

He wore a pair of old black-and-white Chuck Taylor Cons. In one hand he held an unlit cigarette, in the other a brown paper bag—business end of an aluminum can stuck through its opening, tab popped. He seemed quite in control of his faculties and he was. But as he approached, the scent of alcohol surrounding him seemed to overwhelm the fresh morning air—air as fresh and upstanding as it could be at ten o'clock on a humid midsummer morning on the soon-to-be-searing asphalt of Harlem.

"Hi," he said, sounding almost self-conscious. "I'm Earl."

The man was an intriguing contradiction. His voice possessed a certain strange resonance: low, with a gravel edge that undercut its memorable, mellifluous tones with betrayal. His skin was dark, rich, and deeply textured, his body surprisingly lean after all these years. Legs, still strong. But missing were two lower front teeth, which seemed to make his face, when you looked close, appear hardened, worn. Old.

Endless tracks ventured down his arms, their railroad lines darker than that of his darkest days, the maze of scar tissue an eerie sort of avant-garde reminder of the bad habit that had nearly killed him. Whose aftereffects were slowly killing him now.

"Curious?" he asked as he offered up his arms.

Before a response could be formulated, he said: "It's from the White Lady. . . ." Heroin. The old days. "You know, on the streets I still hear people say, 'There goes the Goat. He *used* to be the baddest dude in the world. But drugs brought him down.' People tried to show me the way, but I didn't want to listen. At the time, I really enjoyed doing it. Later, I found out it wasn't shit. It lost me my whole career."

Back in the late 1950s and early '60s, Earl Manigault soared over every park in New York City. He could entertain the crowd, picking quarters off the top of the backboard during warmups—and, legend still has it, making change on the way down.

He could spin, shake defenders almost at will, with command of a repertoire of moves unmatched and unparalleled. Though just a thinly built, six-foot-two forward, he often challenged the likes of Wilt

Chamberlain, Connie Hawkins, and Lew Alcindor—later, Kareem Abdul-Jabbar. Manigault would often throw it down on them.

Just because of what it meant; what it said.

On the uneven asphalt courts blended into the fabric of a neighborhood bordered by a world of burned-out buildings and burned-out dreams, he dominated the playground game with a flair and panache that earned him a street reputation as a player with few, if any, equals. So struck by his ability, his game, Jabbar once called him "the best basketball player his size in the history of New York City." In fact, on the night Jabbar had his jersey retired at the Los Angeles Forum, someone asked him to name the greatest player he'd ever faced. "That," he said, "would have to be the Goat."

The Goat. The nickname given Manigault by those who could not pronounce his last name, butchering it to something sounding like *nanny goat.* The Goat.

On the streets, in the parks, the name came to command respect.

"No question," Johnson said that morning in the eighties, "but that from fifteen feet in you *weren't* going to stop this man. From the foul line to the basket, if he put a move on you, he *had* you. *Period.* You had to get it in your mind that you had to face the embarrassment. He might put it down backward on you. Anything he wanted. The other nine players, two referees, and everyone watching knew *he* was the center of attention."

"I still remember the first time I saw him," Bob McCullough, Sr., recalled. "I walked into this gym and there was this kid playing with weights on his ankles. I said, 'Why don't you take them off, so you can move?' He told me, 'Oh, it's all right.' Then, like he was runnin' up a wall, he came in and dunked something fierce.

"The man could defy the laws of gravity."

But for some there is a wicked gravity. It's called the streets of New York. Its lure is illicit, its power overwhelming. Only the most strong-minded can overcome it.

Earl Manigault couldn't.

As a result, the Goat never made it out of the playgrounds and into the National Basketball Association, though he briefly played in the old Eastern League.

Instead he became a heroin addict by his late teens, a convict by his early twenties, and a symbol to the likes of Joe Hammond, Fly Williams, Red Bruin, Richie Adams, Lloyd, and a host of others who followed in his wake, of everything both good and bad about the inner city, its playgrounds. Its players.

"Sometimes," Johnson said, "no matter how good a person you are, you can't help but fall prey to the sidewalks of New York."

Some men are afraid of success, some merely too impatient to wait for it to come, and so they fail. And some, like Earl Manigault, simply wake one morning to realize the reality that sometimes talent isn't nearly enough; that due to no particular fate, their chance for success has passed and, with it, their hopes and dreams.

"The city," Manigault said, "can take it all away. For every Michael Jordan, there's an Earl Manigault. We all can't make it. Somebody has to fail. I was the one."

On the streets of New York there is a phrase used to recall the pure days, the time when life was unadulterated, uncluttered by all those societal constraints—things like the need for education, need for a job—that seem to hold a man down.

It goes, simply: *back in the day.*

Those words evoke memories of a simple time; time spent on the playgrounds, time when command of a basketball alone could make a man a god.

For Lloyd, it was the time he spent alone at night shooting a ball. For Joe Hammond, the time he tap-dunked home a teammate's miss after sailing into the lane at Rucker Park while pros like the great Dr. J stood by helpless.

For Fly Williams, it was a time when he ruled the parks, ruled college ball; before he wound up in the old Eastern League wrestling an eight-foot-eleven, 1,875-pound bear named Victor in a publicity stunt that earned him a paltry $300.

"I thought I won," he said. "The bear got on Johnny Carson."

For Earl Manigault, it meant a time before two heart operations made him old before his time, a time before jail and before nodding out on street corners robbed him of friends. A time before heroin robbed him of most of his talent and, for a while, all of his ambition. A time before he ever dreamed he'd lose his virgin veins.

Back in the day, the world was a playground and a basketball, nothing more. And Earl Manigault was as close to a god as a mortal dare be.

With what later became referred to on the streets as *stupid-fresh springs*—that is, supple jumping equipment—it seemed he could leap to the moon if he wanted.

In Harlem, decades after the fact, they still recalled how the Goat dunked a ball backward *thirty-six* times in a row to win a $60 bet. And they remembered how major-college recruiters flocked to its playgrounds as the stories of those dunks and his shot-blocking ability spread like the word on the street. Manigault already was considered one of the premier players ever to play in the city when he led Benjamin Franklin High School to the Public Schools Athletic League championship in the 1961–62 season.

"The good old days," he called them that afternoon back when. "We was young. And everybody was looking to make some sort of reputation."

Like the players who followed, Lloyd included, Manigault honed his skills during endless hours of practice in the parks, borrowing moves from the best players of his day and working them into his game; making them his own. As a kid, he would sneak out of his bed at night, jump down the fire escape of his apartment on Ninety-Fifth Street and West End Avenue, and head up to the park on 130th Street and Seventh Avenue—site of the old Rucker Tournament—to work on his game. His goal, like the goal of every kid in Harlem back then, was to earn a spot on the roster of a Rucker League team.

When he finally did, he often faced the best the NBA could offer—

from Chamberlain, Hawkins, and Alcindor to the ungodly Black Jesus, Earl Monroe.

"There were so many bad guys out there," Manigault recalled with a fondness as he sat that morning in the new Rucker Memorial Park, at 155th Street and Frederick Douglass Boulevard. Located across the street from the Polo Grounds Houses—built on the site of the old Polo Grounds stadium, home to the New York Giants baseball team before it fled to San Francisco—Rucker was one of the few litter-free parks in the city, regarded as a shrine. "Wilt Chamberlain, Dick Barnett, Oscar Robertson," Manigault said. "When you went to sleep, you'd *envision* ways to be like that. Sometimes you couldn't even go to sleep. My mom used to put me in bed and as soon as she shut the door, I'd climb out the window and go to the park. I seen Jackie Jackson taking quarters off the top of the backboard and I went home and dreamed about doin' it. I seen Connie Hawkins and Elgin Baylor and I said, 'Listen, I'm gonna do that, too.' You took a little bit from each guy and put it all together into your own thing." Owned it.

Manigault was the master of the in-your-face dunk. Size of an opponent was immaterial. Like the time Manigault, Alcindor, Hawkins, Johnson, Jackson, and Bob Spivey, who had played at Marquette, went down to Riis Park for a day at the beach and before long found themselves on the basketball courts. They hadn't gone to play; in fact, Manigault wore dress shoes—*not* sneakers. Still, finding his path to the basket blocked on one possession by both Jackson and Hawkins, Manigault did what he did best, dress shoes and all.

"I got the ball and I came through the middle," he said, thinking back. "I went right down the middle on Hawk and Jackie and I dunked it. *Put it down.*"

Embarrassed the Hawk. "If you were small, like I was," Manigault said, "you had to put fear in people." Image, ego, and reputation were at stake.

"So many people would always be there to watch you defend your title," he said. "They would be callin' your name when you went on the court. I was always jumpin' around, 'cause if I didn't, my knees would have been shakin', I was *that* nervous. But you were always thinkin', 'How can I capture the crowd?'"

Back in the day, not many men could capture a crowd like the man who seemed able to outleap the gravitational boundaries of planet Earth. He was the man who could do the unthinkable, something he called simply, the double dunk.

Manigault would take off at the foul line, jam the ball through the hoop, catch it, and slam it through again before being reunited with the ground.

A metaphysical experience.

Johnson recalled one game at Laurinburg when Manigault was offered a direct challenge. "We were playing in Durham [N.C.] at Hillside High School and before the game some guy came up and said, *'Who's the Goat? You the Goat?'* Then he said his name was the Goat, too. He said there was only room for one Goat on the court. Well, Earl must have scored thirty-five that night and pinned the ball on the glass two or three times on the kid. After the game, the kid came up and apologized.

" 'You're the Goat,' he said."

But being the Goat, the man who could soar over basketball courts at will, was hardly enough to enable Earl Manigault to reach escape velocity on the streets of New York City, where he proved to be all too earthbound. Too human.

Dismissed from Ben Franklin in his senior year after being accused of smoking marijuana in the locker room, a charge that, more than thirty years later, he still denied, Manigault managed to earn his degree at Laurinburg—he graduated second to last in his class—then continued his struggles in the classroom at Johnson C. Smith University, the traditional black college in Charlotte, North Carolina. But after less than one year there, and after a falling-out with the coach, who was tired of trying to help him, Manigault found himself back in New York; on the streets, no future in sight.

"I never realized you could make a living playing basketball," he said.

Maybe it was immaturity; maybe insecurity. Whatever it was, it hit Manigault. Hard. "I thought it was over," he said. "That's when I went right to the bottom."

"It was really a matter of two years, when his game went from the ultimate to the damn-near ridiculous," Johnson said, a sadness in his voice. "It was a tough time for all of us. It was a difficult time for him and damn difficult for the people close to him."

And it was all because of drugs.

———

David Daye wore a T-shirt that read, "Crack Wars: Use Your Brain." As he said, "I ain't 'bout none of that. Thing is, you got to understand what all that can do to you."

This was the mid-1980s. Daye was just seventeen. He was standing in Montebello Park, not far from I.S. 59 in Springfield Gardens. The place wasn't really called Montebello; it's just that no one could pronounce its real name: Montbellier. The name hardly mattered, though, because, as Daye said as he and a handful of friends stood around under one the baskets, "This park is dead." It didn't look dead. It was clean, well ordered. Off to one side of the court, two older gentlemen played checkers on one of those permanent stone checkerboards that have long vanished because of vandalism in most parks. Kids were playing ball.

"Wait until dark," Daye said. "You'll see."

Dusk settled in and with it came a changing of the guard. Kids moved off in search of refuge as an older and more threatening element moved in. A drug element. Folks who, when they talked of *rock*, didn't mean basketball.

And it wasn't that way only at Montbellier.

It happened at Marcus Garvey Park over on Mount Morris Park West in Harlem. And at Reader's Digest in Manhattan, Ajax in Jamaica; at 66 Park on Stone Avenue in Brownsville, the place where Lloyd Free first became World B.

It happened because a number of kids no longer felt it was worth the risk to go to those parks, to endure the threat of physical harm merely to play ball. It happened because some of the kids who once played ball had gone to the other side.

"You see heroin, cocaine, and reefer—even whores—in some parks," Daye said. "It's the drug element. At other parks, it's more subtle. See, you want to play in a park where you don't have to worry about no one trying to take your bike, your bag, your money. . . . *Your life.* Sometimes you won't even play because of that. But sometimes, if you want to play bad enough, you'll go to a park like that anyway.

"Just so you can shoot around.

"Now, I ain't goin' to be no dealer," he said. "I got a job as an apprentice butcher in a meat market. But I knew kids who used to play every day. Really good players. Some started selling drugs, and now it's 'No more ball.' See, sometimes, you see someone driving a BMW and you're walking. You say, 'I could use some easy money, so I could get one, too.' Sometimes, the environment just gets to you."

———

Billy Thomas learned about the environment firsthand. Where he came up, over on 143rd Street and Third Avenue in the Bronx—the Patterson Projects, once home to the legendary Tiny Archibald—trouble was something dealt with on a daily basis. It seemed as if folks sometimes had to fight their way in and out of hallways, guns drawn.

Drugs and violence were commonplace.

It had been in those projects that Thomas, known on the street as "Billy Bang," first learned to ball. From there he took his game to Lehman High School and became an all-city player back in 1975. But Billy Bang found trouble—or, trouble found him—as he became the victim of a street shooting. And, though he refused to explain how all that trouble came about, he said it forever changed his life. Consigned him to the projects; robbed him of a future because it kept him from basketball.

It is terrible that kids see it that way, that they see basketball as their only escape. Terrible, because sports are overemphasized—on TV, in school, in the neighborhood—and so they put all their stock in their athletic future as a means of escape, neglecting what is really important. School, education. As Thomas said, as he echoed a common lament on the streets: "I had one 'bad experience' and it cost me. I turned to the streets. It was my decision. I didn't think I had nothing else. That's the thing. You do a stupid thing and it could be the end for you. It's so easy to get sidetracked." Around his neck, Thomas wore a medallion with two revolvers and inscribed with the words *Billy Bang*. On his hand he wore a three-finger diamond ring that spelled out *Billy*. All of it was for show, Billy Bang Thomas said, noting he'd learned a valuable lesson: that if you fight the streets hard, sometimes you can beat them. Or, at least, not let them beat you down, steal your soul. At the age of twenty-six, Thomas said that back then he was at least fighting back. He ran a summer league team for kids, called Orange Crush. He said he'd taken a stand against drugs, urged others to do the same.

"Like, I was goin' somewhere in a cab one day and the driver up front was doin' crack, while we were drivin'. I had to say, 'Can you let me out, 'cause I can see you ain't interested in gettin' me where I want to go.' But that's the problem. Nowadays, with crack and all the other drugs, it's gettin' harder to avoid trouble. It's like, if you have some money you have to decide, 'Do I buy a loaf of bread or drugs?' If you go to the store, maybe it will be one where you can even buy them in the same place."

Such was the environment in New York, where dealers—some just kids, like Lloyd was back in the day—sometimes plied their trade seated on milk crates propped up against storefronts; maybe from inside those stores themselves. And such was life in New York, where even the best sometimes fell prey to the environment.

"That's why education is so important," Ron Brown, then an assistant basketball coach at West Virginia University, said, talking about the dangers of the streets and their associations. "I always tell kids, 'If you can play ball in New York, you can go to college in the United States.

And if you can go to college in the United States, you can get an education, make a better life and get out of the environment.' It's that simple."

Brown came up in the Bronx River Projects on 174th Street and Bronx River Avenue. It wasn't the worst neighborhood in the world. Still, it was one where advice—stuff like, "Don't sit by the window at night with the shades up," the understanding being that doing so only made you a target—was geared toward survival.

Unlike a lot of folks, Brown listened to that advice. All of it. He went to school. Got an education at Evander Childs, then at the John Jay College of Criminal Justice. Worked for an organization called the New York City Criminal Justice Agency, assisting the impoverished who had run afoul of the law. Eventually he'd become a coach. First at Pratt, a small college in Brooklyn; later at West Virginia. He wasn't a star, would never be a star. But he'd been smart enough to use basketball to change his life.

Because of that, the first thing Brown said he told all potential recruits—even players he wasn't personally recruiting, but those he met and interacted with out on the recruiting trail—was this: "'I went through the same doors you want to go through. I sat in the same desks you want to sit in. Listen to me: get an education.'

"You try to reach who you can," he said. "If you don't get an education, you lose. If you leave school without a degree, the only place you're going is home.

"A lot of guys from New York City didn't make it," Brown said. "Guys who went to jail, guys who were on drugs. You don't even have to mention names. People in the streets know who they are. The problem is, often you're around people who are just interested in getting by. You lose perspective of what is important. But if you've got an education, you got a chance to be successful. If you keep your record clean, you got a chance to be successful. If you stay away from drugs, you got a chance to be successful. But if you strike out in any of those areas, you don't have a chance.

"I've seen a lot of players who were good on the courts but who didn't have enough life components to stay out of trouble off them.

It's sad. Real sad." Of course, sadder still is that sometimes, no matter how hard a man fights it, no matter how hard he works to do the right thing, he still ends up a victim of fate.

————————

Ends up like Herman Knowings, the infamous "Helicopter Man of Harlem." Back in the day, folks said Helicopter could jump so high that he once went up to block a shot—and wound up sitting in the basket. Wasn't true. But he was a man who had serious *ups*; streets could attain serious altitude. Could leap, could soar. And often he did. Against the best the streets and the pros had to offer in the old Rucker League.

Earl Manigault recalled how one time Helicopter leaped skyward to block a shot, something he did with lightning quickness and amazing regularity, only to find he'd been faked by his man. With no other options, Helicopter treaded air like a swimmer treading water—hovering until his man got called for a three-second violation.

"It isn't just a story," Manigault said. "It really happened. I seen it."

That legendary jumping ability allowed Helicopter to soar over his competition. Folks in Harlem remember with pride the summer of 1968, when Helicopter was selected for a team called the Colonial All-Stars in the Rucker Tournament. There was a game against the Rucker Pros, a team loaded with players, among them five players from the New York Knicks—Howie Komives, Nate Bowman, Emmette Bryant, Willis Reed, and Freddie Crawford, who also managed the Pros. It seemed like it would be an overwhelming match for Knowings, who was six foot five. But it wasn't.

"I'm not going to mention names, because they are my friends," Bob McCullough, Sr., once said. "But there was one play where the Pros brought the ball down, and Copter blocked a shot. *Whap!* The guy passed the ball to a teammate, who tried to shoot. *Whap!* Blocked again. The next guy passed the ball to a third Pro. *Whap!* Blocked again. Get the picture? Copter blocked three shots in a row by professionals."

But while Helicopter could soar over the parks, like with Manigault, his ability did not guarantee him fame and fortune. Folks in the NBA wouldn't give him a shot because he was a center—one who was far too small to play the position in the pros; one they said couldn't shoot well enough to become a small forward or a guard in the NBA.

And so, though he briefly played in the Eastern League and with the Harlem Globetrotters, Helicopter had to get a job that made him just another mortal. So many others had squandered their chance to drugs, to crime. To the streets.

Herman Knowings, it turned out, was just the wrong-size guy with the wrong game. Nothing more, nothing less. All of which consigned him to the fate of the workingman, a man who, unlike a lot of other legends, really was playing by the rules.

It was terrible, then. Because, founder of his own taxicab company, Helicopter was driving his hack to earn a living one night in April 1980 when another car jumped a divider on the 145th Street Bridge. It was the one obstacle he couldn't rise above.

The car crashed into his cab. Killed Herman Knowings, dead.

He was thirty-seven.

———

Bricks littered the abandoned, rubble-strewn lot on Frederick Douglass Boulevard in Harlem, a scene that evoked images of war-torn Europe and Asia; bombed-out cities like London, Dresden, Stalingrad. Hiroshima. Razed high-rise buildings lined the street, their remains now little more than ankle-deep. Others that remained stood only as empty shells, long converted from living space to space for the walking dead; places for shooting up, for smoking crack. Places for all sorts of bad things; name the bad thing.

"Heroin heaven," Earl Manigault said as he pointed out the car window to the desperate, bleak surroundings. This was where he'd shot up all his heroin, he said. "Right here. Every grain of it. *This* is where I fucked up my career."

This was from the days long after the golden era of Harlem had faded into the past; long before the renaissance put it square on the comeback trail. Out near 115th Street, reminders of what a lost world it had become in the interim were visible mere feet from the wreck-age of those forgotten buildings. In war-torn, war-ravaged cities, men who'd had no role in the destruction walked in tatters, rags, scavenging for morsels to feed aching, empty stomachs; searching for the strength to reclaim what they'd once had. Here some found the answer in drug and other illegal activities, trying to blot out the real problem: their environment, their lack of resources.

Their lives.

"You got to understand, there's a lot of frustration here," Manigault said. "Life here is *hard.* That's why some of the richest guys in the world come out of this neighborhood. If you're willin' to go in for 'the Fast Life' as your means of escape, you can make five thousand dollars a day on the street. Sometimes, people just see that as their way out. You have all your sucker friends. There is jewelry, cars, women. You don't think consequences. You go for the easy money. There is not a block in Harlem that doesn't have the bad stuff. Matter of fact, here the bad stuff is all around us. But, while the bad stuff is on every block in Harlem, on every other block there are at least five ballplayers, I guarantee you, badder than *any* cat in the NBA. They could all be there." That they're not, Manigault said, was due to human frailty.

Here Manigault went for the life, too, realizing that lack of foresight meant he was never going to make it off the playgrounds. Realizing that, for him and so many others, the courts where they earned their reputations were all that stood between fame and a life destined to end in a potter's field. From being anonymous, forgotten men.

Soon he had a hundred-dollar-a-day habit. And soon he was going out on the streets, down to the garment district to steal mink coats, out to the mom-and-pop groceries to take whatever he could from the register. It was both pitiable and poignant. And seeing it, some of the local dealers, out of compassion, simply began to give him the goods.

"I was the Goat," he said, explaining the vastness of the fall. "They told me that I could have as much as I wanted. They didn't want to see me stealin' for it."

In 1969, the year the Milwaukee Bucks made Kareem Abdul-Jabbar a rookie millionaire in the NBA, Earl Manigault was first arrested for possession and spent eighteen days in the Manhattan House of Detention, better known as The Tombs. There, he said, he kicked his drug habit and overcame his desire to commit suicide. But that did not save him from a transfer to Green Haven, a medium-security prison in upstate New York, where he served sixteen months of a five-year sentence.

Later, in 1977, he gave in and started using drugs again and one day, with nothing better to do, he hopped into a car with some friends and headed off to do a robbery in the Bronx. Where Manigault ended up was in the Bronx House of Detention and, later, the maximum-security correctional facility in Ossining—the famed Sing Sing.

"We had a plan to steal six million dollars," he said of the short-sighted game plan. "But we got busted. They figured I was the ring-leader. I got two years."

Decades after he first made his reputation, Earl Manigault re-mained a legend on the streets of New York. A shy, almost apprehen-sive speaker, one whose speech showed great care and forethought, he displayed a gentle, human quality. That alone made it difficult to un-derstand how he once turned to muggings and robberies to support his habit. It also filled those who met him with compassion for a man who wanted no pity, a man who never physically hurt anyone except himself, then hurt himself so badly it cost him his most valuable pos-sessions: his ability and, for a time, his pride.

It made you want to cry for the time, back in 1965, when he re-turned to the famed Rucker Tournament, the place where he'd made his reputation, only to lose his balance, stumble twice and fall, embar-rassed. It made you wonder about the self-inflicted pain he must have endured, earning his only shot at a pro career in 1970—it wasn't long after Bill Daniels, then owner of the American Basketball Association's Utah Stars, read about him in *The City Game* by Pete Axthelm—only to discover that, at age twenty-five, Manigault had abused his body so badly it would no longer respond to his commands.

Manigault, a man of compassion, a man without a sense of self-pity, seemed to find a bright side to it all. He smiled, nodded gratefully when, on his return to Harlem, strangers stopped on the street, whispering: "The Goat. It's *the Goat.*"

"The things I done comin' up. I shouldn't be here, right now. Just as far as bein' alive, I appreciate it. I thank the Lord every morning. I'm the last of the crew."

He remained especially proud of his legs, which were clean, unmarked. Unspoiled. Not at all like his arms.

"When the veins in my arms were full, it was tempting to go to my legs," he said. "But I always loved my legs. No matter how bad it got, I always went to another spot in my arms. I must be a rich man. Just look at my arms. All of my money is in my veins."

Come from a place like this and perhaps the greatest homage you can pay a man is to say he survived. Earl Manigault was a survivor.

He lived hand-to-mouth in Charleston, South Carolina, where he'd been born; where years before he'd moved back in with his mother, as well as two of his seven children, Darrin and Earl, Jr. He'd gone south trying to prevent his life from again heading in that direction, too; trying, he said, to protect the interests of his sons.

He was in his forties—"forty-bucks, plus," he called it, that morning back then and he said he'd worked odd jobs, painting houses and mowing lawns. He had been doing work for the local recreation department before heart problems caused him to be laid off for a time and still, wherever he went, he made a sincere effort to advise others on how to avoid the dangers that felled him. He was living proof, he said, of what can happen to a man. No matter how good or well intentioned.

"What I try to tell them is that they have a future," Manigault said as he walked through the playground at Ninety-Eighth Street and Amsterdam, the one locals had come to call Goat Park in his honor. "They just have to give themselves a chance. I say, 'First, see what you can do out there. The drugs will always be there.' If that's what they want to do with their lives, do drugs, then they can always come back to it. But if they give themselves a chance, maybe then they won't get sidetracked."

"He is a guy who I have a lot of respect and admiration for," Johnson said, "even after everything he's done. I respect him for kicking the drug scene. I respect that he gave it his best shot and was able to survive the streets as well as he has. I don't think there's an individual who has had to face the adversity he faced through the years and still looks so good. The older I get, the more I see kids today play basketball, the more I respect him and the way he played. I wish somebody had videotape back then. Because right now his game lives only in our memories."

The pole stood better than a hundred feet tall. It rose with a certain majesty and defiance above that old, lifeless lot on Frederick Douglass Boulevard. At its apex, someone years before had placed a basketball hoop. Legend had it that, once, back in the day, Earl Manigault had jammed a ball through that basket. He never did, of course. But as he said, "I'm the only man alive who could have done it. The *only* man."

A moment later, he turned and walked away.

It was sad. But what with Earl Manigault serving as a visible reminder of what could happen, and what with Len Bias dead from cocaine, Lloyd and Red Bruin having been arrested for drug violations, all while folks out on Guy R. Brewer Boulevard were still cutting deals, you had to ask what it would take to make some understand.

"Maybe people who seen these things happen to someone big in basketball might say, 'Yo, money, like maybe this can happen to me,'" said Rynell Calloway as he stood that afternoon at I.S. 59 talking about the death of Len Bias—or, as the June 30, 1986, issue of *Sports Illustrated* called his tragic passing, *Death of a Dream.*

Calloway was precocious, slick. Streetwise. He was from 138th Street and Lenox Avenue in Harlem, had come to visit friends in Queens. He wanted to believe that the death of Len Bias, that the death and misfortune of so many others, would make a difference. But he knew the streets, knew the score. In his heart, he had doubts.

He was thirteen.

"There's peer pressure all around you," he said. "So much that it's kind of tough not to get involved in the life. But you have to have a strong mental mind. Sometimes you can look out the window and see people die. You read about it in the papers. You have to know that you can get hurt, that those things is something you shouldn't do. That's why what happened to Len Bias is a dis to all of us. We all have dreams that we can be the man, be in the NBA. He had his dream come true and he let it become a nightmare. Face it, the man fucked up. And now we know we can't fuck it up, too.

"Thing is, it ain't always that easy, 'cause lots of people just figure, 'Hey, a little reefer here, a little crack there helps keep the doctor away.'"

All too often it is easier said than done.

"Here's a guy, everything going for him," Craig Davis, a twenty-year-old student at LaGuardia Community College, said. "Money. The Celtics. He was going to make it. He did make it. And then, he goes and kills himself with drugs. You just have to shake your head and say, 'Look what happened to Len Bias. Look what can happen to me.'"

After all, viewed from a distance, there can be a certain enchantment to the life, with its lure of material wealth and good times. But more often than not, that promise remained unfulfilled. Once its hooks had been set, a soul was almost never delivered *from* evil, but rather to it. And the usual result was that a life of promise, of potential, was sapped of its strength and of its goodness, only to be left abandoned; ruined.

Or worse.

Sometimes a few were able to escape its clutches and gain a second chance. Sometimes a few were able to survive. Sometimes a few were lucky enough to be granted a virtual clean slate and a chance to start over from scratch. But precious few were ever that fortunate. Lloyd was. He had not died. He had been issued a warning rather than a penalty. He had been granted a chance to make amends before it was too late. Lloyd still had his talent. He still had his youth. He still had a chance for a normal life. All he had to do now was make an effort to save himself.

Now, if only the message could get through.

Topeka, Kansas

A cold wind blew hard across the frozen ground outside Landon Arena, its teeth gnawing to the bone despite the best efforts to keep warm. It was a vicious wind, the kind that stabbed at you, sapped your strength; the kind that seemed only too at home on a late November morning in a lonely, barren place like Topeka, Kansas.

Across the lot Lloyd raced the brisk morning air as he made his way from the rental car to the offices of the Topeka Sizzlers. It was time for practice and already the sound of basketballs could be heard from on the court inside the arena.

It was days before the start of the 1987–88 Continental Basketball Association season. Everyone seemed anxious; rightfully so. A month out of inpatient rehabilitation for his substance abuse problem, Swee'pea had barely made it to the gym on time.

Barred from playing at UNLV, Lloyd had signed with Topeka that September. Faced with possible jail time, he'd agreed to a plea bargain and under the terms of that agreement, Lloyd had pleaded guilty in Clark County District Court to a misdemeanor charge of attempting to purchase a controlled substance.

He was ordered into a three-month-long drug rehabilitation program; was required to undergo urinalysis on a twice-weekly basis at a local hospital. He also was fined $600 and $200 in court costs. But a month after entering the program, he'd tested positive for cocaine and marijuana. Because he'd violated his agreement, Lloyd found himself faced with additional penalties. That was, until David Chesnoff, the Las Vegas attorney, worked out a deal. Chesnoff talked to Sizzlers owner Bernie Glannon, who knew Jerry Tarkanian, and asked if he was interested in signing Swee'pea. Glannon flew to Las Vegas, met with Lloyd and Chesnoff, then spoke to Larry Brown, who, Glannon said, ironically, was "extremely high on Lloyd." A plan was worked out. Lloyd received permission from the court allowing him to enter a rehab program in Topeka.

Lloyd entered the Keystone Program at Memorial Hospital in August, a twenty-eight-day program, but hospital spokeswoman Debbie Norton said he completed it in forty-five days. "That it took him forty-five days to complete the program," she said, "should in no way reflect a relapse. Some people just take longer than others. Treatment is a very personal kind of thing. You have to identify the problem, then you have to find the right way to treat it. Addiction is a disease and, because it is a disease, that means that it may be different with each person. There is no thirty-day quick fix here."

The Keystone Program used group therapy in its treatment and was recognized by both Alcoholics Anonymous and Narcotics Anonymous. It also had an outpatient aftercare program that lasted fifteen months but was not mandatory. Norton said that, in the case of someone like Lloyd, who had a cocaine addiction, the use of any kind of chemical—alcohol included—would be considered a setback in his treatment.

"It's just too bad he is such a hot item, right now, so early in his recovery," Norton said after Lloyd was released weeks before the season. "That puts a lot of pressure on him. It's a pretty difficult position for him to be in, because, as I understand it, if he suffers a relapse, a million people the next day are going to know about it.

"It won't be easy."

A member of the Sizzlers' front-office staff, Brad Marten, said Lloyd understood how hard it would be. As part of his contract, he would be required to submit to random urinalysis and would have to maintain his attendance in the aftercare program.

"He said drugs were bringing him down," Marten said. "I don't know if that is just lip service, because he's pretty good at telling people what they want to hear."

What Lloyd said was what he'd always said. That this was his "last chance." That he planned to stay in Topeka for two seasons, then move on to the NBA.

That he'd learned his lesson.

"Topeka's not so bad," he'd said upon his arrival in Kansas. "It's not like I have to spend my entire life here. From what I hear, the scouts aren't worried about me on the court. All I've got to do is keep my nose clean, keep myself clean off the court."

And what, he wondered, would be so hard about that?

———

Out on the court, rookie guard Cedric Hunter talked with veteran swingman Ron Kellogg. The two had been teammates back at the University of Kansas. Nearby, another former Kansas teammate, second-year forward Calvin Thompson, was shooting jumpers while Chip Engelland, a second-year guard from Duke University, joked with Brian Rahilly, a center from the University of Tulsa. Other players milled about.

Lloyd quickly changed and took a seat on the sideline between Jo Jo White, the former all-star guard for the Boston Celtics, and Sizzlers coach John Killilea.

"Yo, what's up?" he said, pretending not to notice their concern.

Both gave him the once-over, then turned back to their conversation—discussing game strategies. It was just after 9 a.m. Practice was about to start.

There were drills, followed by a scrimmage with Lloyd at the point and White at off guard. It was a strange combination, the kid and the old man. Lloyd was twenty, without a grasp of the fragile situation he now was engulfed in, where one misstep could jeopardize his chances of reaching the NBA.

His new backcourt mate reeked of maturity, of refinement; the son of a St. Louis minister, youngest of seven. A man who understood the game within the game; had paid his dues and achieved his success, including two NBA titles and Olympic gold.

White had seen his career come and go, was back in basketball more as a teacher than a student. Lloyd was street. He wore sneakers and sweats and a blue leather jacket—"the real *jimson*," he called it; the real thing. White was gentrified. Topcoat, high-style suit; imported leather gloves, shoes. All the trappings. Top-shelf, the best.

White was forty-one, had been a first-round pick out of Kansas back when Lloyd was two. Lloyd had just six years on his eldest son. White had been a seven-time all-star with the Boston Celtics, had led them to NBA championships in 1974 and 1976.

He had come to Topeka not only to see if he could still play the game—a scenario that seemed somewhat of a guise, though he was still slender and graceful and his game still had its delicious moments—but also, it seemed, as part of the reclamation project whose ultimate goal was to save Lloyd from himself.

Bernie Glannon did not hide the fact that part of White's job description was to work with Lloyd, to be a steadying influence on him. To *babysit* him.

White went along with it partly because John Killilea—"Killer"—had been one of his coaches with the Celtics; because he thought he might want to coach, too.

"You've got to understand he never had to work for anything," White said of Lloyd in an aside just before practice began that morning. "People have always told him how good he is, how talented he is, and he believed that he could get by on that alone, rather than trying to develop and refine that skill. He doesn't understand the seriousness of what he has, of where he is. He wants to be something, but doesn't understand the price you have to pay to get there," he said, his voice serious. "Part of the reason I'm here is to help him understand the price he has to pay."

The two seemed to work well together. Lloyd made a sound pass; White offered a word of encouragement. Swee'pea slacked off, got sloppy; Jo Jo busted on him, *scolded* him, then took a moment to offer a friendly word of advice. Lloyd respected his new mentor. He knew what he was, knew where he'd been. He knew why he was there.

"Jo Jo's my man," Lloyd said. "Jo Jo wants to see me make it."

But the questions remained: could White be a significant factor in the battle to spark Lloyd toward success; could he really make Lloyd understand what it took?

Results had been favorable. White stuck around after practice, shooting, running drills. Eventually Lloyd got the hint and began to stay late, too. White taught him the tricks of the trade, veteran moves; skills acquired during a twelve-year NBA career—a surgeon teaching the intern a bevy of intricate new operating techniques.

Lloyd seemed to hang on his every word. *Sometimes.* He'd worked harder than he had ever worked before, sure. But despite White's best efforts, Lloyd still had a tendency to slack off. He still didn't hit the weights as often as he should, still didn't run as often as he should. He rarely attended his aftercare program at Memorial Hospital.

And sometimes, just coming down the court during practice it was apparent he didn't push himself as hard as some of his teammates. "The trouble with him is he's kid-minded," White said of his charge, the start of the season just around the corner. "He's as green as the god-damned grass in Kansas."

———

Willie Glass stripped the ball, broke loose from the crowd, raced down court. The swingman, known as "Hollywood" back on the 1984–85 NCAA Final Four team at St. John's University, had just been cut by the Los Angeles Lakers, his problem an all-too-common one. He had talent, but he was six-foot-five. And undersize swingmen who can't handle the ball and who can't shoot it from downtown don't cut it in the NBA. So Glass found himself in Topeka. A place, he knew, that was the court of last resort.

"I've got to give it my best shot," he'd said. It was all he had left.

As he ran down the left wing, Hollywood made sure that desire was known. There was fury in his action, venom in his eyes, as he leaped at the foul line, soared skyward. As he reached the basket, arms outstretched, he sent a thunderous two-handed tomahawk dunk crashing down over the head of Jerome Batiste. It was raw hunger, the actions of a man in desperate want of a job; in desperate *need* of a job. A man who knew that only a last-ditch effort in this, his final preseason scrimmage, could save him from being released by late afternoon. From seeing his dream die a tortured death.

While Glass fought hard against the odds, in the background Lloyd trotted down court at half speed, as if not to care one way or the other, drawing icy stares from John Killilea. As the scrimmage continued on around him, the trot turned into a noticeable limp. Moments later, as Glass and the others living on the edge of basketball oblivion sweated it out, Lloyd stopped altogether, walked off the court, grabbed an ice pack, and pulled up a seat—as if to inform the staff he was seriously done for the day.

It was 10 a.m. Practice was less than an hour old.

"What's wrong now, *Youngblood*?" Killilea shouted, his voice colored with a hint of disdain and contempt. This was an act he'd seen too many times; he'd grown tired of the kid stuff. Lloyd looked at Killer, winced. He looked wounded by his words.

No faith, coach? No trust?

"Hurt my knee yesterday liftin' weights," Swee'pea explained, sounding as if he might *never* be able to *ever* practice again. "Can't run no more."

"Too bad, Youngblood," Killilea said flatly. "Final cuts are today."

He shook his head in sympathy. Like he was paying last respects. Lloyd stared him down for a moment. *Seriously?* Then, you could see it: the lightbulb going off. No sense taking a chance, he thought. He really did want to make the team, no matter how he'd acted; no matter how childish his cry for attention. Lloyd dropped the ice pack, the towel, and ran back onto the court, his limp suddenly, *miraculously*, cured.

Killilea looked heavenward for an answer to the riddle of the sphinx. None came. Across court, assistant general manager Bruce Carnahan let out a laugh. He explained to a bystander how this had become an all-too-familiar occurrence at practice.

"Oh, he's hurt, all right," Carnahan said in a mock-serious tone. "He slept on his knee wrong last night and his *brains* drained out through his ears."

The scrimmage went on. Lloyd was just being Lloyd.

It was lunchtime and most of the players had scattered in search of food and a brief respite from the morning practice when Lloyd, dressed in gray sweats, red-striped Avias, a red Sizzlers jacket, and a CBS hat, reached the outer offices. It was the final day of double work-outs and, by the time lunch was done, Killilea would have his decision on who was going and who would remain. Lloyd appeared worried, the incident from the morning session fresh in his mind. Then he saw Al "Quake" Quakenbush, the beat reporter from the *Topeka Capital-Journal,* standing in the hall near the exit. He stopped cold.

"What you think?" Lloyd asked Quake, insecurity in his voice. "Think I'll get cut?" Quakenbush seemed taken aback. "No, Lloyd. I think you're going to make it."

"How you know?" Lloyd asked.

"Why, you worried, Lloyd?" He looked it, Quake thought, even if he was trying hard to act complacent. "I don't think you should be worried, Lloyd."

Lloyd stared at Quake. "Who *you* been talkin' to?"

"Go to lunch, Lloyd," Quake said. "You're safe."

Lloyd shrugged, then walked out the door. Quake shook his head. Like most here in the heartland of America, it was obvious he didn't know what to make of him.

Down the hall, Bernie Glannon pushed back into his chair. "You know," he said, "Lloyd is the backbone of our team and I've never, for what may be selfish reasons, denied that. But here we are making Lloyd live a life of responsibilities for the first time in his life. We don't just hand him a wad of money and be done with it."

Glannon was in late middle age, his hair silvered, face rutted, nose bulbous. He had a gentle but firm quality that suggested the time when

your father's father had become your grandfather; it was probably the
result of his having raised six children.

Glannon had allowed Lloyd to live in his house in Overland Park,
Kansas, before moving him into his own place in Topeka. He'd even arranged for his daughter, team office manager Kristi Gillam, to teach
Lloyd how to open his first checking account. It was Glannon who'd
found Lloyd an apartment in the complex where Killilea lived.

It also was Glannon, seeing Lloyd in a 1980 Mercury with rotting
floorboards, who'd arranged for him to use his own leased 1987 Ford
Taurus station wagon.

But Glannon also made it clear those courtesies came with a price.
He'd instilled values in his children, first among them respect for others. He demanded that if Lloyd used his car he be responsible for giving teammates a ride to and from practice. He demanded that if Lloyd
lived in his home he be treated like family, not as a guest. He'd held
Lloyd responsible for keeping his room clean. He'd held him responsible for locking doors, doing dishes, turning out the lights. So it figured
that, when Lloyd abused his privileges and Glannon received a phone
bill that included a call to New York for 101 minutes, he treated Lloyd
as if he were his son.

"I promptly handed him the bill," he said.

Not all of his actions were out of love. Part was good business.
After all, Glannon owned a professional team, was a businessman, one
who understood the value of a sound investment. A travel agent by
trade, he'd turned a modest stake of $25,000 into a small fortune—with
eleven offices nationwide—by the time he'd sold in 1984. And he understood that despite Lloyd's fragile state, with the right tact, the right
amount of effort, and a little bit of luck he might also prove a valuable
commodity—a player who could be a bona fide star, who could be his
best venture yet.

"But," Glannon said, "even though some of what we do is for selfish reasons, out of our interest for the ball team, I think Lloyd can see
the difference in what he has here. Here, Lloyd does not receive special
privileges. He is given his per diem like anyone else. Not first, not last.

But when he gets on the bus. Still, there is no question that I am more concerned where he is at all times of the day than I am with other players. I do call Lloyd several times a day, just to see what he is doing. But at lunchtime I don't go to the restaurant where many players hang out, to see if he is with nine girls or drinking four glasses of whiskey. And I don't go over to his apartment, walk in, and check around, looking in the cabinets and under counters. That isn't my job. I just like to make sure he is not hanging around somewhere and getting into trouble."

As then–CBA commissioner Mike Storen explained, "We're not a social center. We're not going to do this for Joe Smith, the slow, heavyset guard who can't play. The fact is that the owner of the Topeka franchise has taken an unbelievable personal interest in the case. He is damn near living with him. Sure, it is because he is such a good player. But he also understands that, left to his own devices, this kid might never bridge the gap between failure and success. Maybe it's the greater fool theory.

"Maybe it isn't."

When Killer walked out of his office after lunch, he appeared shaken. He'd just met with Willie Glass, told him to pack his bags. "Cutting him really bothered me," Killilea said. "He worked so hard. But he just didn't have the size and we just didn't have a spot for him here. He was just in the wrong place at the wrong time."

Down the hall Lloyd sat, waiting. Back from lunch, he was talking to the secretaries, killing time before afternoon practice. Killer spotted him.

"*Youngblood!*" Killilea called. "Step into my office."

Lloyd grimaced. "This is it," he said. "I'm cut." And down the hall he walked, ever so slow, looking much like a man headed toward his own execution.

John Killilea was a tough man, a slick Irish kid from Quincy, Massachusetts, who knew what from what. He wasn't the kind to let folks get over on him.

"I don't like to prejudge anybody," he'd said of Lloyd, early on. "But in the middle of our first conversation I had to stop him and say, 'Let's stop the street con, okay? Start talking straight.' It was like he was saying everything I wanted to hear. You could see him working for an angle. But after you've been around as long as I have, you can see through it. You almost start thinking three or four sentences ahead."

Though the meeting lasted little more than minutes, Killer used the time to explain about effort and hard work. He told Lloyd that, while he'd worked hard, he still needed to see more both on and off the court. He would no longer stand for moments like the one that had disrupted the morning session. He stressed the need for self-discipline. He had hope that, somehow, the message had gotten through.

"The thing I look for is abnormal behavior," he said. "Is he abnormally tired? Is he screwing things up in practice? Lloyd has not shown any of those signs. But still, I am concerned, because in Lloyd I see the possibility of self-destruction as well as the possibility of greatness. It is in his lap. But attaining success is more than just saying he is the master of his fate. He still has to learn how to be the master of his fate."

Despite the hard-line warning, Lloyd left all smiles. "I'm goin' to be here," he announced to the front-office workers. "See, that's 'cause I been workin' hard. I work hard, don't I?" he asked the receptionist. "I work harder than anybody, right?"

She just stared at him, incredulous. "Next to who?" she said.

Minutes later Lloyd was out on the court, shooting, when his teammates arrived back for afternoon practice. But he was hardly serious, limping, hopping on one foot. As he did, he fired jumpers from beyond three-point range. He hit five straight.

"Yo," he said to Cedric Hunter. "Bet you five bucks."

"You kiddin'?" Ced said.

"C'mon, bet you five bucks," he said to Ron Kellogg.

"You crazy, Lloyd?" Ronnie said. "I ain't betting you."

"Five bucks a shot, c'mon. Bet you," Lloyd said to Calvin Thompson, laughing. All the while, he fired shot after shot clean through the net— just like he had that first afternoon way back when at Andrew Jackson. Thompson pretended to ignore him. Still, Swee'pea went from teammate to teammate until he had gone through them all, no one willing to take the deal. Finally, he got bored—and went and sat down.

Practice went without a hitch. Lloyd played well, ran hard, did everything he could do to do the right thing. He distributed the ball to teammates, made shots, worked on defense. He made an effort. Even Killilea seemed impressed. Afterward there was a team meeting. The next morning the Sizzlers were scheduled to make the first trip of the season. As players packed their stuff, Lloyd came across a schedule card. He studied it a moment. "Look at this," he said. "By my name it says, 'School: Vegas, UNLV.' *Ha!* Check that out. Can you believe that, man?"

"Yeah," Thompson said, with a laugh. "Can you imagine Lloyd in school? Wouldn't *that* be funny? Just imagine, Lloyd Daniels in *Back to School.* Just like Rodney Dangerfield." He began to mimic Lloyd. Everyone in the locker room was in stitches, cutting on Lloyd. Laughing hard, now. "Pretty funny, isn't it?" Thompson said.

"Man," Lloyd said. "Me in *Back to School.* That's funny, man. Me and Rodney. I got that tape, *Back to School.* Man, can't you just see me?"

It was funny. And very sad.

———

About to start the first trip of the season—the kind of road trip teams take in a professional minor league: long and wearisome—Wednesday, November 18, began in the small hours of the morning for the Sizzlers. The team would bus from Topeka, catch a flight out of Kansas City, change planes in Denver, then fly to Casper, Wyoming. All for a game the following night against the Wyoming Wildcatters. From there it would be a six-hour bus ride Friday morning to Rapid City, South Dakota, for a game Saturday night against the Rapid City Thrillers. The following morning the itinerary would be reversed and late on November 24, a week after leaving Topeka, the Sizzlers would return home—three games into a grueling fifty-four-game regular season.

This was a new experience for Lloyd. He'd traveled before, trips to Las Vegas and Hawaii with the Gauchos. But he'd never traveled so much in such a short span.

He was first at the arena, an hour early. "Didn't want to be late," he said.

Apparently, the talk with Killer had had an effect. He'd even brought a paper, the *Cap-Journal*. The sports section had a page with the head shots and bios of each player. Lloyd saw his picture. Even if he couldn't read the type next to it, he knew what it meant.

"Why they pubbin' me?" he asked. "I ain't even played yet. I might ain't goin' to play. How 'bout that happens? You know, here I might don't start. I'm serious. You think I'll play? I say I might don't start. So if I ain't, why they pubbin' me?"

Publicity meant expectations and expectations meant scrutiny. Lloyd hardly liked scrutiny. Worse, there also was an article that quoted UNLV coach Jerry Tarkanian. As he'd said before, Tark said how Lloyd may be the best he'd ever seen. On the bus to the airport in Kansas City, those quotes were causing undue grief.

Teammates also got on Lloyd about the main focus of the article, which reiterated the allegations leveled in *Newsday* by Arnie Hershkowitz, Steve Cropper, Ricky Collier, and a host of others—all of whom alleged UNLV had committed NCAA violations when it had recruited him. Among the alleged violations were the illegal use of a car, as well as the providing of cash, clothes, and free meals at hotels in Las Vegas, not to mention the arrangement of jobs for both Lloyd and Steve Cropper. Detailed in the investigation was the guardianship arrangement with Mark Warkentien.

"How 'bout that motorcycle it says you got at UNLV?" a teammate asked.

"I didn't get no bike," Lloyd said. "They made that up."

"How 'bout them pots and pans and that used color TV it says you got?" asked another.

Lloyd fired back: "People talkin' shit."

"Yeah?" Ced said. "I don't think so. I think Tark loves you, man. I think Tark loves you so much he wants to *bone* you, make *love* to you." Everyone laughed.

Lloyd laughed, too, nervous. His teammates were merciless and he didn't really know how to respond. "Yeah," he said finally, self-conscious. "I *done* Tark."

Cedric laughed so hard, he nearly fell out of his seat.

The ironic thing was that, in a figurative sense, Lloyd had. The twenty-year-old with the third-grade reading level had bummed up Tark's multimillion-dollar basketball program. Big time. A month earlier, UNLV president Robert C. Maxson had announced that an in-house investigation had resulted in a report that included "conflicting testimony" from the parties involved in the incident. The investigation committee had recommended the matter be passed on to conference officials and the NCAA.

"I think anybody knowledgeable about basketball had to know that the NCAA was going to look into the recruitment of Mr. Daniels," Maxson said then.

Just two days after Maxson released the report, the NCAA informed UNLV it was doing just that. It was investigating. Tarkanian and Warkentien maintained the program was innocent of all allegations. The NCAA, as usual, refused direct comment.

But one administrator at UNLV said members of the school athletic department wondered whether the program would be forced to "close down because of the Lloyd Daniels Recruiting Violations Investigation by the NCAA. I have never in my life seen anything like this kid and his publicity. Not only does he make every paper from coast-to-coast for his ability and [his] coke bust, he now creates fury in the basketball department and the NCAA is out to get us." Only time would tell.

But now, as the laughter died down and the bus plowed onward, Lloyd stretched out across two seats and fell asleep. Later, he also slept on the plane.

Landing at Stapleton Airport in Denver, Killilea turned to Pat Ditzler, the team equipment manager, who'd been assigned to keep an eye on the oft-troubled rookie during the trip, and said, "Did you get Youngblood off the plane?"

"I went back and shook him awake," Ditz said.

"You know," Killer said, "we're going to have to take Youngblood by the hand the first couple of flights. Just to make sure he gets where he's going."

Killilea knew what he was up against.

During his career as an assistant coach with the Boston Celtics, Milwaukee Bucks, and the then–New Jersey Nets, Killer had seen more than a handful of players self-destruct, among them Norm Van Lier, John Lucas, and Micheal Ray Richardson. Richardson had become the first player "banned for life" by the NBA in February 1986, testing positive for cocaine use for the fourth time. "Sugar," as he was known, was now with the Albany Patroons in the CBA. Lucas, meanwhile, had undergone treatment and made his way back into the NBA with the Bucks. He'd organized a program to counsel players about dependency problems in conjunction with an aftercare program.

It was the strangest of coincidences that, walking through the airport terminal, Killilea should run smack into Terry Cummings and members of the Bucks.

Milwaukee, having faced the Denver Nuggets the previous night, was leaving town. The Sizzlers, bound for Casper, were passing through. As Killilea stopped to talk to a few old friends, Lucas, of all people, walked over. "Is the kid here?" he asked Killilea.

Killer nodded, pointed to Lloyd—and waved him over.

Lucas shook Swee'pea's hand and pulled him off to the side, and there, in the middle of a crowd racing to catch planes bound for who-knows-where, one recovering addict trying to recapture the luster of a faded career took a moment to advise a recovering addict with the future still ahead of him on how to avoid the pitfalls.

"You and I are in the same boat," Lucas told Lloyd. "I'm going on with my life. You can go on with yours. Lean on people. *Call me.* I have two years of sobriety. You have a month. But we're both just a day away. You have to take it day by day."

For ten minutes Lucas talked. For ten minutes, Lloyd listened.

"I needed help with drugs," he said. "I should admit that, 'cause I had a problem. I had a big drug problem. But now I'm realizin' that. I'm dealin' with it one day at a time. That's what John Lucas was talkin' to me about. He said, 'Just call me when you need someone to talk to. We'll talk.' He said he cared. I appreciate that. I really do."

As Lucas said as he headed off to catch the flight to Milwaukee, "If my ten-minute conversation can carry him for a week and somebody else can carry him for a week after that, then he may be able to accumulate recovery time. But I could talk to him until I was blue in the face. Until Lloyd Daniels is ready, nobody can make it work."

———————

Once John Lucas left, so did Lloyd. There was a two-hour layover between flights and, hearing there was major stock on the block—a huge selection of ladies, that is—Swee'pea and Ron Kellogg wandered off to scout the terminal, went off to work a variety of pickup lines on a variety of nondescript women. Moderately successful, they met a few, though most, either unsure of the men's intentions or merely appalled by their neanderthal approach—more often than not, "Hello," being: "Yo, babes, *wha's up*?"—simply walked on by, usually causing Lloyd to fall into a familiar response: calling out women in crude fashion.

Still, when the two finally returned to the gate a half hour before flight time, they were surprisingly a few names and phone numbers greater to the good.

And Lloyd and Ronnie were still laughing about that when an older gentleman walked over. "Excuse me," he asked in a distinct midwestern drawl, his words casting light on his naïveté, "but are you fellows some sort of athletic team?"

Ronnie and Lloyd looked bemused. Here were more than a half-dozen men, almost all of them in their twenties, none shorter than six foot five, save Cedric, who was a tad under six foot, standing around with carry bags that read "Sizzlers."

"Ah, yes sir," Kellogg said in his most polite voice, as he tried to suppress a quiet laugh. "We're basketball players. We play for the Topeka Sizzlers in the CBA."

The man looked at him. "CBA?" he said.

"Yeah," Lloyd said. "The *Crazy* Basketball Association."

The man smiled weakly. Everyone else laughed, Killer included. The laughter subsided moments later when it was announced that the flight was ready to board. John Harris, a rookie forward from Brooklyn, and Kevin Graham, a longtime minor-league player, had also gone to roam the terminal. Despite having been paged for the previous half hour, the two of them were still AWOL. Nowhere to be found.

Knowing a good teaching example when he saw one, Killilea decided to broadcast a policy statement. He announced that the pair would be left behind.

"Well," he said, glancing toward Lloyd in the process, "if they're not back by the time we're ready to leave I guess they'll just have to find their own way to Wyoming."

Lloyd chuckled, until he realized coach was serious. Until he realized that fines and suspensions also were possible consequences for missing a flight.

"Hey," Lloyd said to Ced and Ron Kellogg as he and his teammates walked across the tarmac toward the staircase leading to the ancient, propeller-driven DC-3 that would carry the team on to Casper. "Know what? John just cut himself. He missed the plane, man. I thought that'd be me, know what I'm sayin'? I thought that'd be *me*."

Harris and Graham showed up just before the doors closed and the staircase was removed. As they found their seats, even Lloyd breathed a sigh of relief.

Lloyd and Jerome Batiste were already seated when Jo Jo, Ron Kellogg, and Ced entered what passed for the hotel restaurant later that night in Casper. Interestingly enough, their orders had already been placed. Interesting, because neither was what you might call a speed-reader. Interesting, because when you really can't read and you order from a menu you really can't read, well . . . it's kind of disaster waiting to happen.

"Hey, what you guys order?" Kellogg asked.

"We got fish," Batiste said.

"What, like a filet?" Kellogg said.

"I don't know," Batiste said. "It's right here." He pointed to the menu to a spot where it read "Stuffed Rainbow Trout," and said: "The waiter said it's good."

Kellogg made a face. Just as he did, the waiter arrived at the table with two orders of trout. He placed one in front of Batiste, the other in front of Lloyd. Each looked at the other for a moment, stunned. The trout was whole. Head, tail, *eyes* included.

Lloyd shot Batiste a quick look, winked. His expression said: *Follow me, follow my lead.* Swee'pea then shot the waiter one, too. "Yo, man," he said, in all earnestness. "I didn't order this. I ordered steak. Didn't I order *steak*?"

The waiter, a fair-haired man in his twenties who, it was painfully obvious, had never been outside of rural Wyoming, much less been face-to-face with a seasoned veteran of the street con, seemed dumbfounded, *gob-smacked*. He checked, rechecked his order pad. "No, sir," he said. "You both ordered the rainbow trout. See?"

"No," Lloyd answered, polite but certain. "I think we both ordered steak. *Right, Batman?* Didn't you order steak? I *heard* you order steak. I ordered steak, too."

Batiste nodded in agreement, as Ronnie and Ced laughed under their breath. Again the waiter checked the pad. "No, sir. I think you ordered the trout," he said.

Knowing a dead end when he saw one, Swee'pea switched gears. "Oh, but man," he said, on the fly. "I just remembered I'm allergic to fish. Yeah, I'm allergic. Ain't I allergic, Batman?" Knowing when to keep his mouth shut, Batiste again nodded.

"See, man, that's why I couldn't have ordered no fish. See, I forgot. I'm allergic. Sorry, but I can't eat no fish. I'm real sorry. But I know you'll do right by me and my man here and bring us the steak. I'm real sorry 'bout that, but I can't eat no fish.

"I *just* remembered."

With that the waiter, flustered and blushing over his "mistake," as well as over the stares he was beginning to draw from the other diners and waiters, agreed to return the trout and bring out two steaks. Before he left, and as Ronnie and Ced seemed about to burst out laughing, the waiter stopped. He apologized for the inconvenience.

As he walked off, Lloyd turned to Batman.

"Damn," he said. "No way I was goin' to eat *that*."

"Me neither," Batiste said. "That thing had *eyes*."

"Know what?" Lloyd said. "I think yours was still alive, man. I thought I see the tail move, right on the plate. I thought I seen the tail *move*."

There was laughter all around.

Later, long after the waiter had returned with two fine sirloin steaks for Lloyd and Batman, White, who'd been reserved and introspective throughout the meal, began to talk about his time in the NBA. Seeing what had happened, he wanted to make a point about education and, knowing the players respected what he'd done in pro ball, figured they just might listen. He spoke about intelligence, about how some people have nothing else going for them except ball. He talked about the need to listen. And learn.

"You know," White said, lapsing into street talk to drive his point home, "some boys that's playing ball got an IQ so low that, lose one point and they's a *rock*."

Cedric laughed. So did Lloyd and Batman. Ron Kellogg looked on, intent.

"They can't read nothing," White said. "They can't get by off the court. They don't know how to handle things. Without a ball, they're lost."

The message was aimed square at Lloyd. But soon Kellogg, who was thoughtful and polite though hardly book-smart, told Jo Jo he knew just what he meant.

Ronnie had gone to Kansas, like Hunter and White.

"I'm not the world's best reader," he said. "In fact, in college one time we had to go around to the local grammar schools and talk to the kids. Remember, Ced? I went to one class, first grade, and I had to read a book. It was hard. I got to a word I didn't know—I don't know, it was *vomitizing* or some shit—and I didn't want to be embarrassed, so I looked at a kid in the front row and said, 'Now, I know it's a hard one, but let's see if you know that word,' and he told me. I was like, '*Whew,* got through that one.'

"I had to read to three classes. So, each time, I read the same book. By this third class I had it down cold." No one at the table, least of all Jo Jo, said a word.

It was only after the table had cleared and everyone had gone back to their rooms that Lloyd began to talk about his situation, though he was not eager to do so.

For all of his smoothness in conversation, all of his good-natured humor, his laughter, and his curious and inquisitive nature, Lloyd was a notorious introvert when the conversation turned to him. He didn't like to talk about himself, his background, or the events of his life. For years, he'd kept from even his closest friends details about how his mother had died, details about all but the simplest aspects of his past. Ask him a question he didn't like and he would just as soon quit talking. Stand up, leave.

That world was all he owned. It was a treasured possession, maybe his most. And he wasn't, if he could avoid it, willing to share it with just anyone.

"People," he said, after some hesitation, "they don't know for real about my life. They don't know my life right now is great. They don't know that now my life is smooth. They don't know I'm not gettin' over on that fast life no more. Yeah, I messed up a whole bunch of times. I messed up in Vegas, fucked up *good,* messed up some people. But I think I'm doin' fine right now. I got a real good opportunity here. I met a lot of people in Topeka who want to see a kid like me make it. I'm goin' to get myself right."

Almost under his breath, he added: "*I am.*"

His voice, usually so smooth, had begun to falter. He stumbled over his words, caught himself. Stopped himself, dead in his tracks. He started again, but a tear welled in the corner of his eye. He fought it. Only after a bit did he continue on.

"All the shit they's talkin' is nothin'," he said. "The only one I let down was myself, understand? I had my chance. I didn't do what I was supposed to have did. But I can't feel sorry now. In rehab," he said, "I was in real tough condition. Ten weeks, I couldn't even touch a basketball. That's because goin' through those weeks in there, I couldn't worry 'bout no basketball. I had to worry 'bout gettin' straight. It was tough. You got temptation everywhere. You got to learn to fight it.

"But if you want to get high, you'll get high. In New York City or even in Topeka, if you want to get high, you're goin' to get high. Especially in a small town like Topeka. Everybody knows where you can get it. If you want it, you'll know how to get it.

"You know who got it. Simple."

Just one week before, Clyde Thompson, the twenty-five-year-old brother of Calvin Thompson, had been shot outside a social club down on Sixth Street in Topeka. Everyone had heard about the funeral and that police were checking into alleged drug connections in an attempt to find a motive. Somehow, though, that didn't seem to be what this was about. It was something else. Something more personal, closer to home. Lloyd pushed himself back from the table; raised himself from the chair.

"We'll talk later," he said. Then he walked out.

"The crux of his entire situation," Killilea said over a casual lunch the next afternoon at the Casper Hilton, "is responsibility. What he has to do now is take responsibility for his own actions. What we are trying to do here is to teach him through association. When a person comes out of rehab and goes back into the same environment he was in, it is difficult to keep that situation from happening again. But here, if Lloyd can learn by example and absorb maybe just ten percent of what he sees going on around him, he can improve his situation and take control of his life. And, if he can learn to take control of his life, he has a chance to succeed."

Killilea sounded doubtful that it would be as simple as he'd made it sound. Perhaps it was his own skepticism; perhaps it was just that others—former Houston Rockets teammates Lewis Lloyd and Mitchell Wiggins, suspended from the NBA for drug violations, among them—had failed when faced with a similar shot at success.

"As far as I'm concerned, Lloyd Daniels is a great talent who has got to learn a lot about things going on in the real world," Killilea said. "He has lived in a basketball world almost all of his life, where he was able to get what he wanted and do what he wanted because of that talent. But he's in the real world right now. Here you either adjust to things or you fall by the wayside.

"In the NBA they have the three-strike rule. I hate like hell to say this is it for him, that if he doesn't do it now his life is ruined. If he were to falter, you would hope he could get it together enough so he had something else going for him, maybe not just be a basketball player. But what else does he know at this stage? He has some study habits. He has some social skills. But his interest right now is basketball. Basketball and hanging out on the corner. The harshest thing for Lewis Lloyd and Mitch Wiggins, two better-than-average pro players, was to be put on the street for two years. The point is, you can deny your problems and deny them, but everybody has to know that, if those problems don't get solved, no matter who you are, eventually the roof has to fall in.

"I saw an end result with Sugar. And so you say, 'How many times can someone start over?' After a while, your skepticism grows and grows and grows."

An hour later, Swee'pea walked into the hotel gift shop, grabbed a deck of playing cards, dropped $2 on the counter, and turned to walk out. Told the bill was $2.97, not $2, he turned back to the cashier, pointed to an acquaintance standing near the counter, talking, and said: "*He's* got it." Then he left. So much for responsibility.

The Casper Events Center was located on a low, barren hill. You could see it from the hotel lobby. Around midmorning the team bused over to the arena for a walk-through. Stuck without a return ride to the hotel after practice, players were forced to scramble down the steep talus slopes of the hill for a mile-long walk back.

Along the way Lloyd, who had not played a game of organized basketball in the year since he'd appeared in those two games at Mount
San Antonio, was asked what the first game of the season would bring.
"It ain't no big deal," he said, trying to hide his apprehension. "Ain't no
big deal at all. I can't be worried. It's just another game."

Nightfall brought with it a different attitude. Almost five thousand
fans packed the arena before game time, interesting since this hardly
seemed to be basketball country. Casper, after all, was an oil boom
town gone bust. The team, known as the Wildcatters, was even named
for oilmen. Here real folks watched rodeo.

The University of Wyoming nicknamed its teams the Cowboys. License plates were all adorned with a bucking bronco ridden by a cowboy. Even the Events Center was built for cowboys and indoor rodeo,
with basketball as an afterthought—even if the university had created real interest in the sport by reaching the 1986 National Invitation
Tournament championship game, led by Fennis Dembo. It was almost
odd, then, that a large number in the crowd seemed to know of Lloyd.
When warm-ups began those people started to get on him. Bunches of
fans showered him with obscenities.

"You're nothing, Lloyd!" one screamed. "You're a fucking jerk!" A
majority of the comments, in fact, were of the four-letter variety, replete with the usual choice accusations. Though his teammates soon
began to take notice, Lloyd tried not to let the catcalls bother him.

But it was apparent they did.

As Lloyd walked to the bench, one man let loose a vicious barrage.
Lloyd glared at him. "Don't understand?" the man yelled. "Read my
lips . . . *if you can.*"

On the public address system, music blared. First, "The Boy from
New York City." And then "Another One Bites the Dust" by Queen. As
Ron Kellogg said afterward, "It seemed like they were trying to tell him
something." He'd said as much to Lloyd, the two of them on the bench
there, telling him, "You better listen to them songs."

Lloyd started the game, but he started slow. With Topeka down,
5–0, he hit his first pro attempt, a jumper from the top of the key. Later,

with the Sizzlers behind, 9–4, he drew a foul on a nice lean-in move, making both free throws, much to the crowd's disappointment. Soon, though, it became apparent Lloyd was doing something he almost never did. He was forcing his game. Adding heavily to the problem was that his teammates didn't seem to understand his game. No matter what they did, no matter where they moved on the floor, they always seemed a step behind him. Part of it was that Lloyd lacked structure to what he did. He'd never really been part of a team, having played only about fifty games in high school and just two in college.

Part of it, though, was that he and his teammates had practiced the plays for the better part of a month and they were running them as if they were machines, following chalkboard diagrams to the letter, like a competition skater trying to trace a figure on the ice. All the while, Lloyd was going on instinct, reading the defense, understanding where his teammates should be if they really knew the game, knew it like he did.

He was passing the ball before they knew how to get there.

Once, he found Kevin Graham cutting backdoor along the baseline and hit him in the chest with a pass. It startled Graham—and the ball bounced off his hands, out of bounds.

Another time it was Kellogg who lost the handle on a nice feed, not realizing until too late that Lloyd had found him open. By the time the half was over, Lloyd should have had at least seven or eight assists, spectacular ones.

Instead he had three.

He had seen several fine passes go for naught, mishandled by teammates. He also had been burned several times on defense by a variety of players, ranging from the Wildcatters' star, Boot Bond, to A. J. Wynder, a rookie guard from Fairfield University. Worse, Lloyd had gone one-for-seven from the field. Topeka trailed, 72–57.

The second half began no better. Soon the Sizzlers were down twenty.

Then Killer switched White to the point and Lloyd to shooting guard. Suddenly the team came alive. Lloyd hit two straight shots to

cut the lead to fifteen and, though he received a delay-of-game warning for tapping the ball out of bounds after a basket—"a damn playground move," Killer called it later—and was called for a three-second
violation, he lifted his game. He played better defense, holding the two
men he switched off guarding without a basket for the remainder of
the contest. He hit five of six shots from the field. His two free throws
trimmed the deficit to 108–103 with 4:19 left.

Time winding down, the score tied, 114–114, the ball came to him.

Lloyd moved down on the wing, set, and fired a baseline jumper
from eighteen. There were twelve seconds left on the clock.

In another time, in another game, the shot would have gone. Would
have fallen the way it did back at Jackson in that game against Whitney.
This time, though, it was off the mark. It hit the rim, fell away. Wyoming won on a basket at the buzzer.

"He made mistakes that a young kid, a rookie, is going to make,"
Killilea said after the game. "The kind a kid with four years of college
would make. There were times he tried to force it. There was the tech,
when he put the ball in, then hit it—a playground thing. But, on the
whole, he did all right."

"I don't think he was very pleased with what he did," White said.
"He made some mistakes. But I told him that was to be expected. You
tuck it away, you learn from it."

"It was a lot of fun being back there after a year," Lloyd said as he
sat in the locker room, still draped in his uniform. "I wasn't never nervous, just happy to be out there again. I think I did all right, all right
for a rookie, a young guy. But I could play better, you know that. A
couple of times I came down, made mistakes. But I knew it would be
tough. I thought, a little tougher." He paused a second. "Damn. That
was a shot I was supposed to made. It wasn't no problem, though. I'll
get it back."

The unofficial count had Lloyd with eight assists. The official count
was not as impressive, though still not bad. The final result? Daniels,
Lloyd: twenty-two points, five assists, one steal, and just two turnovers.
Lloyd Daniels was now a pro.

A young Lloyd. (Family photo)

John Valenti and Ron Naclerio in 1990, the year *Swee'pea* was published.
(John Valenti)

John Valenti and Ron Naclerio, twenty-five years later. (John Valenti)

Lloyd and John.
(John Valenti)

Lloyd at Mt. Rushmore with
Sizzlers teammates Jean Batiste,
John Harris, and Kevin Graham.
(John Valenti)

Lloyd, John Valenti, John Killelea,
and Ron Kellogg at Mt. Rushmore,
November 1987. (John Valenti)

February 18, 1991

Mr. John Valenti III

Dear John:

Just a quick note to say thank you from the library at the
Naismith Memorial Basketball Hall of Fame. Your book,
"Swee'Pea and Other Playground Legends, Tales of Drugs,
Violence and Basketball" makes a great addition to our
library collection.

Playground ball sometimes gets overlooked in the history of
the game. Playing in the playground is the backbone of the
game of basketball. Without it, basketball would be nowhere
near as successful as it is today. Your book highlights the
tragedy of the playgrounds. I think people needed to hear
about the lost legends of the playgrounds, not just the
successful.

I thoroughly enjoyed reading you book. Congratulations on
opening my eyes on what really goes on in the playgrounds.
The book is going to be a big seller in our gift shop, as
well as a great addition to our library. Thanks again for
the donation.

Sincerely,

WAYNE PATTERSON
Research Specialist

c.c. Mr. Joe O'Brien
     Executive Director

Naismith Memorial · Basketball Hall of Fame
BOX 179 · 1150 W. COLUMBUS AVENUE · SPRINGFIELD, MASSACHUSETTS 01101-0179 · (413) 781-6500

Basketball Hall of Fame letter. (John Valenti)

DICK VITALE, INC.

Bradenton, Florida 34209

September 18, 1990

John A. Valenti III

Dear John:

Please use the following for your book:

> "This is an explicit description of youngsters
> chasing a dream, but going about it in the wrong
> manner. Life on the streets, "shooting the rock,"
> thinking this is the easy way to big bucks only to
> find themselves at a dead end. It is spelled out in
> dynamic form in this text."

Hope this is want you need. Take care.

Enthusiastically,

Dick

Dick Vitale

A note from legendary NCAA Basketball broadcaster Dick Vitale. (John Valenti)

Earl Manigault, the Goat. August 1986 at Rucker Playground, Harlem.
(Chris Gerlich, *Newsday*)

Ron Naclerio coaching Benjamin Cardozo, PSAL City championship game, 2015. (John Valenti)

Andrew Jackson High School coach Chuck Granby with Lloyd on the sidelines at the Martin Luther King Jr. Tournament, Nassau Coliseum, January 12, 1986. (Dave Pokress, *Newsday*)

Lloyd battling against Moses Scurry of Eli Whitney, November 21, 1985, at Andrew Jackson High School. Both Lloyd and Scurry were later recruited by UNLV. (Bill Davis, *Newsday*)

Lloyd surveying the court as Andrew Jackson faces Wyandanch in the Martin Luther King Jr. Tournament at Nassau Coliseum, Uniondale, NY, January 12, 1986. (Dave Pokress, *Newsday*)

Richie Adams, "the Animal." In jail, Rikers Island, July 1989.
(Dave Pokress, *Newsday*)

Karlton Hines at Gauchos Gym, Bronx, May 1993. (Jim Cummins, *Newsday*)

Kenny Anderson signing letter of intent to Georgia Tech. With mother, Joan Anderson, and Archbishop Molloy basketball coach Jack Curran. Briarwood, Queens, November 1989. (Phillip Davies, *Newsday*)

Kenny Anderson with the New Jersey Nets, driving past Patrick Ewing. At Meadowlands, April 1994. (Jim Cummins, *Newsday*)

John Salley at the Marcus
Garvey Park playground.
August 1989.
(Richard Lee, *Newsday*)

Mark Jackson playing for a charity
event. (V. Richard Haro, *Newsday*)

Mark Jackson with the New York Knicks,
1988–89 season. (V. Richard Haro, *Newsday*)

Tom Konchalski, high school recruiting expert. At Hunter College, Manhattan, March 1991. (Stan Honda, *Newsday*)

"Hersh." Arnie Hershkowitz, February 1989. (Ed Quinn, *Newsday*)

Benjamin Franklin basketball coach Stan Dinner at The Sports Page, February 1989. (Jim Cummins, *Newsday*)

Ernie Lorch, Riverside Church, December 1985. (Paul Bereswill, *Newsday*)

Lou d'Almeida at Gauchos Gym, Bronx, February 1987. (Tom Kitts, *Newsday*)

Lloyd filming a sneaker commercial for British Knights at the West Fourth Street basketball courts in New York City, July 1993. (Mitsu Yasukawa, *Newsday*)

Lloyd, with the San Antonio Spurs, shoots over Indiana Pacers forward Detlef Schrempf. (Wickedgood / dreamstime.com)

Lloyd's grandmother's house, where he was shot. Hollis, Queens, May 12, 1989.
(Daniel Sheehan, *Newsday*)

Back at the hotel bar, Lloyd, Ron Kellogg, and Ced were sitting around a table drinking Coronas when John Killilea walked in with Quake. Ced, a rookie, and Ronnie, in his second season, both saw Killilea and, almost at the same instant, each grabbed his beer bottle and slid it off the table and down into his lap—worried about making a bad impression on the coach, though both were of legal age and the team had no rules against drinking. Ronnie glanced at Lloyd, who both he and Ced knew probably should not have been drinking, but who hadn't moved, his Corona still on the table.

"Yo, man," Ronnie said. "It's coach."

"So?" Lloyd said.

"Your beer," Kellogg said, motioning with his eyes.

"Yo, be yo'self," Lloyd said. "He knows what's goin' on. You don't have to do that. The man ain't dumb. He knows. Why try to hide? Why not just sit tight?"

With that, Lloyd turned to Killer and Quake, who were moving toward the bar. "Yo, coach," he called out. "How you doin'?"

Killer nodded in acknowledgment and Quake said hello, as Ronnie and Ced just sat there, dumbstruck. Ronnie kept telling Lloyd, "I can't believe you did that. I can't believe you did that," until the shock wore off—and the trio turned their attentions elsewhere. At first, the discussion was about the game. Soon conversation turned to women in the bar. The place was loud and it was packed. A few women were at an adjacent table. Lloyd, Ronnie, and Ced threw out a few lines, some of them true.

It didn't hurt when they mentioned they were ballplayers.

Before long, a couple of girls came over. Lloyd and Ronnie took two and hit the dance floor, but got blown off. Ced had gone to the bar, met two women, and he was talking the talk when Lloyd and Ronnie walked over. One of the women said she was the girlfriend of one of the 'Catters. Ced looked impressed. Lloyd just reached over, took his hand, and palmed her ass. For a moment she looked surprised. Then she smiled.

"Like that, uh?" she said. He nodded.

Lloyd turned to his acquaintance from the gift shop. "Just watch how black boys operate," he said. Being a pro player was about to pay its first real dividends.

Moments later, the two girls and a friend were escorted to their car by the trio. They had to go down the road to another bar and collect a few friends, they said. They promised to come back in five minutes for a party in one of the rooms. A half hour later, Ronnie, Ced, and Lloyd were still sitting in the hotel lobby, waiting.

At around three o'clock, the three of them headed upstairs. Alone.

Wyoming is a desolate place, as places go near the end of the earth, which is what the world here seemed to a bunch of basketball players—most from the inner cities of America—at eight o'clock in the morning on a bus headed across the grasslands from Casper to Rapid City. There is little to see in central eastern Wyoming. The Rockies—with the Teton, Wind River, Salt River, and Absaroka ranges—lie almost due west, well past Hell's Half-Acre and near the Idaho border, their ridges snow covered and hostile by mid- to late November. The state's northwest corner is home to Yellowstone and Old Faithful and north, a stretch beyond Hole-in-the-Wall near Sheridan, the Bighorn Mountains rise to meet the forever-blue skies of Montana. South toward McFadden, Rock River, and Laramie, where the University of Wyoming is located, the Medicine Bows climb toward northern Colorado and into Roosevelt National Forest and Rocky Mountain National Park. But here, headed northeast along Routes 387 and 450 toward the Black Hills of South Dakota, there was nothing save a few hundred miles of golden brown scrub flats; something like a six-hour bus ride worth of them, to be exact.

Much of it was across the Thunder Basin National Grassland—a godforsaken place of indeterminable beauty, once home to the Sioux and the Crow, now home only to endless, tireless rolling hills, ceaseless winds and, at last count, one dead tree.

This was wilderness. Barren, harsh despite moderate fall tempera-tures in the mid-sixties. This was isolation. About as much isolation as a man could stand.

Few of the players paid attention to the view out the bus windows, most opting to catch a few winks. Some stretched out across two seats. Lloyd, who'd used part of his $22 per diem to grab a packaged breakfast at the hotel restaurant, sat back and ate his meal in silence—staring out the window like he was staring at the moon.

"We ain't in the middle of nowhere I want to be," he said, finally, be-fore he went and dozed off, not quite realizing he was here of his own doing.

Teammate Chip Engelland had been watching Lloyd, had been as-sessing him. He was fascinated with Lloyd's ability and skill, was fasci-nated with his game.

Was fascinated with him.

"I heard he had an amazing amount of tools," Engelland said as the bus from the Jackrabbit Lines rolled along Route 450. "It was just stuff I had seen, read. Just squibs in the papers, old basketball folklore. But I tell you, he is amazing. Magic Johnson can learn things about the game from him. From free-throw line to free-throw line, his vision is unbe-lievable. You can see it. He is at home on a basketball court.

"It is in his blood. It's where he lives."

A Duke graduate and an astute observer, the veteran guard harbored no illusions of a career in the NBA. When you go undrafted, make the Sizzlers as a free agent, you come to certain realizations. To Engelland, life in the CBA was an interesting proposition, nothing more. He didn't associate much with Lloyd, other than to trade a passing hello or an oc-casional joke, though he sometimes worked with him in practice.

Still, it wasn't like the two were ever going to be friends.

Engelland was still talking about Swee'pea as the bus turned off the road at the Clareton Post Office, an old weather-beaten shack of a place with a bathroom, a sometimes-working soda machine, and a half handful of tired, lonesome employees whose most frequent visi-tors were always no more than just passing through.

Stepping off, most of the players took a break. Engelland talked.

"Let's face it, this is a major step for him. Being a point guard in pro basketball is like being a rookie quarterback in the NFL. You have a lot to learn. He lacks experience. Right now, he is just making it on his natural skills. But the ones with super talent can make those leaps and not get swallowed up. When he walks on the court, he's the best. Whether it is on a playground in New York City, with ten NBA vets, or in the CBA.

"What he has to understand is that, while he is comfortable now, while he has received some benefits that other people haven't received, you do not get pampered in the CBA," Engelland said. "Believe me, this isn't a pampering league. This isn't no AAU. He is not going to be anonymous in Topeka. People will recognize him and that will put pressure on him. But he has to deal with that. No one is going to be concerned with how he spends his money or if he is eating three square meals a day. He is a professional now. . . . Consider this his education."

Lloyd was working on his education when the bus next stopped again, this time about an hour later, for a lunch break at the Mount Rushmore National Memorial. He took one look at the four faces carved into the mountain and shot a look at Killer.

"Yo, coach," he said. "*Who's* the guy with the beard?"

"Lincoln," Killilea said.

It had been Killer's idea to stop at Mount Rushmore. Most of the guys had fought him on it. Wasted time, they'd said. And as the bus driver turned off the highway north of the Crazy Horse Memorial—which, also carved into a mountain, depicted the infamous Lakota warrior on horseback, pointing off into the distance—even Jo Jo White had voiced his displeasure, yelling: "We don't want to see no fucking mountain."

Engelland, Ditzler, and Killilea had all cringed as a half dozen teammates took up the chorus. Then the bus rounded a bend on the winding road leading to Rushmore and the presidents, faces deep-cut into the rock walls, appeared. The bus went silent.

Players pressed noses against windows.

"Yo, check that out," Lloyd said, turning to his teammates, who all seemed in awe of the moment. Then, he said: "Ain't one of them guys on the dollar bill?"

Washington, Jefferson, Roosevelt, Lincoln. Badlands, grasslands. Crazy Horse, Crazy Basketball Association. All of it; none of it. It was hard to tell just what Lloyd had taken in, was taking in, as he stepped up to the register later inside the cafeteria-style restaurant at Mount Rushmore and bought his meal. The bill came to $3.13.

Lloyd handed the cashier a twenty.

Glancing at the acquaintance from the hotel gift shop, the one he'd stiffed at the register the night before, he pocketed the bills—and left the change. The acquaintance was next in line. With a nod, Lloyd said to him: "There's what I owe you, man."

Later, back on the bus, Lloyd tried to explain just what was going on. Some of it felt like honesty, some like subterfuge. A bunch of it was just all over the place.

"Before, other people was helpin' me through things," he said. "Now I'm on my own. Ain't no one payin' the bills. I pay the bills. I pay the rent. I pay the telephone bill. I'm bein' the man, the way it's supposed to be. Hear me? No one is helpin' me."

He pointed to his coat, a black leather jacket. "See this coat?" he said. "Bought this coat with my own money, I did. No one else bought it. *Me. I'm* workin' hard. *I'm* doin' what *I* got to do. *I* buy my own food. If *I* spend all my money, *I* don't eat. *I* go hungry. If *I* fall, *I* fall. No one else. That's the way it is in the real world, right?"

It all sounded so, well . . . It all sounded so promising.

———

The guys from the Topeka Sizzlers were looking down from the upper deck of the Rushmore Plaza Civic Center as the announcement was made over the public address system. The Rapid City Thrillers were in the process of getting drilled by the Wyoming Wildcatters, but the announcer was focused on other things, on the future.

"Tomorrow night," he said, with the zeal of a carnival barker, "come see the *great Jo Jo White*, the former *seven-time* NBA all-star with the *Boston Celtics*, and, also, *Lloyd Daniels*, the *only* player in the *history* of the CBA *never* to have played in college *or* the NBA."

As the words echoed throughout the arena, Lloyd stared hard at the floor, then hunched down in his seat—as if a thousand sets of eyes suddenly were on him.

"Damn," he mumbled. "Damn."

All Lloyd ever wanted to do was fit in, be just another man in a basketball league doing what he loved to do. But even here, almost two thousand miles from New York, in a metropolis perhaps just two miles square with just two main roads and a population of little more than fifty thousand, Lloyd couldn't find himself a safe retreat.

Even here, folks knew his reputation. Even here, folks knew his past. Even here, in the middle of absolutely nowhere, folks who didn't know him in the least but who acted like they'd known him all his life, were talking about him like some sideshow carnival act. Like some oddity. Like the freak show back in Coney Island.

Lloyd turned to Jo Jo. "Why can't them people just leave me alone?"

Jo Jo White, who knew this world inside and out, who knew it better than anyone else on the team, fumbled up an explanation, that hardly seemed adequate.

So inadequate, actually, that it made the walk from the arena back to the Hotel Alex Johnson feel longer—much longer—than the few short blocks it was down Mount Rushmore Road to Main Street. The night air was brisk. And walking under the stars, in the middle of a universe with no smog and no disturbances, just radiant light and cold, clean air, seemed so peaceful.

And yet White couldn't get his mind off Lloyd, off what had happened back at the arena. Off his feeble answer; off any of it and all of it and none of it, at all.

Within a week, citing his age and his poor performances, Jo Jo White would again retire, just five games into his comeback. But as he walked toward the hotel that night, it was all about Lloyd. "His problem," he said, "is that his attention span is not that long right now. His attitude is good, but you don't know how he'll react when things start getting tough. He is the kind of kid who will go right along with what's going on and so, while he's learning responsibility, at this point it may already be a little too late.

"I think people are being so careful with him because they realize that if he breaks a leg right now, what does he have? *Zero.* They understand he must get his life together off the court. If you have your life together off the floor, you will have it together on the floor. I don't pull no punches. But I'm not going to beat him over the head with advice. I told him once, point-blank, what he has to do. The rest is up to him.

"Right now," he said, "I'm just trying to put time in with him because maybe I recognize things he might not recognize. He has a chance to do something extraordinary with his life, but he also has the chance to end up with zero. There is a game on the court and a game outside. The game outside is the real world; the game of life.

"What he has to learn now is he has to master both."

When he reached the hotel, White went for the elevator. There was a game the next night. All this travel had taken its toll. He wasn't so young anymore; he needed his rest. Near the side lobby was the bar. As White walked past, he spotted Lloyd.

He was inside, drinking Guinness Stout.

Lloyd had been out late. But it was still just 10:30 a.m. Saturday when he knocked on the hotel room door. "Hear about Rod?" he asked an acquaintance.

The *Rapid City Journal* had a short in the morning edition about Rod Strickland, who'd been Lloyd's teammate on both the Gauchos and at Oak Hill. Strickland, now at DePaul, had been ruled ineligible due to academic problems, the article reported.

"How'd that happen?" Lloyd said, shocked. "Why'd he get ineligible?"

Responsibilities, he was told. Strickland hadn't been responsible. He'd missed class, hadn't done well in school. He'd forgotten the lessons he'd claimed to have learned back in Mouth of Wilson. And besides, the world wasn't just about basketball.

There was more to it than that. Much more.

The conversation lasted about fifteen minutes. When it was done, Lloyd swore he understood. Really, truly, understood.

"That's why you got to work hard, right?" he said. "That's why I'm takin' it one day at a time. Know what I mean?"

It was just about two hours later, after a brief walk-through in the arena, that Cedric, Ron Kellogg, and Calvin Thompson started talking about trade rumors as they hung out outside the Civic Center. The Thrillers had just acquired Sean Couch, a former guard from Columbia, who'd earlier been cut by the Indiana Pacers.

Despite having come out of the Ivy League, Couch was a terrific guard. Both book-smart and street-smart, he'd gotten an education both in the classrooms of Morningside Heights and on the playgrounds of Harlem, where his father, Jim, ran a club team called Dyckman. A season later, Couch, who knew Lloyd through club ball back in New York, would last until the final cut on the Knicks—almost making a team that already had two first-round draft picks at point guard in Mark Jackson and Rod Strickland. Here, in Rapid City, someone was going to get cut to make room on the roster for him.

"They've got to make a move," Ronnie said.

Ced suggested one, but Ronnie shook his head. Cal said something, but Ronnie and Ced continued to mull the options.

Lloyd listened, taking it all in.

"Ron," he said, finally, "mean the guys who start the season ain't the ones who get to finish it? Mean you can get *traded*?"

Calvin Thompson laughed. So did Cedric and Ronnie Kellogg. Engelland almost fell over where he sat, pushed hard against the building. "*Mean you can get traded?*" Ced said, mocking the thought. Mocking Lloyd. "*Mean you can get traded?*"

Lloyd stared at them. At all of them. "Well, I don't care if they did got rid of me," he said, finally, amid all the laughter. "I'd just go home."

"I think it's really tough for him," Ronnie said afterward, as he and Cedric, who were both from Omaha, watched the Oklahoma-Nebraska football game upstairs in their hotel room. "Everyone expects so much from him, everyone is watching him. There has been so much publicity over what has happened to him. He has to realize people are just waiting for him to screw up. Waiting for him to go bad. But he also has to realize that he has a lot of people looking out for him, a lot of people who care.

"The problem is you can't really tell what he's thinking, what he's feeling. You can't really tell if he is just saying things to keep people happy or if he really believes it. I don't know. I don't think he knows. I hate to say this, but if he fucks up this time he is going to end up right back where he started, on the street. And I would hate to see that, because the boy has so much talent and you know what happens to folks on the street. He just needs maturity. I care a lot for the kid. It is tough, what he's been through.

"You hope it doesn't happen again, but it is up to him."

As Ced said, "I don't think anybody on this team is going to be his babysitter. You can't say, 'Lloyd, come with me' all the time. He's a grown man. He has to be making his own decisions sometimes. He knows what he should be doing and what he shouldn't be doing; it's just a question of him doing it. He's got to learn to help himself."

That night, Lloyd missed a twenty-five-footer at the buzzer. Fortunately it was only the first-quarter buzzer and Topeka still held an easy lead, 35–25.

It'd also been one of Lloyd's few unsuccessful moments. His blind bounce pass to Batman had handed the Sizzlers a 12–9 lead. His basket and two free throws had extended the advantage to 20–11. His feed to Cal Thompson on a drive had been a sight to see, simple yet splendid; better, it'd kept Topeka in control at 25–20. His off-balance jumper off a pass from Jo Jo White had made it 35–22 before he'd missed the buzzer shot.

The most important thing was that he was comfortable. His performance wasn't restricted by a lack of surety, as it had been the first game. Sure, Lloyd was in want of knowledge on how to work the system. He'd struggled, at times badly, on defense. He'd misread a sideline signal, called time-out at midcourt—when all Killilea wanted was for him to switch guard positions with Jo Jo. He'd forced a couple of shots late, when he tried to do too much down the stretch, drawing criticism from Killer.

But mostly, it seemed, Lloyd had played with confidence.

It was with confidence that he took a pass, spun twice off a defender, and, at the halftime buzzer, hit a jumper from the top of the key to give the Sizzlers a 66–39 lead. It was with confidence that Lloyd easily outclassed the opposing guards—blocking former UCLA guard Montel Hatcher; drawing fouls on Brent Timm, who'd attended Eastern New Mexico, and Darrin Houston, who'd played his ball at Oregon State—all of whom, he knew in his heart, he was better than, despite his lack of experience.

And, after some advice from Killer—"You're forcing shots and you don't have to. You're not alone. You're not alone," Killelea had yelled from the sideline during the fourth—it was with confidence that Lloyd distributed the ball in his special fashion. An over-the-shoulder, no-look pass to Thompson for a lay-in; a behind-the-back pass to Graham for a dunk. All of it on unrefined potential. Like back in the park.

When it was over and Topeka had won, 119–102, Lloyd settled into his locker, feeling for the first time like a member of the club. A real member. In two games, he'd averaged 18.5 points, 6 assists, and 1.5 turnovers. By the time the Sizzlers made their way back to Topeka, Swee'pea would find himself a star on the rise in the CBA.

Imagine what the kid could do when he learned the game.

12

Goodbye, Topeka

Lloyd never seemed to learn from his mistakes. He'd hint at progress, flash glimpses of maturity. Then, with suddenness he'd revert to his old ways.

Unwilling to fight through hard times, he always looked for the easiest way out, clean or otherwise. It happened on the court, where he was brilliant one game, a nonfactor the next, blaming poor performances on injuries or on teammates, never on himself. It happened off court, where his personal life continually hinted at his lack of dedication. All of it raised skepticism over whether he'd ever reach his pro potential.

There was a span during the eight contests played between November 29 and December 20 when Lloyd led the Sizzlers in scoring six times, including three straight games, with highs in back-to-back contests against the Charleston (W. Va.) Gunners—as he outscored guard Kenny Patterson, the former DePaul star from Jamaica, Queens. There was the night he'd strafed the Mississippi Jets for thirty-nine points, which proved to be the second-highest single-game total that season for Topeka.

Those games made an impression on scouts, a good impression, and lent hope to the thought that, somehow, Lloyd might overcome his past and make it.

"He was phenomenal in the transition game," Peter Babcock, then–director of scouting for the Denver Nuggets, said after Lloyd left Mississippi burning, going 17-for-25 from the field in thirty-six minutes of a 140–119 win over the Jets. "They got him the ball in the open court and he either scored or found the open man every time."

But, as Al Menendez, then scouting for the New Jersey Nets, cautioned, "He still has to prove that he's reliable, that he can exist in the pro environment."

For his part, Lloyd felt he was giving a maximum effort. He tried to be on time for practice, tried to attend weight-training sessions. But as the season wore on, it became more and more apparent he still had problems and that they were only getting worse. Time and again, he stated, "Aftercare is more important than ball." Then, time and again, he failed to attend meetings, substituting phone calls for personal appearances.

"I wake up every day thinkin' 'bout the NBA," he said.

But, as Bernie Glannon said: "I don't think Lloyd's ambition is what it needs to be. The guy's plain lazy. When you say, 'Lloyd, you can be a million-dollar-a-year ballplayer or you can be dead in six months,' I don't think he comprehends.

"Lloyd thinks training is getting up to turn on the TV."

If the message was ever to get through, it figured to happen during the first week of January, when the Sizzlers traveled to Albany, New York, for games on consecutive nights against the Patroons. It was here that Lloyd, out of shape and making promises to "work harder," would come face-to-face with what might well be his future.

Micheal Ray Richardson was the best-known member of the Patroons. A four-time NBA all-star, Richardson had been NBA Comeback Player of the Year following the 1984–85 season, when he returned from his third stint in drug rehabilitation to average 20.1 points, 5.6 rebounds, and 8.2 assists in eighty-two games for the New Jersey Nets. But on February 25, 1986, Sugar Ray Richardson, who'd made it through the University of Montana despite being what some described as functionally illiterate, became the first player banned for life by the NBA for violating the league's antidrug rules.

After a tour with a team in Israel—the long-standing joke was that Richardson had gotten Israeli officials to spell it *Isreal*—and a brief stretch with the Long Island Knights in the United States Basketball League, Richardson was working on yet another comeback, with the Patroons. By all accounts, he was doing well, too.

Richardson would go on to lead Albany to the CBA title, averaging 13.9 points, 4.8 rebounds, and 3.1 assists and, on July 21, 1988, he'd even be granted reinstatement to the league by then–NBA commissioner David Stern—though he would instead opt to pursue his career with Bologna in the Italian Basketball Federation.

"He came here, paid his dues, and did everything we expected of him and more," Albany general manager Gary Holle said of Richardson, who, unlike Lloyd, had attended his aftercare program on a near-religious basis. As Richardson said back then: "If you stick with something, then things will work out in your favor."

Serious in his comeback attempt, Sugar put a hundred moves on Lloyd that night in January. Almost all of them worked. He breezed by Lloyd, made plays, handed the ball off, scored. It wasn't long before Killilea, incensed at the lack of effort, sent Swee'pea to the bench. Even Albany coach Bill Musselman, no stranger when it came to speaking his mind, had a few choice words for Lloyd after Albany won, 121–99.

"He couldn't defend against *me*," Musselman said. "He couldn't guard a water bucket. He's a worse-than-average college defender. Print *that*."

At the end of pregame warm-ups the following night, Lloyd stood staring at Musselman. Glaring. He talked trash to Richardson.

"He told me, 'You can't guard me,'" Richardson said. "I told him, 'You can't guard me, either. What'd we do now?'"

In his first nine games, Lloyd averaged a team-high 20.4 points, shooting 55.1 percent from the field. In his next seventeen, he averaged 12.1 points and shot 42.8 percent. He'd placed part of the blame on a knee injury suffered in Charleston, when he collided under the basket with former Georgetown center Michael Graham.

Team officials termed the injury a "slight hyperextension" and said it would have had little effect on his performance.

So what was wrong? Lloyd was less effective, was getting less playing time, and, finally, by the last week of January, was barely getting into games. He appeared a total of six minutes in three games at Pensacola and Savannah, and was benched in another at Savannah on January 27. The following afternoon, Killilea was fired by Topeka and replaced on an interim basis by John Darr. Asked about Lloyd, Darr had once said: "He has great talent, but there are a lot of great talents around. I imagine, if you go to New York, you'd find a lot of other great talents who aren't anywhere."

That afternoon, Lloyd missed practice. Frustrated, Glannon decided the situation had become critical and said he'd ask Lloyd to undergo urinalysis at Memorial Hospital to determine if he was again using drugs. "There are rumors and I don't know if they are only rumors," Glannon said. "But tomorrow, I am going to suggest to Lloyd that, if they are wrong, he take a drug test, undergo urinalysis, and prove them wrong. I have seen his caliber of play deteriorate. There has been a lack of defense, a lack of aggressiveness. I am certain he has not been attending aftercare on a regular basis. In fact, I am reasonably certain he has not been doing anything on a regular basis.

"I just want to find out what the hell is going on. You know, just because he is Lloyd, the rumors will persist all his life. I ask him if there is anything going on and he says no. He told me, 'I won't lie to you, Mr. Glannon. I won't lie to you, Mr. Glannon.' But I am going to be hurt very deeply if that is not the truth. It would just mark another victim of the horrible effects of drugs."

As Lloyd said, "An addict got some of the best schemes in the world. They got the best con in America. They can con anyone. And you're talkin' to the best, right here."

———

What Bernie Glannon didn't know, what almost no one knew, was that Lloyd wasn't only using drugs in Topeka. He also was dealing them.

It had started, he said, with a midnight run to Kansas City. He and a friend were in need of quick cash. The two contacted an associate and made arrangements to deliver a package. After a game one night Lloyd and the friend went to Kansas City, collected the package, and, no questions asked, delivered it same-day express to Topeka.

It was simple, and lucrative. The two did it again. And again. *And again.*

Soon it had become a regular route.

"I was makin' a little money out there," Lloyd said, "[with] a little connection in Kansas City. I was a deliveryman. It was mainly like, you know, ounces, half ounces."

Lloyd had gotten into the delivery business, he said, out of necessity. A CBA salary covers a lot of expenses, as long as a $200-a-day cocaine habit isn't one of them. But that, Lloyd said, was at least how much coke he was using when he played for the Sizzlers. It had started small. He'd been clean, had done his job, had submitted to drug tests. He'd made the extra effort. Then Glannon, convinced Lloyd was straight, decided to have the team stop testing him. That provided a window of opportunity.

Lloyd seized the moment; he started to snort coke.

"I slipped," he said. "My head got bigger. I said to myself, 'They lettin' Lloyd get over again.' They stopped sayin' I had to go to my drug testin'. They tried to be nice to me, let me have my freedom. That was a mistake. See, when I was first out there, I had to go to my testin' and I was cool. Next thing, Bernie said: 'You don't have to go no more.' They didn't want to have to spend no more money, because those tests, they costed money. Then I saw him lettin' me slide, you know. The next thing I know it was like, 'I could go get high, he'll never know.' The disease started comin' back on me.

"I didn't even care 'bout playin' no more," he said, adding: "You lazy, you tired. I ain't goin' to go out there and kill myself. I just wanted to get high."

One month, Lloyd said, he went through $10,000. Soon even the income from his illicit courier service couldn't cover his expenses, both personal and business. The phone was disconnected. Creditors began to make house calls. Worse, the drug crew in Kansas City started to threaten him for cash owed on goods not delivered.

Lloyd was living on the edge.

"I was Swee'pea. A lot of people knew me. They said, 'We ain't goin' to let this punk from the schoolyards of New York City come out here and *house* shit.'"

House. Meaning, steal it.

Luckily, the crew decided it wasn't worth the heat they'd take if they knocked off a couple of pro ballplayers. Still, there was one time when the Kansas City crew pulled guns, knives, and even a few bats—and, as Lloyd said, "threatened to kill us."

The incident should have taught Lloyd something, should have sent him some sort of message to straighten up. It didn't. Because Lloyd decided he still needed coke and cash, and was desperate, he turned to yet another scheme. He began to kite checks. He would go into supermarkets, mom-and-pop groceries, write a bad check; get cash. After all, he was a smooth talker. And he was Lloyd Daniels, star of the Sizzlers.

He had to be fucking honest, right?

"The people knew me," Lloyd said. "I'm goin' to tell you how sick I was. . . . I'd wear my Topeka hat, my Topeka jacket. They already see it's Lloyd Daniels, he plays for the Topeka Sizzlers. And now that's when I really was gettin' over, because they never checked things—it's the Sizzlers, man—so they figured, 'He must have some type of money.'

"I got to feelin' like, 'Nobody can't stop me,'" he said. "I was the man. When I get goin', nobody can't tell me nothin'. One night, one place, I went back and wrote three checks, man. Three hundred here, three hundred there, and three hundred there. The lady was writin' it down like I was crazy. She didn't know what was goin' on."

No one did.

———

Lloyd submitted to a team-ordered drug test on January 29. But, knowing the Sizzlers lacked legal standing to force those results to be revealed and knowing that if they were positive CBA commissioner Mike Storen could ban Lloyd from the league, his lawyer, David Chesnoff, declined to release them. Three days after the test and, still without the results, Glannon placed Lloyd on the injured reserve list—and scheduled a meeting with both Lloyd and Chesnoff to see if the situation could be resolved.

"Bernie has told me there are certain requirements for Lloyd if he is to remain on the team," Chesnoff said during a conversation that afternoon from his office in Las Vegas. "I am not yet aware of what those requirements are, but no one has hidden the fact that this young man has problems as the result of his upbringing."

"It is just one big circus," Glannon said, frustrated. "I have asked the people at the hospital to deliver to me tomorrow, if possible, and Thursday at the latest, a list of what they want him to do with regard to his aftercare. I want them to outline where the meetings are, at what time. I don't want to believe David. I don't want to believe Lloyd. I want it documented—documents signed over to me by Lloyd and David Chesnoff—that Lloyd is being tested and I want to know the results of those tests.

"Right now, I can't confirm drug tests, because I have never been given the results of the tests. I want to know those results. I want Lloyd to report to me daily, so I know that he is at practice, that he has run, that he is going to get into the physical condition he needs to be in to play. Lloyd tells me he is in condition. I said he isn't and *I'm* the final word. The NBA scouts in over the weekend were appalled at the shape he's in. He hasn't put on any weight since he's been here. He hasn't built any muscle. Until he meets all of the criteria, he is staying on the injured reserve list."

Glannon said he hadn't wavered in his support of Lloyd but admitted he was wavering in his patience. Lloyd wasn't in shape, he said. He wasn't playing to his ability.

It was time for him to shape up—or ship out.

"I think it's the first time someone tightened the noose a little bit," Glannon said, adding: "I had NBA scouts sit in this office last week and tell me this is the only way this kid's going to make it. He doesn't agree with me. But right now he doesn't have any choice."

A week later the situation had still not been resolved. Lloyd, who failed to attend practice in the interim, had still not agreed to submit to routine drug testing or attend counseling sessions. He also had made no effort to attend workout sessions. Left with no other choice, Glannon called Lloyd on Thursday, February 11.

He told him he had been cut.

"I called him this morning," Glannon said. "He was apologetic to the fans, to me. He said he was sorry. But I told him to pack his things. He was leaving.

"He just never shaped up, as far I was concerned," Glannon said. "He never gave himself the chance. I don't know what the reason was.

"I don't understand the thing. I certainly did what I could do, including assisting him with the hospital situation, letting him stay in my home, showing him how to do things the way normal people are supposed to do them. But this past week he no-showed a personal appearance with two hundred seventy kids.

"Somehow I can accept him not training. I can, somehow, accept him not going to the hospital, not sitting on the bench during games while he was on injured reserve. But to no-show the kids at a personal appearance? That was the last straw."

Lloyd had missed a meeting with an aftercare counselor, Glannon said. His finances were a mess. There were indications he was running around, doing God knows what.

Twenty-nine NBA scouts had seen Lloyd play for the Sizzlers, Glannon said. He said they'd told him the talent was there, but that Lloyd had showed himself in a "negative" light. "To be a professional means you have got to become responsible," Glannon said, echoing an all-too-familiar refrain. He added: "He was just an immature young man."

Before Lloyd left the team offices for the ride to Kansas City International Airport, he took a moment for one last word with Al Quakenbush, the reporter from the *Topeka Capital-Journal*. "I'm upset to be leaving the Sizzlers," he told Quake. "I just wanted to play ball. I'm sorry things didn't work out. Bernie's a good man and he tried to help me out. The Sizzlers were good to me, but I don't think I'll be back. It makes me worried about my future. I don't know if I can get to the NBA now. I got to keep my fingers crossed that somebody will want me. But it's hard to know if they will.

"If I got to go, I got to go," Lloyd said. "I can't go jumpin' off no buildin's. I'm only twenty years old. There's not that much time, but there's time."

"Maybe," Quake thought. "Maybe not."

Waters, Too Strong

Lloyd couldn't resist the temptation of the streets. The fiasco in Topeka, fast on the heels of the arrest in Las Vegas, had only made that sad fact all too apparent. He was addicted. If not to drugs and to alcohol, then surely to self-destruction.

As a result, no one in America wanted him on their basketball team, despite his vast abilities. Not in the NBA. Not in the CBA. So, what now?

Lloyd was still just twenty.

But he had no skills other than basketball. He'd bounced checks. Debt collectors had begun to hound him. Attorneys for a Topeka law firm claimed he owed thousands of dollars for his rehabilitation stint at Memorial Hospital. He needed a job.

The solution was as convoluted as his past. Not long after his dismissal from the Sizzlers, Lloyd boarded a plane headed to his latest new start in life. When it reached its final destination, he'd found himself as far as humanly possible from New York.

Having considered playing pro ball in Spain, Puerto Rico, and the Philippines, Lloyd instead found himself Down Under. Star of the inner-city playgrounds, Swee'pea was the newest member of a basketball team in Auckland, New Zealand.

Attorney David Chesnoff had come up with the idea. A former graduate assistant coach at UNLV, John Welch, had gone to New Zealand and told Chesnoff that, despite the fact it was hardly a hotbed of basketball, it might be a good place for Lloyd to stage a comeback. The First Division of the New Zealand Countrywide League had just ten teams. They played an eighteen-game schedule, all on weekends. Each team was allowed two imported players and, though the locals were not anywhere near the caliber common to the United States, the league was not without talent. The salary was minimal—$500 a week—but it included use of a house and a car, as well as airfare.

Okay, so the attendance, league commissioner Ross Williams said, was "chicken-feed." In other words, fewer than twenty-five hundred a game in gymnasiums usually owned by the local preparatory schools. Okay, so it was the CBA—*without* perks.

It was still professional basketball. And for Lloyd, that meant a chance for redemption in a place that figured to be a haven far removed from temptation.

There was no drug epidemic in New Zealand. And even though Auckland was the most urban part of this island nation almost a thousand miles off the southeastern coast of Australia—the city, rooted at the narrowest section on the neck of North Island, had a population of just under nine hundred thousand—when it came to moral corruption, save its "skid row" and red-light district, it couldn't hold a candle to New York and Las Vegas. As Lloyd asked of team officials who delivered him from the local airport, "How come the cops here ain't got no guns?" Because there was no need, he was told.

This was where Lloyd would get his act together, once and for all. In New Zealand he could get clean. In New Zealand he could exercise in the unspoiled air. "We're nuclear-free, pollution-free down here," the locals liked to brag—and build strength and stamina as he recorded stats that would assist him in making it to the NBA. In New Zealand he could build a track record for being a reliable professional man, one who'd learned to be mature, who'd learned his lesson.

"It seemed like a good chance for him to prove himself," Chesnoff said. After all, it was reasoned, even Lloyd Daniels couldn't fuck up in New Zealand.

It had been mid- to late March 1988 when Waitemata coach Dave MacCalman asked John Welch if he knew a player from the States willing to come play in New Zealand. Welch himself had joined the team the season before. The Runnin' Rebels had been on a tour of Australia and New Zealand, had faced the National Team, and at one of the games Welch met MacCalman. He'd told MacCalman that if he ever needed a player, he was interested. Within a week, MacCalman called and offered him a contract.

At the time, Waitemata was in the Second Division. As is the case with most foreign professional sports leagues, teams are placed in one of several divisions and then subjected to promotions and relegations based on their seasonal performances—a scenario akin to the New York Yankees or Boston Red Sox finishing last in the American League East and being demoted to Triple-A, while the best team in the International League is promoted to the majors. It is an odd system, strange to Americans. But it works. With Welch in uniform the remainder of the season, Waitemata won the Second Division title in 1987 and earned a promotion to the First Division for 1988.

Seeing what Welch had done for his club, which had only joined the federation a season earlier, in 1986, MacCalman figured he could use another American. So he called Welch: "I need a rebounding forward who can shoot. Do you know anyone?"

Welch offered to make some inquiries. He called Mark Warkentien in Las Vegas. "He has a player who can shoot, rebound, run the floor, and who is so good, he said he is going to be in the pros soon," Welch told MacCalman. Oh, and he was six foot seven.

"God," MacCalman said. "Tell me more."

Actually, there was just one thing Mark Warkentien wanted to know, Welch said. "Is there any *cocaine* in New Zealand?"

As MacCalman later admitted, "Once his past was explained, it did have me a bit worried. I thought, 'This is a player of high caliber, but he must have had a few troubles.' You don't let a guy of that talent slip through the nets of American basketball if he doesn't have troubles. But perhaps, then, I also thought, as I'm sure everyone else who has come in contact with him has, 'Well, maybe I can help this guy. I'll be the one who shows him the light.' Little did I know," he said. "Little did I know."

The province of greater Auckland is divided into four major areas—metropolitan Auckland, its most urban; North Shore; Eastern Auckland or Manukau, as it is known to the locals; and Waitemata. In Maori, the language of the original inhabitants, Waitemata means "strong waters." White water. *Rapids.*

New Zealand's economic structure was based primarily on agriculture and livestock, with wool, beef, lamb, mutton, and produce the chief exports. The bulk of the land is fertile plains with a volcanic central plateau. A western suburb of Auckland, Waitemata is not rural—though its tallest building rose just nine stories.

Lloyd had no idea what to make of it. Any of it.

"Everything was weird down there," Lloyd said later. "Like, different. It was strange. I didn't have no idea, like, how to adjust to things."

In New Zealand, as in other nations once part of the United Kingdom, you drive on the left side of the road, a bad sign for Lloyd, who already had enough trouble driving on the right. In New Zealand, as in neighboring Australia, they didn't just have dogs and cats but also a wide variety of rare, exotic animals: small kangaroos called wallabies; ferocious mini-weasels called stoats; lizards known as three-eyed tuataras; a chicken-sized flightless bird called a kiwi; and hawklike green parrots called keas, a bird that even killed sheep—just to eat their livers.

In New Zealand they talked strange, too; stranger at times than shit folks talked on the streets of New York.

"Even our light switches take some getting used to down here," MacCalman said. "We flick 'em down to turn 'em on, up to turn 'em off."

To get Lloyd acclimated to his new environs, the first thing MacCalman did after he'd fetched him from the airport was to take him up to One Tree Hill, the highest point around Waitemata save the Whangarei Mountains to the West.

"I wanted to give Lloyd a bit of an idea of where he was and of what it was like down here," MacCalman said. As the two looked over the landscape from One Tree, famous because it had once been the subject of a song on *The Joshua Tree* by U2, MacCalman said, "How does it feel to be on the bottom of the world, Lloyd?"

"I better hold on, Davie D," Lloyd replied. "Or, *I'm'll* fall off."

Lloyd arrived in Waitemata during the first week of April, the beginning of fall in the Southern Hemisphere. It was a week before the season was to begin and, because Waitemata was new to the First Division, the team still hadn't worked out all of its organizational problems. Arrangements were still being made to get Lloyd an apartment and a car. Meanwhile, he moved in with MacCalman and his mother, Aline.

The house was in a well-to-do area of Waitemata. It had four bedrooms in the main house, which had a swimming pool, pool table, and jacuzzi. It also had a separate residence for MacCalman, who was a paraplegic and confined to a wheelchair.

MacCalman was twenty-eight then. He had attended college in the States, playing basketball at West Hills Community College in Coalinga, California.

He'd spent two semesters at the junior college in the San Joaquin Valley and, on the very last day of school, had joined friends going swimming in a nearby river canyon. On arrival MacCalman dove in, hit bottom. Broke his neck. Still, he loved basketball. So, when he returned to Waitemata, he was bent on starting a professional team.

It was a small operation, pretty much a one-man show. "We were without major backing and finances," MacCalman said. "We really weren't as well organized as other teams. When Lloyd came, I think he was expecting a lot different treatment than what he got. He thought it was bush-league—and perhaps to him it was."

Nevertheless, Lloyd liked living with the MacCalmans. Within days of his arrival he'd already come up with nicknames for both MacCalman and his mother. He called the coach "Davie D." "And," MacCalman said, "he started calling my mum 'Mumsy.'"

"It was kind of funny, really," MacCalman said. "But he had a natural way with people. He had us laughing. He was just fun to have around." For a while, at least.

———

There were four teams based in Auckland. The day before the season began, members of each of the four marched in a parade down Queen Street, the main drag in the city proper, then gave a basketball demonstration on a makeshift court in Queen Elizabeth Square. The parade, which drew supporters of all the teams—Altos Auckland, North Shore, Ponsonby, and Waitemata—was followed by a news conference.

Lloyd marched, then shot baskets.

A photo of him driving for a lay-in before a host of curious onlookers in the middle of the square appeared the next morning in the *New Zealand Herald* with a caption that read: "New Yorker Lloyd Daniels shoots for goal." Lloyd also talked to a reporter from the *Dominion Sunday Times*, telling him, "I just want another chance. God gave me a gift. It's up to me to use it. That's why I'm in New Zealand."

Still, Lloyd wasn't about to go to the news conference. MacCalman did. He got the first question.

"We've heard about this Lloyd," a reporter from one of the local papers said. "His reputation precedes him. What about it?"

MacCalman was caught off guard. He knew Lloyd had uncommon talent. He'd seen glimpses of it from the very first practice.

But how was it everyone knew about Lloyd Daniels?

"Lloyd came from the depths of New York, a world away from New Zealand," MacCalman said, though he later admitted he really had no idea what that meant. "He is here to improve his skills, to work on his chances to reach the NBA. Any reputation, things about Lloyd, should be left behind. Give him a clean break."

Later, MacCalman thought more about the question. "I got the message," he said. Lloyd might be better known than he realized. His situation might be worse.

Waitemata opened that weekend in Wellington, a city of six hundred thousand located on the southernmost tip of North Island. It was a two-hour flight in a forty-seat turboprop that dipped and darted in the infamous winds that envelope Wellington, which is surrounded by mountains including a number of active volcanoes.

The Exchequer Saints, who'd won the league title the previous season, were top-seeded again in the First Division. Waitemata, with players who were "rookies" to the division, was the bottom seed. No one gave Waitemata much of a chance.

No one, that is, except Lloyd.

In the first minute of the game, Lloyd drew a foul and made both free throws. Two minutes later, he sank a three-pointer. With eight minutes gone, Waitemata was still close, down just 22–18. Lloyd already had fourteen. He had twenty-two at halftime and the Saints, thought to be a sure bet by most in the crowd of twenty-five hundred at Madgwick Stadium, barely led, 52–46. Waitemata was tougher than expected.

This Daniels kid was good.

Then, little more than twelve minutes into the second half, Lloyd got called for his fifth foul. "It was a little push foul," MacCalman said. But Lloyd lost it, started to yell. As he argued, his face inches from referee Robin Milligan, a woman who'd come with Lloyd to the game also began to scream. "Spit on him, Lloyd!" she yelled. *"Spit on him!"*

As Lloyd said later of the incident: "I was cursing him, *sprayin'* him [with spit]."

"We couldn't believe it," MacCalman said. "It was a bad call. Lloyd had been in the country only about five days. He didn't know how to react, so he argued it. But here was his girlfriend telling him to *spit* on the *referee*. I didn't think he actually did spit on him, but there was a reporter there who wanted to make a name for himself and he wrote a story. The next day the paper had a headline, 'Lloyd Daniels Spits on Ref.'

"It made him look bad, though Lloyd actually did admit to me later that he had a way of talking and spraying at the same time." From there things just got worse.

Around the house, Lloyd had done what he was told. Dishes, chores. "My mum wouldn't take any shit from Lloyd," MacCalman said. "And he listened to her. Toward the end, he was telling me she reminded him of his grandmother."

But Lloyd moved out after Wellington and began to share a place a half mile away with Warwick Meehl, a guard on the New Zealand National Team known as "the Ice Man of New Zealand." Apparently he was the New Zealander version of George Gervin. It seemed that, having worn out his welcome so many places, Lloyd should have learned his lesson, have made an effort to work. And work hard. But in his new place, Lloyd had free rein. Left to his own devices, he soon began to run afoul of Dave MacCalman.

It started with the usual MO. Lloyd claimed injuries in practice, said he couldn't run. He was sent to the trainer, who couldn't find anything wrong. Soon he started missing practice altogether. He missed one, then another. MacCalman didn't understand, especially, when Lloyd told him it was just practice—not a game.

"I said to him, 'Lloyd, you're down here to get yourself on the straight and narrow. The letters *NBA* should be a neon sign to you.' But he would just show up, touch his toes twice and go, 'Okay. That's it coach. I'm ready.' Then he would pull up lame and go see the trainer. He was out of shape. He refused to run, lift weights, do the extra things he needed to do. He wasn't trying hard enough.

"We had a few run-ins," MacCalman said. "I'm a taskmaster. But he made it hard for me, a real test. I'd tell him, 'You have to do more than just show up.'"

"I told him the competition sucked down there," Lloyd said. "No ones had no kind of game that could touch me. Why should I have worked? It wasn't nothin'. Besides, I told Davie D what type of player I am. I said, 'I'm not 'bout bein' a *practice* player, Davie D. I'm a *game* player.' But, over there, they wanted me to work.

"You believe that?"

"The question is, 'Does Lloyd want to improve himself?'" Mac-Calman said. "I know he wants to be an NBA player. But I don't think he can rationalize what it takes; the commitment, the sacrifice. He likes to win. He doesn't like to work hard.

"His work ethic wasn't where I would have liked it."

After Wellington, Lloyd led Waitemata to wins in its next two. He had 23 points as the team won by three at Nelson, on South Island, and a game-high 36 points as Waitemata beat Altos Auckland, 94–84, to wreck that team's first game in its new 3,000-seat arena, Chase Stadium. Off the court, though, his actions were becoming more and more distressing. He was having problems with a girlfriend who, Mac-Calman said, was disturbed over talk Lloyd was seeing not just one but *two* other women.

As Lloyd said: "There was all these 'Kiwi Girls' who ain't never had no black boys before and they loved me. How could they not? They *had* to love *Swee'pea*. Them 'Kiwi Girls' was all *over* my dick."

Then there were the drinking problems. Drugs were scarce in New Zealand, but beer flowed like water. Lloyd went out to local bars every night with teammate A. J. Tuitama, a twenty-one-year-old forward from Waitemata. The two would have two, three beers at one bar, then a couple more at another, MacCalman said.

Before long, the coach said, Lloyd was bringing the beer home— usually a few cases a week. And before long, MacCalman realized he had a problem. He was drinking too much," MacCalman said.

It would have been ironic if it weren't so sad.

After all, imagine a man drinking too much beer in a nation often teased mercilessly for its beer drinking?

As MacCalman said of the situation: "We like to drink our beer and we really don't like to hold a man down when he is having a few. But when it begins to affect his work, well, you have to ask him to stop. I never saw him so drunk he couldn't stand. But it got to the point where he was drinking enough that it became a concern."

Now, the New Zealand Basketball Federation had seen its share of Bad Boys from the United States. Just the season before, there'd been a player from Los Angeles who robbed a local service station the night before he was to leave to go home—as if a six-foot-six, bald-headed black man might blend right in down in Auckland. He was arrested at the airport. Another player, loaned furniture by his club, sold it to some locals. "Twice," MacCalman said. He got arrested, too.

Still, no one had seen anyone like Lloyd.

"He took New Zealand by storm," MacCalman said. "Here he was, six foot seven and out of New York, a young man who knew how to hustle people.

"New Zealand is a *back lot*. We were curious, fascinated by a person like Lloyd. Very susceptible. So Lloyd was able to do whatever he wanted. . . . He charged videos from the local shop to other members of the club. He rang home quite a few times, made toll calls, and charged them to other people. There was a liquor store about two-hundred yards from his place. He had a tab going there. He had run amok."

After the Auckland game, Lloyd went to a team-sponsored "after-match" party. He wasn't supposed to stay long. Waitemata had a game the next day and MacCalman told him he was running an early practice, a pregame run-through.

"He swore on his mother's grave he would not let me down," Mac-Calman said. "To me, that was a fairly solemn vow. But he never arrived for practice."

Waitemata lost by three to New Plymouth. Lloyd had just twenty-one.

"That was when I lost all respect for the man," MacCalman said.

The two had it out. MacCalman told Lloyd he was just wasting everyone's time, including his own. Lloyd told the coach he just wanted to go home. "It took us about five minutes to reach a decision," Mac-Calman said. Lloyd was headed stateside.

"I can't believe Davie D said it was for too much drinkin'," Lloyd said. "He knows in his heart that wasn't what it was. I left there because it was borin', because there wasn't nothin' for me to be doin', at least nothin' that I realized at the time. I was homesick, far away from home for the first time. The competition was *weak*, know what I mean? It wasn't nothin'. And, there was a lot of other things I could've did, except that I was a city kid and I didn't know how to appreciate them then. So, I just went to Davie D and said things wasn't workin' out. Then I just went home."

Still, as Warwick Meehl drove him to the airport, he said Lloyd began to have second thoughts.

"Should I go?" he asked. "Think I should go?"

Meehl wanted Lloyd to stay. Deep down, so did Dave MacCalman. But everyone knew it was best for him to leave.

Warwick told him, "Yes."

"You know, he reminds me of Billie Holiday or Charlie Parker," MacCalman said afterward. "He just had a sad beginning, and he doesn't seem able to shake off the scars he carries. People tried to help him. But Lloyd always seems to know all the answers. It is the life he has chosen. People have given him other options. He has looked at them, stayed with them a while. But, in the end, he always goes back to that life. He needs a crutch and his pursuit of that crutch is what has brought him down. We took sort of a gamble. We were told Lloyd was a bit of a time bomb and that, at some stage, he would blow it for himself and for the team. But we felt that New Zealand would be a good place for Lloyd. It turned out that it was just too much of a backwater and too much of a culture shock for him. We weren't sociologists and we weren't in a position to change him. I just wish it could have been under other circumstances when he was here.

"I wish Lloyd could have been *not* so Lloyd Daniels."

Cracks in the Concrete Dream

The streets of New York City were filled with bad associations, sometimes so many that they became impossible to avoid. Associations that came in the form of lifelong friends and acquaintances, people who once seemed good and honorable and who sometimes, when you least expected it, turned out to be drug dealers and muggers and murderers.

There were bad associations that turned out to be neighbors and relatives, turned out to be people you played ball against in the parks and on the playgrounds. Associations with people you'd said hello to, whom you'd grown up with. People you knew. Or thought you did.

And, because of that, what happened was that judgment often became twisted, bent. Blurred. Became corrupted. Or worse, suspended. Forgotten.

This was a lesson Holcombe Rucker tried to teach kids in Harlem back in the day, when, in the 1950s, he laid the foundation for what would become the Rucker Pro League.

Rucker understood the value of associations, of education, because he realized that he, too, could have succumbed to the streets. He had, after all, dropped out of high school to join the army during World War II, and it was only after he came back from the war in 1946 that he went on to earn his high school diploma and a degree at City College.

Rucker saw basketball as a way to reach kids who'd been unreachable, as a hook to teach them sportsmanship, to encourage education, to steer them toward opportunities in business—like Saul Lerner had tried to do with Lloyd.

You couldn't play in one of Rucker's youth-level games until you showed him your report card. That led to the formation of an organization called Each One, Teach One, which had working professionals— from teachers and guidance counselors to police and firefighters—who advised kids on issues ranging from health education to career options and drug abuse. But, the world Rucker tried to make a better place had changed so much since his death in 1965 at age thirty-eight—the problems multiplied, the drugs more prevalent; the moral fiber that once bound community more corroded. Going, gone.

"It's hard to do sometimes," Mark Jackson said, "but you do have to learn to be strong and understand the road you have to take if you want to be successful. It boils down to environment, your upbringing, who you're with, the type of family you have. Those are all key factors, because there's a lot of great players that haven't made it because they became sidetracked and there's a lot of ones, who maybe aren't as good as those guys, who stayed on the right path and became successful. You've got to remember, there's a lot of legends on the streets of New York City."

The then–New York Knicks guard was in the locker room in Madison Square Garden, getting dressed for a game against the Dallas Mavericks. He knew of what he spoke. He'd played both with and against many of those legends—Lloyd, Ron Matthias, Richie Adams, Red Bruin, Pearl Washington, Walter Berry, and Kenny Smith, to name a few—growing up in the Hollis–St. Albans section of Queens. He'd seen some who'd achieved success. He'd seen a bunch who'd not only failed to achieve the dream of making the NBA but who'd missed a chance to turn their basketball skills into something tangible, like an education.

Who'd failed to cash what was an otherwise winning ticket.

Jackson knew because back when he was a student at Bishop Loughlin High School in Brooklyn, he was far from the best guard in New York City.

Pearl Washington had become a national sensation at Boys & Girls, en route to Syracuse; Smith had become an all-American at Archbishop Molloy, turning it into a full ride to North Carolina. Jackson went from Loughlin to St. John's. But, truth be told, it wasn't like he'd been quick to set the world on fire. He was a good player, but far from a sure thing. So, he'd buckled down in the classroom, hedging his bet. And then, with an education as his insurance, he'd acted with unyielding determination on the court, his sights on the NBA.

All of that enabled him to move on, cover his bases, while friends around him fell. All of that enabled Jackson to distance himself from the streets.

So even when, in the summer of 1989, Jackson was subpoenaed and forced to testify as a character witness for an old neighborhood acquaintance, Thomas Mickens, then on trial in Brooklyn federal court on charges related to alleged cocaine trafficking and money-laundering operations, he wasn't touched or tainted by the appearance.

People knew what Jackson was—and what he wasn't—and what he was was a man with a plan. What he wasn't was a thug.

Despite being labeled as too slow, too sporadic, despite being selected eighteenth overall in the first round of the 1987 NBA Draft, he went on to become the first rookie ever to average double figures in assists as he was voted 1987–88 Rookie of the Year—the only non-lottery pick to win the award. Despite his critics, the next season he was named to the East squad for the NBA All-Star Game. Not that Jackson didn't have problems. He had a few.

There was his publicized dispute over having to share his position with Rod Strickland, a dispute that some said contributed to Strickland's being traded to the San Antonio Spurs. There was what some viewed as whining over his treatment in the press, as well as negative reactions toward fans who booed his poor performances.

And there were his shortcomings as a player, most notably that he had a hard time defending almost everyone in the league.

Still, Jackson had made it a lot further than most people ever thought he would. He made the NBA. And he had a successful career: first as a player, then as a television broadcaster, later as a coach. What allowed him to do this, he said, was family.

"I was very fortunate to have good backing, as far as my family was concerned," said Jackson, who had even lived at home during his rookie season with the Knicks.

"That backing was a very influential part of growing up. It kept my priorities straight. It helped keep me away from the wrong people, helped keep me headed in the right direction, helped me with academics, everything. It helped me to stay strong. It helped me to be smart enough to know when to say, 'Yes,' and when to say, 'No.' I'm glad that I had that, because, when I go back to the neighborhood and I see some of the guys still playing, I realize that it's really unfortunate they didn't have that, too."

Unfortunate, because kids without that guidance often never got a chance to be like John Salley or Mark Jackson—or even become a success merely by becoming good citizens. Instead, despite their best efforts, they often get caught up in "situations," as problems are called on the street, their careers passing them by the way Lloyd's was; their lives complicated by the lack of foresight. Bad associations are like that.

Shorty Black hadn't liked the call, it having gone against his team, and so angered, the witness alleged, he'd decided to do something about it late on that summer afternoon on the blacktop courts at Baisley Park. His teammates had protested to the referee; made it known he'd made a mistake.

But the ref said he wasn't going to change his mind, wouldn't reverse the call, a call that, police and confidential informants said later, cost the game for the Supreme Team. Too much had been riding on the outcome: police said as much as $50,000—the cash sum allegedly bet on the game, one allegedly sponsored as a "community service" of sorts by local drug dealers.

And so, Robert Whitfield testified before Justice Lawrence J. Finnegan in New York State Supreme Court, Shorty Black *hit* the referee.

It happened in an instant, too fast for the ref to react in self-defense. Shorty Black, whose real name was Earl Byam, had come from the bench, fist drawn as a lethal weapon, Whitfield testified. A bad call can cost a man and his team a lot in the parks and on the playgrounds of New York City. Though no one other than Whitfield seemed sure who threw that punch, when it was thrown that warm July afternoon and it landed firm, landed sound, it cost Greg Vaughn, the man on the receiving end, his life.

Shorty Black, charged with manslaughter, pleaded innocence. He hadn't been the assailant, he said, but had been the victim of mistaken identity.

A few witnesses testified perhaps that wasn't true; one, Hassen Pinchback, a law clerk who lived in the neighborhood and who'd served as the timekeeper and alternate referee for the game, agreed to take the witness stand despite claiming death threats had been made against both himself and his family. No one, however, offered a lick of proof to substantiate the accusation against Shorty Black and no one, other than Whitfield, that is, had claimed even to have seen him throw the fatal punch.

In fact, other witnesses—including one named Darrin Hall, who said he'd watched the game from outside the chain-link fence that surrounded Baisley Park—told the court it was not Shorty Black at all who was involved on the afternoon of July 30, 1988. It had been someone else, a fact, street-level sources said, was true.

Under cross-examination, Assistant District Attorney John Scarpa had asked Hall: "Are you positive that Earl Byam did not throw that punch?"

"Yes," Hall said, having added his view was "clear enough to see it wasn't Earl." Neither he nor anyone else seemed to know who, though, delivered the fatal blow during the fracas that had spilled onto the court in the aftermath of the controversial call.

Then again, the first law of survival on the streets was to forget a man's face and his name in due haste when hard times come to call.

So, Shorty Black walked clean on the afternoon of June 20, 1989, and rightfully so, since there had been no proof of wrongdoing by him. An eleven-man jury—the twelfth juror had a near–nervous breakdown during deliberations and was excused three hours prior to the delivery of the verdict—found in favor of acquittal on charges of first-degree manslaughter, second-degree manslaughter, and second-degree assault.

"*Lord! Oh, God!*" Shorty Black had yelled in the courtroom when that verdict came in, having grabbed his attorney, Howard Meyer, hugging him for dear life. "Thank you. Thank you, God. Oh, God. Oh, God. Oh, God. *Thank you.*"

_____

Greg Vaughn, relatives said later, had no idea the game might be run by drug lords. He wouldn't have refereed it, they said, had he known. He'd spent a great deal of time preaching the perils of drug usage, after all, and his stature as a recognized teacher and basketball coach—*as a man*—made sure that message got through.

"He was always against any kind of drugs—beer, crack, heroin, cocaine," one former player, Bryan Cromwell, said. "He told us that if anyone ever came in smelling like beer, he'd take him into a room and beat him like if his own son had done it."

His students at P.S. 140, an elementary school in South Jamaica, Queens, and his college players respected that attitude. It meant he cared.

Vaughn, six foot six, 235 pounds, had been a star of sorts at Queens College, a Division II school just off the Long Island Expressway in Flushing, Queens. He'd become the all-time leading scorer and rebounder in school history at Queens, whose alumni included musicians Paul Simon, Marvin Hamlisch, and Carole King, comedians Ray Romano and Jerry Seinfeld, porn star Ron Jeremy, and Ruth Madoff, wife of convicted Wall Street Ponzi schemer Bernie Madoff. His uniform, number 44, had been retired during a ceremony in 1986. After graduation, he'd found modest success, becoming an assistant and then head basketball coach at Medgar Evers College in Crown Heights, Brooklyn, not far from where Lloyd grew up. Later, tired of having to drive across Brooklyn from his day job to his Medgar Evers job, which was part-time and paid little, he resigned to become a junior varsity coach at Prospect Heights High School in Brooklyn. It was more convenient.

The basketball team at Medgar Evers, a Division III school with few resources and far removed from the glories of major-college Division I basketball, often was bad. God-awful, that is. But Greg Vaughn, who knew how to remain in good spirits in the face of hard times, tried his best to take it all in stride. Even when his team once headed into its postseason conference tournament with a record of 2-20, Vaughn kept his sense of humor. "I've got my strategy all figured out," he said. "First, I'm going to go out to a restaurant, sit there all day, and eat until I put on a hundred pounds. Then I'm going to get me a pair of glasses and a white towel. By game time, I'll look like John Thompson and maybe my team will play like Georgetown." They didn't.

Still, Vaughn was having fun. As Shawn Woods, who'd played for him at Medgar Evers, recalled, "He could make a guy laugh at a funeral on Christmas Day."

Despite his nature, despite his fear of what drugs might do to a neighborhood, Greg Vaughn was on a battleground—one through which, despite his stature, even he could not safely tread; one which, despite his background, perhaps even he did not fully understand. Battle lines often were unclear in neighborhoods like South Jamaica, Queens. Sometimes it was too hard to tell the players without a rap sheet.

Some said Vaughn must have known what kind of game he was working, especially since he was paid for his time and especially since Baisley Park, located on Foch and Guy R. Brewer Boulevards near the back of the Baisley Park Houses in South Jamaica, was known in all the wrong circles as the Sniff Bowl.

Whether he knew of the element that joined him in the park that afternoon and looked the other way because those people had once been friends and neighbors, or whether he had no idea, in the end proved moot. Struck in the head by an unidentified assailant, he fell face-first into the ground that afternoon and wound up comatose—left in the arms of Hassen Pinchback, who'd been his friend, as everyone else scrambled through the gates, out of the park and into the recesses of the neighborhood.

Five days later, Greg Vaughn died. He was thirty-three.

On the streets, they call them "vics." They know no colors, no sexes, no ages. No bounds. They are victims, pure and simple. Innocent, involved by happenstance. They are hurt, maimed, changed for life. If they're lucky, that is. Usually, they just die.

Barbara Chiles had been a "vic." That had a lot to do with the emotion her son was feeling when he took the court that night in March 1989. A guard for Columbia University, Tony Chiles, Jr., had played for Riverside Church and knew Lloyd from club games and from the parks. He wore a white headband that read "Mom." He'd drawn a heartfelt ovation from fans at Levien Gymnasium, Columbia's home court.

A week earlier, Barbara Chiles had been found slain in her apartment in the Kingsbridge section of the Bronx, handcuffed to two other women and shot twice in the head, execution-style. One of the other women also died. Police, seeing the situation, called the double homicide a drug-related hit. It was an obvious explanation, one that fit the scenario. Except, Tony Chiles said, it just wasn't true. Couldn't be true.

A senior political science major at Columbia, Chiles would become a basketball agent and later a coach. And that night at Levien Gym, he tried to explain how it all was just a case of his mother being in the wrong place at the wrong time—another innocent victim in a city already filled with too many of them.

"My mother was a good person," Chiles said as he stood outside the locker room after the game, an overtime loss to Yale—the first game since his mother had been murdered. "She had nothing to do with drugs or those situations. If you had listened to the story the police told or read the ones in the newspapers, you would think that my mother was the queen of crack in the Bronx. It wasn't anything like that."

It would take more than a year for police to learn just what had happened to Barbara Chiles, why she'd been murdered. Strange as it seems, the full picture became clear only after the then still-unsolved case appeared on the television show *America's Most Wanted*. It turned out, the NYPD said, the assailants had allegedly kidnapped the other two women, nineteen-year-old Sarray Watson and an acquaintance named Rita Faulk. Watson, Tony Chiles said, had been a casual friend of his brother's girlfriend. She had been to the Chiles home just once, but knew Barbara Chiles worked at Chemical Bank and kept the books for a store owned by relatives. Accosted less than five blocks away, Watson panicked when the robbers demanded money from her and Faulk. So she took them to see Barbara Chiles. And Chiles and Faulk wound up dead.

"It was a situation that got out of control," Tony Chiles said later. "She was a young girl. She panicked. My mother died. . . . An innocent bystander."

Unfortunately, in New York City, it wasn't uncommon.

Laid out in the back of the ambulance, Orlando Antigua tried to comprehend what had just happened to him. Blood was streaming out of the corner of his left eye socket, running down the side of his face. All he could think in that moment was that he was dying. And as he stared at the ambulance ceiling, the worst part was he had no idea why.

It was Halloween night, 1988. Antigua and his friends had been walking along the Grand Concourse in the Bronx. There was a commotion at a discount appliance store down the block. Some kids were arguing with store employees. Antigua stood on a car bumper to get a better view and, as he did, someone behind him—someone he didn't know—threw an egg that landed in front of the store. The next thing he knew, Antigua said, the store manager had drawn a gun—and shot him in the head, grazing him.

"I guess he thought I did it," Antigua said. "He pulled a gun and shot me. I hit the hood of the car. Blood was just coming out. I was panicking. I ran up to him and said, 'Mister, why'd you shoot me?' He just looked at me. He was like in shock."

Some victims of violence turn out to be like Lloyd. Not really victims, but rather folks who are involved—and, in some way, responsible for what they get. Others, like Barbara Chiles, are real victims who don't deserve their fate, and who don't get a second chance.

But sometimes, though not often enough, it seems on the streets of New York, real victims catch a break. They live. They go on to lead good, productive lives.

They turn out like Orlando Antigua.

Just three weeks after the shooting, Antigua made his varsity debut for the basketball team at St. Raymond's High School in the Bronx. And, by the winter of 1990, the six-foot-six junior forward had blossomed into one of the most promising players in the city. He still had fragments of the small-caliber bullet imbedded in his head, near his left temple. "It's hard to take in," he said. "When I saw the X-ray, it really hit me."

Despite the occasional headaches, he decided he could live with that. Even the kidding from teammates. "They called me BH," he said. "For Bullethead."

Because of who he was, how he was raised, Antigua even came to accept that the man alleged to have shot him was cleared of all charges. Four witnesses testified the store manager, who had no criminal record, shot Antigua. Five said he did not.

The gun was never recovered.

"Orlando was just checking out what was going on," then–Bronx assistant district attorney Robert Kelly said of the incident. "An innocent bystander. I don't get witnesses like that in the Bronx. Usually, they're involved in some way or are criminals. But he was a good kid. He wasn't causing any trouble. Half the kids in the city should be as good as Orlando."

"I think how close I was to dying," Antigua said. "It changed my attitude. . . . When something goes wrong in my life, it's just a small thing compared to that."

———

While crack vials littered the streets in most neighborhoods, and while victims made headlines in the tabloids at an alarming rate, drug games mostly went unseen by all except the participants—hired to perform while bets were placed by rival factions. The usual payment to key players, who appeared because the money often was just too good to pass on, at times ranged into the low to mid four figures. For organizers, the stakes were exponentially higher.

One player told of a game one summer at a park somewhere in Harlem. The call went out for real talent, the player said, and some of the best-known high school and college players, even a few former professionals, answered the invitations.

"This homeboy, called himself 'Robocop,' who I think was a real cop and who sometimes worked a few games here and there as a referee, was supposed to work the event," the player said. "It was to involve some top-shelf folks. Robocop showed and met this dude [who had] pulled up in a Benz. He opened the back lid and there it was, a hundred and fifty grand, in cash, just sittin' there in the trunk. Players was each going to be gettin' like five grand to appear. They offered Robocop two grand to call the game.

"He said, 'Think I'm crazy? I make a bad call, the bullets'll be flyin'. I could make myself dead.'" So he went on his way and the game never came off. "Thing was, he was right," the witness said. "This was some dangerous folks. Some *serious* shit."

Often, witnesses said, games were run in parks and playgrounds inaccessible to all but the slickest of the slick and only "known" viewers were allowed in. Watchdogs would ring the park for those games, armed with undergarment Uzis and dressed to the *nines*—in such cases, 9mm semiautomatics or "M&Ms with peanuts," as the gun and its bullets were called—those being the street weapons of choice.

There it was known as "goin' illegal." And illegal guards stood their ground to keep the "unwanted element"—cops, coaches, and, yes, reporters—away from the action, which, witnesses claimed, often included bets being taken out in the open. One afternoon, it might be at the Sniff Bowl, another at Ajax Park in Queens. Yet another at the Mecca in Brooklyn or Mitchell Houses in the Bronx.

Might be anywhere.

"A lot of kids play in drug games," the old Ben Franklin coach, Stan Dinner, said, noting it beat a minimum-wage job. "It's an easy way for some of these kids to earn some money. You can pick up a few hundred bucks if you have the right connections."

"Hundreds, maybe thousands of kids have played in those type games," Ron Brown said, adding: "It's attractive because it's easy money. They don't think about what it really is, so they just don't turn it down. They figure, 'Everybody does it.'"

"Everybody in New York knows about it," Tiny Archibald, who was raised in the environment and knew people who played in those games, said. "It involves high school kids, college kids. There's a lot of people getting paid. People in the front row are handing out money. Some of these kids are driving cars you and I can't afford. You see it. Some guys get five hundred, a thousand a game. The drug dealers, they're buying players. They tell the folks they're betting against, 'I'm gonna bust you by eight. I'm gonna bust you by ten.' They set the line and decide how much to bet. The kids get paid, are getting stuff, on the basis of how they can dictate the outcome of a game."

But there is more to those games than money and bets. Because, scarier drug games and drug tournaments are often "sponsored events," run by neighborhood power brokers who use them to improve their stature, gain respect in the community.

"You know how McDonald's is into community relations?" a local scout familiar with those games said. "Well, your drug dealer maybe would like it to be known that he is willing to give back to the community, too, because it's good for business. So, maybe he sponsors a tournament for the kids. Maybe he buys some shirts for the players. Maybe he buys some trophies or some sneakers and hands them out.

"It improves the way folks view him.

"Think about it. Why did people always protect the Mafia? Because they were scared, but also because the Mafia looked out for the community."

Like bad associations, those contributions often skewed the line between right and wrong. What with all the positives and negatives of the situation, sometimes it was difficult to see all the angles. Though it sounds clichéd, stereotypical even, dealers were viewed as success stories in some communities and, despite the dictums of common sense, often were held in high esteem. It all went back to making cash money, to having juice. To keeping it real.

To doing whatever it took, whenever.

And, the view in some of those communities was at times perverted even more because dealin' folks put back into the neighborhood some of what they took out, unlike the bullshitters and the promise makers who talked a good game but never kept it real. Politicians, after all, promised the world, then often ignored the needs. Cops, too.

"Folks in inner-city environments are constantly faced with poor housing, poor sanitation, high unemployment rates," Bob McCullough, Sr., commissioner of the famed Rucker League, said. When someone showed interest in lending a helping hand, even someone of questionable moral fiber, it was not often rebuffed.

Back in the day, Earl Manigault, who'd tried to heed the advice of people like Holcombe Rucker, ran a tournament for kids at Goat Park. The goal of the Goat Tournament was to teach the kids to steer clear of the streets, of drugs; to place an emphasis on education. What happened next was frightening: To fund his antidrug tournament, Manigault turned to dealers—getting *them* to donate money needed to purchase shirts and uniforms.

"I told them dealers," Manigault said, "you have to put something back into the community. They couldn't argue with the Goat."

Gene Williams, a longtime Manigault associate who'd worked with Each One, Teach One and the Rucker League, argued the logic. But he couldn't argue the results. After all, though he disliked—no, *hated*—the notion of dealers funding tournaments, he said it was hard to dissuade folks from accepting assistance for something positive.

"It takes money to run a tournament and if the Parks Department cannot run the tournament, people feel someone has to. It's bad. It gives dealers exposure and gives legitimacy to what they do. I don't condone it. But what can you do? The message is there anyway. And, it does lend itself to having activities in the community."

The problem, of course, was despite the uncertainties, there remained certain constants. Like the basic law of the streets: *you get what you pay for.* Unfortunately, in New York City, the phrase sometimes took on a perverse new meaning.

———

Vernon Harton had been in his office at Jacksonville College when the phone rang. It was early August 1989; Harton was sweltering in the heat of another Texas afternoon. Still, his mind was on basketball. The fall semester would begin in a month and at Jacksonville, a small junior college in Jacksonville, Texas, that meant basketball season wasn't far behind. So when Harton lifted the phone and heard it was Malloy Nesmith, a returning player from Monroe High School in the Bronx, he'd been ecstatic. Until Nesmith began to talk.

"He said, 'Coach, did you hear the news?'" Harton said. "I was like, 'No. What's going on?' Then he told me."

What Nesmith said was that Karlton Hines, Jacksonville's star recruit, was being held without bail in the House of Detention for Men, The Tombs—charged with second-degree murder.

"Malloy said, 'You can forget about Karlton because he's in the slammer,'" Harton said. "I said, 'He's in the slammer?' and Malloy said, 'Yeah, they said he killed somebody.' As you can guess, it came as a shock. I couldn't believe it. I never had anyone who couldn't come to school because 'maybe he killed somebody.' It's terrible, a guy with all that ability. We heard he couldn't find the classroom, that he didn't always want to go to school. But we hadn't heard whether or not he had ever been in trouble. I guess he is now. After all, they got him for murder. We've crossed him off our list."

Once, Hines had been selected as the best player in Manhattan. That was back when he was a sophomore at Manhattan Center High School—which had once been Ben Franklin—and back when he was on the Gauchos. From there he'd tried to get out of the city, spending a season at Maine Central Institute, where, courtesy of tuition paid by Lou d'Almeida, the six-foot-five swingman averaged 25.1 points, 7.6 rebounds, and 6.2 assists and was offered a scholarship to Syracuse. But, you know the old cliché: *you can take the boy out of the city, but you can't take the city out of the boy.*

And Karlton Hines, well . . . he couldn't leave the streets.

So he left Maine Central.

A spokesman for the Bronx district attorney, Edward McCarthy, said the arrest of Hines stemmed from what was believed to be a drug-related altercation in the Bronx on July 30, 1989. The incident ended, McCarthy said, when Hines "took a broken bottle and slashed the throat" of thirty-year-old Edwin Santos in an alley behind a building on East 156th Street, near old Yankee Stadium. Santos was pronounced dead on arrival at Lincoln Hospital. Hines, who was then just nineteen, claimed self-defense. He said Santos had pulled a knife.

Here he was, a tragic figure.

Selected a preseason high school all-American by no less than *Street & Smith's*, Hines, who'd lost his scholarship earlier in the year when Syracuse heard he'd dropped out of classes at Adlai Stevenson, was now charged with second-degree murder, as well as second- and third-degree assault and resisting arrest. Then, Hines got off.

"It was alleged by the defendant that the other man had pulled a knife on him and that, in self-defense, he took a broken bottle and slashed the throat of the other man," McCarthy said as he tried to explain the decision reached by a grand jury in Bronx Criminal Court. "The grand jury believed that and refused to indict him."

"That afternoon," Tony Chiles, the Columbia guard, said, "Karlton came up to 155th Street and was playing ball like nothing happened. He came straight to the park. He was like, 'Ain't no big thing.' He scored something like thirty-five, I think."

And so, when Harton answered his office phone again, this time in late August 1989, he decided to change his stance when he heard the news. After all, like most coaches, he knew talent when he saw it—questionable association or not.

"Karlton got off, did he?" Harton said. "Hey, well, that's no problem then. I mean, well, if it was only self-defense, I can live with that then. As long as he didn't murder anybody, well, then, *I tell you partner,* he can still play *here* if he wants to."

———

The gymnasium was bathed in a dim, languid, yellow light, the kind you found in all those old New York City high schools in the 1980s; the kind of light that made a place seem old, worn. The two banks of bleachers, one on each side, were full. The teenage kids screamed loud, unchecked, unrestrained. Under one basket, John Salley stepped to the microphone.

It had been forever since he'd been here, though he tried to make it back at least once a year, just to stay in touch; to remind himself where it was he'd come from, and to let students here know that someone out there, no matter how successful, still cared. Was one of them.

"Yo, Canarsie!" Salley yelled over the mic to the kids from Canarsie High School in Brooklyn, the place where he started down a road he'd only dreamed would take him to the NBA.

It was February 1990. Salley was home for the NBA All-Star Break. He wore sweats and sneakers, his own brand; of course, he wore the NBA championship ring he'd won the previous season as a member of the 1989 world champion Detroit Pistons.

The noise died down, attention focused.

"Now," he said, "what I've got to say may not penetrate everybody. But I have one job. And my one job is to get through to one person. And if I get through to one person, then my trip here was necessary. ... I came here to talk about drugs.

"Yeah, I know," he said, as the audience uttered a collective groan. "You figure this is going to be one of those speeches, like, 'Yo, you shouldn't do drugs. You should stay in school. You shouldn't do this, you shouldn't do that.' And then you'll turn around and the person who said that, they're being picked up for using drugs. One thing you're never going to see—and, if you do see it, you might as well call the *New*

York Post and tell them they're lying again—is me using drugs. But I didn't come here to talk like that. I came here to talk to you. I came here to talk about the future. *Your* future."

Slowly, Salley lured them in. Told some jokes, got them to listen, and then, when he had them where he wanted them, in the palm of his hand, the man known as "the Spider" set the trap.

He talked about drugs, about responsibility. About school, the future, hard work.

He talked about success.

"You know," he said, "one of my best friends got killed because of drugs back when I was in college. Another one of my friends got killed because of drugs since I've been in the pros. One of my other friends, he used to be a real good friend, too, has an occupation that I don't believe in. Hear me. Hear what I'm trying to tell you."

His friend Don Washington had been a disc jockey at a party somewhere in Virginia, Salley said. He'd been working at an event where drugs were being used, someone who was high tried to rob him. When Washington fought back, the man stabbed him.

He'd been killed over a gold chain.

The other friend was named Lloyd Harrison and he was killed back when Salley was at Georgia Tech. It had happened during the season. Harrison and some friends had gotten high, then gone into a Laundromat to wash clothes. A man there had crawled into a dryer. Harrison laughed at him. Angered, the guy shot Harrison in the chest.

It was about as senseless a murder as murders go in New York. Yet, it had the unmistakable signs of the kind of things that can happen in a drug environment.

Salley was distraught. And he wanted revenge. He'd gone to then–Georgia Tech coach Bobby Cremins, asked for a plane ticket to New York.

"I asked Bobby Cremins for a ticket home. He said there were three games coming up, but I said, 'I don't care, because my friend got killed, and when we find the guy who did it, we're going to shoot him.' Cremins gave me a one-way ticket. I said, 'What's this for? How am I going to get back?' He said, 'I figure if you kill the guy, you'll be a murderer, too, and won't be coming back—so it won't matter.' I gave the ticket back, because I realized then that this guy didn't kill my friend. . . . Drugs killed him. If there wasn't a drug atmosphere, none of that would have happened. . . . Bad associations spoil *useful* habits."

It was a lesson Salley said he'd been taught as a kid and that had been reinforced as an adult. His mother, he said, always told him there were two paths in life: the easy road and the hard one. Or, perhaps, more accurate: the one with all the shortcuts and the one where you had to work to reach the finish line, where you had to pay your dues.

"One means you're taking shortcuts to get there, cutting corners," Salley told those kids. "The [other] one may take more time. But you learn to play by the rules, learn to overcome obstacles, and, in the long run, learn to be a better person."

Salley was not much of an athlete back in high school. Just a bit over six feet, he had to make the Canarsie basketball team as a walk-on—the seventeenth man on a seventeen-man roster. He grew. But he remained under-recruited, a pencil-thin six-foot-seven forward who had raw ability and heart, but an uncertain future as a major-college player. Georgia Tech took a chance on him because he had potential and because he was the type of kid who would work his hardest to bring that potential to fruition. He was someone who was able to see the future, the way he had when he attended Canarsie—"I got in trouble back then, but only for standing out by the door talking to the girlies," he told the kids at Canarsie. "But I came to class."

Now, Salley made the NBA because, by the time he left Tech he'd grown to seven feet. And because he'd spent countless hours working on making himself better. But that wasn't his biggest success, he said. And neither was the fact that he became the first black player at Tech to have his jersey retired. Or that he would become just one of two NBA players—the other, Tim Duncan of the San Antonio Spurs—to win championships in three different decades.

The real success was that Salley built a foundation for life *after* basketball, for life *other* than basketball, so that, if he didn't make it, he could still be successful.

"As far as living in a certain environment, a lot of times you're born to fail," Salley said later, as he sat in the coaches' offices at Canarsie. "You're in a situation where you're not going to win—I don't want to be that negative—but where the system doesn't want you to win. Still, sometimes people slip out. I just happened to be the one to slip out that time. See, if you grow up your whole life looking at people pimp, you're going to be a pimp. If you grow up your whole life looking at drug dealers, sometimes that's the way it goes for you.

"My environment was that I watched my father get up at four thirty in the morning and not come back to the house until five o'clock at night. He'd watch Walter Cronkite and go to sleep. He drove a truck. He worked hard. In other words, I had a positive example.

"What I try to tell these kids, kids who might not have that, is that what you have to understand when everybody's running around and patting you on the back—or when people are running around putting you down—is that, in the end, it's only going to be you. *Yourself.* When you were born, you were born by yourself. When you die, you will die by yourself. And if you want to be a success in life, you have to do it by yourself. No matter what your situation is, no matter how it was that you started off in life."

Salley tried to be a role model for kids because he'd seen others do the same when he was younger. He'd sat at clinics and listened to Bernard King, then with the Knicks, talk about success—having come out of Fort Hamilton High School near the Verrazano Bridge in Brooklyn. He'd told kids they could do the same.

Salley listened. He listened to King and to others like World B Free, who'd come out of Canarsie with Geoff Huston to make the NBA, yet who still came back. "Those guys gave me hope," he said. "They made me think about things."

As he said: "People ask me who my idol is and I tell them, 'Malcolm X.' They ask me why and I tell them it's because he went from a negative to a positive. He was in jail, he was a bad person. He took drugs, he sold drugs. He was, at times, a pimp for women. He was put in jail for his negativity. He went to jail, educated himself, read every book that he could possibly read to the point where he had to wear glasses. He came out, took a religion that he felt was of his feeling and conscience. He took people from what you would call the gutter to become upstanding human beings and I think that's important. He told people, 'Follow your conscience and let it be your guide.'"

In the late 1980s, Michael George still lived in the neighborhood where he'd come up in Harlem; in the shadow of the St. Nicholas Projects—St. Nick, on the block—on 131st Street. He still had the same friends, those who were left; still took his runs in the park where he'd played ball as a kid. Back when he'd been a player. Not a legendary one, but one who still got his share of time on the neighborhood playgrounds.

He'd won the 1970–71 Public Schools Athletic League B Division City Title, the small schools title, at Bronx High School of Science—teaming in the same back court with Steve Lappas, the TV commentator and former assistant at Villanova and head coach at Manhattan College, who'd coached Rod Strickland and Harry S. Truman to the PSAL City Title.

Later, George was a sports reporter for the *New York Post*.

He also once was a member of a drug team.

It began when he and some friends were approached by a summer league coach who needed players. George was among those who agreed to play. The coach, this guy named Darryl, had a fine team; one of his best had been a starter in the Atlantic Coast Conference. Darryl also was a drug dealer, but since he treated his team right, some of the guys thought it was easy not to mind his occupation, George said.

"You could always go to Darryl and borrow five hundred for new sneakers," he said. "Know what I'm sayin'? He took care of his crew. He wanted us to be the best. To be respected. Now, some of us wasn't about drugs. But that didn't affect the way he treated you. His team was a reflection on him, on his business. Things had to be done right.

When we went to games, we went in a black pearl limo. Darryl would send over three limos to take his team to the games. We used to go from Manhattan over to Brooklyn, pull up at maybe eleven o'clock at night in front of these projects, and pile out of this limo—steppin' out in style to play our game. We would intimidate people just because we played for someone who could afford to send us in limousines and have them wait around for us while we played the game. It was a whole social thing. There were guys who couldn't play for Darryl and guys who wanted to."

To some of the crew, the impressionable ones who didn't have their head, the lifestyle was one they then chose to follow. Not only did Darryl use his team to enhance the reputation of his drug business and earn a little side cash with some well-placed bets on the games—but he used his team to recruit employees, who became his street-level dealers. But the one constant understood by Mike George, and not understood by most of his teammates, was the consequences of making such associations. Which was why George eventually quit.

There was the brutality of street-level corporate takeovers, drug-related hits, which happened when you least expected them.

"Darryl got killed," George said. "And the setup was that Darryl probably got killed by someone on the team, this guy named Hilton, and everyone knew it. See, Darryl got killed in his apartment. Darryl was the kind of guy who always came to the door with his gun cocked, because of the nature of the business. But Darryl didn't have his gun when he got two in the head. He left it in his desk drawer. So everyone figured it had to be someone he knew. Hilton lived in the building. Hilton wanted to move up in the organization. And Hilton was the guy crying loudest at the funeral.

"But it wasn't long before Hilton got set up, too," George said. "He was in the community center hangin' out when someone came runnin' in and said, 'Hilton, there's someone outside needs to see you.' Hilton went outside and took three in the chest."

In other words, choose your friends well.

It was because it often was difficult to tell the good from the bad that the game between the Rastafarians, a posse whose trade was alleged to be marijuana, and the Supreme Team, a crew, as members of drug gangs were known, whose business was alleged to be crack cocaine, came to be refereed by Greg Vaughn.

Perhaps that was how Boo Harvey, then the point guard at St. John's, also came to be a participant. Harvey told St. John's athletic director Jack Kaiser he'd considered the contest to be "a pickup game."

He'd also denied knowledge of players having been paid, though it seemed unlikely a player of Harvey's stature—someone who grew up in the infamous Forties Projects in South Jamaica—wouldn't have known the game was funded by drug dealers and that certain players would receive money.

"There's always heavy betting on these games," one police source said, "and [gang members] probably would want to let bettors know it's going to be happening. Players would have to know."

Some street-level informants even told police that Harvey, who had performed for the Supreme Team, had been paid for his appearance. "A drug game?" the police source said. "Fifty thousand? Someone was paid. You know the 'name' players must have gotten some cash to be there."

Harvey, who refused public comment on the situation, denied he was paid. Kaiser for his part said, "I'm not Sherlock Holmes. I have to believe my man. We did have a special session with Boo and he steadfastly said he did not get paid and said he did not know if anyone got paid. I asked questions, he gave me answers. Boo was very candid. He said that, at the time, he did not consider this to be a big thing. He was in his own neighborhood, on his own playground. We told him there was this necessity to watch acquaintances and friends and where he hangs out. But these are probably people he has known all his life. Kids, you know, can easily rationalize."

"You hear rumors and you read things in the paper," then–St. John's coach Lou Carnesecca said at the time. "Drugs, gambling. It's all conjecture. This referee was a nice guy. He must have thought it was all right to be there. Boo did, too."

Though the NCAA eventually suspended Harvey for one game for having appeared in what it termed "an unsanctioned summer-league game," in reality the suspension was irrelevant. Of importance, really, was what his participation illustrated: that money, drugs, violence, and basketball are inextricably linked in the inner city.

They are part of life, part of death.

Like Mike George and Greg Vaughn, Boo Harvey was only dealing with people from the neighborhood, a neighborhood in which he had received mixed messages all his life. Chances were, as Kaiser suggested, he'd known most of those people since childhood and never once questioned their motives or their business. To him, to Mike George, to Greg Vaughn, and to a host of others, they were acquaintances; people to play ball with, against. That some might be drug dealers or doctors was not a factor.

To him, to them, they were just folks from the block.

Perhaps that was why, when those in the neighborhood got together to hold a three-day memorial tournament at Baisley Park in an effort to raise money for widow Robin Vaughn and her six-year-old son, Darryl, more than a dozen uniformed housing police officers had to be called out to patrol the area. It seemed someone had called 911, reporting that local residents had been seen placing bets on the games.

———

All this, John Salley said, was why it was important for little kids to see him, to see he was, as he said, "tangible." It was important that they see other positive role models. People like his teammate Vinnie Johnson, who'd come out of the city and now talked to kids about success. People like Rolando Blackman, who'd graduated from Grady High School in Brooklyn and become an NBA all-star. People who'd turned their lives around like Bernard King and Chris Mullin.

People who'd become positive examples, like Len Elmore, who'd come out of New York City to have a fine NBA career, then went to work as both a television commentator and an assistant district attorney in Brooklyn. People like Ricky Sobers, World B Free, Kenny Smith, and Kenny Anderson. People who'd made it, were making it.

"You know," Salley told his audience that afternoon at Canarsie, "when I was in school, like the fourth grade, I had a friend in my class named Darryl Littles. When we got to the fourth grade, Darryl Littles couldn't read. Now, it wasn't the school's fault. You can't say it was his parents' fault. It was Darryl's fault. We was in a science class and the teacher said, 'Darryl, read this paragraph.' Darryl said, 'I don't have my glasses on. I can't see.' Good trick, right? The next time, the teacher called on Darryl and Darryl had his glasses, had his glasses on and, when he was asked to read, he said, 'I can't. I got a headache.' Everybody was going, like, 'He can't read. He can't read.' And Darryl was like, 'I can read. I just got a headache.' I said, 'Darryl, you didn't know the word, did you?' He said, 'I knew the word. I knew the word. I just didn't feel good.' Let me tell you something. When Darryl finally told me he couldn't read, he was embarrassed. My mother helped him learn how to read. I helped him learn how to read. Darryl's a sergeant [in the military] now. And you have to read if you want to make sergeant, because you have to take tests. What I'm trying to say is that, if a brother like Darryl can make a change in a little bit of time, then anybody can change—if they want to."

As one kid from Brownsville, then–Canarsie basketball team member Dwayne Carter, said afterward, "This meant a lot to me. I can understand, relate to it. A couple of my friends have gotten shot. One got shot in the head. One got shot in the back over a girl and another was shot 'cause of drugs. It means a lot for him to come down here and tell us that it don't have to be that way. Maybe it will make a difference."

For the sake of those whose futures hung in the balance and had yet to be decided, you could only hope the kid was right.

Van Nuys, ASAP

The list of those eligible for the 1988 NBA Draft contained a dozen college underclassmen, so-called early entries, when it was announced on May 18.

Most of them were expected. Guard Rex Chapman announced he was leaving the University of Kentucky. Tito Horford, a seven-foot-one sophomore whose controversial enrollments in Houston and Louisiana State had once been nullified by the NCAA, was done at Miami. Charles Shackleford said goodbye to the good folks at North Carolina State; Jerome Lane was out at Pittsburgh. And guard Rod Strickland, the junior from New York City who'd teamed with Lloyd at Oak Hill Academy and whose college career had best been described as "checkered," had thrown in the towel at DePaul.

But one name on the list caught nearly everyone by surprise.

Lloyd Daniels, Jr., whose well-chronicled past was already being heavily scrutinized by a host of curious-but-cautious NBA officials, had announced he was entering the draft.

"I'll go to an NBA camp," he said, sounding unconcerned about the concerns, "and, if it doesn't work out, I'll come back to the CBA. No harm done."

To declare himself eligible, an underclassman had to submit a written letter to the league announcing his intentions to forfeit all remaining college eligibility. Lloyd, of course, already was ineligible to play in college, since he'd played as a pro.

Making a formal declaration somehow felt desperate. And it was met by many of the league executives with skepticism, cynicism, and disbelief.

Acting as an agent, Las Vegas attorney David Chesnoff, who'd filed the required letter in March, said of Lloyd, "There's no question he can play in the NBA. It's just a matter of his learning to accept discipline—making games, making practices. It's called maturity. That has to come from him. He knows what the score is now. All he wants is a chance to show what he's got. He realizes this could be his last chance."

With former Houston Rockets guards Mitchell Wiggins and Lewis Lloyd having been banned from the league for a minimum of two years for drug violations—and, with Micheal Ray Richardson still awaiting reinstatement, Chris Mullin having just completed treatment for admitted alcohol abuse, and Nets forward Orlando Woolridge having become a recent guest in the Alcohol and Substance Abuse Program in Van Nuys, California—there seemed little chance of Lloyd being selected by any team.

A high-ranking official, in fact, said NBA commissioner David J. Stern might even warn all teams that a contract with Lloyd Daniels would not receive automatic approval, if at all. That seemed possible, too, considering what had happened three years earlier, when the Cleveland Cavaliers selected Tulane star John "Hot Rod" Williams.

Implicated in the point-shaving scandal at Tulane, Williams did not have his contract validated until he had been acquitted on sports bribery charges. That was a year after he was taken by the Cavs.

Though some NBA executives remained unconvinced Lloyd could ever straighten out his life—as Peter Vecsey, the viper-tongued columnist for the *New York Post*, wrote: "Lloyd Daniels entered the NBA Draft because his life-long ambition is to receive an expense-paid vacation to Van Nuys"—several teams did express at least marginal interest. Gathered at the American Museum of Natural History in Manhattan on May 20 for the NBA Draft Lottery, which would determine the draft order, a bunch of general managers and scouts assessed Lloyd's skill and his chances of being selected.

"I would give him a chance," then–Indiana Pacers general manager Donnie Walsh said. "He has to get himself squared away, but I see someone drafting him. No one will waste an early pick, but I think someone will take him. We will consider it."

"With his previous background and his involvement in things, teams will think about it seriously before they bring him in," Phoenix Suns general manager Cotton Fitzsimmons said. "But I think someone will . . . take a look at him. I would question that he might go in the first three rounds. But he'll probably get invited to a camp."

Seattle SuperSonics head scout Gary Wortman said while most underclassmen weren't mature enough to survive in pro basketball and questioned whether Lloyd was "ready for the rigors of the NBA," he also said he'd seen Swee'pea with the Topeka Sizzlers—and said the Sonics just might take a shot. "It's difficult to say where he'll be picked, but I think he could even be a first-round pick. It'll be interesting."

As one general manager, who asked not to be identified, said, "If Daniels showed up at the Chicago pre-draft camp and showed that he could play NBA-caliber basketball, teams would be interested. We wouldn't scratch him off *our* list."

Others weren't so sure. Some said that, in the interest of self-protection and self-preservation, their clubs would avoid Lloyd at all cost. As then–New York Knicks director of scouting Dick McGuire said: "We have no interest in him. None at all."

"I think it is a little too early to assess his situation," said Nets general manager Harry Weltman, whose team had lost Richardson and Woolridge to drug issues in the three previous seasons. "I am not positive Lloyd can play in the NBA and people will have to take a strong look into whether he has made any advances in dealing with his life."

With the draft still a month away, some said there might be time for the jury to reach a favorable verdict, for teams to weigh the positives against the negatives, take a chance, select him.

But, considering the disaster that followed the 1986 draft—Len Bias died and draftees Chris Washburn, William Bedford, and Roy Tarpley all found themselves in rehabilitation for substance abuse—that chance figured to be *fat chance.*

As Marty Blake, NBA director of scouting, said: "There's only so many strikes you can give a guy. At one time, I assumed Lloyd Daniels had talent. Now, I haven't the vaguest idea where he might be drafted—if he gets selected, at all.

"It's a tragic case."

———————

Lloyd wasn't taken in the 1988 NBA Draft. Rumors and reports of his personal problems in Topeka and Waitemata, New Zealand, as well as his problematic educational background, caused teams to shun him. His only chance was to get invited to a rookie camp somewhere, though he'd still have to prove he was clean—and had the ambition necessary to make it in pro basketball. So he went to Los Angeles and joined a team in the L.A. Summer Pro League.

The Summer Pro League is where draft picks work to improve their games before camp and undrafted players work to be seen—in hopes of getting invited to camp.

Lloyd held his own in Summer Pro, where he went head-to-head with folks like Orlando Woolridge, Benoit Benjamin, and Reggie Miller. He became friends with UCLA guard Pooh Richardson at Summer Pro. And he received favorable reviews from scouts who'd seen him there and liked his game. But the scouts also noticed that Lloyd still seemed to be having issues. As some teammates said, Lloyd sometimes arrived at games "high" and "reeking of alcohol"—something he later admitted was true.

The subsequent lack of interest in signing Lloyd to a free-agent contract amid the whispers was another warning sign for those who knew Lloyd's demons best.

"Lloyd was preparing to go to the CBA," former guardian Mark Warkentien said. "But he was not ready. We brought him to Las Vegas and proposed he enter rehabilitation. Me, my wife, David Chesnoff, Sam Perry—we all sat in my living room until all hours of the night until we convinced him to reenter rehab."

"For a while, it seemed he was getting real healthy," Chesnoff said. "But soon you could see he was getting lazy again. I said to him, 'Lloyd,

I get the feeling you've been disregarding your health.' He said, 'Ches, I really want you [guys] to find the best program you can.' He realized he was strung out. That he wasn't playing to his full potential. He was staying up late and partying. He said he had had enough."

"I didn't think I had a problem," Lloyd said later. "I thought I could do it on my own. I was in denial. I thought I could still get high and play ball. But you know the old sayin', 'You can't do two things at once.' You got to pick one thing. If you goin' to get high, you just got to get high. You got to say, 'Can't play no ball no more.' If you want to play ball you got to say, 'Can't do drugs no more.' I couldn't do that. I tried, but I couldn't do that. I knew I needed to get me some help. I knew I could have been better in L.A. if I wasn't gettin' high. I finally realized drugs and basketball don't mix."

On October 24, Lloyd, who'd suffered relapses after two previous stints in drug rehabilitation, entered the Alcohol and Substance Abuse Program Treatment Center at Van Nuys Community Hospital in Van Nuys, California. Otherwise known as ASAP/Van Nuys, the center served as rehab central for the NBA—with fourteen players treated there for dependency problems over the course of the previous four years.

Unable to get into the NBA, onto the roster of an NBA team, Lloyd had still managed to become a member of its most exclusive club.

For the next three months, Lloyd would serve as the cornerstone for what could have been a contending franchise in the NBA in 1988–89. Forget the Lakers. Forget the Pistons. At various times, Lloyd was in Van Nuys with Duane Washington, Dirk Minniefield, David Thompson, William Bedford, and Roy Tarpley. Lloyd Daniels, the self-proclaimed new Chris Washburn when he was at Laurinburg, even got to meet the original model at Van Nuys. Chris Washburn turned out to be his roommate.

"We was all addicts, all addicts," Lloyd said of his new friends. "But, how'd you like to coach that team? We had the all–Van Nuys team. All of them was my boys. Chris Washburn's my boy. Roy Tarpley's my boy. We was all lovely together."

The ASAP treatment center had become associated with the NBA in 1985, when Dr. David Lewis, the program's founder and director, signed a contract to serve as an exclusive "rehab and detox" facility for the league's players—a situation that would enable his program to administer to the specific needs of addicted athletes. There had been a growing concern among NBA teams, as well as the rest of the business community, that the use of recreational drugs was having an effect on the ability to conduct business. Publicity generated by revelations of drug-addicted athletes threatened the league's success, tarnishing its most marketable asset: its image.

What ASAP/Van Nuys offered was a chance for self-help. A chance to come clean and come back. Part of its attraction was that the program offered a chance for basketball players to play basketball while they submitted to more conventional treatment, something that seemed to make treatment more palatable.

More embraceable.

"We're the only drug treatment center in the country with NBA-approved breakaway backboards," Lewis once said. It was rehabilitation and rebounds. "Physical exercise is helpful in recovery," he said. "It is a perfectly good addiction."

Of course, part of the rehabilitation process at Van Nuys remained traditional. The twelve-step program developed by Alcoholics Anonymous—a program in which an addict must first admit he is powerless over drugs or alcohol—was used. Part of the treatment program also required daily sessions with counselors, all of whom were themselves recovering addicts. Days were structured to allow patients about an hour and a half of free time, though players, who often awoke at 6:30 a.m., spent as much as three hours a day playing basketball and volleyball, riding exercise bikes, and swimming laps. There were nightly counseling sessions, as well as group therapy.

Patients began rehabilitation on the east wing of Van Nuys Community Hospital, where they slept in hospital rooms in hospital beds.

There were no televisions and no telephones. Only after they had shown progress toward their recovery were they moved to one of the six bungalows—"Clean and Sober Houses," as they were known—on the hospital grounds, which were surrounded by a six-foot-high fence.

The average stay at ASAP/Van Nuys lasted forty-five to forty-eight days at a cost of about $500 a day. In Lloyd's case, some of those bills were paid in advance by David Chesnoff with a portion of the more than $20,000 to be charged to Medicaid.

Or, against Lloyd's future earnings.

"If you willin' to work it, it works, man," Lloyd said. "All you got to do is take one day at a time. If you want to work they program, it'll work. It's up to you. You got to be one hundred percent clean. You got to say, 'I need help.' That's the only way you goin' to make it in life. It's just a mind-over-matter thing. You got to realize, say to *yo'self,* 'Do I want to come out of here with nothin' or do I want to be somethin'?'

"That's what it is."

But Lloyd didn't always approach Van Nuys as rehabilitation on the road to the NBA. Often he treated it as one big party.

As an "expense-paid vacation."

The afternoon Lloyd entered the hospital, the first person he saw was New Jersey Nets guard Duane Washington—not to be confused with Dwayne "Pearl" Washington, the all-American from Boys & Girls High School in Brooklyn and Syracuse University who also played with the Nets, as well as with the Miami Heat. And the first thing Lloyd and Duane did when they met in the hall was exchange high-fives.

"Here," one witness said, "you figure this is going to be a serious thing. Then you see that. I've got to tell you, it made me wonder."

Wonder all you want. But at least Lloyd now had a real chance. What was the alternative? To end up like Micheal Ray Richardson, Mitchell Wiggins, and Lewis Lloyd, banned from the NBA because of not being able to conquer a drug problem? To end up like Earl Manigault, Joe Hammond, and Fly Williams, never having had the chance to succeed at a pro career because of a drug problem? To end up like Len Bias, dead because of drugs? To wind up like Richie Adams, dying a slow death?

Flora Adams spoke with a heavy heart, the kind you get when you are forced to watch your son make a shambles of his life. Once, she said, back when her son Richie used to be regarded as one of the best basketball players in New York City, she used to think that someday he'd make the NBA. He was that good, had that much talent.

"He had a future," she said. "Know what I'm saying?"

She was in her apartment in the Andrew Jackson Projects near the Grand Concourse in the Bronx, no more than a few blocks from Yankee Stadium. It was a neighborhood where, in the 1980s, the landscape, cratered with the battered hulks of burned-out tenements, often mimicked the tattered dreams of its residents.

It was the neighborhood that had given life to her child, to her children. The neighborhood where, years before, her son first headed down the road to ruin.

It had been a simple beginning, she recalled of that time. Junior high school. Some wrong-minded friends. A mugging out there on the Concourse.

Later, it became more complex. Much more. Drugs, muggings to support a bad habit. Stolen cars, armed robberies. Name it.

"I don't understand," she said. "I raised four kids. I have two daughters and they were never in trouble, never did no drugs. My baby . . . I never had no trouble with him. But in this building I'm in, mostly everybody is on crack. Everybody my son Richie hung out with is on crack. All the girls, the young girls, is on crack. You know, he's not a bad child. If you knew him, you'd like him. You would. Evidently, he was just weak. One of the weaker ones. He was a follower. He trusted everyone."

These were painful words. Words of anguish. As she'd spoken, her eldest son, the drug addict, was across the East River—in a jail cell over on Rikers Island.

There Richie Adams, the former star forward from Benjamin Franklin High School and UNLV—the man once known in the parks as "the Animal," for the ferocity of his game—sat in a jail uniform awaiting sentencing in New York State Supreme Court, First Judicial District, following his guilty plea on May 16, 1989, to a count of robbery, first-degree, and two counts of grand larceny, fourth.

A spokeswoman for the Manhattan district attorney, Colleen Roche, said the then-twenty-six-year-old Adams had been arrested after he tried to steal money "by placing a gun to the jaw of a woman at a cash machine" in Manhattan on September 25, 1988. Fifteen days later, he "snatched a purse" from a woman in an apartment building in Manhattan. Then, on April 30, 1989, Adams was arrested while out on bail, caught stealing the purse of a sixty-eight-year-old woman in Grand Central Terminal.

As if to document how much of a wreck he had made of his life, Adams, who was six foot nine, 210 pounds and who had no front teeth, grabbed the purse at 5:04 p.m.—in the middle of an evening rush-hour crowd. He was wearing a UNLV sweatshirt. As Roche said, "He wasn't real difficult to identify."

And so, Adams now sat in Rikers, declared a predicate felon due to his numerous offenses, facing years in the state penitentiary.

"I told him," Flora Adams said, "'You know, you are one of those people out there in the street that I'm afraid of.' He just sat there and gave me the strangest, saddest look. What could he say? I told him, 'That was somebody's *mother* you robbed.'

"It was all quite disappointing to me."

———

On the basketball court, removed from his penchant for self-destruction, there seemed little reason ever to be disappointed in Richie Adams. Despite his thin, wiry frame, he could dominate games. Could intimidate opponents, could be strong; make his own decisions, the right ones. Back then he was to be feared, a player's player.

The kind who owned the park.

"If Lloyd Daniels is Magic with Larry Bird's jump shot," Orlando Magic forward Sidney Green said, "then Richie Adams was a smaller

Bill Russell. That's the only comparison I can make. That's how much of a great player Richie Adams was. I would have to put him high on the charts of all those I have played against.

"No problem, he could play in the NBA."

How good Adams could be came in eleventh grade when Gary Springer, then a senior at Franklin, got hurt prior to a game against Charles Evans Hughes. Hughes had guard Steve Burtt, who'd later star with Springer at Iona College before going to the Golden State Warriors, and Kevin Williams, who later played for the Nets.

"Richie came in and had something like forty-two points with twenty-two rebounds and eleven assists," Franklin coach Stan Dinner said. "It was, without a doubt, the greatest performance I've ever seen in high school, college. No, anywhere."

"The ball would come off the rim," Springer recalled of that game, "and he just was going over everyone. Once, Richie threw it down so hard they had to stop the game until the rim and backboard stopped shaking."

But, off the court, another pattern began to emerge. Not only did Adams "borrow" Stan Dinner's car without permission. And not only did he arrive high for a playoff game against Stevenson. He also began to steal things from local stores, steal things from his own friends and teammates. Sometimes, friends said, he stole to help people, sort of a latter-day playground Robin Hood. Dinner recalled the time when a girl in school told Adams she'd been without food and was hungry.

"She was pregnant. She said, 'Richie, I got nothing to eat.' Richie went out to the supermarket and loaded up. . . . He put it all under his coat and came back."

Sometimes, though, Adams just stole.

"I think he was a kleptomaniac, maybe, he would steal so much," Springer said. "He was good at it, too. He'd walk into a store and come out with soda, cookies, crackers; anything anyone wanted. But there was a time me and Lonnie Green was sitting with him in a pizza place and the guy put Lonnie's change on the counter. We turned around for a second and, when we turned back, it was gone. Richie had taken it.

He gave it back when we asked. He said it was all a joke. But I think he was calling out for help, though. I really think he needed some serious help."

Like Lloyd, Adams had started smoking marijuana when he was just ten. He started snorting coke at eighteen. Overnight, he became moody. One minute he'd be laughing. The next he wouldn't talk to anyone. Often he mingled with people he should not have associated with. He almost always refused to listen to good advice.

"Intellectually, he was smarter than anybody we had," Dinner said of his players back at Franklin. "Now, I don't know what that means, but he wasn't a dumb kid. This kid had brains and he wasn't a bad kid. Richie would give you the shirt off his back. He just didn't listen to the right people. He was self-destructive."

Because of his bad attendance record, dating back to his days at Alfred E. Smith, Adams failed to graduate from high school. He later earned his GED and attended Massachusetts Bay Community College. Then he went to UNLV. But the team had Green, then a senior who played the same position.

So Adams rarely played as a sophomore.

Sitting behind Green made Adams jealous, according to Joe Bostic, who ran a private elementary school in Bedford-Stuyvesant and was a longtime friend of Adams and other players from the city—including Lloyd, Mark Jackson, and Walter Berry, all of whom played at one time or another for his summer league team, the Wiz.

"In his heart, Richie knew he was better than Sidney," Bostic said. "He knew he should be starting, should be playing. It hurt him, bothered him. He couldn't be patient. He started to act stupid."

Danny Tarkanian, the coach's son and a player for the Runnin' Rebels, was perhaps the closest to Adams during that time.

"More than once," Danny Tarkanian said, "he told me that he was a manic-depressive. During some practices, he would just go sit in the corner and not talk to anyone. I mean, he wouldn't move. Guys would say things to him. Dad would try to get him onto the floor. But Richie just sat there. It was like he was in another world."

The situation got worse after the season. Adams's grandmother died. Days later, so did his girlfriend's mother. Distraught, Adams refused to go to school. He refused to leave his room, sitting in bed for hours with shades drawn, smoking joints.

"You couldn't talk to him," Flora Adams said. "He was in his own world."

By the time he returned to Las Vegas, he'd missed too many classes and was forced to sit out the year as a redshirt, which was fine with Jerry Tarkanian. Adams had become so much of a problem, his coaching staff didn't want Adams back.

Danny Tarkanian convinced his father to give Adams another chance. Tark did. And Adams responded, not only on the court—he was named conference player of the year two straight seasons, averaging 15.8 points and 7.9 rebounds with 45 blocks as a senior—but also off it, where he showed a remarkable ability to work with children. "He'd prop his hat sideways," Jerry Tarkanian said, "and sit with the kids. The other guys would have taken their showers, left the arena, and he'd still be there laughing, signing autographs, talking to the kids. The other players would leave with their girlfriends. Richie would leave with the kids to go get ice cream."

The problem was, Adams was a lot like those kids. A follower, he always seemed to follow the wrong people, hoping to find the Pied Piper. A follower who seemed to make the wrong decision every time his life neared a crossroads.

Touted as a legitimate pro prospect, he joined the Long Island Knights in the United States Basketball League—a summer semiprofessional league run out of small college and high school gyms—to earn money before the NBA Draft. Then, when he was selected by the Washington Bullets, it was learned he'd been arrested earlier that very morning in the Bronx, driving a stolen car. "He had gone out to Long Island to pick up his paycheck from the Knights," Flora Adams said. "He said the cab didn't wait for him and he didn't have cab fare to get back. He knew he had to get to the draft."

And so Adams took a car from the parking lot outside the gym.

"It was wrong," Flora Adams said. "But that is the way he is. He didn't mean no harm."

"The amazing thing," Tarkanian said, years later, still in disbelief, "was that the police gave Richie a polygraph test and he passed it. He wasn't lying. He really believed that he had just *borrowed* that car. To him, he hadn't done anything wrong."

Given probation, Adams went to rookie camp with the Bullets in Princeton, New Jersey, but eventually was released. It seemed team management didn't look highly on the fact that he snuck out of camp each night and went home, one time leaving pro camp in order to return to the Bronx to appear in a drug game—for $100.

"Some of his friends came out to see him at the hotel," Springer said, recalling the situation. "His get-high buddies. Richie climbed out the window, actually hung out on the window ledge, and went with his so-called friends." As Flora Adams said, "Every night, his friends would go over and get Richard and every day the coaches from the team would come here, pick him up and bring him back."

After that, Richie Adams bounced around for a while. He played for two years in Argentina on a team that Springer was also supposed to join.

"But," Springer said, "the guy mailed my plane ticket to Richie and Richie cashed it, a twelve-hundred-dollar ticket. That's when I knew [he] was off the deep end."

Jerry Tarkanian also sent Adams a plane ticket, one to Las Vegas, where he had several jobs lined up for him. One was as a valet at an exclusive club; another was bartender, a job Tark said would earn Adams a minimum $50,000 a year. Adams cashed that ticket, too.

Later, Tarkanian sent a nonrefundable ticket.

"I was supposed to meet Richie at one for a four o'clock flight," Joe Bostic said. "All I had was a phone number of the place we were to meet. I called at one. No Richie. I called at two. No Richie. I called at two thirty. No Richie. Three. No Richie. Finally, he showed up at the place and called me and said, 'Joe, come get me now.' It was three fifteen and, of course, there was no way we could make it."

Dinner even arranged for Adams to play in Yugoslavia.

"I called a representative of the team and said, 'I'll meet you tonight at eight o'clock with Richie.' Richie met me at eleven a.m. and was with me all day. Around seven p.m. he says, 'Coach, I'm hungry. Give me some money and I'll go get a sandwich.' I said, 'Great, Richie. Go get me a coffee, too.' I gave him a few bucks.

"I didn't see him again for four months."

"You know," Tark said, "it's hard to understand this drug thing, what makes these kids do this. Why can't these kids reason? Why couldn't Richie reason? Why couldn't Lloyd reason? Why can't any of these guys see what they've given up when they do this? Why can't a guy who's making a million dollars a year in the NBA reason? I don't know. I don't understand."

"Sometimes," Bostic said, "these guys just don't have the internal strength to say, 'No.' It's just like Swee'pea. If tomorrow, you could take Swee'pea out of his environment, change his mentality, Swee'pea would be a pro within a year. There is no doubt in my mind that there aren't fifteen ballplayers in the country better than Swee'pea. I'm talking about the pros, anybody. There is nobody I've seen that Swee'pea is not, offensively, equal to or better than as far as making something happen—including Magic, Joe Dumars, any of them. But people like Swee'pea, people like Richie, people who find this kind of trouble, they just don't understand the ramifications of what they do. It's just that, for all of them, the siren's song of the streets is stronger than anything you can tell them. It's stronger than anything you can say."

———

The games were incredible at Van Nuys, like outtakes from an NBA *Jam Session,* except that these stars were patients—and the games were played on the confines of the undersize, outdoor court. Sometimes, Lloyd went head-to-head with Tarpley, the seven-foot center from the Dallas Mavericks, dunking on him or embarrassing him with a move that would see him tell Tarpley, "Go get your sneaks, man." At times Tarpley would return the favor. "Showin' him some," Tarpley said.

Sometimes Lloyd and Tarpley made sure to be on the same team, going against Minniefield and Thompson, both of whom were smaller. Sometimes Lloyd and Washington went against Minniefield and Washburn. Other times, Lloyd went one-on-one against Washburn or Washington. Almost always, Lloyd came out on top.

"What used to get me pissed off," Lloyd said, recalling those games, "was that they would say to me, 'Don't worry, Lloyd, you be in the NBA one day.' I knew I should. They all knew I should, too. Like Chris Washburn. He was *dookie*, hear me?"

In other words, Swee'pea said, Washburn wasn't *shit*.

"He couldn't stop me. And Duane Washington? He had one hand. *Naclerio* is better than him. I told him, 'I can't believe *you* made the NBA.' And even if, like, David Thompson could still jump, I still had a better all-round game than all of thems, hear me? I was better than all them guys. Like, Roy Tarpley is supposed to be the 'Player of the Nineties.' Right? He's the 'Player of the Nineties.' That's what they call him. Well, I used to serve Roy Tarpley. Ask him. I used to serve him all the time."

"He did," Tarpley said. "He tricked me a couple of times, put a couple of playground moves on me. But I told him, 'Life isn't all about basketball.'"

Not that Tarpley had a right to talk. He'd grown up in Brooklyn and Queens and had moved, first to Mobile, Alabama, and then to Detroit, before he attended the University of Michigan. There he became an all-American and led the team to consecutive Big Ten titles. Selected seventh overall in the 1986 NBA Draft, he fast became a force in the league, winning the NBA Sixth Man award over Thurl Bailey of Utah for the 1987–88 season—finishing among the league's rebounding leaders despite being a reserve. But off the court, Tarpley had major problems. In the summer of 1987 he had been admitted to Van Nuys for treatment of a substance abuse problem.

On January 5, 1989, when Lloyd was nearly finished with his rehabilitation, Tarpley was readmitted to Van Nuys—his second NBA violation.

Still, Tarpley understood he was weak, that he had a problem. He admitted that he'd stumbled a number of times and said he was now working hard to overcome his addiction. But he couldn't say the same about Lloyd.

"We played against each other all the time," Tarpley said. "He was fun and I really had a good time with him. I really got to know him, we got to know each other because you're all on the same level in there, have the same sickness, disease. He's a very talented guy. He's got all the physical ability in the world. But there's a question of maturity, being responsible; being responsible for yourself and making the right decisions. In order to make it, you have to be dedicated, willing to go that extra mile. I didn't see that from him. I don't think he wanted to work that hard. His biggest problem was maturity. There comes a time when you have to be mature. Some people take longer than others. It is tough. I know it's been hard for me. But you've got to want it. And you have to want it bad. He wants it one day and the next, like, it's no big deal. You've got to want it all the time. It's not an easy process. It's a one-day-at-a-time thing. He got a great sense of humor. He got a nice personality. But he can get carried away with it sometimes. He doesn't know when to stop. You know, like, a joke is a joke. Like okay, man, enough is enough is enough. He likes to make people laugh. But you can only laugh so much and then it's time to get serious. And, a lot of times, when people tried to get serious with him, he was still there fooling around. It seemed like it never sunk in."

———

Richie Adams—inmate No. 89T2957—had called from a pay phone at Bear Hill Correctional Facility in Malone, New York. And now he was laughing about a move he'd made earlier in the week, a 360-degree tomahawk dunk: the kind he used to do with lightning regularity on national TV; the kind once pictured in *Sports Illustrated*. "They gave me a job working in the gym," he said. "I'm still the same. I still got it."

He'd been in so deep this time that even the high-priced lawyer hired by Danny Tarkanian and his father couldn't get him off.

So he'd gotten the maximum: four-and-a-half-to-nine years at Bear

Hill, a medium-security prison in the Adirondack Mountains, so far north in New York State that it was no more than a long jump from Canada, not a hundred miles southwest of Montreal.

This was drug rehabilitation for Richie Adams, rehabilitation for him and a million other addicts in America. Playing ball, biding his time until he could get back on the streets. Still, you had to wonder how much different it was from the rehabilitation Lloyd was going through at ASAP/Van Nuys. Sure, Adams didn't have the counselors. Certainly it didn't cost as much. But would rehab change Lloyd, cure him?

Could prison really rehabilitate Richie Adams?

One of the reasons UNLV had implemented its drug testing program back in 1985 was Adams. The coaching staff suspected he was using drugs—specifically, cocaine—and wanted to catch him red-handed, get him treatment, Jerry Tarkanian said.

But the program, then in its infancy, lacked teeth. The school had no power to take formal action. The first positive test would result in a meeting with the violator. Counseling, optional. A second violation meant coaches would meet with the player's parents. Counseling, mandatory. The third time a player tested positive, he'd be suspended. Two tests were given that year.

Adams failed twice.

But, partly because he lacked leverage and partly because he couldn't afford to lose his best player and still win basketball games, Tarkanian never took action against him.

After all, UNLV was headed for a 28-4 finish in 1984–85, was headed for its second-straight conference title, after going 29-6 with Adams in 1983–84. So, instead, what Tarkanian did was sit Adams. For *portions* of games.

Then again, Richie Adams wasn't about to listen to anyone—not Tarkanian, not his assistant coaches, not counselors—who offered advice on how to get a handle on his drug problems, all of which explained why, after all the years, all the efforts, he was behind bars for drug-related robberies; why he'd never sought treatment.

"I didn't *have* to rob," Adams said. "I just did it because I was stupid. I'm still the same Richie. I did stupid things 'cause of Richie. But you lose your mind so much, it makes you go out and do some stupid things. Drugs make you so unaware of things. It made me crazy, to go out and rob someone in front of fifteen thousand people. I was walking down the street, saw an opportunity to rob somebody. I just went out and did it. You think, 'If police chase me, I'm going to get away. If they catch me, I'll get out soon.' To me, I make problems for myself. It was my problem. Now that I'm getting older, I realize this thing was hurting me. It is hurting me. I said I would stop some day, and this is what it got me. I went to jail."

"You know what the sad thing is?" basketball scout Tom Konchalski said. "It is that we know and care about Richie Adams because he is six foot nine and a great basketball player."

Flora Adams sat in her apartment in the Jackson Projects. She was fifty-two years old then, having worked most of those years to make a better life for her children and grandchildren, two of them—Richie, Jr. and Richelle—Richie's children by two different girlfriends. She'd always made sure there was a roof over their heads. She'd always made sure there was enough to eat. She'd made sure their clothes were clean. And still, this had happened.

"You know, the first time he ever got arrested, I was ashamed," she said, trying not to sound guilty as she explained that she still spoke with her son on a regular basis, except now always by phone. "I was embarrassed. I used to visit him. But I felt like the criminal, so I don't go no more. It still hurts me, knowing that it's my child who did these things. I never thought I would have a child who would do things like this."

The last time she'd seen Richie, she said, he looked better. His face, once drawn and gaunt from self-abuse and drugs, had filled out. Even though he was still missing his front teeth—she'd found his dentures, broken, while cleaning earlier that week—she said, with a certain irony: "Richie *always* looks better when he's locked up. . . . It's sad to say, but I told him he looked like my child again. I mean, you wonder what made it all go wrong with him."

She and her son's friends—the real ones, the ones like Sidney Green and Stan Dinner and Joe Bostic and, yes, even Jerry Tarkanian—often wondered just what would happen if Adams eventually were to get out of prison. It was difficult for them to admit it, but they all were duly skeptical about his prospects. Any prospects.

"Richie's history," Dinner said then. "You hate to say it, you really do. But he's twenty-six years old and he's history. He's yesterday's news. I mean, what can you do with him? What are you going to rehabilitate him to do? What can you teach him to do? You're going to teach six-foot-nine Richie Adams to do what? Tell me. He has no skills. He don't have a degree. He's a basketball player. What can a basketball player do with no education? What?"

What indeed? After all, how could you treat a person for a problem when a major part of their problem was their environment, when it's *themselves;* factors over which you had no control? How could you treat a person who didn't *want* to be treated?

All her life, Flora Adams tried to lead her son down the right road and couldn't. She tried to save him from himself and couldn't. Instead he'd always fallen prey to his weakness, to his environment. To his addiction. To his impulses. To who he'd become.

"I always ask myself, 'Was there anything different I could have did?' But I did the best I could for him. My children were never hungry. They were never dirty. They always had a roof over their heads. I think I did good by these kids. It worked with three of them. But Richie, he lacked the strength to make it, keep away from the streets. . . .

"I'm not blaming nobody. He has his own mind. . . . Sometimes, I ask him, 'Richard, don't you wish you could start over again?' and he'll say, 'Yeah.' I still love him, but I am disappointed. If anyone could have made it, it could have been him."

———

Lloyd still had a chance to make it. Even he knew that much. So he tried hard to heed the advice of the counselors at ASAP/Van Nuys. In the house, where each patient was assigned chores—sweeping, cooking, cleaning—he always tried to do his on time, with precision. "There was days I had to sweep the floors," he said, "and days I had to do the dishes. It wasn't no big deal. It was what you had to do."

When the patients met at night for their group therapy sessions, Lloyd tried to be open and explain how he felt, explain why he was the way he was.

"You had to share thoughts with the other people," he said. "I told them how I used to be out on the streets, how I got a problem. The idea was to get your feelings out. You'd see guys break down. I cried one day. I'm not ashamed. I cried.

"You realize things when you do that, you really do."

Perhaps the person who tried hardest to make Lloyd understand his situation was David Thompson. Once, back in the day, Thompson had been known simply as "the Skywalker"—the guard who leaped over centers and other mere mortals in a single bound. An all-American, he'd soared to spectacular heights in college and in 1974 had carried North Carolina State to its first NCAA championship. He'd gone on to become an all-star in the NBA, one night back in April 1978, scoring *seventy-three* points in the final game of the season while trying to win the league scoring title. He didn't.

But he had become one of only three players in NBA history at that point—Wilt Chamberlain and Elgin Baylor were the other two—to have ever scored more than seventy in a single game, and, only Chamberlain had ever scored more.

But Thompson was a cocaine addict—a cocaine addict who also liked to drink. When his career ended in 1984, he was left with nothing. No wife, who'd left him, taking their children; no house, which he lost to the Internal Revenue Service, which took all his possessions in lieu of the $810,461 he owed to forty-one creditors, as well as in back taxes; no self-esteem, which he'd lost long before he'd ever lost his material possessions; and, no employment. Thompson filed for Chapter 11 bankruptcy in 1986.

Eventually he'd taken a job with the Charlotte Hornets, where he'd served as a community liaison, speaking to groups about the dangers of substance abuse. But, having failed to heed his own advice, Thompson slipped in the fall of 1988.

On December 15, he found himself a patient in Van Nuys.

"He told me straight up, as a man, 'Hey, look at me,'" Lloyd said. "'Look at me. I been there. I got an NCAA ring. I played in the NBA All-Star Game. And now I got to work for the Charlotte Hornets. In the *office*. 'We'd talk 'bout life, personal life, me an' David T. . . . He'd say, 'Look at Chris Washburn. Look at these other boys. Is that how you want to end up?' He told me, 'Lloyd, live a wrong life and you'll be back. Either you'll be back or you'll be dead. Remember that,' he said. 'Remember that.'"

Of course, Lloyd told him he would.

"The thing with addiction," Thompson said, "is you can feel that you want to do it, get yourself straight. But, while you say things that you genuinely mean, the second you go out with the wrong people, take that first drink, do that first drug, it all goes down the tube. I think Lloyd really wanted to stop. But one thing he had to realize was that alcohol is also a drug and would lead him right back into all his problems. See, but he didn't want to give things up, give it up completely. You've got to be willing to change your playmates *and* your playgrounds. Because, if you go out with your old buddies, you have to realize they're going to persuade you to take a drink or do drugs before you persuade them not to. But it seemed Lloyd could never come to grips with that.

"The idea is to do it one day at a time," Thompson said. "You can't say, 'I've got to stop for the rest of my life.' You just have to say, 'One day at a time.'

"It becomes as hard as you make it. The center is a lot like going to school. You learn the medical reasons behind why you drink or use drugs, then you learn the physical and the emotional aspects of your dependencies. But it also becomes one addict talking to another, learning to understand what another person has to say about it. If you can identify with what another addict has to say, then you can get rid of your guilt, the negative feelings. A lot of people who use alcohol or drugs have done things that they regret and they have to be able to forgive themselves before they can move on toward recovery. But you have to be honest to go forward. Honesty. That's the key.

"You have to be honest, open-minded. You have to be teachable. You have to be willing to go to whatever lengths to do what you have to do to stay sober.

"Rarely has anyone failed who followed the path. But you have to want to be sober for you. Not for basketball, not for your family, not for your kids. But for you. That means you have to be honest about it. I don't think Lloyd ever understood that."

———

Lloyd was in ASAP/Van Nuys for eighty-five days, from late October 1988 until almost February 1989. Then he spent a handful of weeks in a halfway house near Sherman Oaks, California. "He was a much different guy," Chesnoff said of his recovering client. "He was much more mature, much more goal directed."

Jodie Tarkanian, Tark's daughter, recalled how Lloyd came to visit her for dinner while he was in the halfway house. They went to basketball practice at UCLA—"We went to talk to Pooh," Jodie said. "He was like, 'Pooh, my man. Pooh, my man'"—then made a spaghetti dinner and went bowling. "He said he was doing good," she said. "He came in, helped with the dishes. He had even tried to help me cook. He was talking about the NBA. He said, 'This is my *last* chance. I *have* to do well this time.' I kind of got the feeling that he really wanted to do well. But he just didn't know how."

"In my opinion, he had to stick with ASAP and with the halfway house, play in the summer league again, spend a whole season in the CBA and, maybe the next year, an NBA team would pick him up," Chesnoff said. "But he would have to really live and work hard. And I don't think he could do that. Instead, Lloyd went back to New York.

"Against my advice, he went back," he said. "That was a problem. That's not exactly an environment best suited to staying out of trouble. I've been in that neighborhood with him. They sell crack on the street corners, not baseball cards."

"I went back," Lloyd said, "and in 'bout a month I had some problems. I didn't follow no aftercare. I got big-headed, said, 'Yeah, you could smoke a joint. It ain't no big deal.' Everybody thinks. 'Oh, I could drink, as long as I don't do cocaine' and 'Oh, I could smoke as long as I don't do cocaine.' Well, I didn't do no coke for two weeks. Then I had a relapse.... I didn't have the sense to realize what it meant to stay clean."

He just couldn't do what it took to ensure his future.

The Entourage

Lloyd had been standing around, talking with friends, when boxer Mike Tyson walked into the Entourage Cafe that night. Tyson was then the undisputed heavyweight champion of the world. And Lloyd? He was straight out of rehab at Van Nuys.

"Yo, *Mikey Boy!*" Lloyd called out. Suddenly Tyson was all smiles.

"Hey, Lloyd," Mike Tyson said as he came walking over.

The group of friends—Jamal Faulkner, the all-American from one of the best high school teams in the nation, Christ the King; Syracuse-bound center Conrad McRae; star guard Lawrence "Future" Pollard; even Arnie Hershkowitz and Ron Naclerio—just sat there stunned, speechless—*dumbfounded*—as Lloyd exchanged high-fives, low-fives, shakes, smiles, and a hug reserved for long-lost homeboys with Tyson.

"Mikey and me is B-Boys," Lloyd said later. "We got history."

The two had met earlier in the year through a mutual friend and, knowing they both came from the same area of Brownsville, had begun hanging out together. Tyson had been through his divorce with Robin Givens, and his world was in turmoil. Lloyd represented the old days, someone from the 'Ville, from back when life was simple. Simpler. From a time when Iron Mike could just be Mike. So the two would hang out, go to clubs, go drinking. They were the new odd couple, yet still much the same.

But, Hersh cautioned, "Mike Tyson thought Lloyd cared about him, because of where they were from, you know, as friends. But Lloyd looked at Tyson as money for Lloyd. Lloyd looks for the next guy he can cling on to. He'll parasite off anybody.

"Tyson just happened to be the richest anybody he knew."

Despite his alcohol and substance abuse problems, Lloyd spent an awful lot of time at the Entourage, most of it, drinking, Hersh said. The Entourage was located just outside the boundaries of midtown Manhattan, a preppie hangout frequented mostly by kids in their early twenties home on vacation or just out on the town. It had become a place for Hersh, Ron, and their summer league players mostly because Hersh knew the manager—a guy named Dave Liss. The players, other than Lloyd and the pros who used to drop in, were mostly still in high school and never drank. But they ate after games. Ron and Hersh paid sometimes. Other times Dave, the manager, picked up the tab.

Lloyd was at the Entourage a lot, Hersh said, mostly because it was a place where he could bum money, the way folks said he had coming up. So he'd hang out, ride Mike Tyson's coattails, maybe welch off some of the other guys. Or he'd straight-up ask to "borrow" a five-spot or a twenty, or, Hersh said, anything he could get his hands on.

The thing was, Hersh said, times had changed.

Back when Lloyd was a star on the rise, a kid with a future, Hersh, Sam Perry, and a bunch of other folks had been more than willing to spot Swee'pea some meal money, some carfare, some hanging-around cash—anything, pretty much—just because.

Now? Now, Lloyd was a has-been, a might-never-be, and his act had grown old and tiresome. An annoyance. They were tired of him asking, tired of him always having his hand out, tired of him looking for marks. Tired of him in general.

Then one night at the Entourage, Hersh said he'd made one last deal with Lloyd. As usual, he said, Lloyd hit him up for a twenty. Hersh told him only in return for a favor. Conrad, Jamal, and Future needed a ride home. Hersh flipped Lloyd his car keys.

"I told him, 'Be back in an hour.' I figured he'd be back in three."

It turned out, Hersh would be lucky to get it back at all.

A terrible driver, Lloyd was on the Brooklyn–Queens Expressway headed for Conrad's place near Long Island University in Brooklyn. Jamal was in the front passenger seat; Conrad was in the backseat with

Future, who lived over near Boys High. But Lloyd didn't know where to get off and the three other guys didn't drive.

This was in the days before nav systems and cell phone maps and GPS and so the four of them, almost literally, were traveling by the seat of their pants.

"Hey, where you get off? Where do you get off?" Conrad yelled to Lloyd from the backseat.

"I don't know, man," Lloyd said. "I ain't sure."

"What's the matter?" Conrad said. "Can't you read the signs?"

"Yo, man. Don't play me!" Lloyd yelled back to McRae. "You don't know me well enough to play me. Play me and I'll kick your ass. I mean it."

"Ah," Conrad said. "You can't read, can you, man?"

He started laughing and making fun of Lloyd. And then, all of a sudden, Lloyd turned around, *reached* into the backseat, and began to fight with McRae—in the car, on an elevated section of the BQE, going well over fifty-five miles per hour. "What'd I tell you, man?" Lloyd said. "*What'd I tell you?*" Jamal had to grab the wheel.

At six thirty the next morning, Hersh called Ron Naclerio. "Ron, you're not going to believe this," he said. "Lloyd *stole* my car."

It was three days before he got it back.

———

Lloyd had blown his chances in high school, Las Vegas, the CBA, and even in New Zealand, and now he was laying waste to the strides he'd seemed to have made during rehabilitation at ASAP/Van Nuys. But, while Lloyd busied himself with the bars, with searching the streets for crack cocaine, back in Queens the kid who'd once earned himself "a little name" in the local parks and gyms had reached his senior year.

He'd fulfilled his promise.

Kenny Anderson was now six foot tall and, though still a willowy 170 pounds, had become the most sought-after high school recruit in America. The previous fall he'd narrowed his college choices to five schools: Syracuse, North Carolina, Georgia Tech, Georgetown, and

Duke. Then, after much anticipation and suspense, on November 9, 1988, he announced he'd committed to Georgia Tech.

Word on the street suggested schools had offered six-figure payments to entice Anderson to sign. But Georgia Tech coach Bobby Cremins, as well as Pierre Turner, Vincent Smith, and Anderson himself, all laughed at that and said that, at best, suggestion of such a figure was ridiculous and, at worst, it was nothing short of scandalous.

Still, such rumors served to confirm Kenny Anderson's status as the most recruited player in the nation, just as his selection of schools was confirmation Team Anderson had been successful in taking a kid with raw talent, a kid who was immature, and guiding him safely home. When Duke announced it had signed Bobby Hurley, Jr., the star guard out of St. Anthony's in Jersey City, New Jersey, a team selected as the 1989 national high school champion by *USA Today*, Anderson was unfazed—since he had *choices*. So what if Georgetown coach John Thompson and his Hoyas eventually signed Andrew Jackson guard Dave Edwards? Anderson simply eliminated Georgetown from consideration. When Joan Anderson decided Syracuse coach Jim Boeheim was "too cold," as she'd said, her son was not frozen out of an offer. And though North Carolina had come after him hard, when Anderson ruled out playing for the Tar Heels he was able to speak his mind on the reason. "I don't want to be another horse in Dean Smith's stable," he said—though he'd later apologized for the remark.

Still, the point had been made. Kenny Anderson had had choices, had been afforded the chance to decide his *own* future. He'd had options and his options had been not only five of the most prestigious basketball schools in America but also five well-respected academic institutions. The Kenny Anderson who began life near the Forties Projects had a limited future, despite basketball. The Kenny Anderson who would come out of Archbishop Molloy with a B-minus academic average and 2,621 career points—at the time, the highest total ever in New York State—had the world at his feet, which explained how he wound up his senior season as the *Parade Magazine* National Player of the Year. And it partially explained why, upon his graduation, Kenny

Anderson's high school jersey ended up enshrined in the Basketball Hall of Fame.

As Tom Konchalski, the high school basketball scout, said when asked where Anderson ranked as a basketball player and a person, "There are only three people that Kenny Anderson ranks behind: the Father, the Son and the Holy Ghost."

"If it wasn't for them, that support network, there's no telling where I could have been," Anderson said. "I might have tried to get over on people, I might have gotten sidetracked. It was hard. It was a lot of work. But you have to make a sacrifice to avoid temptation. You have to realize that there is a lot of bad out there. I think those people helped me realize that. I think that it helped me stay focused on what I had to do."

Of course, the shame was that most kids never learned that lesson, never had anyone to help them learn it. Because they weren't as talented as Kenny Anderson or because they didn't receive such good advice or didn't listen, instead they often wound up not like Kenny Anderson but like Lloyd Daniels, Jr., or Richie Adams or Earl Manigault.

Cast adrift, their futures bleak.

―――――

Hersh had given up on Lloyd. Written him off. Like everyone else, he'd grown sick of the headache. So, in a deft move, Hersh passed Lloyd off on Ron.

But Ron also had grown tired of the aggravation, the act. He could only bang his head against a wall so many times. The only times Lloyd ever called him anymore was when he needed something. Cash, a ride, a favor. Cash. And so, when Kevin Barry stepped into the picture, offering to help Lloyd, Ron thought it was a good idea.

Barry had met Ron through friends. Because he ran the Give a Kid a Chance Foundation, a nonprofit organization to assist underprivileged children, Ron figured maybe he could bring new resources—and a new perspective—to the effort.

After all, Barry had been dealing with kids like Lloyd forever, it seemed. All the way back to his friendship with old boxing trainer Cus

D'Amato, which was how he'd first met Mike Tyson. Which, eventually, was how Lloyd had met Tyson. Now Barry was going to do his best to save Lloyd. Letting him move into the house with him and his sons in the Marine Park section of Brooklyn. Buying him clothes, food.

"This guy was mesmerized by Lloyd," Hersh said. "He really felt he could make the difference. But he was getting conned by Lloyd."

Kevin Barry insisted that wasn't the case. That he'd made demands of Lloyd, that Lloyd had responded. That Lloyd, honestly, was getting help. That he, Barry, really, truly believed that, given time, he could have gotten Lloyd straightened out.

"I was teaching Lloyd things like how to brush his teeth," Barry said, "how to change his clothes. No one had ever shown him the right way to do those things. It was like he was twelve years old. It was like he was Rain Man or something."

And so, Kevin Barry was putting forth an effort, was trying.

And Hersh? Hersh had cut his losses, so to speak; run. The incident with the car was the final straw. He no longer had the strength to deal with the situation. Lloyd, he said, was for *gornisht helfen,* Yiddish for hopeless, beyond help. A lost cause.

Besides, Hersh said, Swee'pea was yesterday's news.

"He's at an age where, if he can't take care of himself, I don't want to be a part of him," Hersh said one night in April at the Sports Page, run by ex–Ben Franklin coach Stan Dinner. "This kid is twenty-one years old and he is finished. People I know told me that he has been blackballed from the NBA. For life. The Knicks and the Nets said they are never going to touch him. I don't want to see the kid die. But I don't want any part of him. He came in the other night. He was all drugged up. He was drunk. He was like, 'Let me have some money. I'll pay you back as soon as I make it. I promise.' But the things we allowed him to get away with when he was young—the things like 'Give me ten dollars, give me twenty'—we won't let him get away with anymore. Back then he was a celebrity. And you want to be associated with celebrities. But to me the kid is poison now. Double-X poison. You know what I mean? To me the kid is *poison.*"

Two weeks later, Lloyd got shot.

Operation

It had been a rough night. Now, on a bench near the elevators, anxious relatives gathered and sat, motionless, not quite sure what to make of the situation.

They'd been summoned to Mary Immaculate Hospital in the early morning hours and, what with the operation over and the sun reaching toward the noon sky, all they could do now was sit and wait for the latest word on Lloyd. It was difficult, the waiting. Down the hall, behind a set of ominous wooden doors with wire-reinforced windows, Lloyd slept, heavily sedated, in the intensive care unit.

There was a blandness to the room. It was an awful, sick-feeling place. A place where the patients hovered in limbo, between life and death; where the nurses whispered. A place where the monitors used to record vital signs emitted a steadfast, monotonous beat, their deadtime rhythms an eerie reminder of the inner battles being fought for the very souls of the suffering.

For all their nuisance, those machines confirmed that Lloyd was, indeed, alive. Still, he didn't look so good. A drainage tube, filled with blood-tinged fluid, protruded from the wound in the left side of his neck, another from the wound to the right side of his abdomen. Gauze covered the wound to his left shoulder. At one point that morning the detectives had come to Lulia Hendley and asked to take the clothing Lloyd had worn when he'd been shot.

"They said, 'Just in case he dies, we need it for evidence,'" she said. "Then, my heart sank. I said, 'No, not Junior. This is my oldest grandchild.' I thought then he was gonna die."

She was not alone.

Downstairs, a television crew waited out the morning. The local all-news radio station, 1010 WINS—the one that said, "You give us twenty-two minutes, we'll give you the world"—reported the shooting on its broadcasts. A few reporters and at least one photographer spent part of the morning and much of the afternoon in the hospital searching for tidbits of information. The severity of the situation became apparent around midmorning, when a wearied, bleary-eyed man walked through the front door at Mary Immaculate. He seemed shaken as he moved toward the front desk.

He wanted news, he said. He wanted it now.

"I'm his father," the man said as he rubbed his work-swollen hands. "I'm Lloyd Daniels, Sr."

Many years before, he had abandoned his son, had perhaps, condemned him to this fate. All that was forgotten as he stood at the desk and asked his question. "Is he alive?" he said.

Yes, he was told. But no one knew for how long.

Annie Sargeant walked down the hall looking tired, as if her feet hurt to do so. She looked worn, and the green cloth coat, the green kerchief thrown over her still-uncombed hair, did nothing to help her appearance. It was apparent she'd been up all night, or most of it, anyway. She'd just come from seeing her grandson in the ICU.

"He was in pain," she said. "You could tell he was in pain."

She reached her hands into her pockets, searched for a tissue, but found none. She was near the hospital doors now. There she stopped for a moment as a reporter asked her a question about the shooting. Early reports from police, he said, were that it had been drug related. Sargeant had raised Lloyd back on New Jersey Avenue.

When drugs were mentioned, she got defensive. "It wasn't no drugs," she said, adamant. "It wasn't no drugs, I can tell you that. He was robbed. Somebody robbed him. He didn't mess with that stuff. He didn't mess with no drugs. It wasn't no drugs."

Her daughter, Barbara Stephens, moved to her side. "Mama," she said, prodding. "Mama, *c'mon*. Don't talk to these people. You don't have to talk to them. Just shut your mouth and let's get out of here. *Now*. C'mon, mama. Let's *go*."

As mother and daughter walked out through the main entrance, another relative, who asked not to be identified, just shook her head. "I don't know why she said that it wasn't drugs," the woman said, seriousness in her voice. "You could have predicted this would happen. Anyone could have predicted this would happen to him. It's because of what he be into. It's what he be into that caused this." The implication was clear.

"Why did this happen?" Ron said. "Because he was reading Shakespeare and his tutor didn't like the way he was reading it. *Come on*. In *that* neighborhood, who knows why? It could be anything. But you have a pretty good idea. It *had* to be drugs."

It was, of course, related to drugs. But the incident that led to the shooting and the actual shooting itself had not happened the way relatives had first explained it; the way it was reported in the papers and on the news. In reality, Lloyd had been drinking Olde English with his aunt, Sherry Baptiste, and decided he wanted to get high. So he went out on the block and, down around the corner of Francis Lewis, he found a young kid, maybe sixteen years old, selling crack. Lloyd walked over to him and demanded his goods. When the kid refused, Lloyd, who'd done this several times before, beat the shit out of him—and stole his crack, about a hundred dollars' worth—before running off.

Angered, the kid and his partner, who was also some juvie wise-ass, decided to follow Lloyd home. They did. They found him.

And they shot him.

"I know these jokers will kill you," Lulia Hendley said. She'd seen the assailants come to the house, had seen her grandson, seen Junior, get shot. "If you take they crack, I know they'll shoot you. I know they will. . . . They'll kill you. They really doesn't care. They give it to you one way or the other, whether you live or die, they don't care."

Word was there was a contract out on the shooters. In fact, when the triggerman found out whom he'd shot, he'd sent word through the grapevine. "They said to say he was sorry," Hendley said. "But you can't change something that's been done."

As one person said, "You know how many drug dealers who knew Lloyd have also put the word out, 'Get this kid.' The kid's dead who did this."

"Hey, they shot Lloyd Daniels. They shot Swee'pea," another said. "These guys had a better chance of living if they had shot a cop."

Not many of the folks who knew Lloyd were surprised to hear the news he'd been shot. Most of the reactions were similar. After the initial shock, whatever emotion they'd shown soon vanished. The news had perhaps been inevitable, they'd said.

"You know, it's sad I tell you," Gauchos director Lou d'Almeida said. "Goddamn. I saw him earlier this week. He stopped over at a game and said, 'Hello.' He told me he was working on getting a tryout some-where. . . . I told him, 'When you're ready to do it, when you have some good news for me, give me a call.' And now this."

"We've been waiting for this call every day since he left," Kristin Gillam, daughter of Topeka Sizzlers owner Bernie Glannon, said. "Tell you the truth, we kind of expected it."

"You can say it was the path he was walking," Waitemata coach Dave MacCalman said when a reporter called his home in New Zea-land to tell him the news.

"It's like if your father is ninety-nine and has been terminally ill for ten years," Ron said. "You know what's going to happen. It's still a shock when it does."

"It's too bad," ex–Sizzlers coach John Killilea, who'd become an assistant with the Houston Rockets, said when he heard. "As a basketball person, you say it was certainly a shame because of his ability. But to hell with his talent. It's too bad for this to happen to anyone. This is a problem with society. The educational system didn't do a bit of good for him. The culture didn't do a bit of good for him. He wasn't prepared to step out of his environment, didn't have the ability to sever that bond. But I also guess you couldn't force him to do what had to be done, either, so he became just another one of those guys in the trenches. You knew nothing good was going to come of it."

"I was hoping nothing like this would happen," Dave Jones, a Gauchos coach who met Lloyd at age fourteen, said. "You always hear things on the street. I just hoped the street life would never catch up with him. You know, he was here last week working out, working hard because he wanted to do this. He watches NBA players and knows he's better than half the guys he sees. He just listened to a lot of the wrong people."

As d'Almeida said, "When I watch all these playoff games on television I think, 'Hey, I'd like to see what Lloyd would have done here, what he would have done there.' People always say he is the most incredible talent they have ever seen. I see Magic Johnson. I see Michael Jordan. Then I see Lloyd. Boy, oh boy. It's sad."

"You know," d'Almeida said, "it's unbelievable how many wrong turns he's taken, especially when you consider how many good turns he could have taken.

"They say a cat has nine lives. He may have one left."

That Lloyd survived getting shot was due to circumstance and coincidence, as well, it turned out, as to the luck of the draw. The night he was shot an ambulance crew just happened to be on a meal break in the neighborhood and, once the 911 call was received, arrived at the shooting scene in less than five minutes. And Dr. Walter F. Pizzi, chairman of the Department of Surgery of the Catholic Medical Center of Brooklyn and Queens, the organization that ran Mary Immaculate, said Lloyd received immediate and proper medical treatment from those paramedics, who also knew to transport him to Mary Immaculate—the only hospital in Queens with a level-one trauma unit.

Dr. Pizzi had implemented the trauma unit because of lessons learned during his association with an ex-colleague, a renowned thoracic surgeon who'd written six books on medical techniques developed during his own tenure at Harlem Hospital, where he had been a pioneer in the field of trauma surgery and an advocate of specialized emergency trauma care units before his death in 1985. More incredible, that colleague also had saved the life of Dr. Martin Luther King, Jr., after the famed civil rights activist was stabbed by a deranged woman during a 1958 book signing in Harlem.

Explaining how Dr. King had been brought to the ER with the weapon, an eight-inch-long letter opener, still embedded in his chest, millimeters from his aorta, and how he'd led a biracial team of surgeons who had skillfully removed the blade, saving Dr. King's life, that colleague told reporters, "He was a sneeze away from death."

That colleague, the one who'd saved Martin Luther King? Whose theories had led Pizzi to institute the trauma center at Mary Immaculate, which saved Lloyd?

Dr. Emil A. Naclerio. Ron's father.

"It's a small world," Ron told Dr. Pizzi when he met him for the first time at the hospital as Lloyd recovered from being shot.

"A very small world," Pizzi replied, noting that the trauma center had actually only been operational less than a year.

"You know how close this kid was to death?" Ron said later, echoing the words of his father. "A high school overtime period away. That's why I find this incredible."

"It is because of that center that Lloyd is alive," Dr. Pizzi said, noting that Ron's father, his late colleague, Dr. Naclerio, "was a distinguished chest surgeon, one of the first to promulgate trauma care in New York City hospitals." As Pizzi later said of Lloyd, "He was the right patient for the right hospital at the right time. He had the right care from the scene. The paramedics did all the right things. There was a team of trauma surgeons ready for him. Everything happened perfectly and the system worked."

As Ron said, "I'm glad it did."

Lloyd was asleep when Ron went to visit him that afternoon, hours after the shooting. "How're you doin'?" Ron asked him, when he finally opened his eyes.

"I don't know, Ron," Lloyd said in a bare whisper. "I don't know."

"You're going to make it," a nurse standing near the bed told Lloyd. He tried to force a smile, but couldn't. "Ron," he said, "I screwed up big-time. I'm lucky to be alive, ain't I? I was real close. I almost died. Maybe God still wants to see me play."

"God and the devil were fighting for you," Ron said as Lloyd again tried to force a smile. "They were choosing up a game.

"He didn't look good," Ron said afterward. "I mean, he looked like he was going to make it. But you could tell he was bad. He had all these things in his nose. He was attached to all these machines. He was in pain. He was scared. He told me he thought he saw the world, his life, pass before his eyes. He said he saw his mother. Hopefully this struck a nerve. He said it did. I think he finally realized he's not invincible."

"It was a major thoracic wound," Dr. Daniel L. Picard, the director of surgery at Mary Immaculate and the doctor who'd operated on Lloyd, said as he stood in an office just down the hall from the ward. "One bullet hit him in the right side and penetrated his right lung. Two other bullets struck him in the left side of the neck and the left shoulder. The damage was pretty extensive. It was close to the vital organs. He lost about six pints of blood. But he was lucky. The prognosis for recovery is good.

"I will make no prognosis, however, for his sports career."

Dr. Picard didn't have to make a prognosis, because, the shooting just hours old, back in St. Albans, folks on the street had already begun to form opinions.

It was the afternoon after the shooting. As Lloyd continued to recover in his hospital bed, down in Jamaica Park, in the playground where Lloyd used to play ball, kids talked about the legend who had become, in their words, a "bum."

"He was still the best out here, the best ever in this neighborhood," seventeen-year-old Anthony Johnson, who'd played against Lloyd, said. "He could shoot from anywhere, pro three-pointers like they were nothing. But he didn't seem to care anymore."

As another player, nineteen-year-old James Stanton, said, "He

wasted his talent, hanging out with the wrong crowd, the wrong people, the wrong influences."

Down at the corner of 203rd Street, a man in a New York Giants
jacket selling five-dollar vials of crack offered an assessment that
seemed to summarize the entire situation. "We knew him here," he
said. "Came around a lot. He was a basketball player. Once."

A basketball, autographed by Michael Jordan, who was also a Brooklyn native, sat on a table near the hospital bed in Room 613. Lloyd,
shadowed by the rack that held his intravenous solution, was standing
at the window. There were flower arrangements, including one from
Jerry Tarkanian and the basketball staff at UNLV.

It was a little more than a week since Lloyd had been shot. Already
he was up and walking around, walking the halls, biding his time 'til he
could get out.

"You want to know how dumb I was?" Lloyd said. "I saw the gun
and still I came out on the kid, like I was a *gangsta* or somethin'. The kid
was like, 'Where's my money?' He wasn't goin' to let me *house* him like
that. He wasted two bullets in the air. Then, when I didn't hand it over,
he shot me. I came rushin' at him, we was tusslin' and then he shot me
two more times and I went down. I was so surprised to be shot. I was
scared. That's what I remember, bein' scared. I was like, 'Don't let me
die, God. Don't let me die.' All I could remember was like how in *Star-
sky & Hutch* when the bad guys got shot and like when they closed
their eyes they was *dead*.

"I was like, 'You got to hang on, hang on. *Don't close them eyes.*' I
thought that, like, if I closed my eyes, I was dead. So I never passed out.

"I should be dead," Lloyd, whose recovery had been called a "medical miracle," said. "I know that. God always say that if you do crazy shit,
you goin' to get it back someday. Well, man, I tell you, that happened
to me. Because of that, all I watched the first few nights here was them
God shows, one service right after another. Today I feel a little better.
I may watch some wrestling today. I don't want to mess up no more."

On the table, next to the basketball from Jordan—"Get well, Lloyd. All my best, Michael Jordan," it read—there were letters and get-well cards, hundreds of them. In fact, it seemed they were working over-time downstairs in the hospital mailroom to keep up with all the cards and letters that had come in from around the country. There were letters about Jesus, letters about God. There was a letter to inform Lloyd that he had been enrolled in the "Priests of the Sacred Heart."

There were letters from ex-addicts who advised Lloyd to "be strong." There were letters from ex-addicts who told Lloyd it wasn't a crime he'd been weak. There was a letter from a girl who wanted Lloyd to come live with her in Toledo, Ohio. As if anyone, *ever*, wanted to live in Toledo, Ohio.

There was even a letter from a girl in Queens who identified herself as the president of an organization called LLDA. It stood for "Leave Lloyd Daniels Alone." She'd started it because, she said, Lloyd was "being exploited by the media."

Lloyd also received a letter from a woman who wrote: "I don't know you, but I am going to say it like it is: 'Are you crazy or what? Are you?' I never met you personally, but I heard of you through newspapers and TV. 'Are you a man or what?' You, with such talent . . . and such beau-tiful height. If I was able to travel—and, I'm not rich that I can afford to go by cab, you see I'm sixty-six years old and homebound—I know I would slap your face and probably do it a few times! What right do you have to ruin your life? Have you no value on your life? I will say this to you, Swee'pea, and remember this. Picture yourself deep in a grave turning to bones for the rest of your life while worms eat you up! I care—and your family cares, the world cares. Do *you* give a damn?"

A former police officer wrote to tell Lloyd he once had a drinking problem, but was now sober. "I haven't had a drink for eight years," the man wrote. "Not one drink and not one drug. No pot. No speed. No beer. No hard stuff. No nothing, and I feel good about it." The man went on to explain to Lloyd that he could get clean, too.

All it took was work.

Perhaps the most heartfelt letter came from an athlete who'd been there before, who'd suffered a relapse of his addiction, who was again fighting hard to overcome it. It came on the official stationery of the Charlotte Hornets, and included a team hat.

"I'm sorry to hear about your present situation," ex–Van Nuys rehab mate David Thompson wrote. "I hope that you will be okay and will come through this just fine. I am very concerned about you and your future. God sometimes puts people through things to make them realize how precious and important life is. I hope you take this situation and make it a positive one for you. Things in my life are so much better today because of me staying clean and sober. Today, I am celebrating five months sobriety.

"Lloyd, you know if I can do it, so can you," Thompson wrote. "You have a lot of people that care about you and want to see you make it. It's still not too late! You have really got to try and get your life in order before it is too late! If I can help in any way, don't hesitate to call. You need to get out of New York. Enclosed is a Charlotte Hornets hat. Keep this hat and use it as a motivating factor. If you are serious enough, you can be there or with some other team. You've got too much talent to waste it on the streets.

"God was with you this time. Lean on him. He won't let you down."

"You know," Lloyd said, when asked about all the cards and letters, "people still love me. They still want to see me do well. But God, he don't like ugly. . . . I keep gettin' these lessons in life, but I ain't never learned. I want to learn now."

"You're just a lollipop," Ron said. "What are you *gonna* do with *this* chance?"

"I stay right, now," Lloyd said.

"Whether that will wear off in a month or two, who knows?" Ron said later, outside the hospital. "Now he just has to do what he says. Sooner or later you have to get up on your own two feet and do what you're supposed to do. He still has a chance. I know this sounds stupid. But maybe those three bullets saved his life."

Con Man

The television was on. Lloyd was stretched out on the couch in the living room, Kevin on a chair near him, and it was there Swee'pea fought, without much success, to stifle a yawn. It was almost midnight. Back in the day, that would have meant it was just about time for Lloyd to go out, hit the town; to break the night, stay out 'til dawn, in search of liquor, in search of crack. In search of a good time. Any good time.

Instead, here he was, home; drained and wearied. Not from self-abuse and drugs, but from a long, hard day of work.

Leaning back, Lloyd stretched his arms, sighed.

"Yo, Kev. Like, I'm exhausted. It ain't easy, all this workin' out stuff."

Kevin Barry laughed. "Welcome to the real world," he said as Lloyd made a face; grimaced. "No one said this was going to be easy, Lloyd," Kevin added. "You know this isn't going to be easy. But you can do it. You know you can." Lloyd nodded, sure.

It had been just three weeks since Lloyd had been shot, a week since he'd been released from Mary Immaculate. Yet he had just spent five hours running, lifting weights, working to get back into shape; had even gone out and beaten Ron in a game of one-on-one. The scars that remained on his neck, chest, and abdomen served as a brutal reminder to how close he'd come to death, but now he sat and talked about the future. A future once bright and promising; one now, at least, still salvageable.

"It ain't easy," Lloyd said. "Ain't nothin' in life is easy. Gettin' shot ain't easy. But whatever happens before, happens. I just got to say, 'I fucked it up.' But, like, we all fuck up. Hear me? I can't take back my past. All I can do is make a future. It's up to me now to make a future, know what I'm sayin'? No one else. It's up to me."

He pressed back into the couch, turned away for a moment, thinking. How had he come to this place? How had he come to find himself in such dire fucking straits? Could he ever do what was necessary to make things right? Honestly, he didn't know.

"I'm goin' to do it this time," he said, when he turned back. "I *got* to do it. I ain't Superman now. I know that. Can't take no more bullets. I *got* to get well now. No bullshit this time. I want it. I want it bad. Those who help *theyselves* make it. You know, that's what they say, 'Those who help *theyselves* is the ones who's goin' to make it.'

"You heard that, right? So, I got to take it one day at a time now. One day at a time. I learned that. I *think* I learned that. Gettin' shot helped me learn it."

"You know," Kevin said after Lloyd had gotten up, gone inside to bed, "I think now the true person has come out of Lloyd Daniels. Every night, he prays to God. Every night. He has been working hard. And I mean really hard. He knows he is on his last legs. You know what they say, 'You have to hit the bottom before you hit the top.'

"A couple of weeks ago, I would have told you it was over," he said, clicking off the TV. "But I think he has hit bottom. You would hardly believe the turnaround."

Most mornings, Lloyd woke at eleven then headed to the local gym, the Brooklyn Health & Racquet Club. There he'd lift weights for hours under the supervision of trainer Joey "Boy" Fortunato, whose job it was to make sure Lloyd got back into competitive shape. Fortunato worked him on the leg machines, had him bench weights, ran him on the track, had him ride an exercise bike to increase his strength and stamina. After lunch and a late afternoon rest, Lloyd returned for night sessions.

"The guy was soaking wet every day," Fortunato said. "People couldn't believe it. It was every day. I'm serious. . . . No drugs, no beer, no alcohol. You could not believe the resilience in this kid, the convalescence in such a short amount of time."

It wasn't long before Lloyd had regained much of the weight he'd lost after the shooting. Where once he'd been accused of drinking a case of beer a day, Lloyd, whose weight had dropped to 177 pounds in the hospital, had boosted his weight to 190—each day drinking a *case* of a high-calorie, high-protein nutrient mixture.

"That's fifteen cans to each case," Kevin said.

Kevin, Ron, and Tom Rome, the agent, even made plans to enroll Lloyd in an outpatient drug and alcohol rehabilitation program and, until the logistics could be worked out, formed a network that enabled them to keep someone with him twenty-four hours a day, seven days a week. Team Daniels, they'd called it.

"He is constantly, constantly, constantly occupied," Kevin said.

As Ron said, "You know what they say about horses? Well, we're leading him to water."

There were positive signs, too. When Ron mistakenly ordered a beer at dinner one night, Lloyd said to him, "Go ahead, Ron. I know I can't have no beer."

"He went out for a run around the block one night," Kevin said, "and all these little kids started running along with him. It was like a scene out of *Rocky*. Except Lloyd was telling them, 'Don't do drugs.' People come up to him on the street and say, 'Hey, we want to see you play again.' You cannot believe it. This is amazing, the change."

One night Lloyd picked up a doll of the *Popeye* character Swee'pea that Kevin had bought for his son, John. Ron was there when it happened. "Yo, Ron," Lloyd said. "We got to ask Tom. When I make the NBA, can I still use 'Swee'pea' or do we got to get permission? We'd be stealin' it, right? He had it first."

The moment was good for a laugh, but everyone agreed it showed Lloyd was thinking about the future. Still, it remained to be seen just how long the good times, the sober, drug-free times, would last. Would it be long enough for Lloyd to make a serious run at the NBA? Would it be long enough for him to just get on with his life? Would it be an hour, a day, a week, a month, a year? No one really knew for sure.

"I just feel so confident that this could happen this time," Kevin, the eternal optimist, said. "I know it could. The past, we can't change. Now it's all the future. All the future, all the future. This could be the time it happens, the time he makes it."

"I'm keeping my fingers crossed," Ron said. "If you didn't think you could win this game—had no chance of winning—you'd forfeit. Walk away. But look at this kid. He was shot in the neck and the bullet just missed the jugular. He took one in the chest and it just missed his heart. If the ambulance broke down on the way to the hospital, he was dead, anyway. And here he is out of the hospital and playing ball. You have to believe there is a reason. Maybe this time, he finally got the message."

It sounded so familiar, the refrain.

———

The kids surrounded Lloyd outside the entrance to the subway stop near the park at West Fourth Street. "Swee'pea!" one yelled out. "Give us your autograph?"

One after another, Lloyd signed, scrawling his name, almost illegible. He continued to do so as he walked toward the park and later, even as he changed out of his street clothes along the fence. Lloyd had come to Manhattan to get a few runs with some serious folks, to see where he stood. With word on the street he might show, the kids came, too. In New York City, performance reviews more often than not are rated on fan appreciation: of a dunk, a shot, a pass, a move. With the crowd lined four-deep in places, Lloyd understood full well the critics were out in force.

He wasted little time showing them what he could still do.

The court at West Fourth, along Sixth Avenue around the corner from Bleecker Street in the West Village, was notorious. A box, games there were more like a steel cage match than basketball. Rules were that there are no rules. Dunks, jams, flagrant fouls. Body-on-body. Anything; name it. But on an afternoon when the mercury soared into the nineties and he himself had a temperature of 102—the result of a bout with the flu—Lloyd raised the game to high art at West Fourth.

While others dunked, he shot. While others shot, he passed. While others looked on, uncertain, he buried shots they hadn't even dreamed of. And while others stood awaiting his next move, he made passes they were certain couldn't be made. When he was done, he'd amassed 21 points—with a ridiculous 24 assists.

"Bullets don't stop my man Lloyd!" someone shouted out.

Yelled another: "He's had more chances than the law allows! But the man still got it!"

Indeed, he did.

One night that summer Lloyd dropped forty on Ricky Sobers. Another night, on a team that featured Syracuse-bound Conrad McRae, as well as a host of other local high school and college stars—Jamal Faulkner, Shane Drisdom, Wilfred Kirkaldy, Future Pollard, Effrem Whitehead, and Duane Causwell, among them—he hit seven consecutive three-point jumpers in the second half of a game to be voted the most valuable player at a tournament in New Cassel, Long Island.

Soon Tom Rome received new interest in his client. The Harlem Globetrotters wanted Lloyd to come to camp in the fall. A team in Greece offered a contract worth more than $100,000. A team in Spain asked to negotiate his rights. A team from the Italian Basketball Federation offered a concrete deal, outbidding the team in Greece.

Several NBA teams also made inquiries, Rome said.

"It has gotten to the point where the kid has got to do it himself," Rome said. "He has got to go to a camp. . . . Show what he can do. It's not such a big leap for him."

"All I need is a chance," Lloyd said. "I can't even think about failin'."

Asked what he was doing different to ensure success this time, Lloyd issued a straightforward answer.

"Workin' hard," he said, "and pissin' clean."

———

It all sounded good. The problem was, as usual, that it wasn't true. Lloyd had been enrolled in an outpatient substance abuse program and had been asked to submit to urinalysis. But, Tom Rome said, Lloyd often failed to attend the aftercare meetings. And he proved unwilling to submit to drug tests. As Kevin Barry said, "Why is it every time he's supposed to take a drug test, he's nowhere to be found?"

The answer was soon apparent.

There was a meeting with Dr. Pizzi when Lloyd agreed to urinalysis. When the test was to be administered, Lloyd changed his mind—and refused to take it.

"The idea was for him to start proving that he was clean so he could build a good track record," Ron said. "And Lloyd agreed to take the test. But then when we got down there, he said no, he wouldn't take it. I was really pissed off. We got into an argument over it. I told him, 'You piece of shit. Why are you going back on your word?' He said, 'C'mon, Ron. Don't you trust me?' I said, 'No, I don't trust you. Why should I trust you?'

"He said he felt there was no reason for him to have to prove that he was clean, that he should be trusted. I started yelling and told him, 'Look, if you're not going to do it, let's get the fuck out of here, because I don't want to have to deal with none of your bullshit.' He tried talking to me, but I said, 'Just shut the fuck up. No more of your shit. Get in the fuckin' car, I'm dropping your ass off at Kevin's. I can't deal with any more of this.' He kept on telling me, 'Yo, I'm clean, Ron. I'm clean.'"

The problems were sporadic.

For a week Lloyd would be fine. He'd work out, meet his obligations, and all was well. Then one night he'd leave the house—and wouldn't come home.

"You know what they say about the monkey on your back?" Kevin said. "Well, it's almost like he has this monkey inside him and that monkey sleeps almost all the time. But, when he feels the need for a mind-altering drug, the monkey goes berserk."

Kevin thought the best solution was to get Lloyd out of New York.

For better or worse, he took him to the Sugar Ray Leonard–Thomas Hearns fight—in Las Vegas. He saw his former attorney, David Chesnoff, and his former guardian, Mark Warkentien. Arrangements were made for Lloyd to join a Dutch basketball team on a ten-game tour against teams from the World Basketball League (WBL)—a professional league for players under six foot five.

Two of the games on the tour were scheduled to be in Las Vegas, where the team, Computerij Meppel of Meppel, Holland, would face the Las Vegas Silver Streaks—a WBL team operated by former Topeka Sizzlers owner Bernie Glannon.

"The pay will be minimal," Glannon said. "But it'll be the opportunity to play ten games. I'll encourage that if I'm convinced Lloyd is straight."

WBL commissioner Steve Ehrhart said Lloyd could appear because opponents on nonleague teams faced no height restrictions.

"He claims he has straightened out, and we are giving him a great opportunity to prove to people that he has done that," Ehrhart said, explaining the scenario. "He approached us. He was very open about his background, his ups and downs and his problems. This seemed like a fair opportunity for him to either put up or shut up. The American public will now get a chance to see what he is all about."

And it did. Because, arrangements made, Lloyd never arrived at the first practice session. Perhaps that was no surprise, considering there were many indications he was having problems in Las Vegas—among them, a source said, that he'd been seen at the Leonard-Hearns postfight party draining drink glasses, while warning the partygoers in a slurred voice, "Don't do drugs. Drugs'll kill you. Don't do drugs."

Ronnie Lott, then an all-league and future Hall of Fame defensive back for the San Francisco 49ers, pulled Lloyd aside. "Do you know how much money they'll pay you if you only stay clean?" Lott told Lloyd. "You could have a good life."

Everson Walls, then a defensive back for the Dallas Cowboys, offered advice, too. "You've got to come through this," he told Lloyd. "You could do so much."

Finally, UCLA guard Pooh Richardson, who'd just been drafted by the Minnesota Timberwolves, said: "Lloyd, be real. Wake up and see what you're doing to yourself."

But the advice, as it had back at I.S. 59 in Springfield Gardens following the death of Len Bias, fell on deaf ears. And once back home, the trouble continued.

One afternoon, an undercover NYPD policeman spotted Lloyd in Eleanor Roosevelt Park, off Houston Street near the Bowery in Manhattan. "We make about five hundred, six hundred collars a year in that park," that officer, Detective John Kanovsky of the Manhattan South Narcotics Unit, said. "It's a park known for drugs. If you're there, you're not there to play ball and you're not there to meet friends. I saw him milling 'round. He was wearing a red sweatsuit. I walked over and said, 'Hey, Swee'pea. How you doin'?' He looked at me, realized that I was a cop, and said, 'Oh, okay.' He made believe he was dribbling and shooting." Then, he said, Lloyd walked away.

So much for rehabilitation.

It was midnight when Kevin, Ron, and a friend got to Gerard Avenue. They'd come from an affair at the New York Athletic Club on Central Park South. They were dressed in suits and to the people that lined the streets that time of night, they must have looked more like a couple of narcs than guys in search of a friend. The block was a shambles and there was danger all around. Just a block or two from Yankee Stadium, back then it was in one of the worst sections of the Bronx. It certainly was not the best environment for a man with a bad habit. Yet it was here Lloyd had come to live with a cousin.

Ron stopped the car in front of the building on Gerard. Fearing it might get stolen, he and Kevin got out—and locked their other friend inside.

"You got to see this street," Ron said afterward. "It was the middle of the night, but everyone was out, drinking, doing drugs, selling drugs. It was the type of block you could get killed on and, here we are, we got suits on and people are looking at us. I mean, this was shady. We walked into the building and these two addicts are standing there and they see us and figure we're cops, so they start to run. We walk over to the elevator and hit the button, but this woman comes over and, in Spanish, she says: 'No trabaja.' In other words, it *don't* work. So, we walk the six flights to the door and, when we get there, we knock. We're knocking, knocking. We hear noises inside the apartment and Kevin goes to me, 'I hope we got the right one. I don't want to die.'

"With that, Lloyd steps out and shakes our hands. He goes, 'Yo, Ron, Kev. How you guys doin'?' No sooner does he say that than two gunshots ring out in back, in the alley outside the window, and, I mean, this ain't no bullshit. They were *gunshots*."

"I'm like, 'Lloyd, get your stuff and let's get the fuck out of here,'" Kevin said. "But Lloyd was like, 'C'mon, that's just the way it is up here.'"

Back in the car, the four drove a few blocks to the stadium, the old stadium, and there Kevin, Ron, and Lloyd got out for a talk alongside the outfield wall.

"Is this what you want to do with your life?" Kevin asked Lloyd. "If it is, then keep doin' it and I don't want to hear from you no more."

"No, Kev," Lloyd said. A bullshit story, Kevin called it, Lloyd saying, "I don't want this. I was just checkin' it out for a few days. Really, I was just checkin' it out."

As they stood there under the El—the elevated IRT subway tracks up on River Avenue—cars, trucks, and buses went past. And, as they did, folks leaned out the windows. This was twenty-five years before the famous Derek Jeter commercial, the one where he hops out of the car service ride and walks one last time to Yankee Stadium as long-time fans and admirers stop him and say goodbye; wish him well.

This night, fans were yelling well-wishes, too. Yelling them to their playground hero.

"Hey, Swee'pea. *Stay clean!*" one driver yelled. "Yo, Lloyd!" yelled another. "You can do it!" It was a strange kind of sad, Kevin and Ron thought.

Just a strange kind of sad.

Lloyd came home the next afternoon, but Kevin was sure it wasn't because of what'd happened up in the Bronx. It was July 21, 1989. Mike Tyson had left tickets for Lloyd, Kevin, Ron, and Joey Boy for his fight against Carl "the Truth" Williams that night at the Convention Hall in Atlantic City. And, Kevin said, Lloyd didn't have a ride.

Whatever the case, the four headed to Atlantic City and arrived to find the fight had ended moments before—a knockout by Tyson in ninety-three seconds.

The postfight party was at the Convention Center. LeRoy Neiman said hello and told Lloyd he'd seen him down at West Fourth Street.

"I'll be out there drawing you soon," Neiman said.

Rick Pitino, just named the coach at Kentucky, came by. "How are you, Lloyd?" he said. The coach, who'd recruited Lloyd at Providence, had a beer in hand. "Damn," Lloyd said to Kevin. "The man should watch his liquor and stop worryin' 'bout me."

Heavyweight contender Evander Holyfield also stopped to talk with Lloyd. "You look good," Holyfield said. "Watch those bullets."

For a while, Lloyd shot the shit with Charles Oakley, Charles Barkley, and Benoit Benjamin. Then Kevin ran into Linda Taylor, wife of Lawrence Taylor, the all-world linebacker for the New York Giants. Kevin had met L.T. at a golf outing with Fran Tarkenton. He'd met Linda through her husband. Linda had suffered through the drug addiction of her husband. Kevin figured maybe she should talk to Lloyd.

"She was like, 'Let me give you a lecture,'" Lloyd said, recalling that talk. "She said, 'I understand what you're goin' through. My husband, you know, he's workin' his problems out. It's tough, but hang in there. Take it one day at a time.'"

It went in one ear, out the other.

As Lloyd said, he was paying more attention to his celebrity status. "Hey," he said, "everyone was admirin' that night."

From there it was all downhill. Too many nights, Kevin said, Lloyd didn't come home. When he did, Kevin said he either smelled of beer or appeared high. A few times Kevin locked Lloyd out of the house. Other times the two sat all night talking about his problems—which Kevin said included much more than drugs and alcohol.

"The kid was a con man," Kevin said.

There were the phone charges, which were all to hotline numbers. Kevin thought Lloyd was calling the sex phone or something. Turned out he was wrong. "The bill was one hundred and fifty dollars," Kevin said. "They were *Freddie* bills—you know, Freddie Krueger from *Nightmare on Elm Street*. Can you believe that? I thought it was sex calls and it was *Freddie* calls. It's like he's twelve years old."

Of course, there was more to it than that. There was the twenty dollars Lloyd "borrowed" from the paper route run by Kevin's son. There was the twenty-five he "borrowed" from the local pizza boy. "He told him, 'Oh, don't worry. Kevin'll pay you back,'" Kevin said. And then there was the ten dollars he "borrowed" from the kid who lived next door.

"He told the kid, 'Oh, my grandma is sick and I got to go see her before I go to training camp with the Boston Celtics. That's why I need the money.' He told the kid, 'When Kevin comes home, he'll pay you back. Just ask him.'

"You know," Kevin said, "when this kid isn't on drugs, he's the nicest kid in the world. But at times like that, when he is, he isn't worth knowing."

Finally, Kevin kicked Lloyd out of the house for good.

"I don't understand the attractions that lead someone away from success," Tom Rome said later. "Kids like Lloyd still respect that success, that NBA success, but they refuse to do what is needed to achieve it when it is right there in front of them.

"It's the existentialist dilemma. It's a bizarre combination of skills and nonskills, refinements and nonrefinements. I equate basketball to a high form of dance. It's art. And yet a guy like Lloyd is artless when it comes to figuring out how to stay on a team, how to stick with a program. There has got to be a root cause. Maybe it's that kids like him are not encouraged to develop responsibility. Maybe it's the environment. Maybe it's that they expect the world owes them a living. I don't know. It's the Lloyd Daniels Mystery. We don't want him to be the next Fly Williams. But it could be," Rome said, "that he'd rather be 'Lloyd Daniels, the Playground Legend' instead of 'Lloyd Daniels, the NBA Legend.'"

Go figure.

Back in the 'Ville

The building was brown outside now. But, despite a fresh coat of paint, the old apartment on Jersey Avenue still failed to make much of an appearance. Maybe it was the wrought-iron gates, needed to protect the remaining windows from unwanted late-night inquisitors; maybe it was the broken building door, which, without a doorknob of any type, blew open and rattled on its hinges in the brisk midwinter breeze.

Maybe it was the skewed, hand-painted number—No. 508, New Jersey—that adorned the arch over the door. It still looked unclean. Looked worn, looked used.

Litter clung to the low fence that surrounded the unkempt front yard.

The neighborhood, well, it still looked like a scene from some tired old war movie—a dead dog decaying in the vacant lot behind the building; an old, abandoned fire truck overturned amid the rubble in the lot a block over. Across the street, in a postage-stamp-size playground, a handful of little kids played, thankfully still too young *not* to remain impervious to the elements—their time of awakening in the years to come. Maybe. If they got those years.

"Mrs. Sargeant!" Ron yelled as he stood at the door. *"Mrs. Sargeant!"* Above him, in the second-floor window, eyes peeked out from behind a tattered, drawn curtain. *"Mrs. Sargeant!"* Ron yelled again.

Still, no answer.

Uneasily, he pushed open the unlocked front door to the building and stepped into the hall. It was a hideous orange, dark and unlit. Bare wires hung from a broken fixture overhead. Nearby, one agonizing drop at a time, a pipe leaked its contents onto the floor; a floor that seemed to disintegrate beneath his very feet. In front of him, the stairs also appeared to crumble as they reached achingly toward the second-floor landing. Ron knocked on the first-floor door. As he did, a noise startled him. *"Mrs. Sargeant?"* he said, maybe not scared but definitely concerned. No, he decided, the noise was from behind him, footsteps of a man coming down those rickety old stairs.

"Who you lookin' for?" the man said, matter-of-fact.

"I was looking for Mrs. Sargeant," Ron said, the man sizing him up. "I'm a coach. I used to coach her grandson, Lloyd Daniels. I heard he was around here."

"The tall kid who played basketball?" the man said.

"Yeah," Ron said. "That's him."

"Saw him yesterday, I think," the man said, letting his guard down. Changing his tune. "Haven't seen him today. Might have gone to the YMCA to shoot around a bit. Mrs. Sargeant, though, she ain't here. She went to stay with her daughter, I think."

"Do you know where?" Ron asked.

"No," said the man. "But, if I see him, who'd I tell him was lookin'?"

"Tell him Ron. He'll know. Tell him to call Ron."

Lloyd had been home a couple of weeks now, ever since he'd left Moline, Illinois, where he'd lived the previous three months. He'd gone there, five months after the shooting, to play for the Quad City Thunder in the CBA. He had done all he could there, too—attended a rehabilitation program at the United Medical Center of Davenport, Iowa, submitted to regular testing; *pissed clean*—and had made the team.

"We were all a bit skeptical," then–Thunder coach Mauro Panaggio said, "but he has been very positive, very cooperative. His biggest problem seems to be that he was one of those individuals who learned how to run before he learned how to walk. Somewhere along the line, that catches up to you. It is obvious the talent is there. But it still needs to be educated, still needs to be refined. It's up to him."

Things being what they were, Panaggio and his staff weren't about to wait for that to happen. This was pro basketball and Lloyd lasted just four games with the Thunder. The ironic part was, for once he'd managed to stay clean. It was just that Quad City had a chance to acquire George Gervin, the former ABA and NBA all-star and future Hall of Famer, who was making a comeback at age thirty-seven. Gervin, the player Lloyd had most often been compared to, played the same position. With a choice between a has-been who still had marquee value and a never-was who could find trouble at any corner in town, Panaggio made his decision. Quad City cut Lloyd.

Back in New York, Swee'pea disappeared into the streets. A few old friends, a few dealers who were still around, had heard from him. But Lloyd seemed to move through the neighborhood like the night wind, elusive. He'd be one place one day, gone the next. His grandmother, Lulia, hadn't heard from him. Neither had Kevin or Ron.

So Ron Naclerio took to the neighborhood, to Lloyd's old haunts, in an attempt to track him down. He wanted to make sure his old charge was at least still alive.

After stopping by New Jersey Avenue, Ron checked the schoolyards. He went to 192 Park, went to P.S. 202. He stopped by the YMCA on Jamaica Avenue near the cemetery, but folks there said they hadn't seen Lloyd. He checked the projects over on Linden, over on Mother Gaston—but no one had seen Lloyd. So he took one last run to Jersey Avenue. At least, he figured, he could leave a note for Annie Sargeant.

But this time Ron opened the door to the building to find a man standing there—his coat on, a dirtied ski hat on his head, cigarette in hand. He looked haggard. "I'm Lloyd's uncle," the man said. "You lookin' for Lloyd?" Ron stared at him, dumbfounded. "Yeah."

"Well," the man said. "I could take you to him. He's in the projects. It wouldn't be no trouble. A few bucks should take care of it. That wouldn't be no trouble, *right?*"

"Yeah, whatever," Ron said with a nervous laugh.

"Good," Lloyd's uncle said, demanding ten dollars. "Let's go."

Lloyd was stretched out under the covers in the bottom of a low bunk bed, his face buried in an open bottle of Vick's VapoRub, when Ron walked in. "Yo, Ron man," Lloyd said without moving from the bed, when he saw his longtime friend and mentor. "What you doin' here? I ain't seen *you* in a while."

"What do you mean, what brings me by here?" Ron said, stunned and in near-disbelief. "What are you, sick or something?"

"Yeah, man. I got me a cold."

"No," Ron said, shooting Lloyd a nasty look. "I mean, what are you, *sick*? I came by because no one's heard from you. Everyone thinks you're dead."

"Well, I ain't dead," Lloyd said.

"Yeah. You ain't dead."

The television was on. The Chicago Bulls were playing someone on national TV. "*Go Michael J!*" Lloyd yelled as Michael Jordan went in for a jam. On the wall over the bed hung three posters: one of Jordan, one of Magic Johnson, and the one of Lloyd. "You know," Lloyd said, "someday . . ."

Ron cut him off at the knees. "Shut the fuck up, *someday*. You know, you used to be all right. Notice how I said, '*Used to.*'"

"What you mean, all right?" Lloyd said. "What you mean, 'Used to be'?"

"Like I said . . ."

"I told you, man, I'm *sick*. You know, I think that's 'cause my girl might be pregnant. Know how the men, *theys* sometimes get sick when they girls get pregnant? Ain't that right? Well, I think my girl's pregnant, 'cause I been sick a bit lately, like in the mornin's. But I still been playin' ball all the time. I still got it. I do. I mean it.

"I still got a chance. I know I do."

Ron shook his head. At the foot of the bed Lloyd's cousin, Randy Stephens, sat laughing. "Ah, Lloyd," the kid said. "Man's doggin' you. Doggin' you big-time."

Stephens was fourteen, and a lot like Jermaine, Lloyd's fifteen-year-old half brother who lived in Charlotte, North Carolina, whom Lloyd had never met. Both Jermaine and Randy had reputations for being good ball players who could make things happen.

Better, both were good students, too.

"I've got a ninety-four average," he said. "I go to school all the time." Around the room, which was his, hung a bunch of certificates—some for his "excellent attendance record," some for his work in school, and some for his "good citizenship."

"The kid's all right, Ron," Lloyd said, pointing to his cousin. "He got a good game.... He even goes to school. He ain't like me."

"Someone here got brains, then," Ron said.

For an hour, Ron and Lloyd went at it; back and forth. Ron getting in his digs, Lloyd trying to explain how he still had a chance, Randy laughing every time Ron got in a shot. At one point, Randy switched the channel, found a TV game featuring UNLV. Moses Scurry was in. So were Stacey Augmon and Larry Johnson.

"I guess it's a good thing you weren't on that team," Ron said to Lloyd, who would have been a senior then for the Runnin' Rebels. "I don't know if you could handle being the second-best player behind Larry Johnson, which is what you'd have been."

"You know that ain't true, Ron," Lloyd said.

"If it ain't," Ron said, "when are you ever going to prove it?"

Lloyd looked away, grabbed the bottle of Vick's—and took still another sniff.

Out in the hall that led to the living room, Annie Sargeant stood with her daughter, Barbara Stephens, Randy's mother. "You think Lloyd's ever goin' to make it?" she asked. "He keeps sayin' he will, that some teams is interested in him. I think he could. He could, right? What you think? I think he could go somewhere—Europe. They say *theys* got some ball teams in Europe that likes him—and do good.

"I think he just needs one more chance."

"Yeah," she was told. "Yeah, sure."

The shame was Lloyd would have fit well with the UNLV team that won the 1990 NCAA championship. One, he could play. Even Jerry Tarkanian would have been hard-pressed to claim Lloyd wouldn't have started at one of the guard positions for the Rebels. And, based on some of the situations that team got into, it seemed Lloyd wouldn't have been out of place. Not only did that Rebels team talk real trash to its opponents—one Loyola-Marymount University player said, "On the court, other teams go, 'Where's your jump shot?' These guys go, 'Where's your *mother*?' and, before you can answer, they go, '*In my hotel room!*'"—but the players also did things like run up their phone bills. In fact, during the season six players were suspended for a game each for failure to pay their hotel phone bills. One was Moses Scurry.

Of course, earlier in the season, Scurry also had been academically ineligible for a handful of games. The six-foot-eight, 205 pound forward had been suspended for another game—after he punched Utah State University coach Kohn Smith during a scuffle. "How was I supposed to know he was the coach?" Scurry asked in the aftermath. "He had a *sweater* on. I thought coaches wear *suits* and *ties*."

Despite his run-ins, Scurry was still playing well and by the end of the season he even graced the cover of *Sports Illustrated*—pictured in action from the NCAA Championship Game in Denver, where UNLV routed Duke, 103–73.

Still, during the 1989–90 season no one in America really was on top of his game as much as Kenny Anderson. Just a freshman, Anderson had come into Georgia Tech and become an instant success. As the season neared the end, he was leading the Atlantic Coast Conference in assists, was a shoo-in for NCAA Division I Rookie of the Year, and was part of a new collegiate legend: "Lethal Weapon 3," the nickname given the three-guard offense that teamed him with Brian Oliver and Dennis Scott.

"I'm not going crazy or nothing," Anderson said near the end of the season, which also saw Georgia Tech earn a berth in the 1990 NCAA Final Four. "But I feel like I was touched this year, you know, touched by God or something. I mean, my year has gone so well that I don't know what else to think. All this happening to me has been incredible. It feels like a repeat of my freshman year in high school, it really does."

———

Lloyd was remembering the old days, too, as he sat in a booth at an Italian restaurant in Flatlands, Brooklyn, near Mill Basin, talking about his life and where it had gone wrong. He'd ordered his food and, unable to read the menu, had reached his decision on what to eat after asking everyone else at the table what they were going to order.

He was drinking a beer.

"You know," he said, between bites of his meal, "I've had a fucked-up life. People wanted to see me make it. But people couldn't be with me all the time, so I was fuckin' up. If I could do it all over, I'll put my hand on the Bible, I would do it different. You don't know how hard it is comin' up in a rough life.

"People made it easy for me, so I ain't goin' to use it as no excuse. I ain't goin' to use that as an excuse, you know, cryin' my head off sayin', 'That's why Lloyd didn't made it.' But you look, you probably couldn't have made it, comin' from my background. You see where I live. Don't I live all over? Do I got one steady home? Tell me I'm wrong. Do I have one steady home? Look at New Jersey Avenue. It's fucked up over there. My grandmother don't even stay there no more. You see how fucked up it is. Did you go inside? Rats be all in there, roaches be all over. I'm tellin' you straight up, as a man, a lot of people couldn't come up in my life. I ain't got to use that as no excuse, 'cause I had that basketball ability to take my grandmother and my family out of that.

"But I never learned how to do things like nobody else," he said. "I never had no one to show me. I needed somebody hard on me. I didn't have that."

As he sat there, it was easy to feel compassion for him, for all that he had missed in life, for his bad beginning, for the rough times. But he was twenty-two years old now, old enough to know better, old enough to be responsible for himself.

After all, though some had tried to use him, exploit him for his basketball talent, many along the way had tried to help him make a better life, had tried to steer him clear of trouble, show him the right path. But Lloyd had always just refused to listen.

He had refused to listen to the advice of teachers who wanted to help him in school. He had refused to listen to all the coaches who tried to teach him self-discipline, who knew what he could do if he only put his mind to it. He had refused to listen to friends who were looking out for him. And he had refused to listen to those who only wanted to see him make the simple effort needed to enable him to find success.

Wasn't he to blame, too?

"I could still make some camp," he said as he finished the last drops of his third beer. He motioned for the waitress, who brought still another, spilling it on the table as she did.

"Okay," she said, trying to make a joke of it. "Who's the alkie?"

"What'd she say?" Lloyd said, with a laugh. "She call me an *alkie*?" Told yes, he turned to her. "Well, then I guess you should get me another one."

It was as if, despite all he had been through, he just couldn't comprehend that he had done this to himself, that he remained the difference between success and failure, that he needed to change things if he wanted them to change. After all these years, Lloyd still knew the right things to say—but not how to act on them.

The con man had conned himself.

"Like I said, I could make a veteran camp," he said. "I ain't braggin' or nothin', but I killed some rookies last summer. I killed some rookies. If I'm straight, man, I can play with anybody. Ain't no one can play with me, you know that. I still got the thirty-footer. I think my J is better now, even. I just got to get back humble, I got to get back humble now, man, 'cause I still got it. I just got to get clean. I'm tryin' to work hard. I'm playin' ball every day. I swear to God, I'm playin' ball, man. I be in the parks, just shootin' around. Remember how I used to do? I'm workin' hard, just keep my skills up there. I'm tryin' to get back, no one ain't got to lead me. I'm doin' it now.

"For once in my life, I'm not [lying to] myself. The man's tryin' to do somethin'. If I don't make it, if I can't make it big-time, then somethin's wrong, hear me?"

"The kid's a goner," Ron said later, as he sat behind the wheel of his car, the engine running. "He's gone."

It was 10 p.m. It was pitch black out. And here, on a side street in the heart of embattled East New York, Lloyd had asked Ron to stop the car—so he could take a piss on the side of a van parked on the street in front of some row houses.

"I got to take 'Herbie Love Puppy' out for a walk," he said, as he hopped out. "This ain't goin' to be in the book, is it? You ain't goin' to put *this* in the book?" As Lloyd stood outside under the winter night sky, two teenage girls came walking down the block and, seeing Lloyd relieving himself in public, one covered her eyes and the other walked around the far side of the van. "Hey, ladies," Lloyd said with a smile, still taking his piss. "Herbie wants to say hello. Say hello to Herbie."

"You're sick," Ron said as Lloyd got back in the car. "Just sick."

"Ain't goin' in the book, right?" Lloyd said. "No one wants to read 'bout Swee'pea takin' a piss, right?"

"Not unless it's clean piss," Ron said. "Not if it isn't clean."

"I'm tellin' you, man," Lloyd said as he was being dropped off, "this time it'll be different, Ron. I mean it. This time, I'm goin' to make it, man. I am. I tell you, I am."

"He's a goner," Ron said again as he pulled away, leaving Lloyd standing on the street, alone in the night. "That's it, I think." He shook his head. "He's gone."

The power lift moved across the floor dragging its cargo with it and it wasn't until he'd stacked the cartons on the floor that Lloyd Daniels, Sr., stopped, and sat for a moment. He was forty-two, a five-day-a-week stock clerk in the basement of Pergament's in Lake Success, New York. He was lean, in good shape, and his face still looked young, though perhaps just a bit tired of all this. On each of his leather work gloves was written "Pops." He was, after all, about twenty years older than all of his coworkers.

"I don't really want to talk 'bout Lloyd," he'd said politely. "You wonder when the kid will ever realize what he's done to himself. You wonder when he'll ever get it together. The thing is, you can't tell these kids nothin' nowadays. They have to learn it all for themselves. That's just the way it is with them. That's all I can say.

"I can't say nothin' more 'bout it. 'Bout nothin'."

Then the man, who'd rarely spent time with his son, took his gloves, put them back on, dismissed himself from the conversation, and went back to work. It was strange, because the words echoed almost in an exact fashion what Lulia Hendley had said about him, her eldest son. That you couldn't tell him anything; that he'd had to learn it all for himself. "Maybe that's just kids," she'd said. "You just hope *theys* learned it right before it's too late."

Lulia was seated in her living room. Behind her were portraits of all the family members. In the next room, her grandchildren screamed as they ran back and forth across the floor.

"You know," she said, "I had a son, died at twenty-six. Got shot. Shot three times with a thirty-eight in the back. He had been connin' peoples at card games and God knows what else. Then one mornin', a Saturday mornin' I think, right down on Jamaica Avenue in front of the Blue Chips, somebody shot him three times in the back. His name was Hollis, Hollis Daniels. Junior's uncle. I had to go out there and identify him. It wasn't real pretty. But he had been hangin' out with his crew. It was what he wanted from life. You couldn't tell him nothin', either."

She was asked what this all had to do with her grandson. She said it had everything. She'd heard all the stories. She said she felt it was hopeless, the situation. Where she used to laugh and joke with people about Lloyd—"Junior's goin' to make me an old *man*," she'd once said—now she became serious; quite serious.

She hadn't seen Lloyd since he'd been shot.

She wasn't sure she'd ever see him again.

"I don't know," she said, her voice now barely audible above the noise from the other room. "Junior's a lost cause. I think he's lost in the mist now. He's twenty-two years old and he's not listenin' to nobody. And, you see what's goin' to make it bad for Lloyd is, number one, he doesn't have the education. See, if he had an education, it wouldn't be bad if he didn't make it. He could go out and get him a job.

"But what, what he's goin' to do? Tell me, what's he goin' to do? He don't know how to do nothin' else but basketball. That's it."

She looked down. There was a tear in the corner of her eye.

Generations had passed in her family, as they had passed on the streets and in the parks, and still little had changed. Folks were still making the same mistakes. Folks were still finding the same trouble. And, in all honesty, Lulia could hardly see if they would ever get better, ever work out. "Sooner or later," she said, "he'll kill *hisself* with drugs or booze or get killed hangin' out in the wrong place. I hate to say it, but that's my gut feelin'. He'll die a young man. If he don't convince himself he has a problem, then he'll die a young man. He's going in the wrong direction not to die a young man."

Then, that strong-willed woman began to cry.

Epilogue

Lloyd Daniels didn't die a young man.

And though more than twenty-five years after the first publication of *Swee'pea* it still seems hard to believe—the drinking and admitted drug abuse, the problems with school and with the law, that he was shot and nearly killed—Lloyd Daniels proved everyone wrong. His grandmother, Lulia; the experts.

Ron Naclerio. Me.

First, Lloyd found a good woman who believed in him, who helped get him back on track just when he seemed lost for good. Then, Lloyd said, he found God.

Finally, he got clean and sober long enough to change his fate. And on October 16, 1992, he made his National Basketball Association debut for the San Antonio Spurs in a preseason game against the New York Knicks in Albany, New York.

The Knicks won, 96–90. The outcome was irrelevant, as was the fact that Lloyd, who shot 0-for-5 from the field in the first half, was a perfect 5-for-5 in the second half—finishing with 12 points, 7 rebounds, 1 assist, and just 1 turnover in 25 minutes. Because, afterward, Swee'pea declared: "I'm in The Show."

Knicks coach Pat Riley called Lloyd "a prodigy."

"I thought it was a thrill playing against him," Knicks guard Hubert Davis said. "He was everything and more that I've heard. . . . He's a legend in his own right."

Unfathomable as the whole scenario was, it was more unfathomable considering the depths to which he'd sunk after being shot. Cut by the CBA Quad City Thunder, back on the streets of New York, Lloyd had latched on with the Miami Tropics in the minor-league United

States Basketball League (USBL)—the self-proclaimed "League of Opportunity"—for the 1990–91 season. It was there that *Sports Illustrated* writer Douglas S. Looney caught up with him, penning a piece titled: "Legend or Myth? Lloyd Daniels was a storied playground basketball player, but his life—and his once bright NBA prospects—have taken a sorry turn." The story ran on July 8, 1991. It wasn't kind.

"Like Zsa Zsa Gabor," Looney wrote of Lloyd, "he's mostly famous for being famous. Look closely at his game and it unravels like a ball of yarn."

Writing of watching Lloyd mail it in during a game against the little-known Philadelphia Spirits at Holy Family College in northeast Philadelphia, Looney quoted then–NBA director of scouting Marty Blake, who'd once raved about Swee'pea, as saying, "This guy can't play. He's a myth." And then–Indiana Pacers scout Al Menendez, who'd fawned over Lloyd as a high school player, told Looney, "I think his talents have been blown completely out of proportion. He's like a hero by word of mouth."

One NBA player-personnel director told Looney that Lloyd had "reached his level," meaning the USBL. And John Killilea, who by then was an assistant coach with the Houston Rockets, told him, matter-of-factly, "He'll never make it."

In fact, Looney wrote that another member of the Tropics—remember the Terminator, Ron Matthias?—had a better shot at the NBA than Lloyd.

Despite the critics, despite the odds, Lloyd continued his long road back from the brink. The unlikeliest road back. He played for the Greensboro City Gaters in the little-known Global Basketball Association and was named MVP of the All-Star Game and then league MVP—averaging 24.3 points, 6.6 rebounds, and 3.9 assists in 63 games, his first full season since high school. He played for the USBL Long Island Surf.

Along the way, Lloyd said, something inside him changed.

The seeds were first planted back in 1990. That August, just a few months before the release of *Swee'pea*, the book, Lloyd was offered a "last-chance" contract with the Tulsa Fast Breakers in the CBA. The coach was Henry Bibby. "I think," Bibby said, "he deserves the chance. But he has to realize this could be his last go-round. He has to be a good citizen on this team, in this town. He has to have the desire and athletic ability I used to see when he played uptown. And he has to understand that drug addiction is there forever. Hopefully, I can get the most out of him. He was a big, big-time player."

At the time, Lloyd was playing basketball in the Starrett City League; that is, a league based in the Starrett City apartment complex in East New York, Brooklyn.

He never made it to Tulsa.

He did, however, get a tryout with the CBA Albany Patroons in October 1990, signing a contract for $525 a week. The only guarantee of the nonguaranteed contract was that Lloyd would have a shot to make the team. Coach George Karl, who'd later coach the Cleveland Cavaliers, Golden State Warriors, Seattle SuperSonics, Milwaukee Bucks, Denver Nuggets, and Sacramento Kings, said Lloyd was overweight and out of shape—and cut him on the final day of camp.

Karl said he'd made his decision after watching Lloyd and wondering how good he could be without drugs and alcohol. Instrumental, he said, was when a player who'd faced Lloyd in high school told him, "George, this guy is ten percent of what he was."

So Karl sat Swee'pea down in his office and told him, "Lloyd, you've got to forget about basketball and get your life in order." As Lloyd later said, Karl was the first coach who'd ever told him to forget about basketball—and to focus on life. His life.

"He was the first one," Swee'pea said, "that had the guts to do that."

The slap in the face woke Lloyd. But it was a woman he met in Albany—Kendra Dunn—who got Lloyd to see the light. Lloyd told *People* magazine in 1992 that he'd met Dunn, then an insurance company benefits specialist, in Albany on November 24, 1990. (It was the reason, he told *People,* he later took uniform number 24 with the Spurs.) Where most everyone only cared about Lloyd Daniels the basketball player, Kendra made it clear, Lloyd later said, that she cared about Lloyd Daniels the person. For the first time in forever, it seemed, maybe for the first time since he'd become a basketball player, Lloyd had found someone who wanted nothing from him in return. Except love.

Kendra helped Lloyd get sober. She helped him find God. She set him on a path toward finding himself. For once, it seemed, Lloyd stayed on that path.

In Albany, he attended Narcotic Anonymous meetings twice a week. For six months. He took a job at a local Boys Club. "It was an awakening of the spirit, man," Lloyd told *People* in the story that appeared on November 9, 1992. "As they say, God just came to me and he said, 'Hey, Lloyd, I want you to walk the straight line.'"

So, Lloyd went from Albany to the Miami Tropics and the Greensboro City Gaters and the Long Island Surf. There, after a slow start that saw him miss the first seven games of the season with shoulder tendonitis, Lloyd played like a man possessed.

During one stretch he scored 25 points in each of back-to-back games, then had 33 points with 6 assists, 22 points, 10 points with 12 assists, and 21 points with 10 assists before springing for 36 points with 13 rebounds and 9 assists in a 138–114 win over the Tampa Bay Sunblasters—and was named USBL Player of the Week.

He followed that with games of 35 points, 36 points, 22 points, and 26 points with 9 assists, then scored 27 points with 12 rebounds and a record 19 assists in a 131–110 win over the New Haven Skyhawks. It would be his final game with the Surf.

That was because, once again, fate intervened. Jerry Tarkanian had been forced out at the University of Nevada, Las Vegas—ironically because of the sanctions expected as a result of the NCAA investigation into Lloyd's recruitment there and because of the investigation launched following the publication of those infamous photos of Moses Scurry and his Vegas teammates in the hot tub with Richie the Fixer Perry.

And Tark the Shark got hired to coach the Spurs.

Lloyd had averaged 23.7 points, 6 rebounds, and 7.8 assists in 16 games for the Surf. Tark made signing Lloyd a top priority. That happened just two days after he'd gone off in that triple-double game against the Skyhawks.

"He has seen things you or I will never see," Tarkanian told the *Fort Worth Star-Telegram* in a multipage broadsheet article on Lloyd, adding: "Hopefully."

The story, published on August 23, 1992, a few short months after Lloyd signed, was written by Steve Campbell under a headline that read: "Clean Living. Drugs, alcohol, and street life almost killed him. Now, with the San Antonio Spurs, Lloyd Daniels has a chance to fulfill his enormous potential, and he's confident he won't blow it."

Spurs officials declared Lloyd clean and sober, according to the article. Three months prior Lloyd had gone through a rehabilitation program in Houston run by none other than John Lucas, the former NBA star he'd first met at the airport in Denver. The article went on to claim that he was going to church and working hard, doing chores. It talked of him doting on his then–infant daughter, Aubrey—of turning his life around. Of it being good.

"I'm just happy to be here," Lloyd told Campbell. "How many guys do you know that get shot, have a drug problem as bad as I have, and right now, look: I'm twenty-four years old and I'm here. I appreciate that. That's God's work. I appreciate that every day."

That article quoted me, as the author of *Swee'pea*, as saying: "I think he should be a symbol for people, for everybody out there in that situation: No matter how bad things get, you can make it happen. . . . He's living proof you can make it happen."

It quoted Lulia Hendley saying of her grandson, "I don't worry about him going back. When I go to bed at night, I don't have to worry about him getting in trouble. It's a lovely feeling. A lovely feeling . . . He has changed his life around."

"This guy," Tarkanian said of Lloyd, "probably went twenty years before he had three good meals in a week. Seriously, this guy has overcome odds very few people even understand exist today." To which Lloyd said: "I know Coach Tark wants to see me do well more than anybody. Coach Tark is a great man, and not just because I can play basketball. The guy really stuck by me, and I would like the world to know that."

In fact, Campbell reported Lloyd had turned down rookie-camp invitations from the New York Knicks, Atlanta Hawks, and Milwaukee Bucks to play for Tark.

A story in the November 1992 edition of *Esquire* titled "The Lloyd Daniels Affair: The First Last Chance of Two Basketball Holy Fools," once tried to describe and define the indefinable relationship between Swee'pea and Tark, the attraction that seemed to leave anyone and everyone—except the two of them—befuddled and bemused.

At one point the writer, Ivan Solotaroff, asked Tarkanian, "Do you feel angry with Lloyd?" In other words, for all the trouble he'd caused him at UNLV.

"I can't even understand that question, much less answer it," Tark said. "He was just a nineteen-year-old kid with a drug habit and a sixth sense for the game. . . ."

Lloyd, it turned out, would be the least of Tarkanian's problems in San Antonio. One, he didn't have a pure point guard; much to his chagrin, he had Vinny Del Negro. And two, he had many conflicts with ownership, which, following a disastrous 9-11 start, saw Tark fired—replaced, oddly enough, by John Lucas. Lloyd went on to spend two years with San Antonio.

The ride, however, was anything but smooth.

———

Lloyd's first regular-season game was, ironically, against the Sacramento Kings, which featured Philadelphia playground star Lionel "Train" Simmons and former Cardozo center Duane Causwell. Lloyd shot 2-for-8 from the field and scored 6 points with 2 assists, 1 rebound, 1 turnover, and 5 fouls in 24 minutes off the bench. The Kings won, 114–106. Causwell, who back at Cardozo had been referred to by Ron as "Abdul Lollipop," finished with 15 points, 8 rebounds, and 2 blocks in 29 minutes.

But in his second regular-season game, Swee'pea came off the bench to play 45 minutes in a 125–121 double-overtime loss to the Denver Nuggets, shooting 11-for-19 from the field, making his only three-point attempt, as he scored 26 points with 8 rebounds, 6 assists, 3 blocks, and 3 steals—playing guard.

There was a 21-point, 7-rebound, 4-assist performance in Game 3, his first career start, a 104–98 win against the Milwaukee Bucks on November 10. After scoring 16 points on 8-for-14 shooting two nights later in a loss to Atlanta, folks started talking about Lloyd as a serious candidate for the NBA All-Rookie Team—along with Shaquille O'Neal and Christian Laettner. He had, after all, averaged 17.3 points, 5.5 rebounds, 4 assists, and 1.25 steals in 35.3 minutes over those four regular-season games.

"I know I can do things," Lloyd said of being in the NBA. "It's a great feeling. But I never doubted myself. Once I believed I had a drug and alcohol problem, I knew I'd be all right. I just had to come to the belief that I'm going to be an addict the rest of my life. For me, I just take one day at a time and ask God for the strength to stay straight."

"I don't like opera," Ron told the *Star-Telegram*. "But if I change the channel and see Pavarotti, there's something about it. I have to watch. You're seeing something awesome. With Lloyd, it's the same thing. You're seeing greatness."

As NBA veteran Doc Rivers said, having played against Swee'pea, "Lloyd's a great example that if you're living, you should not give up on a person."

On the road, Lloyd came under the watchful eye of his teammate, "the Admiral," former Navy star and future Hall of Famer David Robinson. Still, the remainder of the 1992–93 season was filled with on-court highs and lows. There was a 19-point game against the Cleveland Cavaliers, a 24-point game against the Seattle SuperSonics, and a 21-point game in a 108–103 loss against the New Jersey Nets—a game that saw Kenny Anderson, the Nets point guard, score 31 points with 17 assists, 4 rebounds, and 2 steals. But there also was a DNP— NBA shorthand for Did Not Play—against Sacramento in Game 40, followed by a 4-point performance in a win over the Nets and a 6-point performance in a 133–115 win over the Indiana Pacers. A game when former New York City standout Vern Fleming scored 24 off the bench for Indiana; where former August Martin swingman Sean Green, who'd played against Lloyd at Jackson, had 9 for the Pacers. There was the zero-point game in eight minutes of a 105–103 loss to the Phoenix Suns on February 23, 1993, followed two nights later by a team-high 26 points in 39 minutes off the bench in a 111–104 loss at Charlotte.

Then there was the game against the New York Knicks at Madison Square Garden on March 21—Lloyd's first-ever at the World's Most Famous Arena. John F. Kennedy, Jr., was in attendance. So were a bevy of stars. Lloyd shot 5-for-10 from the field, scoring 13 points. The Knicks won, 115–96, behind 30 points from Patrick Ewing, 25 from John Starks, and 11 from Anthony Mason.

Lloyd got a sneaker deal and did commercials for British Knights. He filmed a spot down at West Fourth Street, where he was—and, will always be—a star.

The Spurs went on to finish second in the Midwest Division at 49-33. They beat the Portland Trail Blazers, 3 games to 1, in the first round, but fell to Phoenix, 4–2, in the Western Conference Semifinals. Lloyd appeared in 77 games, starting 10. But, he averaged just 9.1 points, 2.8 rebounds, 1.9 assists, and 1.3 turnovers, converted to shooting guard after Lucas replaced Tark. He shot 44.3 percent, 33.3 percent from three-point range.

In two seasons with the Spurs, Lloyd would earn the annual NBA minimum—$140,000 in 1992–93; $182,000 in 1993–94—as he followed the 1992–93 season with 5.7 points a game in 1993–94. He not only played on the same team with David Robinson; in his second season, Lloyd also became teammates with "the Worm"—the controversial star bad boy and future Hall of Famer, Dennis Rodman.

Lloyd also teamed with J. R. Reid, the same player he trounced that summer back in Five-Star Camp, who played 66 games for the Spurs in 1992–93, starting 24, as he averaged 9.9 points a game. Reid earned $1.25 million that season and almost $1.82 million in 1993–94—when he averaged just 9 points a game.

The difference in salaries was the difference in career paths. And reputations. The road taken by Lloyd had cost him a million dollars a year, if not more. Much more.

———

Kenny Anderson had no such troubles. Or so it seemed.

He came out of Archbishop Molloy to help Georgia Tech to the NCAA Final Four as a freshman in 1989–90, hitting the game-tying shot to force overtime en route to a win over favored Michigan State in the Sweet 16, before Tech fell to the eventual champ—UNLV. Then he led Tech to the NCAA tournament in 1991, averaging 25.9 points, 5.7 rebounds, and 5.6 assists a game, before declaring for the NBA Draft. Anderson was taken second overall, by the New Jersey Nets. He spent fourteen seasons in the NBA, playing for the Nets, Charlotte Hornets, Portland Trail Blazers, Boston Celtics, Seattle SuperSonics, New Orleans Hornets, Indiana Pacers, Atlanta Hawks, and Los Angeles Clippers. He was an all-star with the Nets in 1993–94, his third year in the league, a twenty-three-year-old averaging 18.8 points, 3.9 rebounds, 9.8 assists, 1.9 steals, and 3.2 turnovers a game as the team went 47-35 under Chuck Daly—losing a first-round series to the Knicks. He finished with 10,789 career points. He also made $63.4 million, though he never made the NBA Finals.

But, despite his success, Anderson, the kid who'd first made a name for himself back at Lefrak City and Lost Battalion Hall, suffered his own share of setbacks.

The website for an anticipated 2015 documentary on Anderson called *Mr. Chibbs* featured a quote that read: "Basketball is easy, life is hard." Anderson said as much when he appeared with the Rock, Dwayne Johnson, on the reality TV show *Wake Up Call* on TNT in January 2015. As *Washington Post* reporter Dave Sheinin once wrote,

"If Kenny Anderson has learned anything—and he will tell you he has learned plenty—it's that the game, and life, can unspool on you faster than you can spell phenom."

The first thing Kenny Anderson did after being drafted by the Nets was keep a promise, buying a house for his mom, Joan, who'd guided him through thick and thin. It wasn't long, though, before his life got, well . . . complicated.

Anderson had eight children by six different women. He spent money like there was no tomorrow—on houses, on cars; on having a good time—and ended up filing for bankruptcy protection in 2005, citing a net worth of $150,000 and monthly expenses of $41,000. He said he always made sure his kids—and their moms—were provided for.

He said he always tried to do the right thing by them. By most accounts, he did.

But Anderson, who said he'd never even had a beer until he got to college, was living on the edge. At one point, he told the *Washington Post*, he had ten cars and was giving money to extended family and friends to help out. He was having a hard time saying no, to anyone, to anything. "I spent my entire life dedicated to the game," he said on the official website for his documentary, "and when I got there, I went a little crazy."

As Anderson told Sheinin, "I was ignorant. My accountant and my people told me—and I should've listened—like, 'Yo, you only need two cars.' But, I was a kid. . . . I was generous. I didn't say no. I used to have it bad, people calling me, crying, I used to be like, 'Aw, damn, man.' They were struggling. It's hard. . . . So, I helped."

Anderson, it seemed, helped everyone but himself. And then when his mother died, suddenly, in October 2005, he said he was lost.

"After she passed, it changed my perspective on everything," Anderson told me in a phone conversation in 2015.

His finances were in ruins; his life was not in much better shape. He lost his passion for the game, retired from the NBA, played a season in Lithuania, then retired for good. In 2011 he took a job coaching basketball at the David Posnack Jewish Day School in Davie, Florida. But in April 2013, Pembroke Pines police officers spotted his car weaving at 4:30 a.m.—and Anderson was arrested and charged with driving under the influence. He was released on $500 bond, according to the *Palm Beach Post*. But as a result, his coaching contract with the school was not renewed for 2013–14.

He later pleaded no contest.

It was unclear if the Team Anderson structure, designed to keep Kenny Anderson on the road to success, had protected him too much from the associated perils of success.

Where Lloyd had no structure, was forced to deal with life, with the streets, with the world, with very little guidance, on his own terms, looking back it seems possible Anderson was sheltered so much that he wasn't exposed at all to the ways he might get burned. That he wasn't educated on how to keep himself from getting burned.

Too sheltered? "Possibly," Tom Konchalski, the high school basketball recruiting expert who'd known Anderson since he was just a kid, said. "Possibly."

It was all with good intentions, of course.

Those who cared about Anderson—his mother, who'd suffered her own heartache; Archbishop Molloy coach Jack Curran, confidants like Pierre Turner and Vincent Smith, who both saw greatness in him— teamed to keep him on track, to keep the elements at bay. In retrospect, maybe they needed to let him get his feet wet. Maybe they needed to let him suffer setbacks, to fail, to know failure just a little bit.

After all, Anderson, now a grandfather, said he didn't even understand the basics of taxes, not even a sense of what he'd owe Uncle Sam on his NBA paychecks.

Today Anderson is married, is working on his role as a father. His house is paid for, there's money in the bank, and he is working toward becoming a coach again.

"I've never run from any of my problems," Anderson told the New York *Daily News*, "and I never blamed anyone for them. . . . I take full responsibility for everything. I've failed. I've failed in marriage. I've failed as a father. But, you know, failure is good in some ways. It lets you see what you have to build, what you have to do.

"I'm going in the right direction."

Anderson, though, caught a lot of heat when he joined Dennis Rodman and other former NBA stars on a tour of North Korea in 2014, meeting with and playing before Kim Jong Un. He told TMZ that Kim actually treated him "very well" but he admitted he was ignorant about alleged atrocities committed by the controversial dictator's regime. The *Daily News* suggested Anderson and his teammates should have read three pages on the Human Rights Watch website: "Food Shortages and Famine," "Torture and Inhuman Treatment," and "Executions and Political Prisoner Camps."

He later apologized for making the trip.

———

The 2015 NBA All-Star Game was held at the Barclays Center in Brooklyn. As part of the promotion for the game, the league issued a poster called "A History of New York City Basketball." It was a map of the five boroughs. Notable players, coaches, programs—even journalists—associated with all levels of the game were cited in each.

A number had ties to *Swee'pea*, the book. Lloyd was one of those featured from Queens, highlighted with a photo of him in uniform for the San Antonio Spurs.

The mention was brief: Lloyd Daniels, Jackson High School.

But there he was.

A host of others were there, too, accompanied by highlights. Kenny Anderson was pictured with the Nets, above an info box that read: "Only four-time All-City selection; won two Catholic School titles; 2,621 career points; NBA All-Star in 1994."

Duane Causwell was cited. So were Kenny Smith, Kevin Joyce, Brian Winters, Vern Fleming, Anthony Mason, Bob Cousy, and "college coaching icons" from Queens, among them Rick Pitino, Bobby Cremins, and Jim Valvano. Al McGuire had his own box. So did Lou Carnesecca. I.S. 8, the intermediate school where Ron Naclerio taught for years—where future NBA stars Stephon Marbury and Rafer Alston, subjects of the dedication page in the original edition of *Swee'pea*, once teamed to form what surely is the best backcourt in the history of middle-school basketball—was highlighted. So was Alston. As were Jack Curran and Chuck Granby, who'd coached Lloyd at Jackson.

Ron also was among those recognized, which was fitting.

His Cardozo team was the defending PSAL New York City Champion in 2014–15, before falling to Wings Academy in the 2015 PSAL Final at Madison Square Garden, and he ended the season as the fourth-winningest high school coach in New York State history—one win behind Granby. Curran was first, with 972 victories in 55 seasons at Archbishop Molloy. The late Ed Petrie of Long Island's East Hampton High School—and who was, ironically, Curran's teammate with the Rye Pioneers, a club team from Westchester, in the 1950s—was second at 754. Retiring in 2014, Granby had 722 wins.

Ron entered the 2015–16 season with 721 victories and made fast work of grabbing the record, winning his first two games to move ahead of Granby. The record fell before a full house at Cardozo on December 1, the Judges handling a pesky Francis Lewis team, 88–72, before a horde of reporters, fans, friends, and school alums—among those in attendance, Duane Causwell and former Knicks coach Stu Jackson.

Afterward, Ron received a proclamation from Mayor Bill de Blasio, recognizing his feat in becoming the all-time winningest coach in the 112-year history of the PSAL, as a banner with his sketched portrait and the slogan "Naclerio 723" was unfurled to wild applause. For his part, Ron told the crowd that while he'd once dreamed of leaving Cardozo for his shot at coaching a major college team or in the pros, he'd come to realize his appreciation for staying put; in the place that'd always been home.

"My dream was to coach St. John's or the Knicks." Ron, who'd taken over a 1-21 team in 1981, going an amazing 22-4 with thirteen of those same kids the following season, told the packed gymnasium, "It never happened. But I realized the break I probably really got was the break that I didn't realize: the fact that I never left Cardozo."

Winner of city championships in 1999 and 2014, coach of more than a dozen NBA players when you consider his work at Cardozo and on the playgrounds, Ron is now the dean of New York City high school basketball coaches.

Once known in New York City basketball circles as "Nutsy," he now has a new nickname: "the Teacher." Not only is he known on the national stage but a crew has filmed pilot episodes for a proposed television show about his work with at-risk kids. He is a terrific coach.

Of course, many others joined him on that historical map.

Notables from Brooklyn included Fly Williams, World B Free, Chris Mullin, Bernard King, Pearl Washington, Mark Jackson, John Salley, Stephon Marbury, and Brooklyn natives Julius Erving and Michael Jordan. The Bronx list featured Ed Pinckney, Kemba Walker, Jamal Mashburn, Rod Strickland, and Donnie Walsh, while historical figures from Manhattan included a host of familiar names, among them Kareem Abdul-Jabbar, Walt Frazier, Dean "the Dream" Meminger, Cal Ramsey, Walter Berry, Steve Burtt, and Earl "the Pearl" Monroe.

Holcombe Rucker was recognized, as was Rucker Park.

"If Madison Square Garden is the 'World's Most Famous Arena,'" the highlight box from the historical map read, "then Rucker Park is the world's most famous public court."

Connie Hawkins, Pee Wee Kirkland, Jackie Jackson, Tiny Archibald, Herman "Helicopter" Knowings, and Joe Hammond, "the Destroyer," were all cited.

Of course, so was Earl Manigault. The Goat.

Tom Konchalski was among those recognized for contributions to the basketball landscape. As were Howie Garfinkel, Dyckman coach Jim Couch, Wheelchair Classic founder Hank Carter, *The City Game* author Pete Axthelm, *Heaven Is a Playground* author Rick Telander, and the late *Daily News* reporter Bill Travers. Or, as every high school player in New York City once knew him: Mr. Travers.

All in all, pretty cool.

———

A lot else has happened since the first publication of *Swee'pea*.

Duane Causwell came out of Cardozo, went to Temple University, got taken eighteenth overall by the Sacramento Kings in the 1990 NBA Draft—and spent eleven seasons in the league, mostly as a backup center, with the Kings and the Miami Heat.

The kid who Ron Naclerio once said "couldn't walk and chew gum at the same time" made $17.6 million in his career, despite averaging just 4.9 points, 4.2 points, and 1.4 blocks in 541 games. To this day, I remain convinced the New York Knicks would have won an NBA title if they'd taken Causwell with the seventeenth pick in 1990 instead of University of Maryland forward Jerrod Mustaf. Causwell would have been the perfect backup to Patrick Ewing. Instead, Mustaf came and went, his career spent mostly in Europe. And the Knicks had backup guys like Eddie Lee Wilkins, Tim McCormick, Patrick Eddie, James Donaldson, and, ultimately, an aged Herb Williams. Meanwhile Alston, the legendary "Skip to My Lou," came out of Cardozo to play one season at Fresno State—for Jerry Tarkanian. Drafted by the Milwaukee Bucks in the second round of the 1998 NBA Draft, Alston played eleven seasons in the league, averaging 10.1 points and 4.8 assists in 671 career games for the Bucks, Toronto Raptors, Miami Heat, Houston Rockets, Orlando Magic, and New Jersey Nets. His Bucks team, coached by George Karl, lost to the Allen Iverson–led Philadelphia 76ers in the 2001 Eastern Conference Finals. His Orlando Magic beat the LeBron James–led Cleveland Cavaliers in the 2009 Eastern Conference Finals, but fell to Kobe Bryant and the Los Angeles Lakers in the NBA Finals, 4 games to 1. He made a career $28.1 million.

His former backcourt mate at I.S. 8, Stephon Marbury, who went on to star at Abraham Lincoln High School in Brooklyn, also had a pretty good career. To say the least. Drafted fourth overall by Milwaukee out of Georgia Tech in 1996, Marbury went on to play thirteen seasons with the Bucks, New Jersey Nets, Phoenix Suns, and New York Knicks. He scored 16,297 points with 6,471 assists—a 19.3-point, 7.6-assist average—in 846 career games, becoming a two-time all-star and earning the nickname "Starbury." He earned a staggering $151.1 million. En route, he was featured on the cover of *NBA Ballers,* was mentioned in Spike Lee's *He Got Game,* and appeared with Kenny Anderson in the video for Big

Pun's "Watcha Gonna Do." After the NBA, Marbury went to China in 2010, playing for the Shanxi Zhongyi Brave Dragons and Foshan Dralions before joining the Beijing Ducks in 2011. As of 2015, the Coney Island native had won three Chinese Basketball Association titles with the Ducks, had been honored with a national postage stamp and a statue of himself outside the team arena—and had starred in a bizarre Chinese musical stage production about his life, called simply *I Am Marbury.*

Even Sean Green, the former August Martin star who'd played against Lloyd at Jackson, made the NBA out of Iona College: three seasons for a total of eighty-four games with the Indiana Pacers, Philadelphia 76ers, and Miami Heat, earning $885,000.

There also were many strange twists.

Future Pollard went on to become the basketball coach at Jefferson Campus, a group of specialized schools located on the site of the old Thomas Jefferson High School, where Lloyd once played. Thomas Jefferson—T.J. or *Jeff,* as it was known—which counted actors Jimmy Smits, Shelley Winters, and Danny Kaye; former heavyweight boxing champion Riddick Bowe; NBA players Phil Sellers, LeRoy Ellis, and Sidney Green; musicians Lil' Fame and Frukwan; and the former CEO of Goldman Sachs, Lloyd Blankfein, among its alumni, was closed by New York City in 2007 for chronic underperformance and poor graduation rates. The new Jefferson Campus is now the site for the High School for Civil Rights, FDNY High School for Fire and Life Safety, the Performing Arts and Technology High School, and the World Academy for Total Community Health School, better known as WATCH. Pollard led Jefferson into the 2014 PSAL Playoffs, where it lost in the finals, 55–54, to Ron's team from Cardozo.

Tony Chiles, who'd lost his mother to senseless violence when he was back at Columbia University, also got into coaching. An assistant under Steve Lavin at St. John's University, Chiles lost his job when Lavin was let go in 2015—to make way for Chris Mullin. He was immediately hired as an assistant at Fordham University.

Orlando Antigua, the innocent bystander who survived being shot in the head in the Bronx, went on to much-deserved success as well.

He came out of St. Raymond's in the Bronx to play in the Big East at the University of Pittsburgh, then became the first Hispanic ever—and first nonblack player in fifty-two years—to play for the Harlem Globetrotters. He became an assistant coach at the University of Pittsburgh, took a job on John Calipari's staff at the University of Memphis, became a trusted assistant to Calipari at the University of Kentucky, and then was named the head coach at the University of South Florida in 2014. He is the head coach of the Dominican Republic National Team.

He also has a new nickname.

"Bullethead" is now known as "Hurricane."

There were other strange twists, as well. An infant when his father appeared in court in Syracuse, Anthony Bruin, son of Red Bruin, grew up to play basketball at Iona College in New Rochelle, New York. There he teamed with the sons of two former big-time stars for the Gaels—Steve Burtt, Jr., and Gary Springer, Jr., whose father had been on those wild teams with Richie Adams back at Ben Franklin—to lead Iona to a 23-8 record and into the 2006 NCAA tournament. The Gaels lost a first-round game to Louisiana State, after leading by five points at halftime. Bruin played four seasons at Iona, scoring 12.2 points a game as a senior in 2007.

And Burtt, whose father is the all-time leading scorer for Iona with 2,534 career points, finished second all-time—with 2,034.

Then there's Quinton Hosley, a New York native who went undrafted out of Fresno State in 2007. He became a naturalized citizen of Georgia, the nation, and has fashioned an enviable career playing in Turkey, Spain, Italy, and Poland, where his team, Stelmet Zielona Gora, won the Polish League title in 2013. The six-foot-seven swingman, who grew up in Denver, has a reverential nickname on the playgrounds of New York, "T2," which actually is short for "Terminator 2—The Sequel," in reference to his father, the Terminator. Yes, Hosley is the son of Ron Matthias, who nearly made good on that assessment by *Sports Illustrated* writer Douglas S. Looney back in 1991, going to free-agent camp with the Atlanta Hawks—making it to the final cut.

Years after first speaking with him on a long-distance telephone call, I got to have lunch with Dave MacCalman—"Davie D," who'd coached Lloyd with Waitemata—when he came to town to participate in the wheelchair division of the New York City Marathon, which he completed. A world-class Paralympic athlete with gold and silver medals to his credit, in 2011 MacCalman became the first person in New Zealand and one of the first worldwide to be fitted with a robotic exoskeleton built by an Auckland-based company, Rex Bionics. The device allowed the six-foot-five MacCalman the chance to stand again—and, to take his first steps in more than three decades.

"It is hard to describe what it has been like to be back on my feet again," MacCalman told the specialty report, *Disabled World*, adding: "I'm looking forward to . . . being able to stand around and socialize with family and friends."

The world-record holder for the quadriplegic pentathlon, MacCalman became a member of the New Zealand Order of Merit in 2000 for his services to disabled sports—and said he now looks forward to having a chance to walk his daughter down the aisle at her wedding. Strapped into the Rex, Davie D also looks a little like the Terminator.

Schwarzenegger, *not* Matthias.

Dr. Daniel L. Picard, who saved Lloyd's life at Mary Immaculate back in 1989, now is, according to records, assistant professor of surgery at Johns Hopkins.

Chip Engelland, who teamed with Lloyd back on the Topeka Sizzlers, has been an NBA assistant coach for more than ten years now—with the San Antonio Spurs. A sought-after speaker, clinician, and advisor on shooting technique, Engelland, a former ball boy for the legendary John Wooden with his 1975 NCAA championship team at UCLA, played in Canada and the Philippines after his stint in the CBA.

And remember Mark Warkentien? The former assistant at UNLV, at the center of a firestorm when he became Lloyd's legal guardian, became a scout for the NBA Seattle SuperSonics and in 2008–09 was named the NBA Executive of the Year while with the Denver Nuggets. In 2011, Warkentien was hired by the New York Knicks as a consultant to the then–president of basketball operations, Donnie Walsh.

The Knicks, as well as Madison Square Garden, the NHL New York

Rangers, and WNBA New York York Liberty, all are operated by the Madison Square Garden Company. The chairman is James Dolan, who is chief executive officer of the Long Island–based media giant Cablevision. Before agreeing to sell the cable company and paper to the French media giant Altice in 2015, Cablevision owned *Newsday*.

Which meant that, by strange coincidence, Warkentien and I later became teammates of sorts—both of us, ultimately, working for the same boss.

The most tragic figure from *Swee'pea* remains former Ben Franklin High School and UNLV star Richie Adams. Released from prison after serving time for that daytime robbery at Grand Central Terminal, Adams, the onetime playground star and two-time Pacific Coast Athletic Association Player of the Year, beat to death a fifteen-year-old girl named Norma Rodriguez at the Andrew Jackson Houses in October 1996. The medical examiner said Rodriguez, a freshman at Morris High School, died of head and neck injuries, a result of being "repeatedly stomped" by her assailant.

Detectives from the NYPD found a bloody print from a size 13 ½ basketball shoe at the scene, leading them to Adams, who lived in the Bronx project. In September 1998, the six-foot-nine Adams, "the Animal," was convicted of first-degree manslaughter and was sentenced to twenty-five years by acting state supreme court justice Gerald Sheindlin.

Adams is now Inmate No. 99A0313. His earliest release date, according to New York State prison records, is March 3, 2018; the maximum one, October 20, 2021.

He is serving his sentence at the Wyoming Correctional Facility in Attica, New York. It's located next to the infamous maximum security prison there.

On hearing the news that *Swee'pea* was headed back into print, friend and former *Newsday* colleague Alan Hahn, now a host at ESPN New

York and a broadcaster at MSG Networks, dropped me a note via Facebook. It read, in part: "The book is basically the first chapter in the beginning of the end of NYC hoops as we used to know it. Just look at the NBA now. . . . Hard to find city products who became stars."

Truth is, the very essence of playground basketball has changed since the first publication of *Swee'pea*. So, too, has the nature of New York City ball.

An article in the *New York Times* written following the announcement of that NBA historical map and in advance of the 2015 NBA All-Star Game noted that, while there might be asterisks to define what qualifies someone as a New York City player, "There will, however, be no asterisk noting that the local game isn't quite what it once was."

Written by Benjamin Hoffman and titled "An Elaborate Tale of Broken Rims and Moxie," the article appeared on February 7, 2015.

"Plenty of theories exist as to why players from New York City high schools are no longer as dominant on the national stage as they were in earlier decades," Hoffman wrote, adding, "There are, some argue, just more good players in more places than there once were, reducing the city's influence." But it's more complicated than that.

One big reason is that, in most neighborhoods, kids no longer play a lot of pickup ball. The best players in the city play on organized youth and club teams—that is, if they remain in the city at all. A lot leave for prep schools. The ones who stay can be found playing either indoors, where wooden floors are more forgiving than concrete and blacktop, or playing highly structured club schedules—sometimes at the mercy of unqualified coaches, and often without exposure to the game as improvisation.

And art.

A big 2014 summertime story on ESPN by writers Myron Medcalf and Dana O'Neil, titled "Playground Basketball Is Dying," explored the state of playground ball in a host of major cities across the United States—and found an appalling lack of unstructured activity. At Rucker Park, ESPN found the court replaced by an outdoor hardwood floor covered by tarp at night, taken up each winter.

"It's not the same," the man who started the Entertainers Basketball Classic, Greg Marius, told ESPN, adding, "When I was growing up, everybody in the hood played basketball. Everybody. Now," he said, "they're all doing something else." Others, however, argue that the scene is just . . . well, it's just different. More structured. Less informal. Part of that is the result of NCAA mandates, which set rules for off-season activities, as well as clearinghouse standards for incoming athletes.

Thus fewer and fewer players are willing to risk injuries, eligibilities, reputations, to things like substandard park courts—and those old drug games. Some consider it progress. Considering the death of artistry and imagination that gave us Earl Manigault, Joe Hammond, and Lloyd Daniels, to me it's a mixed bag.

———

There have been many real deaths, as well, among those chronicled in *Swee'pea*: Stan Dinner, the longtime Ben Franklin coach who once said Lloyd could do everything with a basketball "except autograph it," is gone. (Strangely, in the wake of his death I learned he was related to the stepmother of my lifelong best friend and basketball junkie, Tony Mills.) Gone, too, is Arnie Hershkowitz, who'd befriended all those young up-and-coming players. A remembrance piece in the *New York Times* on March 15, 2013, called Hersh, who'd died of a heart attack while out for a jog nine years earlier, "a high school teacher, street agent, summer league coach and mentor, and a true character of the game." The *Times* reporter David Waldstein wrote: "Some thought that he was like many street agents—an operator looking for under-the-table payments from colleges that wanted him to direct a player their way. But some of those who knew Hersh well said he was never interested in money."

Anthony Mason, who came out of Springfield Gardens High School, Tennessee State, the CBA, and the USBL to play thirteen seasons in the NBA, and who was named winner of the NBA Sixth Man Award in 1995 and an all-star in 2001, died on February 28, 2015, at forty-eight.

Former Dallas Mavericks big man Roy Tarpley, who was in rehab with Lloyd at ASAP/Van Nuys, died suddenly on January 9, 2015.

He was fifty. Former Cardozo guard Greg "Skate" Scott, who teamed with Kevin Story to form a formidable backcourt know as "the Psycho Twins," leading the Judges to that 1986 playoff upset of Lloyd's team at Andrew Jackson, was found dead in Harlem in January 2016—news that Ron, who'd been his coach, called "devastating." One of the most electrifying players of his time, Skate wasn't even fifty.

Kenny Anderson lost his mother, Joan, in 2005. His beloved high school coach, the ever-gracious gentleman Jack Curran, died on March 14, 2013—at age eighty-two. It is impossible to put a number on how many lives he shaped to the good.

Former Manhattan Center star Karlton Hines, who once seemed bound for basketball greatness, who once might have become one of the best players ever to come out of New York City, was shot to death outside an auto body shop in the Bronx in April 1994. A documentary about his life, *The Karlton Hines Story*, can still be found on YouTube. It's been viewed more than a half million times.

Three men central to Lloyd's time with the Topeka Sizzlers also are gone. Team owner Bernie Glannon, who first afforded Swee'pea a shot at making it as a pro, died in November 2008. And *Topeka Capital-Journal* reporter Allen R. Quakenbush—Quake—died on April 24, 1999, at the all-too-young age of forty-four. John Killilea, "Killer," was changing planes at the airport in Denver in January 1996, coming from scouting Boise State at Montana and headed to watch Valparaiso at the University of Missouri–Kansas City, when he reached into the overhead rack to retrieve a bag, had a heart attack—and fell dead. The *Boston Globe* columnist Bob Ryan wrote: "He was 67-going-on-15, a man passionately in love with a game. For John Killilea, there was no baseball, no football, no hockey, only basketball." He was a good man; a very good man, honest to a fault.

One of the greatest playground players of all time, a man who crossed into folklore and legend with a game unparalleled and a nickname and reputation known to millions who never even saw him play, was lost to congestive heart failure at Bellevue Hospital in New York in May 1998. Earl Manigault, forever the Goat, was fifty-three.

Lloyd's grandmother, Lulia Hendley, a sweet, strong woman with a heart as big as her smile, is gone. So is her firstborn son, Lloyd Daniels, Sr., Lloyd's dad. Word is that Lloyd and his father had managed to reconnect, have time, before his passing.

You can only hope that is true.

Of course, one of the most controversial—and most pivotal—figures in *Swee'pea*, Jerry Tarkanian, also left us. Tark died February 11, 2015. He was eighty-four.

"He fought and fought and fought," Danny Tarkanian told the Associated Press of the health issues—including a heart attack, respiratory ailments, and an infection—that finally took his father's life. The same could be said of battles his father fought with the NCAA at Long Beach State, UNLV, and Fresno State.

In fact, though Jerry Tarkanian amassed a career record of 784-202 as a head coach, his official all-time record was altered to 729-201—the result of games vacated due to NCAA sanctions at Long Beach State and, later, Fresno State.

In his memoir, *Runnin' Rebel*, with Dan Wetzel, Tark wrote: "In major-college basketball, nine of ten teams break the rules . . . the other one is in last place." As he said: "And you can't blame those coaches. If they ever told the truth about what really goes on in college athletics or on their own teams, they'd probably lose their jobs. . . . No one *really* wants to tell the truth. But I don't care. My reputation is what it is."

That honesty was why I always liked Tark, despite our differences. And honestly, despite the fact our *Newsday* investigations of his basketball program at UNLV made his life most uncomfortable at times, Tarkanian remained willing to answer pointed questions, face-to-face—going so far as to allow me to interview him and his family at his hotel suite at the Final Four. Which, I admit, I found pretty stand-up.

Following his death, Lloyd went on *The Doug Gottlieb Show*, an appearance that can still be found at gottlieb.radio.cbssports.com, to talk about Tarkanian.

"Tark was like a second father to me," Swee'pea told Gottlieb. "He was a great man. Forget about basketball. You know, he tried to talk to me every day. And he just a real person. You know, me and him used, I used to go over his house, and me and him just used to talk about life; and he just understood what I been through in life."

How? Gottlieb asked. How could Tark understand *that*?

"You know why," Lloyd said, "because he's a real person. . . . You know, he looked at me like I was one of his kids. I never got to play for him, but he never turnt his back on me. . . . That's a real person. He had to see something in me as a human being."

Gottlieb asked Lloyd how big a role Tarkanian played in him finally getting to the NBA and Lloyd said, "You know, you know one of my friends, they laugh, they say, 'Lloyd, I think Tarkanian took that job 'cause of you. To prove everybody that, 'Hey, this guy still got something in the tank and to see what type of person he is.'"

In fact, Lloyd said, right up until Tarkanian died, the two talked at least "once a week." As he said, "You know I miss him and I know he's in heaven now and I know he'll be watchin' over me, you know, keepin' angels around me to make sure I do the right thing. . . . Tark is the type a guy, he don't look down at nobody because everybody make mistakes and you know what? He saw talent like me and you know what he said? 'I'm gonna give this young man a chance.' . . . [We] just had that bond. Lloyd Daniels had that special bond, where another college coach probably would had turnt they back on me after losing their job. Tark never turnt his back. That's a real dude, man."

Shunned by the NCAA but embraced by his players and college basketball fans everywhere, Tarkanian weathered countless political storms to coach thirty-one seasons at Long Beach State, UNLV, and Fresno State, his teams failing to win twenty games just twice. Other than his twenty-game stint in San Antonio, he never had a losing season.

Those accomplishments were recognized with his induction into the Naismith Memorial Basketball Hall of Fame in 2013.

Ironically, Rick Evrard, instrumental to the NCAA investigation of Tarkanian and UNLV relating to the recruitment of Lloyd and the associations with Richie "the Fixer" Perry, later found himself on the other side of the aisle—defending Fresno State when the NCAA launched an investigation of Tarkanian's program there in 2000.

The investigation began after the *Fresno Bee* reported the owner of a local Japanese restaurant claimed he'd given "several thousand dollars'" worth of free food to Fresno State players, dating back to 1995—and that athletic department officials had failed to report the violations. The program had already weathered public relations storms under Tarkanian—altercations involving Ron's former star, Rafer Alston, who'd been accused of assaulting his girlfriend; Chris Herren checking himself into a rehab facility in Utah; two other players arrested and charged with theft and assault following an unflattering piece by Mike Wallace on *60 Minutes*; allegations of possible point-shaving, to name a few—but the restaurant issue signaled the beginning of the end for the longtime coach. He resigned from his alma mater in 2002.

Evrard—whose first NCAA investigation involved the recruitment of Manute Bol to Cleveland State by coach Kevin Mackey, Mackey having been an assistant coach at Boston College during the game-fixing scandal manufactured by Richard Perry and Henry Hill—left the organization for private practice in 1992, joining Bond, Schoeneck & King, a national firm whose specialties include representing athletes and athletic programs in their battles against the NCAA. He said being on the other side of the equation, including representing Fresno State during that NCAA investigation of Tarkanian and his troubled program, helped change his thinking about athletes and the eligibility requirements and standards set in place by the NCAA.

"I think what Jerry was saying was, 'Look, these kids deserve a chance. . . . It's like the Statue of Liberty slogan, 'Give me your tired, your poor, and I'll help them.'"

Evrard said that while Tarkanian might have "gone off the rails a little in how he helped" some of those athletes, the bottom line is that what he'd always said bore some truth: that the mere exposure to college had benefit, even if a kid never graduated.

Evrard earned a football scholarship after being seen by a recruiter scouting Pete Johnson, his teammate at Long Island's Long Beach High

School. Johnson went on to block for two-time Heisman Trophy winner Archie Griffin at Ohio State. Evrard got to play football at Rice University and go on to law school. Because of that, as well as those experiences with Tarkanian and defenses of other athletes and athletic programs, Evrard said he now thinks it's time college officials revamp the system: provide more benefit to athletes and recognize that higher education is not just for academicians.

Even athletes like Lloyd benefit from the exposure, Evrard believes. "Unfortunately," he said, "we try to tighten the academic standards instead of realizing these kids have gifts. . . . It may not be an academic gift; but they have other gifts. My sense is that there does need to be a change to the collegiate system to give student-athletes better opportunities. It's not college eligibility we're talking about.

"It's their lives."

After two erratic seasons, Lloyd was waived by the San Antonio Spurs on October 4, 1994. He signed four days later as a free agent with the Philadelphia 76ers.

His coach there, once again, was John Lucas.

"The one thing you have to understand," Lloyd told the *Philadelphia Daily News* after signing a one-year, nonguaranteed contract for the league minimum, "is that the Sixers aren't giving me anything other than an opportunity. I have to make the team."

Lloyd said, "If you play hard for John, he'll reward you."

Lloyd averaged 11.5 points during preseason, was the third-leading scorer, had 21 points in a win, and, the *Philadelphia Inquirer* reported, "Shot the lights out from three-point range." He made an absurd 58.3 percent of his preseason three-pointers, in fact.

But Lloyd lasted just five games in Philadelphia—six points, three, five, nine, and, finally, none before wearing out his welcome—as the Sixers released him that November 14. The end came as a surprise to Lucas, who said he'd called Lloyd aside to talk to him about slacking off, only to have Swee'pea lash out, forcing his hand.

"He was playing the way he played in San Antonio," Lucas told the *Philadelphia Daily News.* "There, he played well in camp and the pre-season, then seemed to fall asleep when the season started. That's the path he was taking here.

"When I went in to talk to him about it, he started telling me about some other things," Lucas said. "I tried to make it clear, but his response was, 'Well, if you're going to cut me, you might as well do it now.' That wasn't what I had intended to do."

For his part, Lloyd later said Lucas claimed he'd saved his life—and was trying to tell him he should be grateful. Lloyd said all he wanted was more playing time.

"I don't want people to think John Lucas saved my life," he said, adding: "If Luke saved my life, why didn't he save Chris Washburn's? *I* saved my life. John Lucas is not my savior. He's not no God. You have to save your own life. That's what *I* done."

After Philadelphia, Lloyd signed two ten-day contracts with the Lakers and then, on March 14, 1995, signed for the rest of the season. He played twenty-five games in Los Angeles.

He also played with the CBA Fort Wayne Fury, where he averaged 27.3 points, 5.9 rebounds, and 7.4 assists, then went to France and Italy, before signing as a free agent with the Sacramento Kings on November 16, 1996. He lasted just five games, scoring a total of 6 points in twenty-eight total minutes, then on December 26, 1995, signed with the New Jersey Nets. Twice he was in double figures. But he played seventeen games in Jersey before being waived—going back to Fort Wayne. A year later, in January 1998, Swee'pea signed with the NBA's Toronto Raptors and scored 21 points in his first game.

Five games later, he played four minutes against the Minnesota Timberwolves, scoring just two points. And then he was gone. Cut.

From there, Lloyd played in Puerto Rico and Turkey, in the CBA with the Idaho Stampede, and in Greece. He was in the International Basketball League (IBL) and the USBL, playing in Venezuela and China and Portugal, before finally ending his professional career with the Strong Island Sound in the ABA. That was 2006.

He made a good living. In addition to the more than $750,000 he made in the NBA, his then agent, Keith Glass, said Lloyd made at least a half million in Turkey alone. And Swee'pea certainly had his moments. (Check out a YouTube video of Lloyd playing for Scavolini Pesaro in an Italian League game against Benetton Reviso back in 1996. A 98–90 win; Lloyd, 9-for-11 from three-point range, plus a couple of brilliant assists, not to mention a soft banker off the glass on a *breakaway* near the end of the game—a play where any other player would have dunked it—to score 43. It's impossible to know how many rebounds or assists; a box score couldn't be found. At one point, when Lloyd takes a step-back three-pointer from the corner, the Rai Tre announcer, in Italian, even yells out: "Mamma mia!" Seriously. Mamma mia.)

And still, Glass told me during an interview sometime in 2000, "He's all over the place, Lloyd. That's just his personality. He's an absolutely terrific player. Everybody knows what he is, what he could have been. He's just had trouble sustaining. . . . I've had Lloyd for five years—and it always seems like he's been on a ten-day contract."

"I got to see a lot of beautiful places," Lloyd said, missing the irony.

About the time Lloyd signed with the ABA Strong Island Sound, *Newsday* did a story about what had happened to him; about his life. The reporter was Michael Weinreb. He found Lloyd coaching youth basketball at the Jersey Shore.

Lloyd and Kendra had a house near the Shore, in Colts Neck, an affluent area in Monmouth County, just west of Asbury Park. They had three children—daughters Aubrey and Shaina, son Lloyd III—and by most accounts were doing okay.

But Weinreb described a life of incongruous juxtaposition that was and appears to remain always Lloyd Daniels. Coaching youth ball, talking about "the perils facing America's youth," Weinreb wrote, Swee'pea was on his third beer during the interview—a forever recovering alcoholic, "headed to one more."

As the story, "Reboundin' Rebel: A 'New' Lloyd Daniels Leaves Checkered Past Behind while Coaching Kids in Jersey 'Burbs," described it: "Here he is, molding young minds, urging them to take school seriously, ordering them to listen to their parents, and—of all the unthinkable things—imploring them to toughen up on defense."

"These people who drop their kids at the mall? I'd never do that, man. That's the way kids get in trouble. They start smoking marijuana, having sex, all because they got no guardians. . . . Only time I drop my kids off is if they're going to the movies."

Ten years later, it's hard to know exactly where Lloyd is with life. His onetime agent, Keith Glass, once told me Lloyd needed one contract— just seven games—to qualify for an NBA pension. Never happened. And following the publication of *Swee'pea*, Lloyd cut off most of his communication with Ron. And all of it with me.

He didn't speak to us as we updated this manuscript for the reissue of the book. In fact, the only time I'd seen him face-to-face, between 1990 and 2015, was right after the initial release—when he was with the Tropics. He looked at me and said, "Take another step, Valenti, and I'm a gonna swing on you."

During the intervening years I was hired to write a magazine story about him after his NBA career, when he was back with the Long Island Surf. Keith Glass set up interviews; so did the Surf.

Lloyd said he was sick one time; he failed to show on another. After a third time, he contacted the magazine and threatened to file a lawsuit if they published a story. They didn't, paying me a fee instead.

Ron and Lloyd had a similar falling out and didn't talk for years.

Then an independent filmmaker from Minnesota, Benjamin May, undertook a documentary project about Lloyd. Called *The Legend of Swee'pea*, it came about after May raised tens of thousands of dollars during a brief campaign on Kickstarter. A lot of folks, it turned out, remain interested in and intrigued by Lloyd Daniels. The film, featuring on-screen interviews with NBA Hall-of-Famer David Robinson, Jerry Tarkanian and his wife, Lois, John Lucas, Avery Johnson, Tom Konchalski, Howie Garfinkel, me, Ron, and others, including former Jackson teammate Alvis Brown, agents Keith Glass and David Chesnoff, as well as playground historian Bobbito Garcia, made its world premiere at the prestigious NYC DOC Festival in Manhattan in November 2015.

Lloyd was there, at the theater across the street from the famous West Fourth Street basketball courts known as "the Cage." So were many of the film's participants, including both me and Ron. Lloyd and I had a chance to talk, before the showing. He said to me, "It wasn't you . . . I fucked up." It turned out that just two people in the film ended up in tears during their on-screen interviews. One was Lloyd, talking about what happened to his life.

The other was me.

Afterward, during a post-screening question-and-answer session before a packed theater that included reporters as well as my father, my son, and my wife, Beth, Lloyd gave a shout-out over the microphone: "You know I still love you, Valenti," he said. Later, he posed for pictures with me and Ron, and said, "I didn't die, did I? I didn't die."

In the documentary, Lloyd talks about how life is great; about how he shouldn't even be alive. He's also filmed drinking beers as he's talking to the shoot crew. And, though records were not available, the film reports Lloyd and Kendra are now divorced.

The old block in Hollis, where Lloyd got shot and nearly killed way back when, still looks pretty much the same. But the block where he grew up in Brooklyn—New Jersey Avenue in East New York—has undergone a remarkable transformation. The neighborhood still has its dangerous moments: shootings, violence, drugs. But the old buildings have been restored; windows replaced, doors rehung. The street is clean, well ordered. Nice. Some of the houses even have small gardens. It is a neighborhood on the rebound, on the mend. Saplings are growing, trees; trees, growing in Brooklyn.

Even that rubble-strewn lot across from No. 508, the abandoned lot where kids once played in dirt and squalor, has changed. It's fenced in now, with benches under a pergola; there's a jungle gym and a slide. And a plaque out front: Duke Park.

It makes you wonder what might have happened if it had been the block Lloyd was born into, instead of the one he and so many others actually were. Makes you wonder if things might have been different, turned out different; kids, after all, are kids.

Lloyd's daughters are, by all accounts, doing well. Both, college graduates. His son is on track to graduate high school in 2016. Through another strange twist, his coach at Colts Neck is Lou Piccola—the man who coached Hall of Famer Chris Mullin back at Xaverian in Brooklyn.

Lloyd III achieved minor stardom on YouTube in the winter of 2015, hitting two game-winning shots in the span of little more than a week for Colts Neck. He's six-foot-three; a good player, decent. Tom Konchalski said Lloyd calls him each and every week with updates, trying to see if he can help land the kid a basketball scholarship somewhere.

———

During a conversation in 2015, Konchalski called Lloyd's talent "transcendent," said that, despite the drug and alcohol abuse, despite being shot and nearly killed, he'd still made the NBA—and that in itself remains miraculous. But, Konchalski said, "He should have been a ten-year all-star, he should have been a Naismith Hall of Fame inductee. That was the talent he had." Instead, Lloyd became known as the only player in NBA history never to have graduated high school. For most, Konchalski said, stories of Lloyd Daniels and his immense and immeasurable talent, remain like those of apparitions of the Virgin Mother at Lourdes and La Salette, at Fatima and Our Lady of Guadalupe and even Syracuse. That is, that most nonbelievers don't believe those apparitions existed. But for those who were there, who saw with their own eyes, well . . . they believe, because they know in their hearts and in their minds what they saw. Truly saw.

"When Lloyd Daniels took the court," Konchalski told me then, "the other nine players were playing checkers. *He* was playing chess."

Tom Konchalski said he saw that in Swee'pea. Ron Naclerio said he saw it, Jerry Tarkanian said he saw it, Pat Riley said he saw it, Tiny Archibald said he saw it, Howie Garfinkel said he saw it. Al McGuire and his brother, Dick McGuire, saw it.

Even those experts who later claimed his abilities were mere exaggeration—that his talents were no more than myth, legend unraveling in the light of day like a ball of yarn—saw it; saw it, extolled those vast abilities to the world, then recanted.

Me? I believe what those folks all said they saw; what I saw.

I don't think you can step onto an NBA court, against NBA competition, the best in the world, and, flat-out cold drop twenty-five like you're dropping a dime—and not have extraordinary talent and abilities. Lloyd hardly had a foundation of games in high school, had none in college, had barely one full season in some second- or third-rate minor leagues, had been shot, had nearly died, had been besieged by drug and alcohol problems, and walked onto those courts—and, at times, set the basketball world on fire.

And still, I recall seeing Lloyd make a bounce pass in traffic that had the scout seated next to me, Dick McGuire, then with the Knicks, shaking his head in disbelief.

"To have wasted a gift like that," McGuire said with profound sadness.

That, to me, spoke—and continues to speak—volumes.

I saw the best players of a generation—of many generations—play ball. The best in New York City; the best from across the nation. Sure, Swee'pea didn't care much for defense. But his understanding of the game, the pureness of it; the simple, brilliant elegance with which he played it, when he was possessed to play it? His basketball genius?

That was Einstein.

And Mozart. And Shakespeare and Hemingway and Picasso and . . .

And so I wonder what might have been, what could have been, had he cared for the game half as much as he cared for the substances he admittedly abused; had he cared for basketball as an adult, an adult with the world for the taking, half as much as he'd cared about it as that kid who'd snuck out at night to play in the dark. Alone.

For the love and purity of it; the desire. Nothing more; nothing less.

Lloyd Daniels had a gift; *the* gift. The rarest of gifts. The shameful truth is he did far less with it than he rightly should have, which is tragic, maybe unforgivable.

But, for brief moments in time, he was the best basketball player I'd ever seen. That anyone had. Better, in those moments, than I'd seen before. Maybe, since.

Note on Sources

Many, if not most, of the accounts as portrayed in *Swee'pea* are the result of firsthand reporting, investigation, and observation while covering every level of basketball, from the playgrounds to the pros, as a sports reporter for the New York City edition of *Newsday* during the mid- to late 1980s. Additional stories and accounts were the result of firsthand experiences of coauthor Ron Naclerio, who, as a high school and summer-league coach, knew and interacted with not only the best players in New York City, but also many of the best players and coaches in the nation. Because of that we were not only able to gain access to academic, court, and hospital records, but also had behind-the-scenes access to family members, coaches, teammates, and confidants of Lloyd Daniels, which allowed us to tell his story in great detail and depth. Through our acquaintances, we also gained firsthand knowledge of many other stories related to playground ball and its players. What follows, then, is an explanation of other major sources and sourcing that enabled us to flesh out the tale of *Swee'pea*.

Chapter 1. Three-Shot Barrage

Information about other notables with ties to the Hollis, Queens, neighborhood where Lloyd lived with his grandmother, Lulia Hendley, come from the website HollisNY.com, while background on Mike Tyson was supplemented with information from scores of newspaper accounts located and researched through Wikipedia. Scenes portraying the shooting and its aftermath, as well as the operation, were the result of interviews with Lloyd, his family members, and his friends, as well as an exclusive interview with Dr. Daniel L. Picard just hours after he had finished the operation to save Lloyd.

Chapter 2. The Legend of Swee'pea

The sequences at the start of the chapter are based on personal observation and records kept during my coverage of that 1986 game against Wyandanch. Information about other basketball legends, including the greatest pro players of all time and greatest playground nicknames of all time, were culled from the NBA's 50 Greatest Players list released as part of its 50th anniversary celebration in 1996, as well as a Top 100 list announced by *SLAM* magazine in 2011 and the Under Armour Elite 24 lists on ESPN .go.com—supplemented by the tried-and-true basis of all legend: word of mouth. A major background source was the 1970 classic *The City Game,* by the late Pete Axthelm (Harper & Brothers); *Heaven Is a Playground,* by Rick Telander (St. Martin's Press, 1976); and *Doc: The Rise and Rise of Julius Erving,* by Vincent M. Mallozzi (Wiley, 2010). For the record, the name of the *Popeye* character for whom Lloyd is named has been reported as *Sweet Pea, Swee'Pea, Sweepea,* and even *Sweep Pea* since its debut in 1933. I have always used *Swee'pea*—with a lowercase *p*—when reporting stories on Lloyd. Thus the book title is *Swee'pea* not *Swee'Pea.*

Chapter 3. School Daze

Statistics regarding murders and the type of violent crime described in this chapter were based on information supplied by the NYPD, which tracks offenses on a monthly and annual basis, city-wide and by command (precinct), in seven major felony categories: murder, rape, robbery, felony assault, burglary, grand larceny, and grand larceny–auto. Lloyd's academic records were acquired through exclusive reporting and issues regarding truancy were based on reports from various city agencies found online at NYC.gov. Portrayals of street life were the result of observation and scores of interviews with residents, police, and academicians. The *New York Times* reported that, in November 1991, a ninth grader from Sutter Avenue actually was shot and killed by a fourteen-year-old in a third-floor hall at Thomas Jefferson—a footnote to the observation by Lloyd, years earlier, that the school was "a baby Rikers Island."

Chapter 4. Miles to Go

The population figures for Mouth of Wilson, Virginia, were culled from the 1990—and, later, the 2010—U.S. Census. Description of the town, school, and surrounding area were from interviews and other historical research, as well as from a trek there for a high school game. Sourcing for the number of national high school championships for Oak Hill Academy and Coach Steve Smith were from both the school website—www.oak-hill.net—and from the *USA Today* Super 25 poll found at usatodayhss.com/category /super-25. Coach at Oak Hill since 1985, Smith won titles in 1993, 1994, 1999, 2001, 2004, 2005, 2007, and 2012 and his teams had 14 other Top 5 finishes en route to a 950-60 record by 2015, including 47-1 in 2014–15, when the team was ranked No. 1 in the nation by *USA Today* before losing its final game to No. 2 Monteverde (Florida), 70–61. Information about former Creighton University star Kevin Ross came from a January 30, 1990, piece by Jack Curry in the *New York Times*, as well as from court records (*Ross v. Creighton University* at http://openjurist.org/957/12d/410/ross-v -creighton-university) and from the book *The New Plantation, Black Athletes, College Sports, and Predominantly White NCAA Institutions*, by Billy Hawkins (Palgrave Macmillan). Details about NCAA investigation of the University of Kentucky and recruit Eric Manuel were researched through Wikipedia and articles in the *Lexington Herald-Leader*. A search of the IMDb entertainment industry database found no credited appearances on *Playhouse 90* or *The Dinah Shore Show* by New York Gauchos founder Lou d'Almeida. Allegations that Laurinburg Institute was a "diploma mill" and that it had been "blacklisted" by the NCAA were reported by the *Fayetteville* (N.C.) *Observer*.

Chapter 5. Andrew Jackson

Background on the legendary Bob Cousy, a graduate of Andrew Jackson High School in Cambria Heights, Queens, was from both www.basketball -reference.com and the NBA. Game scenarios involving Jackson and Eli Whitney were re-created following extensive interviews with the participants. Background about the TV series *The White Shadow*, which featured Ken Howard as Ken Reeves, a star with the Chicago Bulls who becomes coach at a school in South Central Los Angeles after his career is derailed by a knee injury, is from IMDb. Information about Kareem Abdul-Jabbar and former Archbishop Molloy stars Kevin Joyce, Brian Winters, and Kenny Smith is from ESPN, www.basketball-reference.com, and Wikipedia, while information about Archbishop Molloy, the school, is from www.molloyhs.org.

Chapter 6. Swee'pea and the Strip

In April 1988, the *Los Angeles Daily News* reported allegations that University of Kentucky assistant coach Dwayne Casey had sent an Emery Air Freight package containing $1,000 in cash to Claud Mills, father of Fairfax High School recruit Chris Mills. The story cited shipping records and employees, who said the package "accidentally" opened during transit. Claud Mills and his son denied receiving the cash. Casey denied sending it and filed a $6.9 million lawsuit against Emery, claiming the allegations "defamed his character and violated his privacy." That July, the NCAA announced it had launched an investigation. Kentucky later was charged with eighteen violations and, following what proved to be a Pulitzer Prize–winning investigation by the *Lexington Herald-Leader*, the school admitted in April 1989 to sending the cash—but refused to concede the source was Casey. Casey always denied sending the money; the allegation never was proven. The Millses always denied they received it. In May 1989, the NCAA put the basketball program on probation for three years and banned Mills, who had just finished his freshman season, from playing again for the Wildcats. It also barred another player, Eric Manuel, from ever playing again at an NCAA school—finding he had "committed academic fraud by cheating" on a college entrance exam. Additionally, the school was ordered to "return $350,000 gained from its appearance" in the 1988 NCAA Tournament; the Wildcats were limited to just three scholarships in the following two seasons and were banned from playing televised games in 1989–90 and from postseason play in 1990 and 1991. Mills promptly transferred to Arizona, became a first-round pick—22nd overall—by the Cleveland Cavaliers in the 1993 NBA Draft, and earned more than $37 million with the Cavaliers, New York Knicks, and Golden State Warriors in a career that spanned from 1993 to 2003. The stories were reported by the *Lexington Herald-Leader*, *New York Times*, *Los Angeles Daily News*, *Los Angeles Times*, and the Associated Press; information also was found through Wikipedia and www.basketball-reference.com. The recruiting letters to Lloyd Daniels were all obtained through Lloyd and Ron Naclerio. Allegations regarding Rob Johnson, said to be a street-level recruiter for Syracuse, were from the book *Raw Recruits* (Pocket Books, 1991) by Alexander Wolff and Armen Keteyian, as well as from reporting by the *New York Times*, New York *Daily News*, and the *Post-Standard* of Syracuse, New York. Riverside Church basketball program founder Ernie Lorch was accused of sexual misconduct in 2002, Lorch was hounded by those allegations for a decade until his death in 2012. Prosecutors in Massachusetts got a grand jury indictment against Lorch in 2010, charging him with attempted rape and indecent assault and battery of a person over fourteen years old. The indictment charged that Lorch "assaulted the alleged victim sometime between March of 1977 and April of 1978 during a trip to Amherst [Massachusetts] for a basketball tournament." But Lorch suffered a stroke in 2010 and a Westchester County, New York, judge ruled he wasn't competent to be extradited to stand trial. He died at a nursing home in May 2012, after years battling diabetes and dementia. Sourcing for that information was from articles reported by the New York *Daily News, New York Post, New York Times,* and *SLAM* magazine, found at www.SLAMonline.com. Background about alleged improprieties by Jerry Tarkanian at Long Beach State University were reported by *Sports Illustrated* and found at www.si.com/vault, as was some information about Richie "the Fixer" Perry—from a February 16, 1981, *Sports Illustrated* cover story about *Goodfellas* mobster Henry Hill titled "How I Put the Fix In," and from a June 17, 1991, article by Shelley Smith, edited by Steve Wulf. Stories about Jack Molinas and the New York City college basketball scandal of the 1950s were chronicled in *The Wizard of Odds, How Jack Molinas Almost Destroyed the Game of Basketball,* by Charley Rosen (Seven Stories Press, 2001). The *Newsday* investigations of Lloyd's recruitment by the University of Nevada–Las Vegas, coauthored with star investigative reporter Danny Robbins, were nominated for the Pulitzer Prize in 1987.

Chapter 7. Guardian Angel

The court filings by then-UNLV assistant coach Mark Warkentien seeking legal guardianship of Lloyd were obtained through the exclusive reporting by Danny Robbins for *Newsday* and were a key factor in our 1987 investigation. They also provided insight into Lloyd's learning disabilities, which included previously undiagnosed dyslexia, and were key to the later discoveries of alleged improprieties at the heart of the NCAA investigation into the recruiting of Lloyd by Jerry Tarkanian and UNLV.

Chapter 8. Mount Sac

I conducted some of the interviews with Mount San Antonio coach Gene Victor over the phone, as I did the interviews with the NCAA investigator,

Rick Evrard. Danny Robbins was the reporter with "feet on the ground," as they say, for *Newsday* in Nevada and California—and he obtained court records and conducted one-on-one interviews with key sources in both states. The newspaper graciously allowed me to use much of that reporting as key background material for the Lloyd Daniels story as told in *Swee'pea*, and I remain grateful to this day for all I learned about reporting from Danny, one of the best investigative reporters I've ever worked with. (He was featured in the ESPN 30-for-30 *Pony Excess* for his investigation of the football program at Southern Methodist University.) As for Sig Rogich and his expertise, *Adweek* called the "Tuesday Team," an ad hoc group of advertising all-stars who produced a series of brilliant TV spots that cemented Ronald Reagan's 1984 presidential reelection campaign against Democratic candidate Walter Mondale, "one of the most famous ad-executive teams in U.S. political history."

Chapter 9. Gone Bust

The scene detailing Lloyd's arrest by Las Vegas Metropolitan Police was written based on video of the sting operation obtained from WVBC-TV Channel 3–Las Vegas and later supplemented with exclusive interviews with police and other authorities, Lloyd and his attorney, David Chesnoff, as well as from information obtained through court records. The *Sports Illustrated* story at the heart of the allegations about Tony Red Bruin using cocaine at Syracuse University was an as-told-to piece by *Lexington Herald-Leader* reporter Jeffrey Marx, who shared the 1986 Pulitzer Prize for Investigative Reporting for stories about infractions at the University of Kentucky. Gary McLain alleged that the night before a team of Big East stars, including Bruin, left for a goodwill tour of Angola, several players had gone to Astoria, Queens, to score coke. "Some of us were getting drunk, and after a while one of the players asked if we wanted to get high. 'Yeah,' I said. 'Let's get some cocaine.' We weren't that far from Astoria, Queens, where one of the players knew where to score some. . . ." Bruin was the lone player on the team from Astoria.

Chapter 10. The Life

According to figures available from the U.S. Department of Health and Human Services' Centers for Disease Control and Prevention, National

Center for Health Statistics 2010 National Vital Statistics Report on the leading causes of death (www.cdc.gov/nchs/data/nvsr/nvsr62/nvsr62_06 .pdf), the leading cause of death for black males and females age 15–19, 20–24, and 25–34 was homicide—murder accounting for 44.1 percent, 41 percent, and 26.9 percent of all deaths in those age groups. By comparison, the rates for whites of both sexes were 8.5 percent, 7.7 percent, and 6.9 percent, with homicide a distant third behind accidents and suicide for whites age 15–19 and 20–24—and a distant fifth for whites ages 25–34, also behind malignancies and heart disease. For males, the figures were even more pronounced. The murder rate for white males age 15–19 was 9.9 percent, compared to 50.4 percent of all fatalities among black males of the same age. For white males age 20–24, it was 8.4 percent; black males, 49.2. In the 25–34-year-old group it was 6.1 percent for white males, 35.1 percent for blacks. Background on Rucker Tournament founder Holcombe Rucker, who used basketball as a way to help disadvantaged youth, was sourced through a July 8, 2012, piece by William C. Rhoden in the *New York Times* titled, "A Harlem Light Still Shines" and from the book *Asphalt Gods: An Oral History of the Rucker Tournament* (Doubleday, 2003), by Vincent M. Mallozzi. The story of Earl Manigault was supplemented with background found in *The City Game* by Pete Axthelm and, later, from the 1996 HBO biopic *Rebound: The Legend of Earl "The Goat" Manigault,* directed by Eriq La Salle and starring Don Cheadle as Manigault, Forest Whitaker as Holcombe Rucker, and Daryl Mitchell as Dean "the Dream" Meminger—with appearances by James Earl Jones and Kareem Abdul-Jabbar.

Chapter 11. Topeka, Kansas

The chapter is based on exclusive reporting after I was sent to Topeka to write pieces about Lloyd leading up to his professional debut in the Continental Basketball Association, then on his first road trip with the CBA team to Casper, Wyoming, and Rapid City, South Dakota. Sizzlers owner Bernie Glannon and coach John Killilea allowed me behind-the-scenes access to Lloyd and other team members; I traveled on the team bus and on team flights, staying at the team hotel. That meant I was there when Lloyd tried his "act" at practice and when Lloyd first was introduced to future mentor John Lucas in the airport in Denver; I was also there when Lloyd made his pro debut in Wyoming. I was on the bus as Lloyd traveled across Wyoming and was there to pose with Swee'pea for photos at Mount Rushmore. I saw former Boston Celtics great Jo Jo White as he tried to mentor Lloyd, and I was at the team hotel in Rapid City when Swee'pea knocked on my door one morning to talk about life and basketball. I later wrote a lengthy feature for *Newsday* on my return to New York titled "The Education of Lloyd Daniels."

Chapter 12. Goodbye, Topeka

Accounts portrayed here are based on phone interviews with Sizzlers owner Bernie Glannon and other scouts and officials, as well as on interviews with both Lloyd and his attorney, David Chesnoff. They were supplemented with information graciously shared by the late *Topeka Capital-Journal* reporter Al Quakenbush, whom I'd first met when I'd gone to Kansas to report on Lloyd joining the Sizzlers.

Chapter 13. Waters, Too Strong

The basis for scenarios described in this chapter were the result of interviews with Lloyd and attorney David Chesnoff, as well as long—and very expensive—phone calls to Waitemata coach Dave MacCalman in New Zealand, later supplemented with information obtained from the *Dominion Post* newspaper, and from websites www.stuff.co.nz and www.doc.govt.nz /conservation/native-animals.

Chapter 14. Cracks in the Concrete Dream

The story of so-called drug games, Earl Byam, known on the street as Shorty Black, and the death of referee Greg Vaughn was constructed following interviews with some of the participants, timekeeper Hassen Pinchback, and fans in attendance, as well as from attending court proceedings and records obtained from court and the NYPD, and from sources who spoke on the condition of anonymity. Information about Queens College alumni was obtained through the school website at www.qc.cuny.edu. The tale of victim Barbara Chiles came from an exclusive interview with her son, Tony, and was later confirmed through the NYPD and other law enforcement officials, while background information used to tell the story of fallen New York City basketball star Karlton Hines was based on interviews and court records and other case information provided by the Bronx County district attorney's office.

Chapter 15. Van Nuys, ASAP

Not long after the revised manuscript for *Swee'pea* went through the final editing process, news broke that John "Hot Rod" Williams, the man accused and later acquitted of point-shaving while at Tulane University in New Orleans, had died of prostate cancer. That was on December 11, 2015. He was fifty-three. Williams was the 21st pick—in the second round—of the 1985 NBA Draft by the Cleveland Cavaliers and went on to play thirteen years with Cleveland, the Phoenix Suns, and Dallas Mavericks. According to accounts reported both by ESPN and the *New York Times*, Williams was arrested on March 27, 1985, for "suspicion of point-shaving"—and, according to a grand jury indictment, he'd taken money for "influencing" point spreads in games against Southern Miss, Memphis State, and Virginia Tech. Charged with sports bribery and conspiracy, his first trial ended when Judge Alan V. Oser declared a mistrial, while Williams was acquitted in a second trial after just twenty minutes of jury deliberation. The six-eleven Williams was the fabled "Sixth Man" with the 1988–89 Cavaliers, who went 57-25, only to be eliminated in a first-round series on a last-second shot by Michael Jordan. As for background about life inside the substance abuse program at Van Nuys, several players, among them David Thompson and Roy Tarpley, were gracious enough to share their stories—as well as talk about their time with Lloyd. An interview with Richie Adams was conducted via telephone. An attempt to visit him during his incarceration at Rikers Island was actually thwarted by a rubella outbreak—my then-wife was pregnant with our son, Jarek, and I couldn't afford any possible exposure—and I was forced to bum quarters from the friends and families of jail visitors in order to take the bus from Rikers back to the mainland, a very surrealistic moment, since the guards refused to change the only cash I had for the dollar bus fare. I didn't tell them I was a reporter; they thought I was friends with an inmate. Other information about Adams and his crimes was obtained from court records, state prison records available at nysdoccslookup.doccs .ny.gov, and through interviews with prosecutors at the Manhattan district attorney's office. Statistics about the highest-scoring games in NBA history were provided by the NBA.

Chapter 16. The Entourage

The scene with boxer Mike Tyson was re-created after interviews with Ron Naclerio and Lloyd, as well as with Jamal Faulkner, Lawrence "Future" Pollard, the late Arnie Hershkowitz, and the late Conrad McRae. Additional information about Tyson, aside from personal coverage of the former champion, was culled from *Bad Intentions: The Mike Tyson Story* (New American Library, 1989; Da Capo Press, 1995); *Taming the Beast: The Untold Story of Mike Tyson* (Rough House, 2014); and the *New York Post*, January 5, 2015. The Brooklyn–Queens Expressway, known to New Yorkers simply as the BQE, is an elevated roadway that skirts the western edge of Brooklyn, passing the Williamsburg, Manhattan, and Brooklyn bridges, and traveling through Brooklyn Heights near the new Barclays Center. My grandfather, John A. Valenti Sr., actually was the New York City deputy commissioner of public works during a portion of the construction, which included building the cantilevered section at Brooklyn Heights. At the start of the 2015–16 season, Kenny Anderson remained the all-time leading scorer among private and parochial school players in New York State history, but was fourth overall—behind Lance Stephenson of Brooklyn's Abraham Lincoln (2,946 points from 2004 to 2009), Ryan Creighton of Greenport in Suffolk County, Long Island (2,799 points from 2004 to 2009), and Sebastian Telfair of Lincoln (2,785 points from 2000 to 2004). Among the Top 50, all 2,000-point scorers, remain: Stephon Marbury (Lincoln, 2,078, 1991–95); Lew Alcindor (Power Memorial, 2,067, 1961–65); Christian Laettner (Buffalo-Nichols, 2,066, 1984–88); and Greg "Boo" Harvey (Andrew Jackson, 2,039, 1981–85). Those statistics were obtained from the New York State Sportswriters Association.

Chapter 17. Operation

Through a quirky twist of fate, I ended up outside the intensive care unit at Mary Immaculate Hospital in Jamaica, Queens, not long after Lloyd had been shot. Hearing the news from Ron, I'd driven to the hospital early in the morning after the shooting to find a growing horde of news reporters gathered in the main lobby. But, being a sportswriter I had long learned that you could often gain entrance to restricted areas simply by *acting* as if you belonged—and so while all the other reporters waited for hospital officials to arrange a news conference, I walked past everyone and went upstairs. There I got exclusive access to the surgeon who operated on Lloyd, Dr. Daniel L. Picard, whom I found in a side room and who agreed to speak with me, one-on-one. I also managed to gain exclusive interviews with Lloyd's grandmothers and aunt and also was present when his father, Lloyd Sr., came walking in. All of which allowed me to write a scene story with information no other reporter had. Because of his relationship with Lloyd, Ron also had exclusive access to his hospital room and to information about his recovery in the aftermath of being shot. Background on the trauma unit at Mary Immaculate was from documents that had been left to Ron by his father, Dr. Emil Naclerio. That information also was confirmed by medical experts and through newspaper reports in the *New York Times* of the events portrayed, including the operation to save the life of Dr. Martin Luther King Jr. in 1958. The section on Orlando Antigua was from interviews with the player, as well as from info provided by the Bronx district attorney.

Chapter 18. Con Man

Events portrayed were mostly the result of firsthand observation by me and Ron, supplemented with information culled from interviews with Tom Rome, Bernie Glannon, Kevin Barry, and others with intimate knowledge of the scenarios as written. In yet another quirky twist of fate, NYPD detective John Kanovsky and I once worked together at the same college newspaper, the *Chronicle*, at Hofstra University—leading him to call, out of the blue, with the story of Lloyd trying to score drugs in the Bowery.

Chapter 19. Back in the 'Ville

Much of the narrative at the heart of this chapter centers around a one-day search by us to track down Lloyd somewhere in the East New York section of Brooklyn, followed by a dinner Ron and I had with Lloyd in a restaurant in the Flatlands. Background about the Quad Cities was found at the website www.quadcities.com.

Epilogue

Hundreds of Internet searches, as well as assorted phone and in-person interviews, went into researching and writing the new epilogue to *Swee'pea*—many of the key articles, websites, videos, and other sources were located through use of Google and Wikipedia. Newspaper articles with background on a host of players were then located in the archives of the *Washington Post, New York Times, New York Post,* New York *Daily News, Newsday,* and other publications, including *Sports Illustrated* and *People.* The NBA archives and website provided stats and biographical information. Videos were located on YouTube and Vimeo. Info like background on "Terminator 2" Quinton Hosley, came from his official website t2hosley.com. Info about the Stephon Marbury musical in China came from deadspin.com. Updates on Dave MacCalman, who coached Lloyd at Waitemata in New Zealand, was provided by Rex Bionics and additional information came from Facebook, www.disabled-world.com—and from a note from Davie D passed along through the people at Rex. Under new NCAA rules, for a summer league to be certified, it must: 1. Apply online at least 45 days before the start of the league; 2. Complete a background check; 3. Complete an educational course; 4. Purchase accident insurance. Certified leagues cannot: 1. Charge admission; 2. Earn money via raffle tickets; 3. Earn money via cable TV or radio rights; 4. Hire as staff anyone associated with a two-year or four-year college; 5. Sponsor all-star games of any kind. NCAA Division I players can participate in one league per summer, but only if: 1. The league is NCAA certified; 2. The season takes place between June 15 and August 31; 3. The player receives written permission from the school athletic director; 4. The league is within 100 air miles of the athlete's official residence or within 100 miles of the school that player attends; 5. Only two Division I athletes are permitted on any team's roster. These rules are designed to prevent stacking teams with collegiate rosters, as well as to prevent exposure to those old "drug" games—the kind Boo Harvey was playing when referee Greg Vaughn was struck and killed. They're also designed to prevent athletes from being paid to play in summer leagues. However, under these rules, guys like Ron and Hersh could never take a team of Division I stars to play at a local prison; then again, Richard Perry couldn't coach a team, either. As for the footnote to the coaching career of Jerry Tarkanian: Following the resignation of Tarkanian, who coached the Bulldogs from 1995 to 2002, Fresno State was hit with ten NCAA rule violations in September 2003, in addition to previously self-imposed sanctions—which included a ban on postseason play and forfeiture of scholarships. Among violations cited by the NCAA Infractions Committee were a team advisor and statistician providing academic papers for players, the use of correspondence courses to meet eligibility requirements, and players being given cash and complimentary tickets. As part of the penalty, Fresno State had to return 90 percent of its revenue from participation in the 2000 NCAA Tournament. Its participation in the tournament also was expunged.

Index

About the Authors

John Valenti

A nine-time Pulitzer Prize–nominated reporter for *Newsday*, John Valenti has appeared on scores of television and radio shows, including *Good Morning America*, and had a featured role in the Emmy Award–winning 2013 ESPN 30-for-30 documentary *Big Shot* by Kevin Connolly. *Big Shot* is the story of how con man John Spano managed to fleece Fleet Bank out of $80 million and buy the NHL New York Islanders while claiming to be a Dallas multimillionaire—and, in part, how Valenti led a team of *Newsday* reporters and uncovered the truth, resulting in the arrest and federal prosecution and conviction of Spano. A veteran of more than thirty years with *Newsday*, Valenti has been honored with four top-five finishes in the prestigious Associated Press Sports Editors competition, including first place for Best Enterprise Reporting in 1996 as part of the team that reported a groundbreaking series on sports-related concussions, and first place for Best Investigative Reporting in 1997 for his investigation of Spano. He was the lead columnist on *Newsday*'s "Death on the Roads" series, which earned the prestigious Society of the Silurians Community Service Award in 2004; he was part of a team that took first place in the 2007 Silurians competition for "Death of a Yankee," the reporting of the plane crash that killed New York Yankees pitcher Cory Lidle; and the 2012 first place award by Silurians for Online Breaking News coverage of the 2011 Tropical Storm Irene. He has covered Major League Baseball, the NBA, the NHL, the 1994 World Cup Soccer, major-college sports, was nominated for the Pulitzer Prize for sports stories and issues reported on in 1987, 1993, 1995, and 1996 and for news events and investigations in 2003, 2006, 2011, and 2012, and has covered an array of high-profile national figures, including Michael Jordan, Magic Johnson, Julius Erving, Mike Tyson, Evander Holyfield, Mario Andretti, Wayne Gretzky, Pele, and the first two men to walk on the moon, Neil Armstrong and Buzz Aldrin. He was a candidate for the 1986 NASA-sponsored Journalist in Space Project, abandoned after the explosion of the space shuttle *Challenger,* and recently authored and is offering for sale his first novel, a piece of historical crime fiction based on one of the most famous unsolved child disappearance cases in U.S. history. Valenti lives with his longtime companion, Elizabeth Eser Jose. He has one son, Jarek.

Ron Naclerio

A former intermediate school teacher, Ron Naclerio won New York City Public Schools Athletic League titles at Benjamin Cardozo High School in 1999 and 2014, and is known nationally as "the Teacher." His teams have made 33 playoff appearances in 34 seasons, reaching the Elite Eight 17 times, the Final Four 8 times, and the Championship game 3 times—his 2014–15 team losing in the PSAL Championship Game. He has the most wins as a coach in the 112-year history of the PSAL. A contributor to *Hoop Scoop* and other publications, Naclerio has been a frequent guest on local and national television broadcasts, and, as the starting center fielder on the 1978 St. John's University College World Series baseball team, roomed with future MLB star John Franco while leading the NCAA in stolen bases. He has coached dozens of NBA players, including Duane Causwell, Rafer Alston, Stephon Marbury, and, of course, Lloyd Daniels. His father, Dr. Emil Naclerio, a renowned trauma surgeon, is credited with saving the life of Dr. Martin Luther King, Jr., after the civil rights leader was stabbed in Harlem in 1958.